CHRISTINA OF MARKYATE

This fascinating and comprehensive collection of essays written by scholars from both sides of the Atlantic surveys the life of an extraordinary medieval woman. Christina of Markyate made a vow of chastity at an early age, against the wishes of her parents who intended her to marry. When forced into wedlock, she fled in disguise and went into hiding, receiving refuge in a network of hermitages. Christina thus became a religious recluse and eventually founded a priory of nuns attached to St Albans.

Samuel Fanous and Henrietta Leyser present a vivid interdisciplinary study devoted to the life, work and extant *vita* of Christina of Markyate, which draws on research from a wide range of disciplines. Key topics have been selected in a balanced and comprehensive approach; they cover timeless themes, such as monasticism and eremiticism, as well as topical matters in medieval research, such as gender.

The book begins by introducing readers to Christina's person and life, setting her in a cultural, social and religious context, and presenting the literary back-ground of *The Life of Christina of Markyate*. Further chapters examine themes such as the two traditions of martyrdom, virgin and ascetic, and Christina's alignment with both, the presentation of sanctity and sexual temptation in the twelfth century, and a survey of contemporary hermits and anchorites. It includes a close reading of the *vita*, revealing its markedly hagiographical qualities, and a discussion of the drama of the initials in the St Albans Psalter and what this reveals about the relationship between Christina and Abbot Geoffrey.

Beautifully illustrated, this book provides students who regularly encounter Christina with a research compendium from which to begin their studies, and introduces Christina to a wider audience.

Samuel Fanous is Head of Publishing at the Bodleian Library, Oxford.

Henrietta Leyser is a Fellow of St Peter's College, Oxford, and the author of *Medieval Women* (1995).

CHRISTINA OF MARKYATE

A twelfth-century holy woman

Edited by Samuel Fanous
and Henrietta Leyser

Routledge
Taylor & Francis Group

LONDON AND NEW YORK

First published 2005
by Routledge
2 Park Square, Milton Park, Abingdon, Oxon, OX14 4RN

Simultaneously published in the USA and Canada
by Routledge
270 Madison Ave, New York, NY 10016

Routledge is an imprint of the Taylor & Francis Group

Typeset in Baskerville
by Taylor & Francis Books Ltd
Printed and bound in Great Britain by
TJ International Ltd, Padstow, Cornwall

British Library Cataloguing in Publication Data
A catalogue record for this book is available from the British Library

Library of Congress Cataloging-in-Publication Data
Christina of Markyate : a twelfth-century holy woman /
edited by Samuel Fanous and Henrietta Leyser p. cm.
Includes bibliographical references and index.
1. Christina, of Markyate, Saint, b. ca. 1096. 2. Christian women
saints–England–Biography. 3. Women–England–History–Middle Ages,
500–1500–Sources. I. Fanous, Samuel, 1962- II. Leyser, Henrietta.
BX4700.C567C48 2004
271'.9–dc22
2004005879

ISBN 0–415–30858–5 (hbk)
ISBN 0–415–30859–3 (pbk)

CONTENTS

CONTENTS

ILLUSTRATIONS

Plates

Figures

Tables

ACKNOWLEDGEMENTS

The editors would like to thank the publishers and copyright holders for permission to reprint material from the following works:

Dombibliothek Hildesheim for the illustrations from the St Albans Psalter;

Brepols Publishers for Thomas Head, 'The Marriages of Christina of Markyate' *Viator* 21 (1990), 71–95;

University of Pennsylvania Press for C. Stephen Jaeger, 'The Loves of Christina of Markyate' in *Ennobling Love: In Search of a Lost Sensibility* (1999);

Oxford University Press for R. I. Moore, 'Ranulf Flambard and Christina of Markyate' in *Belief and Culture in the Middle Ages: Studies Presented to Henry Mayr-Harting*, ed. Richard Gameson and Henrietta Leyser (2001).

ABBREVIATIONS

AA.SS	*Acta Sanctorum quotquot toto orbe coluntur*, ed. J. Bolland *et al.* (Antwerp and Brussels, 1643–)
Ælfric's Lives	*Ælfric's Lives of Saints*, ed. and trans. W. W. Skeat, 4 vols. rpt. as 2, EETS OS 76, 82, 94, 114 (1881–1900, rpt. 1966).
ANTS	Anglo-Norman Text Society
Belief and Culture	*Belief and Culture in the Middle Ages: Studies Presented to Henry Mayr-Harting*, ed. Richard Gameson and Henrietta Leyser (Oxford, 2001)
CCSL	Corpus Christianorum, Series Latina (Turnhout)
CCCM	Corpus Christianorum, Continuatio Medievalis (Turnhout)
EETS	Early English Text Society
OS	Original Series
ES	Extra Series
Elkins, *Holy Women*	Sharon K. Elkins, *Holy Women of Twelfth-Century England* (Chapel Hill, N.C., 1988)
Gesta Abbatum	*Gesta Abbatum Monasterii S. Albani*, ed. H. T. Riley, RS 28, 3 vols. (London, 1867–69)
Holdsworth, 'Christina of Markyate'	Christopher Holdsworth, 'Christina of Markyate', in *Medieval Women*, ed. Derek T. Baker, Studies in Church History, Subsidia 1 (Oxford, 1978), pp. 185–204
Koopmans, 'The Conclusion'	Rachel M. Koopmans, 'The Conclusion of Christina of Markyate's *Vita*', *Journal of Ecclesiastical History* 51 (2000), 663–98
Life	*The Life of Christina of Markyate: A Twelfth Century Recluse*, ed. and trans. C. H. Talbot (Oxford, 1959; rpt. 1987)
MGH	*Monumenta Germania Historica*
AA	*Auctores Antiquissimi*
SRM	*Scriptores Rerum Merovingicarum*
SS	*Scriptores in Folio*
OMT	Oxford Medieval Texts
Pächt	Otto Pächt, C. R. Dodwell and Francis Wormald, *The St Albans Psalter (Albani Psalter)*, Studies of the Warburg Institute (London, 1960)

PG	*Patrologia Graeca*, ed. J.-P. Migne, 161 vols. (Paris)
PL	*Patrologia cursus completus*, series Latina, ed. J.-P. Migne, 221 vols. (Paris)
RS	Rolls Series
Thompson, *Women Religious*	Sally Thompson, *Women Religious: The Founding of English Nunneries after the Norman Conquest* (Oxford, 1991)
VCH	*Victoria County History*
Wogan-Browne, *Saints' Lives*	Jocelyn Wogan-Browne, *Saints' Lives and Women's Literary Culture* (Oxford, 2001)

CONTRIBUTORS

Neil Cartlidge studied English Literature at Clare College, Cambridge. After completing his doctorate there in 1995, he worked in Oxford as a British Academy Postdoctoral Fellow at Wolfson College until 1998, and then as a lecturer at St John's College until 1999. He is currently Lecturer in Old and Middle English at University College Dublin. In 2002–03 he held an Alexander von Humboldt Fellowship at the Seminar for Medieval Latin Philology in the University of Freiburg, Germany. He has published two books, *Medieval Marriage: Literary Approaches 1100–1300* (1997) and *The Owl and the Nightingale* (2001).

Dyan Elliott is Professor of Medieval History at Indiana University. Her publications include *Spiritual Marriage: Sexual Abstinence in Medieval Wedlock* (1993), *Fallen Bodies: Pollution, Sexuality and Demonology in the Middle Ages* (1999) and *Proving Woman: Female Spirituality and Inquisitional Culture in the Later Middle Ages* (2004); she is currently working on a study examining the far-reaching implications of Western Christendom's re-encounter with dualism.

Samuel Fanous completed his D.Phil. in Oxford in 1998. He is Head of Publishing at the Bodleian Library, Oxford and is currently co-editing the *Cambridge Companion to Medieval English Mysticism*. He has written articles on aspects of medieval autobiography, hagiography, contemplation and piety, and on medieval women.

Jane Geddes studied History of Art at the Courtauld Institute, London, and later worked as an Inspector of Ancient Monuments with English Heritage. She is currently Senior Lecturer in History of Art at Aberdeen University. Her publications include *Medieval Decorative Ironwork in England* (1999), *Kings College Chapel, Aberdeen, 1500–2000* (2000), and websites of the complete *Aberdeen Bestiary* and *St Albans Psalter*.

Douglas Gray was the J. R. R. Tolkien Professor of English Literature and Language at Oxford. He is the author of many articles and books on medieval English and Scottish Literature. His books include *Themes and Images in the Medieval English Lyric* (1972), *Robert Henryson* (1979), *The Oxford Book of Late Medieval Verse and Prose* (1989) and *Selected Poems of Robert Henryson and William Dunbar* (1988). He edited the *Oxford Companion to Chaucer* (2003).

Thomas Head is Professor of History at Hunter College and the Graduate Center of the City University of New York. He is the author of *Hagiography and the Cult of Saints. The Diocese of Orléans, 800–1200* (1990) as well as numerous articles on medieval hagiography. He is also the editor of, among other works, *Medieval Hagiography: An Anthology* (2000; pb. 2001).

Stephanie Hollis is Professor of English and Director of the Centre for Medieval & Early Modern European Studies at the University of Auckland. She is the author of *Anglo-Saxon Women and the Church: Sharing A Common Fate* (1992) and is currently completing a study of Goscelin's *Legend of St Edith* and his *Liber confortatorius*.

Tony Hunt is a Fellow of St Peter's College, Oxford, a Fellow of the British Academy and of the Society of Antiquaries, and a Foreign Member of the Norwegian Academy of Science and Letters. His interests include the use of French in medieval England, medieval medicine, and editing Old French texts. His publications include *The Medieval Surgery* (1992) and *Anglo-Norman Medicine*, 2 vols. (1994, 1997).

C. Stephen Jaeger is the Gutgsell Professor of Germanic Languages and Literatures and Comparative Literature, and Director of the Program in Medieval Studies at the University of Illinois, Urbana. His interests are German, Latin and French literature of the Middle Ages, the influence of Latin culture on vernacular literature, intellectual history, history of education, courtliness, chivalry and courtly love, and the 'Renaissance of the twelfth century'. His publications include *Ennobling Love: In Search of a Lost Sensibility* (1999), *The Envy of Angels: Cathedral Schools and Social Ideals in Medieval Europe* (1994, pb. 1999), and *The Origins of Courtliness: Civilizing Trends and the Formation of Courtly Ideals, 939–1210* (1985, German trans: *Die Entstehung hoefischer Kultur*, 2001).

E. A. Jones is Lecturer in English Medieval Literature and Culture at the University of Exeter. In addition to his work on hermits and anchorites, he is interested in late medieval devotional literature, and is the organizer and editor of the Exeter Symposia on the Medieval Mystical Tradition.

Ruth Mazo Karras is Professor of History at the University of Minnesota. She is the author of several books, most recently *From Boys to Men: Formations of Masculinity in Later Medieval Europe* (2002), and numerous articles on various aspects of medieval gender relations. She is currently completing a history of medieval sexuality. She first wrote about Christina of Markyate for a term paper in her sophomore year of college.

Rachel Koopmans is Assistant Professor of Medieval History at Arizona State University. Her research interests focus on sainthood, miracles and the processes by which hagiographic texts and images were produced in the high medieval period. Her article, 'The Conclusion of Christina of Markyate's *Vita*', published in the *Journal of Ecclesiastical History*, was awarded the Van

Courtlandt Elliot prize by the Medieval Academy of America. She is currently working on a book on the miracle collections of Thomas Becket.

Henrietta Leyser is a Fellow of St Peter's College, Oxford. Her publications include *Hermits and the New Monasticism* (1984) and *Medieval Women: A Social History of Women in England 450–1500* (1995). She is currently preparing a book on lay piety in England, 1000–1300. She is co-editor of *Belief and Culture: Studies Presented to Henry Mayr-Harting* (2001).

R. I. Moore was Professor of Medieval History at the University of Newcastle upon Tyne, 1993–2003, and taught at the University of Sheffield, 1964–1993. He is the author of *The Origins of European Dissent* (1977), *The Formation of a Persecuting Society: Power and Deviance in Western Europe, 950–1250* (1987) and *The First European Revolution, c. 970–1215* (2001); General Editor of the Blackwell History of the World and a Corresponding Fellow of the Medieval Academy of America.

Kathryn Kelsey Staples is a Ph.D. candidate in medieval history at the University of Minnesota. She is writing a dissertation on daughters and inheritance in late medieval London.

Jocelyn Wogan-Browne is Professor of English at Fordham University. Her most recent publications include *Saints' Lives and Women's Literary Culture, c. 1150–1300: Virginity and Its Authorizations* (2001). She is co-editor of *The Idea of the Vernacular: An Anthology of Middle English Literary Theory, 1280–1520* (1999), *Medieval Women: Texts and Contexts in late Medieval Britain: Essays for Felicity Riddy* (2000), and other collaborative works; she has edited, translated and published articles on literature for and by women in medieval England. She is currently working on various projects in the French literature of England, including a translation series.

A Note on the *Life*

The *Life of Christina of Markyate* survives in a single copy in a manuscript from the fourteenth century, now London, British Library MS. Cotton Tiberius E. 1. Previously in the library of the eighteenth-century antiquarian Sir Robert Cotton, the manuscript was damaged by fire in 1731, losing its initial and final leaves, though there is in fact no evidence that the *Life* was ever complete. It was edited and translated with an introduction by C. H. Talbot (Oxford, 1959, rpt. 1987) in what remains the standard version, now also available in the Medieval Academy Reprints for Teaching 39 (University of Toronto).

Where contributors have used their own translation, the reference given is to the Latin text. In all other cases, references are to Talbot's translation.

PREFACE

The twelve-minute train journey between Oxford (where we both work) and Islip (where we live) is responsible for this book. On such a journey we first met and discovered our mutual interest in Christina; on the next journey we lamented the lack of a book of essays about her; by the third trip we had decided to do something about it. After that the project took on a life of its own. Through Rod Thomson we were introduced to Jane Geddes, who at the time was putting the St Albans Psalter (a Psalter intimately associated with Christina) on the web (and we would recommend that, before anyone reads a word of our book, this website, <www.abdn.ac.uk/stalbanspsalter/english/index.shtml [accessed 4 June 2004]>, should be consulted). Once we had met Jane the opportunity to hold a conference, an idea about which we had originally been very hesitant, suddenly became irresistible, and in August 2003 at St Albans such a conference indeed took place. A word of explanation may be in order here: this is not the 'book of the conference'. Our list of authors for the book had been drawn up and agreed with Routledge some months before the conference took shape and we felt that Christina studies would be better served by, in the main, separating the book from the conference and allowing each to be free-standing; Samuel Fanous, Jane Geddes and Rachel Koopmans alone, therefore, have contributed to both. But we would like to take this opportunity to thank all who attended the conference both for their insights and for their encouragement.

We each have numerous other debts: our contributors have been exemplary, our families and friends forbearing, and Vicky Peters and Faye Kaliszczak of Routledge forgiving. We have every expectation that the Oxford-to-Islip railway line will continue to flourish. Maybe one day it will even take us eastwards to Christina's homeland; we have our hopes.

SBF and HL
The Feast of the Translation
of St Frideswide
Islip

Plate 1 St Albans Psalter, Psalm 105, p. 285 (© St Godehard, Hildesheim)

Plate 2 St Albans Psalter, The Litany, p. 403 (© St Godehard, Hildesheim)

Plate 3 St Albans Psalter, Psalm 118, detail, p.315 (© St Godehard, Hildesheim)

Plate 4 St Albans Psalter, Psalm 132, p. 345 (© St Godehard, Hildesheim)

Plate 5 St Albans Psalter, *The Chanson of St Alexis*, detail p. 57 (© St Godehard, Hildesheim)

Plate 6 St Albans Psalter, David and his musicians, p. 417 (© St Godehard, Hildesheim)

Plate 7 St Albans Psalter, David the musician, p. 56 (© St Godehard, Hildesheim)

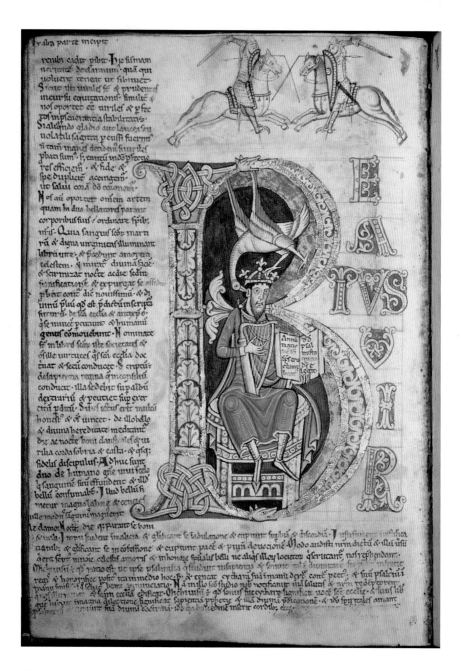

Plate 8 St Albans Psalter, David, Psalm 1, p. 72 (© St Godehard, Hildesheim)

1

CHRISTINA OF MARKYATE

The introduction[1]

Henrietta Leyser

Christina of Markyate (*c.*1096– *c.*1160), hermit and holy woman, was born into a world shaped and scarred by the Norman Conquest of 1066. Already in 1068 a great castle had been built in Huntingdon, her natal home, as well as another in nearby Cambridge; imposing though they were, neither was enough to quell the disquiet against the new regime. In 1069, Earl Waltheof, a major Huntingdon landholder, rebelled against William the Conqueror; in the following year, seemingly in an attempt to forestall further risings in the region, the Conqueror took savage measures against a number of ecclesiastics with East Anglian connections. Native anger and resentment against such treatment spilled over in the summer of 1070 into the remarkable and tangled attack on the monastery at Peterborough and its recently appointed Norman Abbot Turold, a man known to be unsympathetic to Anglo-Saxon sensibilities. 'English people from all over the Fenlands', so the Peterborough Chronicle tells us, joined Danish leaders recently arrived in Ely in the hope and expectation that this was to be the prelude of yet another conquest. Peterborough itself was sacked and burnt and its treasures taken by rebels (led by Hereward the Wake) for safekeeping to Ely. But the Danes stationed there, on learning of the approach of Turold and his band of 'one hundred and sixty Frenchmen ... all fully armed', loaded up their boats with Peterborough's treasures and made for home. Much of this booty was lost at sea, but relics of St Alban were amongst the salvaged treasure and it was while at prayer before these relics, on the eve of his long-planned invasion of England, that King Cnut of Denmark was murdered in 1086. At that moment the last threat to the Norman Conquest disappeared.[2]

Heroic stories of Anglo-Saxon resistance to the Normans were still current in Christina's day, and up to 1154 Peterborough monks continued to chronicle events in English. In Christina's *Life* there is, none the less, not even a whisper of sedition against Norman lordship. Christina's kin had made their peace with their new rulers. Her aunt Alveva had been bedded and made pregnant by that 'firebrand' (as Orderic Vitalis calls him) Ranulf Flambard, right-hand man to William Rufus and one-time administrator of Ely Abbey (hence, one imagines, the opportunity of meeting Alveva).[3] Even after his promotion to the see of Durham in 1099 Ranulf continued to visit Alveva and their children, and, as many of the chapters in this volume will recall, on one such occasion his lustful eye fell on Christina. The depth of the anger Christina's parents felt at their daughter's refusal to fall either into Ranulf's arms or in with his plans makes some kind of sense once their fear that they might lose Ranulf's favour has been taken into account. Prosperous burghers though her parents seem to have been, it is noticeable that their position in the world was far from secure. Sometime after Christina had fled from her home, financial disaster struck the family, who in their plight now had to look to Christina for help. But this is to anticipate; introductory chapters should begin at the beginning and it is high time to turn to the circumstances surrounding Christina's birth.

Typically for a medieval birth we are not given the year (estimates put it at 1096 x 8) but we are regaled with a wealth of detail about the event; one of the pleasures of reading Christina's *Life* is the light it throws, as in this instance, on lay piety. During her pregnancy, Christina's mother Beatrix experienced a prophetic occurrence: whilst sitting in her house she had seen a white dove flying towards her from the monastery of Our Lady (this is likely to be the Augustinian priory founded within the parish church of St Mary's in 1086 x 92, but which later moved outside the town).[4] The dove stayed with Beatrix for seven days 'nestling comfortably and with evident pleasure first in her lap and then in her bosom'. The experience is dated to a Saturday, 'a day specially set aside by the faithful for the devotion to the Mother of God ... between the Assumption [15 August] and the Nativity of our Lady [8 September]' (*Life*, p. 35). Two months later, on 6 November, the feast day of St Leonard, a saint frequently invoked by women in childbirth, Beatrix went to church for Matins and Lauds and for Mass; she commended herself to God, to the Virgin and to St Leonard, returned home and went into a three-hour labour. The child was baptized Theodora.

The intimate scenes of Beatrix's pregnancy and labour immediately pose a question which will re-surface throughout any reading of the *Life* and in many of the chapters in this volume. It is this: what is this *Life*? Is it a record of events told to the author by the actual participants and faithfully recorded by him? A romance (possibilities considered by, among others, Douglas Gray in Chapter 2 and Neil Cartlidge in Chapter 5) or a skilfully constructed piece of hagiography (as Samuel Fanous argues in Chapter 4) we were never intended to take primarily as literal truth? The twenty-first-century reader is likely to want to know, but we need to remember that this is not a twelfth-century question. A medieval reader would always have expected any narrative to have, as did the Bible, at least three meanings: a literal, an allegorical and an analogical; at any one moment one meaning might have precedence over the other and the distinctions might become blurred.[5] Do we, for instance, really know that Christina was born on 6 November, or did this simply seem to be a suitable date, given that St Leonard was frequently invoked by women in childbirth?[6] Are we to believe that her later, momentous visit to St Albans was also on 6 November, as the *Life* avers, or are we to take this as a symbolic way of marking Christina's spiritual re-birth? Was the course of Beatrix's pregnancy actually framed in some way by Marian feasts, or should we take these references to the Virgin as pointers to the relationship Christina will later develop with her and a sign of the protection the *Life* assures us she gave her? All these readings are possible; and it may even be that we do not have to choose between them. Rather more puzzling is the information that Christina's baptismal name was Theodora. It is not hard to imagine that our heroine might have taken for herself a new name once she left the world, and Christina would have been an appropriate choice (St Christina having allegedly been persecuted for her piety by her well-to-do father), but was her baptismal name really Theodora? On the one hand, it is an unusual name for this period; on the other, there is a Theodora in the thirteenth century *Golden Legend* and this Theodora is indeed courted by a rich man offering gifts.[7] There are shades here of our 'Theodora' being offered presents by Flambard. Were oral precursors of the *Golden Legend* already in circulation in twelfth-century England? Or is the name simply the first of a number of signs provided by the *Life* of a certain pretentiousness on the part of Christina's parents or even perhaps of inventiveness on the part of Christina, a mark of her special destiny (following the etymology of the name) as 'a gift of God'?

Let us return to the *Life*. Christina, we are told, was a pious child, strongly aware of her own shortcomings and unusually conscious of the presence of Christ to whom she would sometimes talk 'as if she were speaking to a man' (*Life*, p. 37), a pointer, perhaps, to the later scene when Christina would welcome Christ to her monastery unaware that he is other than a passing pilgrim with 'well-shaped features and a handsome beard' (*Life*, p. 185). Christina's innocence is contrasted with the rather doubtful morals of Canon Sueno, her first mentor ('someone said to her that he was still so stimulated by lust that unless he were prevented by the greater power of God he would without shame lie with any ugly and misshapen leper' (*Life*, p. 39)) and with the frivolous behaviour of her elders. Their party-going, with lots of alcohol, forms an important backdrop to the first part of the *Life*; once Christina has left the world she can put such things behind her. A more enduring problem is Christina's relationships with men which, for better and for worse, form an important theme throughout the *Life* and with which several chapters in this book are concerned (see in particular Chapter 6 by C. Stephen Jaeger and Chapter 10 by Dyan Elliott).

The *Life* gives us the names of over twenty men who in one way or another were important players in Christina's story (and then there is the one who behaved so shamelessly that his name had to be withheld). We should remember also those who had walk-on parts, notably the monks of St Albans. For it was, according to her *Life*, while on a pilgrimage to the shrine of St Alban where her parents had taken her – 'to beg protection' for themselves and for their child (another instance of lay piety) – that Christina decided to become a religious (*Life*, p. 39). The expedition cannot have been lightly undertaken – St Albans is over 40 miles from Huntingdon – but a trip to St Albans would have been an exciting event in the first decades of the twelfth century. St Albans had recovered quickly from the traumas of 1066 and by then was flourishing. In 1101, at

Pentecost, King Henry I had worn his crown there; Henry was present also at the consecration in 1116 of the new abbey church built in place of its demolished Anglo-Saxon predecessor. It is probable that Christina's visit took place just a few years before the consecration, but the building will already have been complete. It is not hard to guess how great an impression it might have made on any pilgrim. The new abbey was enormous – far bigger than contemporary Canterbury – and richly decorated with Romanesque carving.[8] 'When [Christina] had looked carefully at the place and observed the religious bearing of the monks who dwelt there, she declared how fortunate the inmates were, and expressed a wish to share in their fellowship. At length, as her parents were leaving the monastery, having fulfilled all the things they had come to do, she made a sign of the cross with one of her fingernails on the door as a token that she had placed her affection there' (*Life*, p. 39). The next day Christina performed a further ritual. The family had broken their journey at Shillington, and there Christina went to Mass. 'After the gospel [she] approached the altar and offered a penny, saying in her heart "O Lord God, merciful and all powerful, receive my oblation through the hands of Thy priest. For to thee as a surrender of myself I offer this penny. Grant me, I beseech thee, purity and inviolable virginity, whereby thou mayest renew in me the image of thy Son ... " ' (*Life*, p. 41).

Let us now imagine Christina back at home. Enter the wicked Ranulf. The story of his attempted seduction of Christina, of how she thwarted him and of his revenge, needs here only the briefest of summaries; for a full discussion, see Chapter 8 by R. I. Moore. Ranulf, on a visit to his erstwhile mistress, Alveva, lures Christina to his bedroom. Christina escapes and spurns all further advances; Ranulf, in fury, arranges for her to be married to a local lad, Burthred. Christina rejects him. For her, the vow she made at Shillington is sacred. Her family and friends gang up against her; her girlfriend, the fashionably named Melisen,[9] suggests how grand it would be for her to have her own household; finally, in a moment of weakness, Christina yields and accepts Burthred. But does this amount to a betrothal or a full marriage? Thomas Head, in Chapter 7, unravels the complexities of twelfth-century marriage laws, but whatever the uncertainties about Christina's position this much is clear: Burthred seeks consummation, Christina an annulment. Christina tries persuasion and argument, Burthred and Christina's family try every trick in the book – drink, force, sorcery – but all to no avail. For a moment it seems as if Christina may get her way, but her parents are rich and the bishop of Lincoln, in charge of the annulment appeal, is venial. Christina has no alternative but to escape.

Christina's getaway alerts us to a whole network of highly influential hermits scattered around her neighbourhood and beyond; the challenges of classifying such holy men and women is the subject of Chapter 14 by E. A. Jones. The hermit Edwin masterminds the escape, settling Christina at Flamstead with the recluse Alfwen, but not before he has consulted the archbishop of Canterbury about the ethics of the whole venture and has spoken on his way back with hermits 'at various places' (*Life*, p. 85). Ironically the day chosen for the escape is a day when Christina's parents were away visiting 'as was their custom' the hermit Guido (*Life*, p. 89). When they return and find Christina gone, one of the first places they think of looking for her is 'among the recluses of Huntingdon' (*Life*, p. 95). (They are thrown off-track only because Alfwen deliberately misleads them.) Two years later Christina moves from Flamstead to Markyate to live in the hermitage of Edwin's cousin, Roger, formerly a St Albans monk. Five other hermits live with Roger but it is also clear that Roger (perhaps like Guido) had a much wider following; at one point we meet Godescalc of Caddington and his wife, 'people ... of good family, who lived a happy married life under Roger's direction' (*Life*, p. 111). Christina herself is described by Roger, in the one vernacular expression in the text, as 'myn sunendaege dohter' (my Sunday daughter) 'because just as Sunday excels the other days of the week in dignity so he loved Christina more than all the others whom he had begotten or nursed in Christ' (*Life*, p. 107). By all accounts, Roger was a particularly charismatic leader, a supporter of local vocations who had enough authority to be able to protect his followers from outside interference. In Chapter 3, Stephanie Hollis and Jocelyn Wogan-Browne show just how rich and complex the relationship between holy women and their male patrons could be.

Her successful escape to Flamstead to live with Alfwen did not mean that Christina lived happily ever after. In a sense her trials had only just begun. Her relationship with Alfwen seems to have been fraught; her move to Roger's cell, while it brought her spiritual solace, was none the less a time of considerable physical discomfort, confined as she was to a tiny room 'no bigger than a span and a half' (*Life*, p. 103). The fear of being discovered hung heavily over her; perhaps she would yet be 'snatched away', 'handed over to her husband to do as he liked' (*Life*, p. 107). Even after Burthred had at last released her from her marriage vows Christina lived in fear and dread of her old opponent, the bishop of Lincoln, and indeed after Roger's death it was to avoid this bishop's anger that Christina, on the recommendation of the archbishop of York, went to live with the cleric whose name the author of the *Vita* claims to be 'under obligation not to divulge' (*Life*, p. 115). In no time at all the cleric and Christina fall in love. As Kathryn Kelsey Staples and Ruth Mazo Karras make clear in Chapter 11, what is especially interesting about this episode is the frank discussion of Christina's own sexual yearnings; this is no stoical and unfeeling virgin assaulted by some lecherous male. Christina was herself 'so inwardly inflamed that she thought the clothes which clung to her body might be set on fire' (*Life*, p. 117), and though she managed to resist the cleric's advances (even when he stripped before her), none the less the strength of her affections troubled her and subsequently made her pause before making her profession as a nun lest she had in some way damaged her virginity.

Christina finally made her profession at St Albans in *c.* 1131, during the abbacy of Geoffrey de Gorran. The death of the bishop of Lincoln in 1123 had at last given her freedom. Courted, according to the *Life*, by monasteries both at home and abroad 'to add prestige to their places' (*Life*, p. 127), Christina none the less chose to return to St Albans and to take up her long-coveted position as heir to Roger's hermitage. Christina has in consequence long been described as a hermit, sometimes even as an anchorite, but these terms should not be interpreted in their narrowest sense since there is no evidence that Christina ever wanted the solitary life. Many religious women in twelfth- and thirteenth-century England did indeed choose to become anchorites.[10] Christina was not one of them; only during the years when she feared she would be returned to Burthred did she live in strict seclusion. Necessity not predilection drove her to accept the confines of the tiny cell that Roger offered her. After Roger's death, when Christina returned to Markyate, she became the head of a small but informal community that grew along with her reputation, and there is never any suggestion that she or any of her followers sought enclosure. On the contrary, guests of both sexes come and go: Abbot Geoffrey; the author of the *Life*; Christina's brother and her sister; Simon of Bermondsey; these are just some of her 'familiar circle'. When a pilgrim turns up 'quite unknown but of revered mien', Christina welcomes him hospitably 'as she did everyone' (*Life*, p. 183) (realizing only later that the pilgrim is Christ).

Within Christina's own lifetime the opportunities for women to lead the religious life increased dramatically; between 1130 and 1165 at least 85 new communities for women were founded, many by women themselves.[11] Christina stands then at a turning point for English holy women of the twelfth century and we should take seriously her hesitations as to where to make her final profession. Many choices lay before her. The likelihood of her ever going abroad was perhaps slight – the *Life*'s naming of the well-known houses of Fontevrault or Marcigny may be no more than rhetorical embellishment designed to heighten the status of Markyate – but it is all the same not impossible, as the *Life* suggests (p. 147), that Christina at some point considered moving beyond the purview of St Albans. At about the time that Markyate was established as a priory (1145), Abbot Geoffrey was also negotiating with a community of women living nearby Sopwell. The conditions imposed suggest friction: in future, no woman was to be received into the community without permission from St Albans, the women were to be veiled and to live according to the Rule of Benedict and they were to be strictly cloistered: 'guarding the reputation and well-being of the nuns, having made there a house, he declared them to be enclosed there, under lock and doorbolt and seal of the abbot'.[12] For sacramental purposes and for financial security male patronage was essential for any community of women; often, as in the case of Sopwell, it seems to have been dearly bought. Christina in contrast seems to have reached the point where she was able to set her own terms but there was perhaps a protracted period of negotiation behind this. A telling clause in Markyate's foundation charter seeks to preserve the independence of the community from any change in their way of life without the express agreement of the women themselves. Markyate was not a cell of St Albans but of St Paul's in London, but the foundation charter is witnessed by Geoffrey, and there can be no doubt of Geoffrey's involvement in its institutionalization and possibly in these final terms.[13]

Christina's relationship with Abbot Geoffrey fills the last quarter of the *Life* as we have it; the last sentence reads: 'Christina's thoughts were with her dear friend Abbot Geoffrey ... night and day, and she busied herself with his interests by fasting, watching, calling upon God, the angels, and other holy folk in heaven and on earth, sensibly reproving him when his actions were not quite right ... ' (*Life*, p. 193). Strictly speaking, since the *Life* is incomplete and breaks off here, this moment cannot be called a conclusion, but it none the less seems a fitting end. The first time we meet Geoffrey he is presented as a somewhat controversial figure. He had allegedly started his term of office well, 'but as fortune smiled upon him through the support of noble relatives, he began to grow more haughty than was right and relied more on his own judgement than on that of his monks ... ' (*Life*, p. 135). Christina is said to have effected his 'full conversion'. It is therefore more than a little ironical that it is her needs and influence that may themselves have been a cause of dissension between Geoffrey and his monks. While the *Life* suggests only fruitful exchange – 'while [Geoffrey] centred his attention on providing the virgin with material assistance, she strove to enrich the man in virtue ... ' (p. 135) – the later St Albans chronicle, *Deeds of the Abbots*, provides a different perspective:

> ... the abbot constructed the place of the nuns of Markyate from its foundations, giving it rents and tolls from various places for the sustenance of Christina, his beloved, and her congregation of sisters there who were under the regimen and doctrine of Christina, although the convent of St Albans murmured over such expenses and grants ...[14]

Was Christina herself instrumental in some of the negotiations that guaranteed the prosperity of her house? Not all of Christina's advice to Geoffrey need have been strictly spiritual. As a young woman Christina had been the keeper of her father's keys, and her family had set much store on her 'prudence in affairs'; 'if she had given her mind to worldly pursuits she could have enriched and ennobled not only herself and her family but also all her relatives' (*Life*, pp. 67–9). As it was it seems that, even after she had left the world, it was to Christina to whom her family turned in an unexpected (and unexplained) hour of need, 'finding with her both salvation for their souls and safety for their bodies' (*Life*, p. 69).

The most eloquent defence of the relationship between Geoffrey, his community and his beloved Christina is to be found in the initial to Psalm 105 in the St Albans Psalter.[15] Here Christina, her hand touching Christ's, begs for mercy on behalf of the group of monks who cluster behind her. The exact relationship between Christina, the Psalter and St Albans has long been a matter of debate. The inclusion in the calendar of the names of her family and friends has been the starting point for many a speculation. Was this a book made specifically for Christina or only subsequently adapted for her? What messages do the images contain? What function was the book to have? Was this only a book of devotion or did it have a secondary purpose as a schoolbook intended to teach Christina how to read both Old French and Latin? What is the meaning of the inclusion of the story of St Alexis? These are the issues addressed by Jane Geddes in Chapter 12, and by Tony Hunt's study in Chapter 13 on the history of the Alexis legend and its arrival in England.

The St Albans Psalter is a luxurious and costly book; its association with Christina bears testimony to her stature. Rachel Koopmans in Chapter 9 makes the suggestion that Christina was the saint who 'got away'; and that whoever it was who wrote her *Life* glorified the part played throughout her days by the monastery of St Albans in the hope and expectation that she could be annexed by the monks to add lustre to their house. In-house quarrelling spoilt the plan; the *Life* lay unfinished; on her death – and we have no record of the date – no place of honour was found for Christina in the monastery. Links between the priory at Markyate and the monastery withered. It becomes difficult therefore for us to know quite where to place Christina in the history of twelfth-century holy women. The knowledge that Henry II gave her fifty shillings-worth of grain in 1155–56, and that at about the same time sandals and three mitres she had embroidered went to Rome as a present for Pope Adrian, hardly seem sufficient epitaphs for the woman who had once bested that 'firebrand' the bishop of Durham.[16]

Holy women in England are not generally assumed to have made waves. England – at least until the fourteenth century – is presented time and again as a model of orthodoxy; it harboured no heretics and did not suffer extremists. Continental Europe might be home to Beguines, to stigmatics and eccentric mystics, but not England. England was different.[17] But was it? It is surely helpful to consider Christina not only in the company of her English counterparts, the hermit sister of Aelred of Rievaulx, for whom he wrote a devotional treatise, or the recipients of the *Ancrene Wisse*, but – as Elizabeth Petroff suggests – alongside those celebrated twelfth-century European visionaries Hildegard of Bingen and Elisabeth of Schönau.[18] For the extraordinary quality of Christina's visions, their frequency and intensity, is matched by the luminous beauty of the illustrations the St Albans Psalter provided for her contemplation. The aesthetic pleasure these pictures give today should not blind us to the immediacy of their meaning for Christina nor prevent us from seeing her own visions in equally full colours. Throughout Christina's life her spiritual experiences come to her either from something she has imagined or something she has seen: as a small child she talks to Christ on her bed at night as if she could see him (*Life*, p. 37); when she is taken by her parents to St Albans she looks 'carefully at the place'; then, that same evening, she sees herself on her deathbed 'as if the future were already present' (*Life*, p. 39). During some of her worst trials with her parents, a vision of the Virgin to whom she is bidden to offer flowers brings her the assurance that she will triumph over Burthred, envisioned prostrate on the floor 'swathed in a black cape' while Christina herself is arrayed in white (*Life*, p. 77). Images come to Christina both from the natural world, such as a 'large and swampy meadow full of bulls with threatening horns and glaring eyes' (*Life*, p. 99), and from holy lore: 'on the day of Our Lord's Annunciation', for example, 'the fairest of the children of men, came to her through the locked door, bearing in his right hand a cross of gold' (*Life*, p. 107), a vision that draws on illustrations both of the Annunciation and of the Harrowing of Hell.[19]

Christina's marriage to Christ lies at the heart of her vocation but, notwithstanding her steadfast commitment to this concept and even allowing for the power of the vision in which Christina comes to recognize an unknown pilgrim as Christ himself (*Life*, p. 187), it is still through her devotion to the Virgin that Christina's piety finds its most consistent expression. In her home town of Huntingdon it is 'the thought of the Mother of God' and the Hail Mary prayer which give her the courage to defy her parents (*Life*, p. 49); it is Mary who terrifies Burthred into finally releasing Christina from her vows to him (*Life*, p. 109), and it is Mary, as 'queen of heaven sitting on a throne [with] angels of brightness seated about her' (*Life*, p. 111), who promises Christina that she will give her whatever she asks for. During one of the most taxing episodes of her life, when she is smitten with passionate love for her cleric-guardian, it is a vision in which she takes the place of Mary holding the Christ-child to her bosom that frees her from her obsession (*Life*, p. 119); and it will be Mary who cures her too of her worst physical ailment. On Christina's supposed death-bed Mary comes 'with shining countenance [her] head veiled in a snow-white coif, adorned across the breadth of it with gold embroidery and fringed on each end with gold' carrying with her 'a small box in which she had brought an electuary of unusual fragrance' which she herself administers to Christina (*Life*, p. 125). And finally it is Mary who settles her qualms as to whether she can rightly consider herself a virgin despite the many erotic thoughts she has harboured in her life (*Life*, p. 127).

Christina's Marian piety, coupled with her scrupulous conscience, place her firmly in line with the preoccupations and interests of twelfth-century Europe; her love for Mary may have been derived from Anglo-Saxon custom (it is notable that St Albans was a house that staunchly supported the revival of the Anglo-Saxon Feast of the Conception of the Virgin); then again it could also owe much to continental devotional trends.[20] In the mid-twelfth century St Albans could confidently claim to be at the centre of a movement for cultural and religious renewal, drawing on local traditions but showing at the same time no respect for national boundaries. St Alban, the protomartyr of England newly rehoused in a shrine made by Anketil, a former moneyer to the King of Denmark,[21] had called upon Christina, Roger's 'sunendaege dohter' and the beloved of Norman Geoffrey, to 'further his community on earth' (*Life*, p. 127). We hope this volume will contribute to an appreciation of how this rich and nuanced vocation might be interpreted and understood.

Notes

1 I would like to record my thanks to Timea Szell for her particularly attentive reading of this introduction; to Henry Mayr-Harting for conversations over many years about Christina; to Jocelyn Wogan-Browne for support of all things eremitical and to Samuel Fanous for continual editorial good cheer.

2 For events at Peterborough see the 'E' entries for 1070 in *The Anglo-Saxon Chronicle: a revised edition*, ed. Dorothy Whitelock, David C. Douglas and Susie L. Tucker (London, 1961). The best account of English resistance to the Conquest is to be found now in Ann Williams, *The English and the Norman Conquest* (Woodbridge, 1995).

3 The starting point for any discussion of Ranulf Flambard's career remains the study by R. W. Southern, 'Ranulf Flambard', in his *Medieval Humanism and Other Studies* (Oxford, 1970), pp. 183–205.

4 See Alison Binns, *Dedications of Monastic Houses in England and Wales, 1066–1216* (Woodbridge, 1989), p. 136.

5 See Ruth Morse, *Truth and Convention in the Middle Ages: Rhetoric, Representation and Reality* (Cambridge, 1991), both for an analysis of different approaches to truth in the Middle Ages and for a sceptical interpretation of the 'truth content' (pp. 149–51) of Christina's story.

6 Since writing this introduction Tom Licence has pointed out to me that St Leonard is also a saint much favoured by hermits whose chapels were often dedicated to him. See the example given by E. A. Jones in Chapter 14 of this volume. St Leonard allegedly was a sixth-century hermit who helped Clothilda (the wife of Clovis) give birth, but his cult dates only from the mid-eleventh century. For his *Life*, see *AA.SS* Nov. III (1910), 139–209.

7 Theodora's story may be found in translation in Jacobus de Voragine, *The Golden Legend; Readings on the Saints*, trans. William Granger Ryan, 2 vols. (Princeton, 1993), i. 365–8. For the significance of women's names in twelfth-century England see Cecily Clark, 'Women's Names in Post-Conquest England: Observations and Speculations' in *Words, Names and History: Selected Writings of Cecily Clark*, ed. Peter Jackson (Cambridge, 1995), pp. 117–55.

8 See Deborah Kahn, 'Recent Discoveries of Romanesque Sculpture at St Albans' in *Studies in Medieval Sculpture*, ed. F. H. Thompson, Society of Antiquaries Occasional Papers (New Series) III (1983), pp. 71–89. For the history of St Albans in this period see in the first instance *Gesta Abbatum*, i, and among secondary literature the case study presented by Emma Cownie in her *Religious Patronage in Anglo-Norman England* (Woodbridge, 1998), pp. 80–96.

9 For 'Melisen' as opposed to Talbot's 'Helisen' see P. Grosjean's review of C. H. Talbot's edition, *Analecta Bollandiana* 78 (1960), p. 199. I owe this reference to Michael Wright.

10 See Ann Warren, *Anchorites and their Patrons in Medieval England* (Berkeley, 1985), in particular pp. 18–21.

11 The figure is taken from Elkins, *Holy Women*, p. xiii.

12 *Gesta Abbatum*, i. 81, quoted by Elkins, *Holy Women*, p. 47.

13 For the sometimes fraught relationships between women religious and their male patrons in this period see Elkins, *Holy Women*, pp. 38–60; Thompson, *Women Religious*, pp. 54–79; and for Christina and Markyate in particular, Koopmans, 'The Conclusion'.

14 *Gesta Abbatum*, i. 102. For a discussion of the passage and for the translation see Koopmans, 'The Conclusion', p. 677.

15 For the Psalter and full bibliography see
<www. abdn.ac.uk/stalbanspsalter/English/index.shtml>.

For a different perspective from that offered here on the origins of the Psalter see Kristine Haney, *The St Albans Psalter: An Anglo-Norman Song of Faith* (New York, 2002).

16 For Henry's donation see *The Great Rolls of the Pipe Roll of King Henry the Second, AD 1155, 1156, 1157, 1158*, ed. J. Hunter (London, 1844), p. 22. For the gift to Adrian IV, *Gesta Abbatum*, i. 127. For Adrian IV, his English origins and his connections with St Albans see R. W. Southern, *Medieval Humanism*, pp. 234–5.

17 See for example the comment by Warren, *Anchorites and their Patrons*, pp. 21–2: 'On the Continent one discovers religious women as nuns and tertiaries, but also as Beguines, Humiliati, Franciscan tertiaries, and even heretics. English women had fewer choices … The increase in female anchoritism in the thirteenth century in England was a means of containing the spiritual enthusiasm observable throughout Catholic Europe. In a vocation of honoured antiquity English women expressed current sensibilities.'

18 *Medieval Women's Visionary Literature*, ed. Elizabeth Petroff (Oxford, 1986), pp. 136–58.

19 I owe this point to Petroff, *Medieval Women's Visionary Literature*, p. 128.

20 For Marian devotion in England see Nigel Morgan, 'Texts and Images of Marian Devotion in English Twelfth-Century Monasticism, and their Influence on the Secular Church' in *Monasteries and Society in Medieval Britain*, ed. Benjamin Thompson, Harlaxton Medieval Studies VI (Stamford, 1999), pp. 117–36; see p. 121, n.17 for a comprehensive bibliography on the controversy concerning the Feast of the Immaculate Conception. Hilda Graef, *Mary: a History of Doctrine and Devotion* (London, 1963), i. 210–64, remains the best introduction to the Cistercian veneration of Mary and its influence across Europe. It may be worth pointing out that it is hardly likely to be a coincidence that Christina is said to have died on 8 December, in other words on the Feast of the Immaculate Conception.

21 For Anketil and the new shrine see *Gesta Abbatum*, i. 84–7.

2

CHRISTINA OF MARKYATE

The literary background

Douglas Gray

The importance and interest of the *vita* of Christina of Markyate written by an anonymous monk of St Albans has long been recognized by historians of spirituality, but students of the literature produced in early post-Conquest England have in general not given it the same attention.[1] It presents considerable problems,[2] but it also has some fascinating links with the literary traditions of the past and the future, and with the various literary genres of its own period. One of its most interesting features is the way in which it seems to be placed on the edges of a number of these, and to derive not only its individuality but also some of its power from its 'marginal' position. It is a spiritual biography, but similar to a saint's life; it is almost an autobiography based on the reminiscences of Christina (who was, perhaps, as Christopher Brooke remarked, 'given to romancing');[3] indeed, it sometimes also reads like a romance. The monk knew his religious books, but probably, as C. H. Talbot said, 'was conscious also that here was a story to which pure imaginative romance, whether courtly or popular, could offer little competition.'[4] It is, above all, an impressive literary work in its own right. Whatever we think of the questions of 'romancing' and veracity, there is no doubt that the story is an excellent example of narrative art. It is vivid and exciting, both as the story of a twelfth-century girl's tribulations and adventures, and as a spiritual odyssey in which the supernatural, marvels and visions are prominent. The spiritual and the human world overlap and are interfused: this is evident in some characteristic expressions of homely piety, as when the child Christina talks to Christ on her bed at night 'just as if she were speaking to a man she could see; and this she did with a loud clear voice, so that all who were resting in the same house could hear and understand her' (*Life*, p. 37).

Local realism

The use of detail often gives the work a remarkable local 'realism':[5] it offers some fascinating and diverse glimpses of everyday life – a guestroom decorated with tapestries or hangings (*Life*, p. 43); a scene of feasting in hall in which Christina acts as cupbearer (*Life*, p. 49); that the monkish author is writing on wax (tablets) (*Life*, p. 113), etc. – or of behaviour and social attitudes – the way in which Burthred's friends urge him back into Christina's bedroom, reproaching him for being 'a spineless and useless fellow' (*Life*, p. 53); the shame and social dishonour felt by the parents ('her life of poverty will bring the whole of the nobility into disrepute', (*Life*, p. 59)). There are horrific descriptions of Christina's illnesses (*Life*, pp. 103, 123) and of her sufferings in her cell at Roger's hermitage (*Life*, p. 105). Carefully chosen circumstantial details make scenes more vivid: the trembling Christina hiding from Burthred between the wall and the wall hangings (*Life*, p. 53); her escape with Loric (*Life*, pp. 89–93), and later with Godescalc, Roger's disciple, in which they fall off their horse, lose their way at night and have to walk on foot 'groping their way in the darkness as best they could' (*Life*, p. 113).

Emotional drama

The *Life* is notable for its strongly emotional quality. It encompasses the joys and sweetness of contemplation, the tears of longing for heaven and of intense spiritual friendship, and some baser human passions and desires. The emotional states of the actors in the narrative are sometimes portrayed with great precision and understanding: the despair and hope of Christina before her escape, for instance (*Life*, p. 91). We are shown extremes both of anger (the fury of the family, ordering the killing of any companion helping her (*Life*, p. 95)) and of grief (in the brief but moving scene of the death of Christina's brother Gregory, for instance (*Life*, pp. 157–9)). The author is especially skilled in the construction of scenes of intense emotion. An excellent example is found in the two scenes in which Christina hears that her first spiritual adviser, Sueno, has turned against her (*Life*, p. 55) and that in which Sueno, after discovering the truth, grieves bitterly and repents (*Life*, p. 59). Not the least effect of this sequence is to make this first example of an intense friendship convincing on a human level. Emotional undertones make for very dramatic scenes, as in that in which Christina is brought before Fredebertus, the prior of Huntingdon, (*Life*, pp. 61–5), and the intellectual exchanges take place against a background of high emotion. Autti speaks with a 'tearful voice', and Christina, after answering calmly and rationally, bursts out at Fredebertus' suggestion of taking an oath: 'at these words the maiden casting her eyes up to heaven and with a joyful countenance replied: "I will not merely take an oath, but I am prepared to prove it, by carrying red-hot iron in these my bare hands"' (characteristically, gesture and detail are used to emphasize the intensity of the moment). Scenes of excitement – whether caused by fear (as when the sisters see an apparition of a headless body (*Life*, p. 179)), or by joyful expectation (as in the series of urgent questions which express the flurry of Christina's thoughts as she broods on the return of the mysterious pilgrim (*Life*, p. 185–7)) – are impressively done. The conduct of the narrative is careful,[6] and there is an easy balance of dialogue and formal speech.

13

Characterization

It would be rash to talk of characterization in its more modern senses, but the main figures emerge clearly from the narrative. The author does not wish us to waste sympathy on Christina's father and mother, but their emotions are sharply registered. Autti loses all hope after the bishop of Lincoln's first judgement against them, and his distress and injured pride are revealed when he says to his daughter, 'you are even made mistress over me'. His sadness grows from day to day (*Life*, pp. 65–7) – only to be somewhat relieved by the suggestion of his friends that they should appeal to the bishop's greed.[7] Autti and Beatrix are heightened figures, and we will never know how much of their fury – when Autti, 'maddened with anger', drives her out of the house naked, and Beatrix swears that she does not care who would corrupt her daughter provided that it could be done (*Life*, p. 73) – is due to hagiographical hyperbole, but it makes for an exciting story. Burthred, Christina's suitor and husband, is also an interesting figure. He is sometimes simply used as a pawn or shown yielding to the scorn of his friends or (not without hesitation) to the fury and the bribes of her parents. When he first agrees to release his wife he is praised for his 'wise and religious sentiments' (*Life*, pp. 87–91), but he appears much less noble in the scene before the bishop (who has been bribed) when he insults her and boasts of his success. His *furor* takes over until his final penitent appearance.

It is the character of Christina which dominates the book. Even when allowance has been made for hagiography's urge to heighten and idealize, she must have been a remarkable woman. She appears as both beautiful and intelligent (as she demonstrates in her answers to Fredebertus who is amazed at her *prudencia* (*Life*, pp. 61–3)). The author praises her 'moral integrity' (*morum honestas*), her beauty and grace which made her accounted 'more lovable than all other women', and her intelligence and prudence in her actions, which would have made her a great success in secular life (*Life*, pp. 67–9). The undoubted forcefulness of her personality suggests that she fully shared the family trait of determination (or obstinacy), as described by the author, whether the cause was right or wrong (*Life*, p. 67). In her case it sometimes sounds rather like the heroic fault (or virtue) of *désmesure* or *ofermod* in medieval epic. But the clerical author's view is clear: perseverance in good is virtuous, but perseverance in evil is wicked. It is not only humans who feel the force of her determination: anxious for her friend Abbot Geoffrey, she 'stormed God in prayer (*precibus pulsat accumulacius*)' (*Life*, p. 156–7). She is, however, allowed to show some moments of fear and uncertainty. Like other visionaries and saints she is the object of hostile rumours and gossip: some call her a dreamer, others a seducer of souls, others a worldly-wise business woman, or one who loved the abbot with an earthly love (*Life*, p. 173). The author assigns these to malice inspired by the devil; they are part of the tribulations inherent in an 'imitation' of Christ, and confirm her sanctity.

In the midst of her enemies, she has her friends and helpers, sometimes supernatural protectors like Christ and the Virgin Mary, who cares for her from the day of her birth, or the two mysterious phantoms (*fata*) whom the old Jewish woman sees accompanying her (*Life*, p. 75). Among the human friends and protectors, two contrasting figures stand out – Roger the hermit and Geoffrey the abbot – who are the centres of a story of two spiritual love affairs. Roger, the old hermit who instructs and trains her, is a father figure to her, and she is his favourite spiritual child: he calls her in a homely English phrase 'myn sunendaege dohter' (*Life*, p. 107). His uncompromising asceticism is revealed in a certain sharpness of tone (with Edwin, for instance, on learning that Christina had been married (*Life*, p. 83)). Their love comes from their first sight of each other: 'the fire ... which had been kindled by the spirit of God and burned in each one of them cast its sparks into their hearts by the grace of that mutual glance; and so made one in heart and soul in chastity and charity in Christ, they were not afraid to dwell together under the same roof ... Their holy affection [*sanctus amor*] grew day by day, like a large flame springing from two brands joined together' (*Life*, p. 103).

Geoffrey the abbot is a very different person, a man of noble birth and a prelate at the heart of the Anglo-Norman establishment, and from the greater detail available to the author (from St Albans sources and perhaps from a close acquaintance) a fuller picture emerges. His introduction is far from complimentary: 'a certain noble and powerful person' who had begun well as abbot but 'as fortune smiled upon him through the support of noble relatives, he began to grow more haughty than was right and relied more on his own judgement than on that of his monks ... a man of great spirit but obstinate and high-handed' (*Life*, p. 135). Christina's relationship with him gets off to an even more uncertain start than that with Roger, her first message to him (from a vision) being angrily rejected (he apparently shared the opinion of some of her critics that she was a dreamer). However, 'a wonderful though pure love' develops. It is a mutual love (*amor mutuus*), which involves a genuine mutuality – 'he supported her in worldly matters: she commended him to God more earnestly in her prayers' (*Life*, pp. 139–43). She becomes his spiritual adviser (reproving him sharply if necessary). Again the spiritual love is intense: he is regularly called 'her beloved' (*dilectum suum*); she took him to her bosom (*amplectabatur sinu*) in a closer bond of holy affection (*Life*, p. 157); and love inspires the visions in which she sees him (in one she sees herself embracing Geoffrey, and Christ closing her fingers with his own hand (*Life*, p. 169)). With the entry of such an important ecclesiastical figure come allusions to the high politics of the reign of King Stephen. One more relaxed remark however shows that the abbot was a companiable man – he was pleased to be asked to go on an embassy to the papal court, because as he was popular there 'he looked forward to seeing his old friends again' (*Life*, p. 163). In all matters his trust in the advice of his adviser is confirmed: 'the virgin's pure heart had more power with God than the factions and shrewd cunning of the great ones of this world' (*Life*, pp. 165–7). This relationship differs from that between Christina and Roger: it is a mutual one, and here, although Geoffrey is her protector and patron, she becomes his mentor.

Author and scribe

A number of medieval literary works, not necessarily always those involving some cooperation between a literate 'author' and an illiterate or semi-illiterate 'speaker', may suggest some of the ramifications of 'authorship' arising from situations like that of Christina and her monk. There was clearly considerable variety. Straightforward 'dictation' was obviously one possibility. It has been suggested, for instance, that a noble writer like Villehardouin may have dictated his memoirs of the fourth crusade to a secretary. His account has the directness of a popular narrative, and his style owes much to the *chanson de geste* and the popular *conte* that would have been familiar to him. He uses a number of 'oral habits' – formulae, anticipations, recapitulations, etc.[8] Dictation may well have been a common practice in that level of secular society. One would guess that in this case there was little 'input' from a secretary. At the end of the Middle Ages, Lord Bernard Stuart of Aubigny, a Scottish nobleman in the service of the King of France, wrote a brief 'art of war':[9] the preface says that on his last embassy to Scotland he summoned Maistre Estienne Le Jeune, his secretary and chaplain, 'a rediger et escripre ledict livre et traicte' (to redact and write the aforesaid book and tract). It is not clear whether the secretary acted as a simple scribe (an illustration in one manuscript shows the author seated dictating to his secretary) or whether he took some part in the compilation. The latter seems likely, since the 'livret' is based on a work by Robert de Barsat or Balsac, *La Nef des Batailles* (printed in 1502), to which Aubigny added notes from his own experiences, from earlier French military tradition and sometimes from classical sources.

Literary parallels

The composition of two religious texts – the Otherworld Vision of the peasant Thurkill (1206) and the fifteenth-century *Book of Margery Kempe* – presents some interesting and closer parallels to the *Life* of Christina. The 'voice' of the illiterate Thurkill is not as clearly heard as that of Christina, although some of the details of his life are preserved. An excellent study by Paul Gerhard Schmidt[10] explores the possible process of redaction, from the original vision to the written form of the clerical author. The latter's stated intention, to represent the 'visionem simplicis viri simplici eloquio, sicut ab eius ore audivimus' (vision of a simple man with simple eloquence, just as we heard it from his mouth) turns out to be something of a literary topic. Two points made by Schmidt are especially relevant to the making of the *Life* of Christina. He points out the many influences that were at work on the account (which developed over an unknown period of time): Thurkill spoke with relatives, the priest, villagers and their lord, and travelled about telling of his revelations. This is a timely reminder that this kind of composition does not take place in a vacuum, and is not limited to two participants. Allowing the impossibility of distinguishing with certainty between the original and its final literary form, he argues that we should not 'dismiss as suspect all those passages where a literary model can be demonstrated', since the illiterate 'can be familiar with and reproduce literary motifs drawn from sermons, stories or other forms of oral tradition'. The nature of the composition of the *Book of Margery Kempe* has been much debated. She was not literate, or not fully literate, and the priest who eventually wrote the book obviously had some editorial role.[11] However, it seems to be neither a simple dictated record of Margery's own words nor a straightforward clerical narrative. It seems to be an example of a kind of 'collaborative authorship'. Again, we cannot always clearly distinguish the 'voices': we may safely attribute to the priest the doubts he expresses at one point concerning her experiences, but perhaps not necessarily the echoes of the (fourteenth century) meditations of Richard Rolle, which she might possibly have heard herself. Other remarks have the ring of an individual voice and sensibility which most readers would identify as hers; and there are passages which seem to have traces of oral narrative or even direct quotation.[12] Sometimes it seems similar to the modern 'personal narrative' or 'true experience story' in which teller and audience interact in traditional attitudes and use conventional topics and techniques.[13]

The story produced by Christina and her monk, possibly with 'input' from others, and spread over an unknown period of time, seems clearly to be the result of a kind of 'collaborative composition'. There is an interesting oscillation between the voice of the clerical narrator and what sounds very much like the voice of Christina herself. It has been said that 'most of it reads as though she had told him, perhaps many times, what had happened, doubtless somewhat embroidering the original events with each repetition'.[14] However, the clerical narrator's presence is felt throughout, not only in the Augustinian cast given to this providential story, but in comments, and some self-conscious rhetorical embellishments, such as sets of rhetorical questions (*Life*, pp. 93, 157) or a fervent exclamation against Satan (*Life*, p. 173).[15] Often Christina seems very close. We occasionally seem to hear her own turns of phrase: she was so eager to know what had been arranged for her escape that 'as she afterwards averred in my hearing, if she had been given the choice of speaking with the hermit or of having a lump of gold as big as the monastery she was sitting in, she would have set aside the gold without hesitation' (*Life*, p. 87). She sent a messenger to Geoffrey with a proverb – 'tell your master from me: "Tomorrow white stones will be thrown into the pot"' ('a charming proverb', says the narrator, 'which is quoted when success is assured'). She speaks to the Virgin Mary in a homely and familiar way. The result, as in the *Book of Margery Kempe*, is often a striking combination of immediacy and detachment.

Society and language

The *Life* raises some wider literary and cultural questions. One of the 'margins' on which it seems to be situated is socio-linguistic. There was a borderline (not always a rigidly defined one – a non-clerical recluse might be able to recite the Latin Psalter) between the Latin language and culture of the 'clerks' and the vernaculars of twelfth-century England. This seems to be simply assumed in the *Life*: Roger's English phrase 'my Sunday daughter' and Christina's 'charming proverb' are glossed for clerical readers by the narrator. Another borderline – that which divides speakers of French from speakers of English – is easy to exaggerate, especially since most modern inhabitants of England have come to accept monolingualism as a fact of life. Talbot, noting the names of the hermits and recluses, remarks that 'the people with whom Christina was intimately connected seem to have belonged exclusively to the Anglo-Saxon element of the community', and suggests that the eremitical movement was 'particularly strong among the natives of the country' (with the Normans more concerned with 'the organized and disciplined forms of religious asceticism'), that there is 'an undercurrent of national feeling' in the accounts of contemporary hermits, and that 'it is perhaps not entirely by accident' that some of the Normans who are mentioned 'are portrayed in a somewhat unfavourable light' (*Life*, pp. 12–13). We might note, however, that the two Norman Archbishops, Thurstan and Ralph d'Escures, are honourable exceptions, as is Abbot Geoffrey.[16] It is probably the case that Christina, like other English recluses, was 'ministering to the people who were not at home with the Anglo-Norman culture, and who may well have found it hard to make themselves understood by their new French-speaking lords',[17] but the two speech communities, though distinct, surely to some extent overlapped. While some people remained monolingual, others could cope in both languages. No doubt there were other examples of liaisons like that of Ranulf Flambard and Alveva, and the Normans sometimes attempted to legitimize their position by marrying English women. Christina's contemporaries William of Malmesbury and Orderic Vitalis were the offspring of mixed marriages. Christina, like the anchorite Wulfric of Haselbury, was a link between the two cultures. Although her background was Anglo-Saxon, she must have been able to speak Anglo-Norman reasonably well (she communicates with Archbishop Thurstan, who suggests that she might go to the houses of Marcigny or Fontevrault, as well as with Abbot Geoffrey).

Her *Life* also forms an illuminating part of the varied literary culture which was developing in early Anglo-Norman England. Literature in Anglo-Norman reached a high point in the reign of Henry II, but before then was producing distinctive works of considerable interest, especially saints' legends and chronicles (both sometimes revealing an interest in the English past and in English saints).[18] Anglo-Latin literature was well established.[19] It, too, looked both forward and back. Besides the influential masterpieces of Geoffrey of Monmouth on the earlier kings of Britain and the prophecies of Merlin, there was already a series of talented historians interested in contemporary events and also in earlier English saints and history. Henry of Huntingdon (educated in the house of Robert Bloet, bishop of Lincoln, one of the 'villains' in Christina's book) writes his own account in the latter part of his history of the English; in the earlier parts he uses Bede and the Anglo-Saxon Chronicle, and even attempts a translation of the poem *The Battle of Brunanburh* – and even more surprisingly seems to try to imitate Old English verse rhythms.[20] English as a sophisticated literary medium was eclipsed after the Conquest and throughout Christina's lifetime. The Old English Chronicle continued for a time – at Peterborough up to 1154 in a version which contains some powerful passages and which also gives a glimpse into the large changes that were taking place in the language.[21] In some areas of England there was a continuous interest in Old English religious writing. Otherwise, English writing survives in scraps or brief quotations – like the religious song that was taught to the hermit Godric by the Virgin Mary; or is completely lost – like the mysterious English Fables attributed to 'King Alfred' (by that time a traditional figure of wisdom) which Marie de France says she translated. There must, however, have been an extensive body of oral literature.

Christina's book does not seem to have been influential or widely read, but it has intriguing links with the varied writings of its time. The parallels and similarities are often indirect: we must not rashly attribute too much direct knowledge to Christina herself – though we have to remember that the literary genres closest to her *Life* were often more widely disseminated in oral form. Her book is related to a number of these, and also illustrates aspects of contemporary devotional or cultural life which were to prove influential. Some scenes are almost certainly heightened, as is common in hagiography, giving us something which is not quite 'history' but not totally 'fiction'. The narrative is so vivid that there has sometimes been a tendency to regard the book as a totally accurate biography and an exact document of social history, but some caution is necessary.

Biography, hagiography and romance

The *Life*'s obvious link is with the saints' lives, which circulated in literary, but also in oral, visual or dramatic form (her own Abbot Geoffrey had made a play of St Catherine before he entered the monastery). The legend of St Alexis, which has some close parallels to the life of Christina, is found in illustrated form in the St Albans Psalter. A chapel or an altar to Alexis was consecrated at St Albans by Bishop Flambard early in the twelfth century (perhaps *c.* 1115), and possibly, as Dominica Legge suggested, the *Chanson* was sung in connection with this occasion.[22] It is virtually certain that Christina would know this legend. She also knew (by heart) the legend of the virgin martyr St Cecilia, which seems to have been a model for her and her *Life*. We do not know whether she or her hagiographer had heard Benedeit's Anglo-Norman legend of the voyage of St Brendan (written *c.* 1106),[23] or some of the other Anglo-Norman lives which were in circulation. Nor do we know for certain how much her hagiographer knew of the extensive Latin hagiography available, though he would certainly have been familiar with some of it.

It has often been remarked that saints' lives sometimes have a very close affinity with romance, and there has been much interaction over the centuries between the two genres.[24] Perhaps the saints' legends owed something to the older tradition of romance in antiquity (which, for instance, left its trace in the story of Apollonius of Tyre); certainly in the Middle Ages romantic legends like that of Alexis (so close to the story of Christina and perhaps a partial model for it) were influential patterns for pious romances such as *Guy of Warwick*. Although Christina's *Life* shows spiritual forces working – notably in the series of visions given to her – it does not have the many miracles or wondrous happenings often found in romances and saints' lives (magic boats, helpful animals, etc.). Yet parts of it, especially the adventures of the heroine in the first part and its treatment of love, sometimes remind us of romances and may possibly owe something to that genre. It was probably written at or just before the time at which the 'courtly' romance began to emerge: we may perhaps assume that some *romans d'antiquité* and some versions of the Tristan story may have been in circulation in Anglo-Norman England.[25] And the 'tales of Arthur', like those which entranced Aelred's novice, were probably already known even in the north of England.

However, we have to remember that there is a markedly 'romance' cast to a number of saints' legends (like those of Brendan or Alexis), and that the use of the language of secular love to describe mystical love (often coming from the 'Song of Songs') is found in contemporary mystical writing. In the *Life* the intense love that Christina and her friends feel for Christ is expressed in terms which are not unlike those found in St Bernard and his followers. It is in the narrative of her spiritual friendships that the reader of romance may sometimes sense a general parallel – the love of Christina and Roger begins through the grace of a mutual glance, like that of many fictional secular lovers. She has found refuge in his hermitage in the forest, where in surroundings harshly uncomfortable but spiritually idyllic they enjoy the ecstasy of divine love together ('O how many tears of heavenly desire did they shed: on what rare delicacies of inward joy were they feasted!' (*Life*, p. 103)). For all the very marked differences in content and context, a reader might think of the lovers in the forest in the Tristan story. Even the 'detractors' might be compared to those *losengiers* and enemies of love that plague secular lovers. Perhaps we might hear an echo of the language of *fin' amor* in the words Christina uses to console her dying brother, speaking of the Virgin Mary as a noble lady – 'if some noble and powerful lady in the world had called you to her service [*obsequium*], you would have taken great care to appear gracious [*gratum*] in her eyes' (*Life*, p. 159) – but one should probably not press general similarities too far. The profound emotional relationship of Christina with Roger, and especially with Geoffrey, is a kind of intense spiritual friendship subsumed into an ecstatic passion almost identical with erotic love, which is endorsed and blessed in a vision by her divine spouse, Christ, when he closes her hands to help her hold Geoffrey securely (*Life*, p. 169). Their relationship is a mutual one, and one that is extraordinarily real. As Neil Cartlidge remarks in his very perceptive study, 'the portrayal of their love is an exaltation of human love as well as a model of partnership in faith and chastity': like the author of *St Alexis* this author 'is able to accommodate an ideal of mutual loving fidelity to the exaltation of chastity and unworldliness.'[26] The spirit of romance returns at the end of the narrative, as does the memory of the Alexis legend, with the figure of the mysterious pilgrim who visits her, is seen in the choir, but then disappears, like Christ in the story of the journey to Emmaus.

Visual imagery

In the visions the descriptions are especially vivid. Sometimes the images have a tactile quality – when Christ comes to Christina in the form of a small child (*Life*, p. 119) she presses him to her breast and feels his presence within her. Sometimes the imagery, we may suspect, is of a 'popular' rather than a 'learned' kind: the threatening bulls; the toads; the devil's black teeth; the wicked cleric appearing as a savage shaggy bear. Christina is sometimes allowed (or invited) to take part in a scene, as in the elaborate example where in a church a man in priestly garments gives her a branch of leaves and flowers and tells her to offer it to the lady sitting like an empress on a dais near the altar; going down, she passes Burthred and then goes to an upper chamber where she is again comforted by the empress (*Life*, pp. 75–7). They are invariably highly pictorial: Christina is crowned by angels (*Life*, p. 129); she sees Geoffrey 'vested in a red cope, his countenance shining not with a simple brightness but with a brightness mixed with ruddiness, transcending human beauty and glory' (*Life*, p. 149).

Visions and vision-literature were highly prized and very popular throughout the Middle Ages, especially if they were 'prophetic' or eschatological visions of hell and heaven like those of Thurkill, the monk of Eynsham, and others. From this earlier period (*c.* 1126) comes the vision of a thirteen-year-old boy, Orm.[27] The dramatic nature of Christina's experience and visions, especially that near the end of her *Life* of the stranger who appeared in the choir and mysteriously vanished, have suggested links with yet another literary genre, the drama. We can only guess at the kinds of dramatic experience available to Christina and her neighbours and the monks of St Albans. May they have been more varied than the few remaining scraps of information suggest – including perhaps the entertainments of mimi and minstrels, mummings and disguisings, popular festivals? There probably would have been plays on more strictly religious topics. We know that there were already in England 'miracle plays' of saints. Geoffrey's Dunstable play of St Catherine ('quem miracula vulgariter appellamus') sounds like the 'more holy plays' of miracles and the sufferings of martyrs that FitzStephen says that London enjoyed. That it was a school play would suggest that it was in Latin – although it is just possible that if the boys were very young it might have been in French.[28] Sadly, we do not know if Geoffrey continued his dramatic interests after he became abbot. The magnificent Anglo-Norman *Mystere d'Adam*[29] is of uncertain date (perhaps 1146–72) and location, and we do not know if there was anything even remotely like it in the St Albans area earlier. We do know, however, that Latin liturgical drama was well established in England. One liturgical play in particular, the *Peregrini*, about Christ and the disciples on the road to Emmaus ('one of the most remarkable dramas of the paschal cycle'),[30] has been associated with the St Albans Psalter and with Christina's story. The Psalter has three scenes of the Biblical story, the earliest example of a cyclical treatment of it, according to Pächt. In the Psalter, when Christ meets the disciples, he (though not the disciples) is dressed as a pilgrim, in a way which, as Pächt points out, is very close to the description in a stage-direction in the *Peregrini* play of Saint-Benoit-sur-Loire. The cycle has added a third scene in which at supper Christ disappears from sight – a scene which in the plays must have been a very dramatic moment (in the Saint-Benoit play, 'while they were eating … He should steal away furtively, unnoticed as it were'). The expansion indicates, Pächt argues, that 'the theme had become charged with some special meaning and was now of topical interest'.[31] The account of the pilgrim in the *Life* is certainly similar to the story of Emmaus, and is very dramatic. There are differences: in the *Life* he appears at Christmas, not at Easter, and he disappears from the church rather than from the supper table (represented often in art and drama as a 'tabernacle' – i.e. the 'castle of Emmaus'). And in her vision he wears a crown. Do these echoes of the Emmaus story come from a memory of the miniatures or from a liturgical play, or from both? It is hard to be sure. There are only a few references to the *Peregrini* in England, but the European evidence suggests it was generally widespread.[32] It is certainly possible that an example was known to the author or to Christina.

It is somehow appropriate that a note on the *Life* should end with yet another unanswered question. But for all its problems it is a truly fascinating work. It illuminates and is illuminated by so much of its contemporary literature. It looks back in some ways (e.g. in its strongly Marian cast) to pre-Conquest devotion,[33] and forward to the simple affective devotion of the later Middle Ages, and the later literature of recluses. But above all it is a powerful story which presents a woman of remarkable will-power finding not only her chosen spiritual destiny in spite of persecution but also her own 'voice' as a prophet and counsellor, and indirectly as a 'writer'.

Notes

1   Notable exceptions include the papers in this volume by Neil Cartlidge and C. Stephen Jaeger; Bella Millett, 'Women in No Man's Land: English Recluses and the development of vernacular literature in the twelfth and thirteenth centuries' in *Women and Literature in Britain, 1150–1500*, ed. Carol M. Meale (Cambridge, 1993), pp. 86–103; Jocelyn Wogan-Browne, 'Saints' Lives and the Female Reader', *Forum for Modern Language Studies* 4 (1991), 314–32, and 'Clerc u lai, muïne u dame': women and Anglo-Norman Hagiography in the twelfth and thirteenth centuries' in Meale, *Women*

and Literature, pp. 61–85. The present paper makes use of material in Douglas Gray, 'Christina of Markyate', in *Literature and Gender: Essays for Jasodhara Bagchi*, ed. Supriya Chaudhuri and Sajni Mukherji (New Dehli, 2002), pp. 30–49.

2 In the only surviving manuscript it breaks off abruptly. Talbot suggested that it was perhaps an abridgement of a longer work and that it may have been written at the instance of Robert Gorham (abbot from 1151 to 1166) after Christina's death, perhaps for the edification of the nuns at the priory she had founded at Markyate. This view has been strongly questioned by Koopmans in 'The Conclusion', where she argues that it is not a finished or well-honed piece of work, and may have been abandoned, falling victim to factions hostile to Abbot Geoffrey after his death. To a non-historian this sounds convincing. Koopmans also argues that its composition was begun under Geoffrey's tutelage and that it was intended to be presented and dedicated to him. One possible (but not insuperable) objection might be that Geoffrey is treated quite sharply when he is first introduced, and that the vocative *te* apparently addressed to a patron (*Life*, p. 127) could be a rhetorical apostrophe to Geoffrey after death (Neil Cartlidge, *Medieval Marriage: Literary Approaches 1100–1300* (Woodbridge, 1997), p. 112, n. 182).

3 C. N. L. Brooke, ' "Both Small and Great Beasts" An Introductory Study', in *Medieval Women: dedicated and presented to Rosalind M.T. Hill on the occasion of her seventieth birthday*, ed. Derek T. Baker (Oxford, 1978), pp. 1–13 (p. 6).

4 C. H. Talbot, 'A Monastic Narrative of the Twelfth Century', *Essays and Studies* (1962), p. 15.

5 The technique is not that of the realistic novel. A number of characters (including some of her relatives) are only introduced when they are relevant to the narrative of the central figure's experiences – as is quite often found in saints' lives and early 'auto-biography' – a striking case is her brother, the monk Gregory, with whom she had a very close bond, who only appears when he is about to die (*Life*, pp. 157–9). The author's refusal to divulge the names of two characters (*Life*, pp. 79, 115), however, suggests (or is meant to suggest) a closeness to the actual events.

6 Note for instance the self-conscious 'return' as from a digression (*Life*, pp. 69, 157), and the author's approving remark about Christina's telling of the story of St Cecilia (*Life*, p. 51).

7 Bloet's sudden death is recorded with some satisfaction as an exemplum (*Life*, p. 119). Elkins, *Holy Women*, pp. 31–2, notes that in an early version of the *De Gestis Pontificum* (*c*. 1125) of William of Malmesbury, Bloet's death was foretold by the hermit Roger after the bishop had rebuked him for harbouring Christina.

8 Jeanette M. A. Beer, *Villehardouin. Epic Historian* (Geneva, 1968), esp. chs. 3 and 6.

9 Douglas Gray, 'A Scottish "Flower of Chivalry" and his Book', *Words: Wai-te-ata Studies in Literature* 4 (1974), 22–34.

10 P. G. Schmidt, 'The Vision of Thurkill', *Journal of the Warburg and Courtauld Institutes* 41 (1978), 50–64. Interestingly, he cites the case of Alberic, who experienced a vision when he was ten years old, and who later learned to read and write and became a monk: when he read the written account of his vision by one Guido, he was astonished, and accused the redactor of forgery, lies and unauthorized modifications (p. 51).

11 See John C. Hirsh, 'Author and Scribe in *The Book of Margery Kempe*', *Medium Ævum* 44 (1975), 145–50.

12 See Douglas Gray, 'Popular Religion and Late Medieval Literature' in *Religion in the Poetry and Drama of the Late Middle Ages in England*, ed. Piero Boitani and Anna Torti (Cambridge, 1990), 1–28 (p. 11).

13 See Sandra K. D. Stahl, 'Personal Narrative as Folklore', *Journal of the Folklore Institute* 14 (1977); Juliette Wood, 'Folkloric Patterns in Scottish Chronicles', in *The Rose and The Thistle*, ed. Sally Mapstone and Juliette Wood (East Linton, 1998), pp. 117–19.

14 Holdsworth, 'Christina of Markyate', p. 195.

15 Although some rhetorical patterns (e.g. 'hear, then, how prudently she acted' (*Life*, p. 43); or 'what were they to do?' (*Life*, p. 113)) could probably be found in both 'learned' and 'popular' narrative.

16 On a possible attempt to canonize Thurstan, see A. G. Rigg, *A History of Anglo-Latin Literature 1066–1422* (Cambridge, 1992), pp. 52–3.

17 See Henry Mayr-Harting, 'Functions of a Twelfth-Century Recluse', *History* 60 (1975), 337–52.

18 See M. Dominica Legge, *Anglo-Norman Literature and its Background* (Oxford, 1963), chs. 1 and 2. Gaimar's *Estoire des Engleis* (before 1140), for instance, used English material (Legge, pp. 31–2), and contains the story of Havelok.

19 See Rigg, *A History of Anglo-Latin Literature*, ch. 1.

20 Ibid., pp. 36–40.

21 *The Peterborough Chronicle 1070–1154*, ed. Cecily Clark, 2nd edn. (Oxford, 1970). On the survival of Old English, see Christine Franzen, *The Tremulous Hand of Worcester. A Study of Old English in the Thirteenth Century* (Oxford, 1991) and references; N. R. Ker, *Catalogue of Manuscripts Containing Anglo-Saxon* (Oxford, 1957).

22 Legge, *Anglo-Norman Literature*, p. 243 (the prologue to the text remarks 'which we have heard read and sung').

23 Ruth J. Dean, *Anglo-Norman Literature. A guide to Texts and Manuscripts* (London, 1999), no. 504; Legge, *Anglo-Norman Literature*, pp. 8–18.

24 See M. Dominica Legge, 'Anglo-Norman Hagiography and the Romances', *Medievalia et Humanistica* 6 (1975), 41–9.

25 The surviving early versions are difficult to date: that of Thomas is placed in the latter half of the twelfth century by Dean (*Anglo-Norman Literature*, No. 158), that of Béroul is Norman, but likely to have been written for an Anglo-Norman audience (Legge, *Anglo-Norman Literature*, p. 59). Thomas clearly implies that different versions of the story were in circulation (Legge, *Anglo-Norman Literature*, pp. 51–2).

26 Cartlidge, *Medieval Marriage*, p. 113. On the intellectual background, see Peter Dronke, *Medieval Latin and the Rise of European Love-Lyric*, 2 vols. (Oxford, 1965–66), I, ch. 2, and 'Amour sacré et amour profane au moyen âge latin' in Peter Dronke, *Sources of Inspiration* (Rome, 1997), 375–93. See also C. Stephen Jaeger, *Ennobling Love: In Search of a Lost Sensibility* (Philadelphia, 1999), chapter 7; Ruth Mazo Karras, 'Friendship and Love in the Lives of two Twelfth-Century English Saints', *Journal of Medieval History* 14 (1988), 305–20.

27 See Rigg, *A History of Anglo-Latin Literature*, p. 54.

28 Legge, *Anglo-Norman Literature*, p. 311; Catherine Thomas, 'The Miracle Play at Dunstable', *Modern Language Notes* 32 (1917), 337–44.

29 Dean, *Anglo-Norman Literature*, no. 716; Legge, *Anglo-Norman Literature*, pp. 312–21.

30 Otto Pächt, The *Rise of Pictorial Narrative in Twelfth-Century England* (Oxford, 1962), p. 34.

31 Ibid., p. 39.

32 Karl Young, *The Drama of the Medieval Church*, 2 vols. (Oxford, 1933), i. 458–89. William of Malmesbury says that his abbey had a *peregrinus* play *c.* 1125 (Richard Axton, *European Drama of the Early Middle Ages* (London, 1974), p. 163). There was provision for one in Lichfield in the later twelfth century. Lawrence of Durham (d. 1154) wrote a dialogue between Luke and Cleophas on the road to Emmaus; they meet the risen Christ and Thomas's doubts are finally resolved: 'this is the first piece of verse liturgical drama in Anglo-Latin' (Rigg, *A History of Anglo-Latin Literature*, pp. 57–8). As well as the moment of Christ's disappearance, the yearning of the disciples for their master had dramatic potential: in the twelfth-century play from Vic, Catalonia, Mary Magdalen searches for her divine lover and there is a joyful recognition *(Versus de Pelegrino)*, in *Nine Medieval Latin Plays*, ed. Peter Dronke (Cambridge, 1994).

33 See Henrietta Leyser's Introduction to this volume.

3

ST ALBANS AND WOMEN'S MONASTICISM

Lives and their foundations in Christina's world

Stephanie Hollis and Jocelyn Wogan-Browne

Introduction

The history of St Albans Abbey's relations with women is in some ways of relatively tenuous relevance for Christina of Markyate. Sally Thompson pointed out
in 1991 that 'the impression given throughout the *Life* of Christina is of personal
friendship between the abbot and the lady recluse rather than of an institutional
dependence', and this remains true.[1] Rachel Koopmans has recently offered a
detailed historical case exploring the unfinished state of Christina's *vita* and the
failure of Christina's story to be much celebrated in the abbey's history after the
death of Abbot Geoffrey de Gorran in 1146, or, indeed, after Christina's own
death. Christina, she argues, is not a living saint to be treasured but a troubling
liability for the abbey, and one incurred almost exclusively because of Christina's
special relationship with Geoffrey de Gorran.[2] But St Albans did have a number
of associations with women, possibly from the ninth century to the later Middle
Ages. It is important not simply to accept as a generic feature of the historiography of women that Christina had so little apparent afterlife in St Albans (or
that hers remained so isolated as a contemporary female *vita* in twelfth-century
England), but to enquire more specifically into the possibilities and expectations
of Christina's situation.

In this chapter we consider what is known of St Albans' traditions regarding
women in religion and explore some narratives concerning religious roles for a
sense of the possibilities open to Christina.[3] During Christina's lifetime, Geoffrey
de Gorran founded, *c.* 1140, Sopwell Priory, a small Benedictine nunnery close
to St Albans; the hospital of St Julian, subsequently incorporated into the
nunnery of St Mary de Pré in 1194 as a dependency of St Albans, and, in 1145,
Christina's own priory of Markyate, close to the site of the hermitage she inherited from Roger, hermit of Caddington and monk of St Albans.[4] Christina had
also earlier shared the cell of the recluse Alfwen, who was herself under Roger's
spiritual direction, in the village of Flamstead, close to but separate from the
small Benedictine nunnery of St Giles in the Wood, founded in the mid-twelfth
century by Roger de Tosny on land once owned by St Albans but lost at the

Conquest.[5] Christina's initial spiritual formation was at the hands of the Augustinian canon Sueno in Huntingdon. Moreover, St Albans, like other houses, not only devoted occasional institutional provision to women, but received patronage at their hands. From the will of Æthelgifu (990 x 1001) to Matthew Paris's salutation to Isabella of Arundel (d. 1279) as patron of Wymondham (the dependent house long associated with her marital family of which she had the advowson), women donors and patrons had roles in the monastery's history, often as a result of family associations.[6] Both for Christina and for St Albans, a range of religious lives for women must have been imaginable and visible in the contemporary landscape.

More detailed comparisons of Christina's and other stories will be made later in this chapter, but it is worth noting at the outset that Christina's world must already have been aurally trilingual even before she acquired a reading knowledge of written French or Latin. Ian Short has shown how, among solitaries of humbler origin than Christina, English, recitational liturgical Latin, and French were all practised or desired.[7] The great efflorescence of extant Anglo-Norman texts towards the end of the twelfth century occurs after Christina's death, but the first half of the century saw the creation of a number of devotional, hagiographical, historiographical and other texts: the pursuit of a life in religion had a range of pre- and post-Conquest vernacular materials. A Lincolnshire noblewoman, Lady Aeliz de Cundé, widowed in 1140 or 1145, commissioned a commentary on Proverbs: the Psalter commentary made for Laurette d'Alsace at about the same time circulated in England.[8] Geoffrei Gaimar produced his Anglo-Norman Chronicle for Constance FitzGilbert, Countess of Lincoln (probably in 1136–37), using the Anglo-Saxon Chronicle alongside Latin and French sources.[9] Ranulf Flambard figures in Gaimar, as does also the hermit-saint Guthlac of Crowland.[10] Wace's narrative poem on the Feast of the Conception, *La Conception Nostre Dame, c.* 1125–40, circulated widely.[11] It includes an account of how Abbot Elsin [Æthelsige] of Ramsey (the Benedictine Abbey in the Huntingdonshire fens that is the provenance of Christina's Psalter calendar) became (as Christina's Abbot Geoffrey later would do) a supporter of the Feast.[12] By 1121 the Anglo-Norman *Voyage of St Brendan* had been dedicated to Henry I's queen (either Matilda, d. 1118 in most manuscripts, or Adeliza of Louvain, m. 1121, in one).[13] Brendan follows the track of Mernoc, brother of the abbey, who much wanted 'Que fust ailurs e plus sultif' ('that he might be elsewhere and solitary'), and who, in the island to which he has sailed, is so near Paradise that he can hear the angels.[14] Rachel Bullington has drawn attention to the varying linguistic formats of books using the Gallican Psalter (of which the 'Oxford' prose Anglo-Norman translation was made in the early twelfth century): it is extant in a number of different formats and combinations in continental and insular manuscript books from the mid-century on.[15] So too were a number of narratives of religious careers and foundations. *La Vie de saint Alexis* comes readily to mind because of the celebrated early twelfth-century text included in the St Albans Psalter, but this life is itself one of a larger number celebrating flight from the world in various forms. Related subjects of contemporary biography exploring chastity, eremeticism and marriage, for example, include St Giles, beloved only son of wealthy parents who flees marriage for life as a solitary, and St Evroul, a married Merovingian courtier who becomes first an abbot (while his wife enters a convent) and then ultimately a hermit. The Abbey of St Evroul had a monk-chronicler acquainted with England and France in Orderic Vitalis, as well as several dependent houses in England, while relics of its saint received a translation feast at Thorney in the early twelfth century.[16] St Giles has a magnificent later twelfth-century Anglo-Norman biography by Guillaume de Berneville (perhaps a canon of Barnwell, Cambridge): proverbs from this *Vie de saint Gilles* are quoted in a twelfth-century manuscript of Ælfric's Old English saints' lives, and there is an eleventh-century late Old English life from Rochester.[17] Other saints, notably Nicholas and Margaret, also received late Old English lives as well as twelfth-century re-workings in French, these latter probably before the middle of the century.[18] A St Catherine life, which may have been a play, is perhaps the earlier life referred to by Clemence of Barking in her later twelfth-century verse life of the saint.[19]

In the corpus of late Anglo-Saxon saints' lives, a number of which continued to circulate in twelfth-century manuscript copies, Ælfric's conservative reformist treatments of virgin martyrs and abbesses and a mislaid daughter, Eugenia (who becomes a transvestite monk falsely accused of adultery), were supplemented in manuscript collections by eremetic and non-Ælfrician lives.[20] These include Mary of Egypt (a female hermit) and Euphrosyne (a female transvestite monk, presented very differently from Ælfric's Eugenia), St Neot of Huntingdonshire (died *c.* 877), hermit, monk and (according to his twelfth-century life) adviser to King Alfred, and Malchus (a fourth-century desert saint).[21] The holy woman, Veronica, *Vitae Patrum* characters, an anonymous *Life* of Martin, and the late Old English prose Guthlac *Life* all extend and vary the accounts of Anglo-Saxon holy persons offered in Ælfrician hagiography. As with Anglo-Norman, other materials for vernacular religious lives were not lacking: for example an Old English devotional and doctrinal anthology from Rochester of chastity, eremitic and visionary texts (including a *Life* of St Neot of Huntingdonshire and the Old English version of a sermon by Ralph d'Escures, Christina's supporter as archbishop of Canterbury 1114–22), which was owned in the twelfth century by a 'handmaiden' (*ancilla*) of the Virgin Mary.[22]

Stories of British foundations circulated widely in both Latin and vernacular hagiography and historiography. Bede, especially as cited by William of Malmesbury and Henry of Huntingdon, remained an influential source in Latin writings, and the late Old English version of his *Ecclesiastical History* offered several stories of early Anglo-Saxon women religious in the vernacular.[23] From the late tenth to the twelfth century, the saints of Britain were the subject of extensive re-invention in Anglo-Latin and then in Latin and vernacular Norman and Angevin historiography and hagiography as the Normans re-wrote English cultural tradition for themselves.[24] The eight female saints added in the St Albans Psalter calendar have often been remarked: the virgin martyrs of the universal church included in it have an obvious relevance to Christina's struggles with her parents and Burthred. But by the time she was using the Psalter, still more important to Christina may have been the figures of Hild and Frideswide, as, on the one hand, a churchwoman who gave counsel to lay persons of all ranks, and, on the other, a native virgin martyr who was both an eremitic saint and a foundress (see further below, p. 39). These two saints do not appear in St Albans or Ramsey calendars and seem notably not to have been widely culted at this time.[25] Etheldreda of Ely, also included, is important as a married woman saint who retained her virginity through two marriages and became an abbess, but perhaps she figures here also in her role as the leading Anglo-Saxon saint. She signifies a tradition in which Christina, as the reader for whom the Psalter was modified, was thought to partic- ipate or within which she wished to be seen.

In this setting, no single precedent or rationale for Christina's career emerges, but this seems appropriate in several ways: in her *vita*, she is, after all, a figure of multiple and varying significance, engaged in different kinds of religious practice and roles as her career develops, and a range of narrative types and models by which she is received and understood by her contemporaries attach to her life. Moreover, in spite of the existence of various institutions and models, Christina seems to have been representative of many women in religion in the twelfth century in that she could not simply inherit her career through institutional structures but had to make it up as best she could as she went along.

Women at St Albans

On her first visit to St Albans with her parents, Christina marks the sign of the cross on the monastery and subsequently vows herself to religion: 'When the girl therefore had looked carefully at the place and observed the religious bearing of the monks who dwelt there [*inhabitancium monachorum*], she declared how fortu- nate the inmates were, and expressed a wish to share their fellowship [*consorcii eorum*]. At length … she made a sign of the cross with one of her fingernails on the door as a token that she had placed her affection there' (*Life*, p. 39).[26] The *Life* shows Christina as intent on formal profession as a religious here, though in what way Christina might have seen herself sharing in monastic fellowship is impossible to determine. St Albans itself at first glance appears to have long- standing relations with women in several kinds of religious lives from at least the ninth to the fifteenth century. But the record, even in a house with such impres- sive administrative and historiographic resources as St Albans, is far from continuous. The abbess-governed double communities of earlier Anglo-Saxon England did not survive Viking raiding or the tenth-century Benedictine reform. Whatever precedent female communities were associated with St Albans before Christina's time must rather be sought in less formal and less well-documented groups. Matthew Paris relates in the *Gesta Abbatum* that the fourth abbot of St Albans eradicated various errors introduced by his predecessors; he removed *sanctimoniales semi saeculares* from the immediate vicinity of the church to the almonry and ordered them to be much stricter in sleeping, eating and prayer, and required them to attend the canonical hours in the 'greater' church.[27] Reference to the fourth abbot (Wulfnoth) dates this to the reign of Alfred. There is a letter to Alfred from Archbishop Fulk, which condemns, among other bad English customs, women living in proximity to men in orders[28] (new foundations of the Alfredian era are said to have been single-sex establishments). Matthew may be recalling a tradition relating to the reform of a double monastery, or some less formal community containing men and women. Matthew also relates that Abbot Paul (1077–93) regulated the discipline and habit of women living in the almonry and constrained their freedom.

Does this mean that there was a continuous tradition (for over 150 years) of women associated with the monastery? Or were the women whose way of life was 'reformed' by Abbot Paul perhaps women who had taken refuge in the St Albans almonry during the Norman invasion?[29]

In her survey and gazeteer of pre-Conquest women in religion, Sarah Foot comments: 'There is no mention of the presence of religious women [at St Albans] in the Domesday Book, nor are there any further references to women at the abbey after the time of Abbot Paul, unless it were thought that the establishment of the dependent priory at Sopwell were an attempt to regulate the status of women attached to the community. The evidence of the early Sopwell charters preserved in the Register of St Albans corroborates the suggestion of the *Gesta Abbatum* that the priory had an eremitical origin, which implies that it was distinct from the congregation of women based at the almonry.'[30] Christina's visit to St Albans (perhaps in 1111–12, *Life*, p. 14) is too early for the foundation of Sopwell (*c.* 1140):[31] perhaps she wanted fellowship with the monks by joining a group of women carrying out St Albans monastic duties of help to the poor in its almonry, or perhaps she wanted to be a religious woman living near the monastery. Foot argues that in the late Anglo-Saxon period, at least from the mid-tenth century onwards, there was an increase in the number of women who pursued a religious vocation outside the cloisters, either alone or in small groups. Such women, she suggests, were more typical of female devotion in the late Anglo-Saxon church than were the women who were members of cloistered communities (which consisted chiefly of eight royal Wessex nunneries and Barking). Women who pursued a religious life outside the cloisters typically took a vow of chastity; at least some wore distinctive clothing.[32] These vowesses are referred to during the Benedictine Reform period as *nunnan*, as distinct from *mynecenu* (monastic women).[33]

The best documented (particularly in wills) are high-status widows who gathered a small community around them and lived on family lands; these arrangements tended to be short-lived, since the lands generally reverted to their male kinsmen (or to the church) after their death, or after two or three lifetimes.[34] Vowesses also included unmarried women – Ælfric's homily on Judith is addressed to a virgin vowess (and includes strictures on the scandalous behaviour of *nunnan* as a class).[35] It is possible that the increased number of women pursuing a religious vocation in the world may represent a choice on their part (a preference for a more informal, less regulated lifestyle than the nunneries afforded). Foot inclines to the view that they followed a course of action that was in the interests of their families (i.e., property was only temporarily alienated for the use of a vowess).[36]

The lifestyles of vowesses varied considerably. Wealthy widows appear from their wills to have lived very comfortably in the world, perhaps in their own homes. Women attached to shrines resembled recluses more closely. Ælfric's *Life of Edmund* mentions a widow called Oswyn who (in the late ninth century) tended the body of the saint and lived her life in prayer and fasting.[37] In his late twelfth-century Anglo-Norman re-working of Edmund's *vita*, Denis Piramus, monk of Bury, preserves this tradition of Oswen, 'religiuse et almonere', and adds a holy widow whose advice and visions are revered as counsel by the king of the East Anglian Saxons.[38] So also, in the early eighth century, Pega in the *Life of Guthlac* (translated into Old English in the eleventh century) is said to have inherited the hermitage of her brother and had charge of his shrine there (see further below, p. 40).[39] There may also have been a community at Chich in the eleventh century which served the shrine of St Osyth (and the importance of her shrine attendants is upheld in later collections of her shrine miracles).[40] So, too, Christina; according to her *Life*, one of her reasons for wishing to remain in the hermitage she inherited from Roger was that he was buried there (*Life*, p. 127), although the *Gesta Abbatum* subsequently reclaims Roger for St Albans by having him buried in the monastery, not in his cell.[41]

There are a number of references to female religious associated with male monastic communities in Anglo-Saxon England. Foot gazettes these in her *Veiled Women*, arguing that these women were also vowesses (or informal groups of female religious), not regularly organized convents of cloistered women. In addition, she argues that some of these are likely to have been women, alone or in groups, who were tenants of lands owned by the monastic community (which reverted subsequently to the monastery's possession). She considers that we therefore cannot assume that the women were living in close proximity to the monks in these cases. Closest to Matthew Paris's accounts are reports relating to Bury and Evesham. Domesday Book relates that in the new part of the town of Bury lived 'thirty priests, deacons and clerks, and twenty-eight *nonnae* and poor persons who pray daily for the King and for all Christian people'.[42] Foot comments: 'It is unclear what the relationship between the abbey and these vowesses and poor people may have been. Possibly the women were dependants of the abbey, they may have lived in the almonry or have been in some other way connected with charity, judging by their association with a group of the poor; from this account it would not seem that there was a separately constituted and endowed female religious house in the town, nor that Bury was in either the early Anglo-Saxon or Gilbertine sense a double house. It does, however, appear that these women stood in somewhat different a relationship to their male hosts from that of most of the other groups of religious women assigned to this category'.[43] For Evesham, the Evesham cartulary contains a record of the inhabitants of the monastery in the time of Abbot Robert (post-1104); 67 monks and three clerks, together with five *moniales* and three *pauperes ad mandatum*.[44]

In some cases the women associable with male communities were related to high-ranking ecclesiastics: at Worcester in the eleventh century, for instance, they were relatives of Archbishop Wulfstan II.[45] So also at Glastonbury, in one of the best documented cases, the widow Æthelflæd is a relative of Dunstan. Information about their association is given in the earliest life (late tenth century), whose author is known only as B.[46] B explains that, while Dunstan was abbot of Glastonbury, there was a wealthy widow called Æthelflæd who set up little cottages for her accommodation on the west side of the church[47] (which was dedicated to St Mary), 'so that, in that place, she need not stop serving the Lord Jesus Christ by day or night, in her desire for the heavenly kingdom.' Æthelflæd was also related to King Athelstan, and is said to have been generous to him. (B's account includes a description of an occasion when she invited the king and his retinue to visit her: only the miraculous intervention of Mary ensured that there was sufficient mead.)[48] She had already, according to B, had a male friend who was her teacher and priest. He describes her as a *famula Dei*. Dunstan was an intimate friend of hers and loved her for her devout life (he also shared her devotion to Mary). She refers to Dunstan as her 'special friend'.[49] He provided the necessities of life for her, and divine services. He cared for her as a mother when she became ill. She was visited by a divine messenger (in the form of a dove) who imparted to her foreknowledge of her death. She bequeathed her property to the saints of Glastonbury and to the poor.[50]

There are four other women associated with late tenth-century Glastonbury. Halpin thinks that these 'support the theory that some type of unofficial living arrangement existed for women associated with the Abbey of [Glastonbury]'.[51] Foot disagrees: 'The precise nature of their connection with the male community is unclear; although it is tempting to wonder whether the abbey made regular arrangements for the shelter and care of its ageing and widowed female benefactors, this cannot be determined from the sources now extant.'[52]

Recluses and their activities in late Anglo-Saxon England

Anneke Mulder-Bakker and E. A. Jones have pointed to the varied and fluid terminology of reclusion (*inclusa, reclusa, anachoreta, eremita*) and the varying religious and semi-religious lives it embraces.[53] Recent research has also complicated the nationalizing account sometimes met with in earlier twentieth-century scholarship whereby the 'bucolic' recluses of Anglo-Saxon England are contrasted with more refined Norman churchmen.[54] Henry I visited hermits for their medical advice, as well as for their prophetic knowledge. Both Henry and King Stephen visited Wulfric of Haselbury.[55] It is possible that Abbot Geoffrey (builder in 1129 at St Albans of exclusive guest chambers for the queen), once drawn to Christina, was influenced by royal patronage of hermits like Wulfric as well as by Christina's merits in deciding to further the relationship.[56] The beautiful and elaborate Guthlac roll (c. 1200), which commemorates both Guthlac and Pega, testifies to the undiminished prestige of Anglo-Saxon hermit lives in post-Conquest England.[57]

Although not much is known of them apart from their existence, a number of people in the tenth and eleventh centuries seem to have pursued informal and unofficial religious vocations.[58] Goscelin's conception of a solitary religious, on the other hand, seems to have more in common with the formally enclosed anchorites of the later Middle Ages (i.e., an inhabitant of a cell built against a church wall who never left the confines of the cell). He says in *Liber confortatorius* (c. 1082) that he has often longed for a little lodging like Eve's, 'which, however, had a little door for the purposes of exiting to services so that I should not have to do without the open space of a church'.[59] He also tells a story about an anchorite (*anachorite*) called Brihtric who had a wooden cell attached to a church at a fortress not far from Bury; he refused to leave his cell when pirates attacked and was burnt to death when they set fire to the fortress.[60] Whereas Goscelin regarded the primary occupation of a solitary as prayer and reading, Brihtric was an illiterate lay man, and continually repeated the Lord's Prayer and Psalm 50.

Devout women did embroidery and recited the psalms. In the early Anglo-Saxon period there are references to elderly abbesses retiring to become recluses.[61] That the practice was still current in the twelfth century is suggested by the *Life of Modwenna* (composed 1118–35?), patron saint of the Benedictine house of Burton on Trent, who, late in a busy career of founding in Ireland, England and Scotland, takes a reclusive sabbatical on the island of Andressey in the River Trent.[62] We can infer from *Liber confortatorius* that it was possible to become a recluse within a convent in the late eleventh century: Goscelin had hoped that Eve would be a dove in the cloister, not a solitary turtledove, or, if she preferred, that she might be a turtledove in her native land.[63] So too, St Tibba, a seventh-century Anglo-Saxon solitary whose story was revamped and connected with Kyneburga of Peterborough in the eleventh century, seems also to have been a nun.[64] Monks, however, particularly in the early Anglo-Saxon period, not uncommonly moved out of the monastery to a solitary place when they wanted a more serious lifestyle (Roger's predecessors include Cuthbert, Guthlac and Willibrord).

Consulting hermits for spiritual advice was evidently a feature of late Anglo-Saxon society. There is a letter from Abbot Ælfric to the ealdorman Sigefrith on chastity in which he warns him against the advice of 'your anchorite at home with you' as erroneous in comparison with Ælfric's own teaching of 'the holy teaching which the saviour taught' about clerical marriage.[65] Christina's parents consult the hermit Guido, outside Huntingdon (*Life*, p. 89), though they also visit St Albans as a shrine site offering protection (*Life*, p. 39). Rural people, in the absence of priests near at hand, may have regarded holy men (and even women) as their principal confessors and spiritual advisors. Roger the hermit, for instance, 'sent for Godescalc of Addington and his wife, people very close to his heart and of good family, who lived a happy married life under Roger's direction' (*Life*, p. 111).

Christina herself is venerated in her *vita* for her holiness of life, her advice, prophetic and visionary faculties, but not for miracles of healing: only one miracle of healing is attributed to her, and she is reported to have been at pains to avoid being credited with that (*Life*, p. 121). In both this and other cures, her role is strictly intercessory (*Life*, p. 121), while the cure of her own illness is ascribed directly to God rather than to physicians (*Life*, pp. 123–5).[66] Christina may have wished to dissociate herself from any implications of witchcraft or from women healers with a bad reputation. But male solitaries in the *Life*, notably Roger, also seem not to perform miracles of healing. There is a miracle of healing attributed to the recluse Wulfric of Haselbury, but he was a priest. Miraculous healing may not necessarily have been part of the late Anglo-Saxon conception of a living holy person, though it is certainly recorded as a posthumous intervention in shrine miracles.

Spiritual friendships

Early Anglo-Saxon saints' lives depict friendships between bishops and the abbesses of double monasteries; these friendships reflect the partnership of particularly eminent abbesses and bishops as heads of the Church advancing the conversion, and are figuratively associated with the relationship of Mary and Christ's favourite disciple, John (whom the Celtic Church regarded as Christ's apostolic successor). When Bishop Wilfrid died, for instance, Tahtberht, whom Wilfrid had appointed to succeed him as abbot, took the cloak on which his body had lain to Cynethryth, 'the abbess of Bishop Wilfrid', instructing her to keep it for him; Cynethryth subsequently used it to perform a miracle of healing.[67] In his continental mission, Boniface, setting out to meet the martyrdom he foresaw, urged both his appointed successor Lul and Abbess Leoba to carry on with the work he had begun; like Christ on the cross, Boniface commended Leoba to the care of Lul and his senior monks, and left Leoba in possession of his cowl.[68] This paradigmatic conception of the relationship of abbot-bishops and abbesses is echoed in Goscelin's *Legend of Edith* (*c.* 1080); describing Bishop Dunstan's consecration of the church built by Edith, Goscelin depicts him as the 'friend of the bridegroom' who unites Edith in marriage to her heavenly bridegroom and is himself united with Edith as John was with Mary when Christ on the Cross commended his mother into his keeping: Dunstan 'reverently led the Lord's spouse and heavenly queen by the hand, and directed her steps towards the heavenly lamb and the mountain of the daughter of Sion; ... a virgin breathed forth fragrance to a virgin, lily scent to lily scent, and a John was seen to pay reverence to a Mary'.[69] This image of a Trinitarian unity of virgins at the crucifixion is also alluded to by Goscelin in the *Liber confortatorius*, where it signifies the spiritual friendship of Goscelin and Eve, their union in Christ.[70] From this point of view, it is striking that Christina has a vision of herself and Geoffrey as Mary and John at the foot of the Crucifixion (*Life*, pp. 181–3). As with Goscelin's use of this image, Christina's vision defines a spiritual relationship. After an important thematic sequence in which Christina and Geoffrey's friendship in Christ ('in Christo dileccio', *Life*, p. 174) is both calumniated and validated, Christina's vision resolves her dilemma as to the relative places of Geoffrey and God in her love, and marks her spiritual pre-eminence in the relationship. She is on God's right hand, Geoffrey on his left: after initial unease, she accepts these positions as signifying God's importance to her and her role in Geoffrey's spirituality (*Life*, pp. 181–3).[71]

In the late Anglo-Saxon period, however, in keeping with the diminished status of abbesses in the single-sex and more enclosed institutions that replaced the double monasteries, friendships between bishops and devout laywomen assume greater significance in the lives of bishops than their relationships with abbesses.[72] Some of the women mentioned as the friends of bishops appear to have been widows who were living as vowesses in their own homes. The *Life* by B, for instance, relates how Dunstan was summoned to the home of a noble matron who 'asked him as a friend to design a special stole for her for divine worship, with various patterns and forms, which afterwards she would be able to decorate with gold and gems'.[73] But the best example in the late Anglo-Saxon period of an ecclesiastic's veneration of a holy woman paralleling the relationship of Geoffrey and Christina is that of Dunstan and Æthelflæd, who live in an institutional as well as personal proximity (see above, p. 31). It may well be that B's account of Dunstan and Æthelflæd confirms Foot's view that devout women living in the vicinity of male communities were seeking safety, economic assistance and access to the sacraments.[74] Doubtless her family connections were an essential factor. But Dunstan's veneration of her for her holy life is a factor too ('the blessed Dunstan always kept close to this woman, for he loved her above all others for her wonderful behaviour. It is impossible to describe how well and how much he groomed her in holy services').[75] So, too, in the case of Christina and Geoffrey, the connection with Geoffrey is presented by the *Life* as God's provision for Christina's rescue from the tribulations of poverty (*Life*, p. 133), but Geoffrey's reverence for Christina's spirituality and her influence on him is even more heavily stressed throughout the rest of the *Life* (see especially pp. 143–5, 151–3).

As well as these changing and developing Anglo-Saxon traditions, one could note the relationship of Eve, the English nun who became an anchorite in France, for whom Goscelin wrote the *Liber confortatorius*, and Hervé, a fellow member of the anchorite community at Saint-Eutrope; the purity of their relationship was affirmed and celebrated by Hilary of Orléans shortly after Eve's death (*c.* 1120).[76] By contrast, Aelred's vigorous advocacy both of spiritual friendship between men and total segregation of men and women in religion, as in his treatise for his recluse sister, are well-known.[77] There are a number of eleventh- and twelfth-century cases where a relation between a cleric and a recluse is embodied in works produced by the one for the other, but where it is unclear how close or continuous the relationship is. Anselm writes enthusiastically and encouragingly on the spirituality of a small group of women (he calls them *ancillae dei*) under spiritual direction.[78] His terms are both deeply Anselmian and reminiscent of the insistence on the importance of interior disposition that was to make the early thirteenth-century recluse's guide, *Ancrene Wisse*, so influential: 'Do not therefore consider so much what you do, but what you desire: nor so much what your deeds are as the condition of your will'.[79] In the early twelfth century, Godwin, praecentor of Salisbury, writes a lengthy set of *Meditaciones* on the beatitudes for the recluse Rainilva, calling them 'the first teachings of [her] new Christian law', promulgated by her 'nouus legislator' Christ.[80] Hildebert of Lavardin, correspondent of Maud, queen of Henry I, writes to the recluse Athalisa on the value of the virgin life.[81]

From his time in Normandy, Thurstan of York may have known of continental friendships between female recluses and priests, such as that of Eve and Hervé, which may have influenced him in confiding Christina (unhappily as it turned out) to the care of his friend after Roger's death (*Life*, pp. 115–17).[82] Cohabitation in the same cell by male–female couples is not recorded in the Anglo-Saxon period, however (and it is not clear that Eve and Hervé cohabitated), but the practice does have Celtic precedents.[83] Friendships between female recluses and male religious evidently raised suspicions in twelfth-century England, as the *Life of Christina* shows,[84] but also gained acceptance in some quarters. Geoffrey of Burton, for example, envisages friendships between hermits and a woman of much higher rank than Christina, in the case of the Abbess Modwenna. In her reclusive sabbatical on Andressey island in the Trent, Modwenna is brought lives of the saints by a hermit friend.[85] Modwenna's friendship with the hermit Kevin is threatened when a demon tempts him to think the eremetic life is futile by taunting him that, after all his ascetic labour and desert privations, Modwenna is giving greater spiritual friendship to two robbers she has converted and has them 'learning their letters and living with the virgins [i.e., at Modwenna's foundation]'.[86] The angry and jealous Kevin is cured by Modwenna's banishment of his devil and her miraculous provision of a healing bath, after which he and his followers 'joyfully return to the desert [in solitudinem]').[87] These stories no doubt promote the rank of Burton (as embodied in Modwenna), but also suggest that considerable influence over male spirituality could be exercised by female companions in the religious life, especially in male–female spiritual friendship.

Christina's refuges and foundations

Had Christina not been perceived as pre-eminently marriageable, it might have been expected that her parents, wealthy gentry (her father, at least at the time of her betrothal, was head of the Gild Merchant of Huntingdon), would seek for or even set up a small foundation for her, of which she might expect to become the prioress. There were many smaller foundations for women in the first half of the twelfth century, a number of them in Bedfordshire and Hertfordshire, though Huntingdon itself had no new foundations specifically for women until the convent of Hinchingbrooke was established in 1186–90.[88] Christina's high status as biological daughter is notable in her *vita*. It is she, not her mother, who has in her keeping 'the keys which he [her father] had placed in her possession ... Autti was very rich and always entrusted to Christina his silver and gold and whatever treasure he possessed' (*Life*, p. 73). In Anglo-Saxon terms, possession of keys is a definition of the mistress of the house – women were buried with their keys hung at the waist, and Cnut's law code (1018) rules that a wife is innocent of her husband's theft if he brings stolen property into the house, unless she has the key to the place where it is hidden: 'But she must look after the keys of the following: namely her store-room, her chest and her coffer; it is brought inside any of these, then she is guilty'.[89] So, too, the account of Christina at the Gild Merchant's festival recalls the Anglo-Saxon motif of woman as cupbearer. Although *cnihten* gilds, associations of wealthy landowners, existed in the tenth century, the Gilds Merchant are more characteristically post-Conquest developments of the earlier Gilds of Thanes.[90] Christina's appearance as cupbearer is none the less reminiscent of *Beowulf* (the extant manuscript of which is variously dated to the late tenth or early eleventh century). The poem gives a description only of Wealhtheow, the king's wife, in this role, but Beowulf recalls at his home court how King Hrothgar's daughter took round the hall cup.[91] Given such preeminence in the family context, formal entry to a conventual life via parental provision of dowry must have been an impossibly remote prospect for Christina.

The socio-economics of entry to the religious life are commonly figured (among other things) by the retention of virginity in saints' lives. Christina's use of the Cecilia story in defence of her virginity is well-known, but in addition to such martyr saints of the universal church, Anglo-Saxon and Anglo-Norman tradition offer narratives in which women choosing virginity eventually succeed either in entering or founding a cloister. Anglo-Saxon virgin princess saints were particularly the subject of Norman re-invention, and their Latin *vitae* often date from the eleventh or twelfth centuries, incorporating earlier sources where available, drawing on the repertoire of hagiographic convention. The figure of Christina in her *Life* shares some motifs with the *vitae* of these prestigious figures. In catching specifically at Christina's sleeve (*Life*, p. 43), Ranulf Flambard is reminiscent of King Edgar in Goscelin's *Life of Wulfhilda*.[92] When Christina finally arrives at Alfwen's cell, the rhetoric of her change of clothing is reminiscent of the Anglo-Saxon princess saints in their choice of humble habits over purple and silk (*Life*, p. 93).[93] The eleventh-century life of Edith of Wilton by Goscelin shows her resisting promotion to abbess either of her own or other communities, much as Christina is said to resist both Archbishop Thurstan's Clementhorpe in York and the glamorously aristocratic possibilities of Marcigny and Fontevrault across the Channel.[94] Some parallels are particularly apparent in the remarkable post-Conquest lives of St Osith.[95] This Anglo-Saxon princess saint is forcibly married to King Sigher of East Anglia by her parents, but delays consummation of the marriage with excuses and sophistries. After three years King Sigher determines to claim his rights on his birthday, but is distracted by a wonderful white stag running through his hall. While he hunts the stag (to Dunwich, where it leaps into the sea), Osith (in the Anglo-Norman *Life*) veils herself at the altar, since the two priests her mother has sent to accompany her to her new home are too frightened to do so, or (in the Latin *vita*) she is veiled by her priests.[96] On return, the enraged Sigher, confronted with a *fait accompli*, surprisingly accepts the situation, and gives Osith manors with which to found a monastic house. Later, bathing in the woods with her maidens, she is beheaded by Danish raiders, and carries her own head to her church's altar. Her posthumous miracles include becalming the ship of marauding sailors and paralysing Richard Belmeis II, bishop of London. Osith's Anglo-Norman *Life* has been brilliantly examined by Jane Zatta as an account of the obligations of lordship and one very specifically targeted against the bishops of London. This reading emphasizes the saint as the embodied claims of the Augustinian priory of Chich and explores the issues of lordship for the individual and for monastic and church rights.[97] Some of St Osith's land was split into prebends for the canons of St Paul by Bishop Maurice of London (1086–1107) in the late eleventh century, and his successor, Richard Belmeis I (bishop of London, d. 1127) was only prevented from taking more Chich lands for his own hunting by suffering a stroke. He penitently established Chich as a regular house of canons in 1121. One of the principal miracles in the Anglo-Norman *Life* shows the saint working vengefully on behalf of the canons of Chich, crippling with paralysis Belmeis's nephew, Richard Belmeis II, bishop of London 1152–62, who was attempting to confirm grants away from Chich between 1154 and 1159.[98]

Osith does not attempt to convert her pagan husband Sigher of East Anglia, but her refusal of consummation to him is developed and detailed over three attempts in the vernacular version of the life,[99] making it reminiscent of Christina's strategems over Burthred's three attempts on her virginity (*Life*, pp. 51–5). Osith's self-veiling also has its parallel in Christina's vow, made after she first sees St Albans and marks a cross on its church door with her fingernails. On the return journey the next day at Shillington, Christina places an oblatory penny on the church altar, and offers herself to Christ (*Life*, p. 41), an offering subsequently confided to and confirmed by Sueno, canon of Huntingdon, still in secret, on return to Huntingdon (*Life*, p. 41). Thomas Head has illuminated this sequence in showing it to constitute a betrothal vow to Christ.[100] The parallel with the reinvented Anglo-Saxon St Osith suggests that self-dedication was seen as a plausible pre-Conquest custom, a point also supported by the provisions in Anglo-Saxon penitentials for setting aside unauthorized vows of virginity in the event of subsequent marriage.[101] Osith's self-veiling technically defies canon law, but, given the Anglo-Norman *Life*'s strong defence of the saint's prerogatives, it can perhaps be seen as part of the *Life*'s examination of the limits of institutional law, here seen as subordinate to the direct relation between an individual and God as overlord.[102] Osith's death echoes and elaborates her earlier dedication: she carries her head to her church, marks the church door with her bloody hands and advances to the altar on which she places her head, before composing herself between two pillars, facing east, hands folded in prayer. If the metonym of laying her maiden head on the altar signifies Osith's dedication of virginity to Christ, it also connotes the saint's validation of the priory at Chich as her principal location. She becomes an embodied charter for Chich.

Like Osith's Sigher (and other defeated husbands of virgins, such as St Etheldreda's King Ecgfrid), Burthred is brought to the point of being prepared to support his wife's life as a religious: 'I am prepared to release her before God and you, and I will make provision for her out of my own pocket: so that if she wishes to enter a monastery she can be admitted by the community without hindrance', he says to Sueno and Christina's father's chaplain (*Life*, pp. 69–71). Sueno and the chaplain promise Burthred that Christina's continuing virginity will be the guarantor that she freely agrees to his release of her (*Life*, p. 71). It is a sign that she is not being coerced by churchmen perceiving her as a potential resource and demonstrates the characteristic association of virginity with integrity of volition. But unlike Osith or the paradigmatic Etheldreda of Ely (and many others such as Brigid of Ireland, Cuthfleda of Leominster, Eanswith of Kent, Frideswide of Oxford, Mildrid of Thanet, Melangell of Montgomeryshire, Merwenna of Romsey, Modwenna of Burton, Werburga of Ely, Hanbury and Chester, Winefride of Shrewsbury, Wulfhilda of Barking),[103] Christina's preservation of her virginity does not achieve for her a formal religious career in a convent. Virginity must be freely willed and vowed, but requires endowment and assent to be realized as a status. It is not always a necessary and almost never a sufficient condition for a religious life.[104] Burthred subsequently changes his mind about endowing Christina's religious life, and Christina, without dowry or dower and without support from kinsmen, runs away to informal lay reclusion as her best entry strategy.

Reclusion was not cheap either, and many of those undertaking it were married or widowed.[105] Christina has to buy time, while achieving what imprimatur for her status she can. Institutionalizing her status as virgin is as important as the initial escape: the conventional options are formal consent by the bishop of Lincoln to her reclusion, or acceptance in a religious community. Her first direct speech as represented in her *Life* after her escape is 'I wish to have that place to dwell in' in her vision of Roger's hermitage (*Life*, p. 111), about five years after her initial flight to the recluse Alfwen, and shortly after Burthred finally releases her from her marriage vows (*Life*, p. 109). Although both archbishops, and especially Thurstan of York, are represented as supporting Christina, Roger's death necessitates a further period of hiding for her. Only after the bishop of Lincoln's death in 1123 are Christina's moves towards connection with St Albans begun (through the one healing miracle which, as noted above, is so carefully managed by Christina, *Life*, pp. 119–21), and it is almost twenty years later that Markyate is founded. A large part of Christina's career falls within the fundamental paradigm represented by the characteristic development of religious foundations from hermitage to cloister, but in a long drawn-out and tortuous version of the process.

The solitary and the coenobitic life are closely entwined from the very beginnings of monasticism, from St Benedict himself onwards, and the weight of tradition, especially post-Cluniac reform, contributes legitimating force to the trope of eremitic origins for monasteries.[106] Some of the Anglo-Saxon princess saints cited above have eremitic passages en route to their aristocratic abbesshoods. The two twelfth-century lives of St Frideswide of Oxford are a case in point. William of Malmesbury's brief *vita* is expanded in a twelfth-century *Life* ('Life A').[107] In the former, Malmesbury merely relates that Frideswide had taken a vow of chastity; the king set his heart on marrying her, so she fled into a wood to escape him, but he followed her there; she therefore returned to Oxford by hidden ways. He followed her there too but was struck blind at the town gate (and this is why English kings are afraid to enter Oxford or lodge in it). So Frideswide established a monastery there. In 'Life A', however, Frideswide's flight and subsequent sojourn in the wood becomes a period spent as a hermit. An angel tells her to take two nuns with her, and in the nearby wood called Binsey they find a little hut built previously by swineherds, which was completely covered with ivy. Frideswide carries out miracles of healing there, before deciding to return to her monastery in Oxford. So, too, Geoffrey of Burton's *Life of Modwenna* shows the saint repeatedly seeking solitude for herself and her handmaidens and nuns (competing indeed with pigs for woodland food) only to have her establishments effortlessly turn into monasteries and daughter houses.[108] Æthelthryth (d. 835), daughter of Offa of Mercia, refuses Ethelbert King of East Anglia in order to become a hermit at Croyland.[109] St Etheldreda of Ely, in flight from her second husband Ecgfrid, is divinely assisted to a retreat with two handmaidens when St Ebb's Head is cut off by the sea, saving Etheldreda from Ecgfrid's pursuit, and she is able to live there ascetically for some time before founding her Abbey of Ely.[110] Etheldreda's younger sister, Witburga, becomes a solitary at Holkham and East Dereham (with, like Giles, a tame doe as her companion) and is incorporated into Ely Abbey and its holy female dynasty only at her posthumous tenth-century translation.[111] St Dymphna, purported daughter of a British king, flies with her confessor Gerebernus to solitude first at Antwerp and then Gheel.[112]

Stories of the successful solitary or hermit as the nucleus of a convent formed a major genre of *Gründungssaga* in twelfth-century Britain, not only in formal *vitae*, but in cartularies, chronicles and anecdotal reports. The two recluses of Eywood whose rough shelter of wattle is replaced by Geoffrey de Gorran with the convent of Sopwell are but one example. Such stories for women's foundations, as for men's, had a long life in Britain: the fourteenth-century cartulary of Crabhouse in Norfolk, for instance, tells of eremitic foundation and refoundation (with a recluse keeping safe the muniments that enable refoundation).[113] The widely circulating tale of 'Le Miracle de Sardenai' shows an anchoress developing a pilgrimage hostel and eventually a double monastery around her acquisition of a wooden image of the Virgin which grew a coating of flesh.[114] The well-known passage of *Ancrene Wisse* in which the text's initial audience of three sisters (already noted within an early interpolation as having increased to 'twenty now or more … as though you were a convent of Shrewsbury or Chester')[115] are said to have asked for a rule for their way of life is a further instance. In refusing them a formal rule, the author offers them a charismatic account of the superior internalized spirituality of their anchoress status, relegating pragmatic prescription as a mere 'outer rule'.[116] But he may also have been refusing the full burden of care and organization undertaken by some churchmen (notably Gilbert of Sempringham and Robert of Arbrissel) in the face of chronic institutional underprovision for women's lives in religion.

A critical period of transition is naturally the death of the figure around whom a group first gathers. Male succession seems to have posed fewer threats to viability. The hermitage or reclusorium of Kilburn, for instance, founded by the hermit Godwyn under the auspices of Westminster and granted with the permission of Abbot Herbert (1121–*c*. 1136) to the three 'maidens' ('puellae', 'ancillae Dei', not 'moniales'), Emma, Gunilda and Christina, seems to have been established, as Sally Thompson notes, in terms that envisage a growing community with a future, to ensure which the women are to choose a suitable elderly man to be their mentor at Godwyn's death.[117] For Christina the passage from hermitage to cloister is neither quick nor smooth, Roger's death being received initially not as a handing-on, but as the withdrawal of male supervision, leaving Christina unprotected from the bishop of Lincoln (*Life*, p. 113).

Women could inherit property even under primogeniture in the Anglo-Norman period, but usually only in the absence of a suitable male.[118] In the Anglo-Saxon period, however, it was not uncommon for daughters to inherit family property. Christina inherits Roger's hermitage as his spiritual 'Sunday daughter' in the *Life*'s famous English phrase ('sunendaege dohter', *Life*, p. 107).[119] There is an Anglo-Saxon precedent for this in Felix's *Life of Guthlac* (early eighth century). Guthlac at his death tells his servant to go to his sister Pega and tell her that he has avoided her presence in life in order to be united with her in eternity – he also gives instructions for the way in which she is to bury him (wrapped in a cloth sent to him by a female religious). Guthlac tells the messenger the secret of his prophetic and visionary powers: an angel shows him mysteries unlawful for him to utter. (Just so, Geoffrey of St Albans is above all concerned to know the source of Christina's ability to know 'his deeds beforehand', *Life*, p. 151). Guthlac instructs the messenger to tell this only to Pega and Ecgberht the anchorite. Subsequently, Pega translated his body to a shrine, where she took up residence. It became a site of pilgrimage and healing miracles, and there is an account of a miracle of healing performed by her with the aid of some salt consecrated by Guthlac.[120]

Pega is here the inheritor of both Guthlac's hermitage and his supernatural powers. As Hollis has shown, this story reflects a 'soul friend' tradition: it is a mark of particular intimacy to tell someone the secret or the story of your life, and this, like designating someone as the person who is to bury you, appears to be a way of designating the heir to your supernatural powers and charisma.[121] Presumably, then, when Roger wishes to bequeath his cell to Christina and she feels an anxious need of Mary's authorization (*Life*, p. 111), it is not just material inheritance which is involved but some conception of inheritance of his spiritual powers or even leadership of the hermit community. As Roger's pupil, Christina has become the sharer of his secrets and knowledge of mysteries ('de secretis celestibus', *Life*, p. 104). Roger may also have left Christina some money to support herself.[122]

In classic fashion Christina's hermitage becomes the site of her new priory of Markyate under the auspices of Geoffrey of St Albans. But the foundation of Markyate out of Roger's hermitage is on land belonging to the canons of St Paul's Cathedral Church, London (whose bishops are shown as so severely disciplined in the hagiography of Osith of Chich).[123] Roger's original possession of the hermitage is interestingly mysterious (why was a monk from St Albans established on St Paul's land when he became a hermit?). In the *Life* it is said that when he got back from Jerusalem, Roger was 'met at Windsor by three angels clothed in white garments and stoles, each one bearing in his hand a cross over which there were the same number of burning tapers. Accompanying him visibly from thence, they brought him to the site of the hermitage and established him there' (*Life*, p. 81).[124] In going to the 'wilderness', hermits and recluses must sometimes have occupied land on which there were no or uncertain legal claims. The Anglo-Saxon hermit Guthlac, for instance, is shown winning possession of his island hermitage by defeating the demons who inhabited it. Christina's inheritance of Roger's hermitage is legitimated by the Virgin Mary (*Life*, p. 111).[125] But it looks here as if some dispute was involved in Roger's possession of his hermitage, subsequently elided in the St Albans cult of its male hermit-saints.[126]

Christina's largest 'inheritance' of institutional capital, Geoffrey de Gorran's decision to turn her tenure of Roger's cell into the priory of Markyate, is gained only after many years and is also marked by anomalies. The hermitage was located on the further side of the Watling Street boundary between Bedfordshire and Hertfordshire.[127] (The village of Markyate, which developed around the priory on the Caddington side of Watling Street, is now divided between the two counties.) Did Geoffrey de Gorran choose Markyate because he was opposed within St Albans? There was some resentment over his support of women on the part of the monks, though even greater complaint was made about Abbot Warin's perceived diversion of revenues in the foundation of St Mary de Pré.[128] Why not establish Christina on territory securely held by St Albans within his own jurisdiction; why indeed was not Geoffrey's earlier foundation of Sopwell (1140) offered to Christina? Was Geoffrey trying to keep their friendship and its associated expenses independent of St Albans? Geoffrey may well have been aware of the earlier experiment by which the Kilburn hermitage became a priory (but in this case switching from episcopal jurisdiction to dependence on the Westminster monks).[129] Geoffrey was a correspondent of Osbert of Clare, prior of Westminster, who furthered the survival of the Kilburn hermitage after its initial establishment (and over which Gilbert the Universal, bishop of London, relinquished all episcopal jurisdiction), and both men were supporters of the feast of the Virgin's conception.[130] Gordon Whatley, in an important revision of earlier work, has argued that opposition to Osbert and the feast came from Westminster rather than St Paul's, and that the Belmeis family were promoters of regular monastic life, rather than secularists. It is the Belmeis brothers, Dean Ralph and Archdeacon Richard, who lead in the donation of land for the Markyate priory.[131] It may be that in Geoffrey's personal network lies the reason for the willingness of St Paul's to help with the foundation of Markyate. Or was it Christina who wanted a jurisdiction that did not make her house immediately dependent on St Albans? One moreover that gave her recognition outside the informal structures chiefly governing her religious career until then? The Markyate charters make the canons of St Paul's the nuns' patrons, but they also stipulate that neither monks nor clerks are to alter the nuns' way of life without their consent.[132] Was the formal offering by St Paul's of their gift of land at the altar a triumph for Christina such as that of Osith?[133] Christina's passage from inscribing the church door at St Albans to having an altar on which to lay her own charter is longer but no less arduous.

Geoffrey de Gorran's other foundations are more conventionally established and represented in the *Gesta Abbatum*: Sopwell, *c.* 1140, not only has its story of eremetic origins, as noted above, p. 29, but is undertaken with a clear line of dependency from St Albans; with the patronage of baron Robert d'Aubigni and the entry of his sister Amice;[134] and with a reformist agenda signalled in the enclosure and virginity provisions of his charter.[135] Did Geoffrey de Gorran, devotee of the royal female patron of clerical learning, St Katherine, and builder of the queen's guestchamber at St Albans,[136] see himself in the tradition of elite spiritual foundations for women, as already established for instance at Fontevrault? Sopwell maintained its links with St Albans after Geoffrey died in 1147 its Anglo-Norman customary, for instance, giving instructions for the continuing commemoration of St Alban by a weekly chanting of his office.[137]

Geoffrey de Gorran's third foundation, the hospital of St Julian, is usually credited to Christina's influence, but the *Gesta Abbatum* says nothing of Christina at this point and stresses that the foundation is 'consilio et consensu Conventus'.[138] As Rachel Koopmans has suggested, the amalgamation of the hospital with Abbot Warin's 1194 foundation of St Mary de Pré some thirty years after Geoffrey's death could be seen as part of the replacement of Christina as St Albans' 'helper' by St Amphibalus after Geoffrey's death, though it is worth noting that the first master of the hospital was the son of the man who had the founding vision of St Amphibalus.[139]

In her establishments, as in other aspects of her career, tradition offered some possibilities and models but no automatic or easy precedents for Christina, who had to deploy and realize the conceptions and precedents of religious life with originality and persistence. The trope of reform in which we principally hear of the female communities around St Albans (Abbots Wulfnoth and Paul's 'reforms' of the *nunnae* or other women associated with St Albans in the ninth and the eleventh centuries) has a continuing history. In her magisterial 1922 study of medieval English nunneries, Eileen Power used the gift of half a dozen ordinals from the St Albans Abbot Thomas de la Mare (1349–96) in a treatment of the priory as quarrelsome, illiterate and in need of reform.[140] In fact, the changes to the house can equally be accounted for by a declining need of nursing work for leprosy: Richard de Wallingford (abbot, 1328–36) had already regularized St Mary's as Benedictine and de la Mare may have been formalizing a gradual process (one common among smaller foundations) of a hospital becoming a convent, not reforming an unsatisfactory religious house.[141] Power omits to mention the change of function for the house or the fact that it included brothers (as the Anglo-Norman customary makes clear), or for that matter to consider the possible francophone literacies of the house.[142]

In the creation of her religious career, with institutional resources having to be sought opportunistically among informal and personal networks, Christina of Markyate can be seen as representative, perhaps, of many other under-recorded female religious lives. So, too, St Albans: for all the formalization and expansion of its relations with women in Christina's lifetime, its most famous chronicler, Matthew Paris, even as he himself produces saints' lives for royal and noble women in the thirteenth century, knows nothing of Christina in his part of the *Gesta Abbatum* house history. Information about her, added under de la Mare in the revival of St Albans' hermit-saints, contributes more to the capabilities and prestige of Roger than her own achievements.[143] Like Pega, holy woman and sister of St Guthlac, Christina's story was effaced as much as propagated in St Albans historiography.[144] At the same time, it is sometimes possible to catch a glimpse of the ways in which Christina may have turned the absence of institutional power not only into charismatic power, but also into a source of greater freedom of action. The cultural powers drawn on and embodied by Christina are opportunistically seized and outside St Albans' sense of itself; they are not therefore negligible.

Notes

1   Thompson, *Women Religious*, p. 58 (pp. 56–61 for St Albans and women).
2   Koopmans, 'The Conclusion'.
3   For modern accounts of the presence of women at St Albans see W. Page and M. Reddon, 'St Albans Abbey', *VCH, Hertfordshire*, ed. William Page, iv (London, 1914), pp. 367–416 (at pp. 368–9, 373, 375); L. F. R. Williams, *History of the Abbey of St Alban* (London, 1917), pp. 21, 59; David Knowles and R. Neville Hadcock, *Medieval Religious Houses: England and Wales* (London, 1971), pp. 264, 388.

4 *Gesta Abbatum*, i. 77–9 (St Julian's), pp. 80–2 (Sopwell); pp. 201–4 (St Mary de Pré): pp. 95–6 (Markyate); *VCH Herts.* iv. 422–6 (Sopwell); ibid., pp. 464–7 (St Julian's); ibid., pp. 428–32 (St Mary de Pré); *VCH Bedfordshire*, ed. H. A. Doubleday and William Page, i (Westminster, 1904), pp. 358–61 (Markyate).

5 *VCH Herts*, ii. 194; iv. 432–3.

6 *The Will of Aethelgifu: A Tenth-Century Anglo-Saxon Manuscript*, ed. Dorothy Whitelock *et al.* (Oxford, 1968), pp. 6–10 (pp. 40–3 on St Albans' post-Conquest treatment of the will in its own interest): Sarah Foot, *Veiled Women*, 2 vols. (Aldershot, 2000), *s.v.* Standon, ii. 183–6. For Isabella of Arundel's suit over her right to nominate the priors of Wymondham, see *Gesta Abbatum*, i. 407–9: *Monasticon Anglicanum*, ed. William Dugdale, rev. John Caley, Henry Ellis and B. Bandinel (London, 1821), iii. 332; Susan Wood, *English Monasteries and Their Patrons* (London, 1955), pp. 61, 64. For Paris's salutations to Isabella as patron, see Wogan-Browne, *Saints' Lives*, pp. 161–3. For women donors in the late eleventh century, alone or with their families, see Emma Cownie, *Religious Patronage in Anglo-Norman England 1066–1135* (Woodbridge and Rochester, 1998), pp. 84–8, 91, 93.

7 Ian Short, 'Bi-lingualism in Anglo-Norman England', *Romance Philology* 33 (1980), 467–79. Godric of Finchale (d. 1170) miraculously acquires Latin and French according to his biographer, Reginald of Durham; Wulfric of Haselbury (d. 1155) gives the ability to speak French to a stranger, to the chagrin of Brihtric, a local parish priest and friend of the hermit; John of Beverley cures a deaf and dumb youth who is then able to speak English and French and becomes a baker (in a miracle collection of, probably, 1170–80). These stories confirm the social status of French, but they also show the wide range of those who might acquire it or aspire to do so.

8 *Les Proverbes de Salemon*, ed. Clare Isoz, ANTS, 44, 45, 50 (London, 1988–94) iii, pp. 12–14. Aeliz was probably herself a Clare and by marriage a half-sister of William de Roumare, Earl of Lincoln; her second husband was Robert de Cundé of Lincolnshire (d. by 1145 at latest). The author, Sansun de Nanteuil, was probably Aeliz's chaplain. (In the late twelfth century, a Roger de Cundé founded the nunnery of Hinchingbrooke, Huntingdon: see Thompson, *Women Religious*, Appendix A, *s.v.* Hinchingbrooke.) The commentary for the Countess of Alsace is extant chiefly in Anglo-Norman manuscripts (see *The Twelfth-Century Psalter Commentary in French for Laurette d'Alsace (An Edition of Psalms I-L)*, ed. Stewart Gregory, 2 vols. (London, 1990), i, Introduction).

9 Ian Short, 'Gaimar's Epilogue and Geoffrey of Monmouth's *Liber vetustissimus*', *Speculum* 69 (1994), 323–43 (at pp. 327–8).

10 *L'Estoire des Engleis*, ed. Alexander Bell, ANTS 14–16 (Oxford, 1960), Flambard: v. 5,812; Guthlac: vv. 1,635–9, 5,726–7.

11 *The Conception Nostre Dame of Wace*, ed. William Ray Ashford (Chicago, 1933). Lists of extant manuscripts for this and all other texts counted as Anglo-Norman literature can be found in the indispensable Ruth J. Dean with Maureen B. M. Boulton, *Anglo-Norman Literature: A Guide to Texts and Manuscripts*, ANTS OPS 3 (London, 1999).

12 *Conception Nostre Dame*, ed. Ashford, vv. 39–172.

13 *The Anglo-Norman Voyage of St Brendan*, ed. Ian Short and Brian Merrilees (Manchester, 1979), pp. 4–5.

14 Ibid., vv. 87–8; vv. 97–100.

15 Rachel Bullington, *The Alexis in the St Albans Psalter: A Look into the Heart of the Matter* (New York, 1991), pp. 106–7; 201–2.

16 For the life of St Évroul see *The Ecclesiastical History of Orderic Vitalis*, ed. Marjorie Chibnall, 6 vols., OMT (Oxford, 1968–80), Appendix II, i. 704–11. On Old French versions see Janice M. Pindar, 'The Intertextuality of Old French Saints' Lives: St Giles, St Évroul and the Marriage of St Alexis', *Parergon* 6A (1988), 11–21.

17 *La Vie de saint Gilles*, ed. Françoise Laurent (Paris, 2002); *The Old English Life of St Nicholas with the Old English Life of St Giles*, ed. Elaine Treharne, Leeds Texts and Monographs n.s. 15 (Leeds, 1997). Quotations from the Anglo-Norman *Gilles* and Life of St Andrew occur as marginalia in a collection of Ælfric's homilies made in the second quarter of the twelfth century (Cambridge, University Library MS Ii.1.33: see *Ælfric's Catholic Homilies: The First Series*, ed. Peter Clemoes, EETS SS 17 (Oxford, 1997), p. 28, n. 1.

18 Influence is not only in one direction, as is suggested by the existence of a thirteenth-century French prose life of St Godric alongside continental lives of Becket, Brendan, Patrick (Dean, *Anglo-Norman*, no. 530).

19 Only a fragment is now extant (in a mid-thirteenth century collection of saints' lives in Manchester, John Rylands, University Library MS French 6: Dean, *Anglo-Norman*, no. 568: 'Les Vies de sainte Catherine d'Alexandrie en ancien français,' ed. E. C. Fawtier-Jones, *Romania* 56 (1930), 80–104.

20 On Ælfric's distrust of eremitic spiritualities see further Mary Clayton, 'Hermits and the Contemplative Life in Anglo-Saxon England', in *Holy Men and Holy Women: Old English Prose Saints' Lives and their Contexts*, ed. Paul Szarmach (Albany, NY, 1996), pp. 147–75: *The Old English Life of St Mary of Egypt*, ed. Hugh Magennis (Exeter, 2002), pp. 22–5; also his 'St Mary of Egypt and Ælfric: Unlikely Bedfellows in Cotton Julius E. vii?', in *The Legend of Mary of Egypt in Insular Hagiography*, ed. Erich Poppe and Bianca Ross (Dublin, 1996), pp. 99–112: Andrew P. Scheil explores the differences between Ælfric's Eugenia and the anonymous Euphrosyne's life in 'Somatic Ambiguity and Masculine Desire in the Old English Euphrosyne', *Exemplaria* 11 (1999), 345–62. We do not pursue the comparison of Christina's *Life* with Old English saints' lives here, since a detailed and very illuminating paper was given on this topic by Mark Atherton at the Christina of Markyate and the St Albans Psalter Conference, St Albans School, 2–3 August 2003.

21 For a survey and bibliography see Gordon Whatley, 'Late Old English Hagiography ca. 950–1150', in *Hagiographies*, ed. G. Philippart, ii (Turnhout, 1996), pp. 429–99 (at pp. 455–9 for non-Ælfrician saints).

22 London, British Library, MS Cotton Vespasian D. 14: see Mary P. Richards, 'Texts and Their Traditions in the Medieval Library of Rochester Cathedral Priory', *Transactions of the American Philosophical Society* 78 (Philadelphia, 1988), 92–4; and for full contents, N. R. Ker, *Catalogue of Manuscripts Containing Anglo-Saxon* (Oxford, 1957: reissued 1990), pp. 271–7. For Ralph d'Escures see *Life*, p. 84.

23 *The Old English Version of Bede's Ecclesiastical History*, ed. Thomas Miller, 2 vols., EETS OS 95, 96 (London, 1890), EETS OS 110, 111 (London, 1898).

24 Gordon Whatley, 'An Introduction to the Study of Old English Prose Hagiography: Sources and Resources', in *Holy Men and Holy Women*, ed. Szarmach, pp. 3–32 (pp. 15–16); Robert Bartlett, 'The Hagiography of Angevin England', in *Thirteenth Century England V*, ed. P. R. Coss and S. D. Lloyd (Woodbridge, 1995), 37–52; Susan J. Ridyard, *The Royal Saints of Anglo-Saxon England: A Study of West Saxon and East Anglian Cults* (Cambridge, 1988); for Anglo-Norman women saints see Wogan-Browne, *Saints' Lives*, pp. 60–6.

25 See, for an indication, *Anglo-Saxon Litanies of the Saints*, ed. Michael Lapidge, Henry Bradshaw Society 106 (London, 1991), where Hild makes no appearance and 'Friþeswiða' is once included in a late-eleventh century litany, probably from Winchester New Minster (pp. 145–60, 168). On Hild's cult up to the twelfth century, see Christine Fell, 'Hild, Abbess of Streonaeshalch', in *Hagiography and Medieval Literature: A Symposium*, ed. H. Bekker-Nielsen *et al.* (Odense, 1981), pp. 76–99.

26 As this takes place on Christina's birthday, it may imply that she regarded herself as now old enough to vow herself to virginity.

27 *Gesta Abbatum*, i. 11, 59. It is not clear whether Matthew Paris means that the women attended services in the church with the men: a poem by Aldhelm, c. 700, mentions the presence of both men and women at services in a double monastery (*Aldhelmi Opera*, ed. Rudolph Ehwald, *MGH AA* 15 (Berlin, 1913), Carmen 3, pp. 14–18 (at ll. 46–58); *Aldhelm: The Poetic Works*, trans. Michael Lapidge and James L. Rosier (Cambridge, 1985), p. 49).

28 The Letter admonishes 'episcopis et presbiteris subintroductas habere mulieres' ['bishops and priests [not] to have women living with them']: it is preserved in Flodoard of Reims's *Historia Remensis Ecclesiae*, ed. Martina Stratmann, *MGH SS*, xxiii (Hanover, 1998), p. 386, l. 18: text in *Councils and Synods, with Other Documents Relating to the English Church, 871–1204: Part I, 871–1066*, ed. Dorothy Whitelock, M. Brett and C. N. L. Brooke, 2nd edn., 2 vols. (Oxford, 1981), no. 5, p. 13: trans. Dorothy Whitelock, *English Historical Documents c. 500–1042*, 2nd edn. (London, 1996), no. 224 (223 in 1st edn.), p. 887.

29 For Lanfranc's attempts to expel refugee women from female communities, see *The Letters of Lanfranc, Archbishop of Canterbury*, ed. and trans. Helen Clover and Margaret Gibson, OMT (Oxford, 1979), p. 166.

30 Foot, *Veiled Women*, ii. 158, citing Domesday Book, I, fos. 135va–136ra (Hertfordshire), 10, 1–20, and on the charters, Thompson, *Women Religious*, p. 23.

31 Thompson shows good reason for thinking a community had developed at Sopwell before Geoffrey's 1140 foundation, but the evidence does not go back before the charters of Henri d'Aubigni, c. 1107–32, who made his grant to the 'ancillas Dei et servis Dei' at Sopwell when his daughter was old enough to be a member of the group (Thompson, *Women Religious*, p. 24).

32 Foot, *Veiled Women* i. 111–98 (pp. 125–6, 138). Prayers for blessing vowesses are included in Anglo-Saxon pontificals (i. 127–34).

33 Foot, *Veiled Women* i, esp. 104–10. See also, for a list of tenth-century charters granting land to pious women (sometimes referred to as nuns but more often by phrases such as 'cuidam sancte conversatione dedite Christi ancille' or 'cuidam religiose femine'), Bruce Venarde, *Women's Monasticism and Medieval Society: Nunneries in France and England, 890–1215* (Ithaca, NY, 1997), p. 24, nn. 27 and 28.

34 Foot, *Veiled Women*, i. esp. 120–6.

35 'On the Book of Judith,' ed. Bruno Assmann, *Angelsächsische Homilien und Heiligenleben* (Darmstadt, 1964), pp. 102–16. Mary Clayton argues that the intended reader was a virgin vowess living in a community of other *nunnan*: 'Ælfric's Judith: Manipulative or Manipulated?', *Anglo-Saxon England* 23 (1994), 215–27, at pp. 225–7.

36 Foot, *Veiled Women*, i., esp. 171. The temporary nature of women's property – the extent to which they are transmitters rather than owners – continues in post-Conquest society: for a succinct account see Henrietta Leyser, *Medieval Women: A Social History of Women in England, 450–1500* (London, 1995), pp. 83–4, 86–9: Paul Brand, '*In perpetuum*: the Rhetoric and Reality of Attempts to Control the Future in the English Medieval Common Law', in *Medieval Futures: Attitudes to the Future in the Middle Ages*, ed. J. A. Burrow and Ian P. Wei (Woodbridge, 2000), pp. 101–14.

37 *Ælfric's Lives*, pp. 314–35 (at p. 328, ll. 189–94).

38 *La Vie Seint Edmund le rei, poème anglo-normand du XII e siècle par Denis Piramus*, ed. Hilding Kjellmann (Gothenburg, 1935), vv. 3,035–70 (v. 3,038). For the Roman widow's credentials as semi-religious, counsellor and prophetess, see vv. 1,115–295. (The source for this section of the *Vie* is Gaufridus de Fontibus's *Infantia sancti Edmundi*, AD 1148 x 1156 (*Memorials of St Edmund's Abbey*, ed. Thomas Arnold, 3 vols., RS 96 (London, 1890–96), i. 93–103, at pp. 98–9).

39 *Felix's Life of Saint Guthlac*, ed. Bertram Colgrave (Cambridge, 1956, rpt. 1985), pp. 154–6, 168.

40 Foot, *Veiled Women*, ii. 161–2: the twelfth-century Anglo-Norman Life of St Osith includes 351 lines without equivalent in the Latin *vita*, narrating the miraculous cure at Chich of a paralysed Welsh woman from Hereford who subsequently works as a shrine attendant: 'An Anglo-French Life of St Osith', ed. A. T. Baker, *Modern Language Review* 6 (1911), 476–502 (vv. 1065–416).

41 *Gesta Abbatum*, i. 101.

42 *Domesday Book*, ed. John Morris *et al.*, 39 vols. (plus 3 index vols.) (Chichester, 1975–92), ii. fo. 372r (Suffolk, 14, 167).

43 Foot, *Veiled Women*, ii. 49.

44 *Monasticon Anglicanum*, ed. Dugdale, ii. 37; discussed A. Locke, 'The Abbey of Evesham,' in *VCH Worcestershire*, ed. J. W. Willis-Bund and William Page, ii (London, 1906), 112–27, at p. 116; and D. Knowles, *The Monastic Order in England*, 2nd edn. (London, 1963), p. 137 (Knowles's dating of this as 1095–96 is incorrect).

45 Foot, *Veiled Women*, ii. 257–9.

46 'B', *Vita sancti Dunstani*, chs. 10–11 (*Memorials of St Dunstan, Archbishop of Canterbury*, ed. W. Stubbs, RS 63 (London, 1874), pp. 1–52 (17–19)).

47 These cottages were close enough to the church to be visible from the church door (*Vita Dunstani*, ed. Stubbs, p. 17).

48 *Vita Dunstani*, ed. Stubbs, p. 18. Æthelflæd's accommodation does not appear to have been ascetic; at any rate, it was big enough to entertain the king and his retinue at a feast, and there is a mention of Dunstan hearing her talking to her divine messenger behind the curtain hangings (*Vita Dunstani*, ed. Stubbs, p. 19). In this context, the provision miracle for the feast perhaps functions as a reminder of the voluntary poverty of a wealthy woman: a sign of committed asceticism and a holy life, rather than of actual dearth in Æthelflæd's household.

49 *Vita Dunstani*, ed. Stubbs, p. 19.

50 Ibid., pp. 19–20.

51 Patricia Halpin, 'Women Religious in Late Anglo-Saxon England', *Haskins Society Journal* 6 (1994), 97–110, at p. 104.

52 Foot, *Veiled Women*, ii. 96–7.

53 See E. A. Jones's chapter in this volume; Anneke B. Mulder-Bakker, *Lives of the Anchoresses* (Philadelphia, forthcoming).

54 So, for instance, 'Neither place [Marcigny and Fontevrault] would seem to be specially suited to Christina with her less refined, more bucolic Anglo-Saxon background' (Donald Nicholl, *Thurstan, Archbishop of York (1114–1140)* (York, 1964), p. 197).

55 See Edward J. Kealey, *Medieval Medicus: A Social History of Anglo-Norman Medicine* (Baltimore and London, 1981), pp. 22, 55, 72.

56 The ninth-century Durham *Liber vitae* lists anchorites after kings and queens but before abbots, priors and priests (Ann K. Warren, *Anchorites and Their Patrons in Medieval England* (Berkeley, 1984), p. 127). Warren notes that the Pipe Rolls available from 1154 onwards greatly increase the documentation (p. 128), but royal anchoritic support on the part of the early Plantagenets and Angevins continues, rather than inaugurates, a traditionally high status for anchorites and hermits.

57 *The Guthlac Roll: Scenes from the Life of St Guthlac of Crowland*, (introd.) George F. Warner (Oxford, 1928). For Pega see p. 9 and Plates XV–XVI. Godric receives the tonsure under the eye of Abbess Ælfthryth of Rypadun [Repton] in Plate III.

58 Halpin, 'Women Religious', pp. 103–7.

59 'The *Liber confortatorius* of Goscelin of Saint Bertin', ed. C. H. Talbot, *Studia Anselmiana* 37 (1955), 1–117, at p. 34, trans. W. R. Barnes and Rebecca Hayward, 'Goscelin's *Liber Confortatorius*', in *Writing the Wilton Women: Goscelin's Legend of Edith and the Liber Confortatorius*, ed. Stephanie Hollis, forthcoming. Goscelin assumes that Eve will never leave the cell in which she has enclosed herself at Angers. He envisages her cell as eight feet square with a narrow window (*Liber*, ed. Talbot, p. 72); the dimensions may,

however, be based purely on numerology, since he draws a connection with the eight inhabitants of Noah's Ark. Eve first became a member of a small anchorite community attached to a cemetery church (St Laurent), dependent on the nunnery of Le Ronceray. She later moved to the anchorite community at Saint-Eutrope where Hervé was a member: see A. Wilmart, 'Eve et Goscelin [I]', *Revue Bénédictine* 46 (1934), 414–38.

60 *Liber*, ed. Talbot, p. 67.

61 So, for example, Leoba checks that all her convents are in order and then retires to what sounds like a hermitage with some of her 'famulabus Dei', *Vita Leobae Abbatissae Biscofesheimensis Auctore Rudolfo Fuldensi*, ed. G. Waitz, *MGH SS* xv.i (Hanover, 1887), pp. 118–31 (p. 130), (*Anglo-Saxon Missionaries in Germany*, trans. C. H. Talbot (London, 1954: repr. 1981), pp. 205–26 (p. 223)); see Stephanie Hollis, *Anglo-Saxon Women and the Church: Sharing a Common Fate* (Woodbridge, 1992), p. 275.

62 *Geoffrey of Burton, Life and Miracles of St Modwenna*, ed. Robert Bartlett, OMT (Oxford, 2002), ch. 37, p. 154 (on the date of the *vita*, see p. 1, n. 1).

63 *Liber*, ed. Talbot, p. 36. Hilary of Orléans, in a commemoration of Eve written shortly after her death, *c.* 1120, appears to have believed that she was already living as a recluse before she left Wilton ('Thus for a while she served God in a cell'); 'Die Gedichte und Mysterienspiele des Hilarius von Orléans', ed. Nicholas M. Häring, *Studi Medievale*, 3rd ser. 17 (1976), 915–68 (p. 926, l. 53). The tradition of nun-anchoresses continued (Ann K. Warren, 'The Nun as Anchoress, England 1100–1500', in *Medieval Religious Women I: Distant Echoes*, ed. John A. Nicholas and Lillian Thomas Shank (Kalamazoo, 1984), pp. 197–212), but the larger proportion of anchoresses were laywomen.

64 P. Grosjean, '*Saints Anglo-Saxons des marches Gauloises,*' *Analecta Bollandiana* 79 (1961), 161–9 (p. 168).

65 'Eower ancor æt ham mid eow'; 'þa halgan lare þe se hælend tæhte' (*Angelsächsische Homilien und Heiligeleben*, ed. Bruno Assmann (Kassel, 1889; rpt. Darmstadt, 1964), introd. Peter Clemoes), no. 2, pp. 13–23 (p. 13, ll. 4, 11).

66 This cure is also witnessed by the dream of one of her handmaidens (*Life*, p. 124), in which a vision of the Virgin curing Christina is reminiscent of a story in *Ancrene Wisse* pt. 6, told in illustration of the danger of relying on earthly cures (*Ancrene Wisse*, ed. Robert Hasenfratz (Kalamazoo, 2000), pp. 363–4). The vision in effect certificates Christina's as a divinely-licensed cure and no dereliction from asceticism.

67 *The Life of Bishop Wilfrid by Eddius Stephanus*, ed. Bertram Colgrave (Cambridge, 1927, rpt. 1985), ch. 66, pp. 142–4. See further, Hollis, *Anglo-Saxon Women and the Church*, pp. 164–5, 171–2, 188.

68 Waitz, *Vita Leobae Abbatissae*, ch. 17, p. 129, 'Life of Saint Leoba', trans. Talbot, pp. 221–2, and see Hollis, *Anglo-Saxon Women and the Church*, pp. 289–97.

69 *Vita Edithae*, ch. 21, ed. A. Wilmart, 'La Légende de Ste Édith,' *Analecta Bollandiana* 56 (1938) 5–101, 265–307 (at 87–8); trans. Michael Wright and Kathleen Loncar, in *Writing the Wilton Women*, ed. Hollis (forthcoming). Cf. John 19: 26.

70 *Liber confortatorius*, ed. Talbot, esp. p. 31. Goscelin is possibly echoing an image found in a verse on Christ on the cross in Aldhelm's prose *De Virginitate*, ch. 7 (*c.* 700): 'Himself a virgin commended a virgin/ To a virgin for safe-keeping' (*Aldhelmi Opera*, ed. Ehwald, p. 235, ll. 11; *Aldhelm: The Prose Works*, trans. Michael Lapidge and Michael Herren (Cambridge, 1979), p. 64.

71 Jerome and Paula are also cited as a precedent for Christina and Geoffrey at the beginning of this sequence's account of the slander and gossip about their friendship. Abelard makes use of this precedent, as does Goscelin, who likens the friendship between Edith, her mother, Abbess Wulfthryth, and one of the nunnery's chaplains (Benno of Trier) to that of Jerome, Paula and Eustochium (*Vitae Edithae*, ed. Wilmart, ch. 14, (p. 73)). Goscelin's allusions in the *Liber confortatorius* to the correspondence of

Jerome and women also suggest that he regarded it as a precedent authorizing his relationship with Eve; see esp. *Liber confortatorius*, ed. Talbot, pp. 31–2, 35. (In *Letter 65: To Principia*, Jerome reveals that he has been criticized for writing to women and defends himself for doing so by praising them: there is perhaps an echo of this in Goscelin's defensive stance in his prologue to *Liber Confortatorius*).

72 See further *Writing the Wilton Women*, ed. Hollis, 'Introduction'. Again the tradition continues in Anglo-Norman: in Piramus's *Vie seint Edmund le rei*, suspicion of 'amurs' falls on King Offa and the Roman widow for their 'conseil' and 'privité', but is dropped because of the widow being 'de grant aage' (Kjellman, *Vie seint Edmund*, vv. 1153–8).

73 *Vita Dunstani*, ed. Stubbs, ch. 12, pp. 20–1.

74 In the case of Æthelflæda, economic assistance seems to be in conflict with the widow being 'very wealthy', 'praedives' (*Vita Dunstani*, ed. Stubbs , p. 17).

75 Ibid.

76 For the relationship of Hervé and Eve see n. 59 above and the metrical commemoration of Eve by Hilary of Orléans, ed. Häring, 'Die Gedichte … des Hilarius von Orléans', pp. 25–30. It was written during Hervé's lifetime and perhaps at his request ('For the sake of Hervé, her loving associate … send your prayers to his creator that, while he lives, he might protect him from the kindling of sin', v. 39, ll. 153–6). In a reversal of Geoffrey and Christina's roles, Eve serves Hervé 'as her lord' (Hilarius, v. 26, ll. 101–3). In contrast with the suspicions Hilary attributes to his audience, the relationship was approved as pure by Hervé's former abbot, Geoffrey, who wrote three letters to him, the first of which was also addressed to Eve; *Letters 48–50, Goffridi abbatis vindocinensis: Opera omnia, PL* 157, cols. 184–8.

77 See Ruth Mazo Karras, 'Friendship and Love in the Lives of Two Twelfth Century English Saints', *Journal of Medieval History* 14 (1988), 305–20.

78 *S. Anselmi Opera omnia*, ed. F. S. Schmitt, 6 vols. (Edinburgh, 1946–61), iv, *Epistola* 230, pp. 134–5, and, as *ancillae dei* under the *cura* of Robert, v, *Epistola* 414, pp. 359–62 (p. 361).

79 'Nolite igitur considerare tantum quid faciatis, sed quid velitis; non tantum quae sint opera vestra, quantum quae sit voluntas vestra' (*Opera*, ed. Schmitt, v, p. 360).

80 Oxford, Bodleian Library, MS Digby 96, f. 8r. The text in this manuscript gives great prominence to the dedication in its rubricated incipit, suggesting a certain prestige in writing for a holy woman. An edition is in preparation by S. D. Holland (information in Richard Sharpe, *Handlist of the Latin Writers of Great Britain and Ireland before 1540* (Turnhout, 1997), *s. v.* Godwin of Sarum). On the text see Teresa Webber, *Scribes and Scholars at Salisbury Cathedral c.1075–1125* (Oxford, 1992), pp. 123–8.

81 *Epistolae, PL* 171, cols. 194–7, I.21 (before 1121): see Barbara Newman, 'Flaws in the Golden Bowl: Gender and Spiritual Formation in the Twelfth Century', *Traditio* 45 (1989), 111–46 (pp. 128, 145). For an example of the uses made of this widely influential letter, see *Hali Meiðhad*, ed. Bella Millett, EETS OS 284 (Oxford, 1982).

82 Donald Nicholl, *Thurstan, Archbishop of York*, pp. 197–8.

83 See, e.g., R. Reynolds, '*Virgines subintroductae* in Celtic Christianity', *Harvard Theological Revue* 61 (1968), 547–66. Robert of Arbrissel was reproved for similar practices and a later medieval legend of Aldhelm credits him with temptation by a young virgin (Reynolds, '*Virgines subintroductae*', pp. 559, 563).

84 Compare with Eve and Goscelin (who was not a resident at her Wilton nunnery but frequently visited Eve there). He addresses her in the *Liber confortatorius* as a kindred soul; explicit consciousness that their relationship might be regarded differently by others is found only in the prologue: 'May hissing calumny, the wicked eye, the artful finger, the impure gossip-monger and cackler be far from our pure whispering' (Talbot, *Liber*, p. 26). (Christina's *Life* more extensively registers scandalous constructions of her relationship with Geoffrey, see *Life*, pp. 173–5).

85 *Life and Miracles of St Modwenna*, ed. Bartlett, ch. 35, p. 144.

86 Ibid., ch. 14, p. 50.

87 Ibid., pp. 58–60.

88 Thompson, *English Nunneries*, Appendix A. *s. v. Hinchingbrooke*.

89 II Cnut 76.1a, 1b, in *Die Gesetze der Angelsächsen*, ed. F. Liebermann, 3 vols. (Halle, 1898–1916), i. 308–71, at pp. 362–4; trans. *English Historical Documents*, ed. Whitelock, p. 73.

90 For a succinct review of early gilds and scholarship on them, see V. R. Bainbridge, *Gilds in the Medieval Countryside: Social and Religious Change in Cambridgeshire c. 1350–1558* (Woodbridge, 1996), pp. 5–20.

91 'The lady of the Helmings [Wealhtheow] then went about to young and old, gave each his portion of the precious cup' (ll. 620–2): '[Beowulf's recollection of Hrothgar's daughter] At times before the hall-thanes the daughter of Hrothgar/ bore the ale-cup to the earls in the back' (ll. 2020–1), *Beowulf*, trans. Roy M. Liuzza (Peterborough, Ontario and Letchworth, 2000). The Anglo-Norman romance of Horn (1170s?) suggests such scenes continued to be an image of glamour and prestige: King Hunlaf summons his daughter Rigmel 'as was the custom, to carry round the wine/ as his ancestors did: he did not want to break their custom', and Lenburc, daughter of Gudreche of Ireland attends a feast with her mother (*The Romance of Horn*, ed. Mildred K. Pope, 2 vols. (Oxford, 1955), i. vv. 4,132–4, 2,386–94: for a translation see Judith Weiss, *The Birth of Romance* (London, 1992), pp. 95, 55.

92 'La vie de st Vulfhilde par Goscelin de Cantorbéry,' ed. Mario Esposito, *Analecta Bollandiana* 32 (1913), 10–26, ch. 3, p. 16, ll.14–23. Wulfhilda's female relative, Wenfleda, is complicit with the lecherous king's plans (ch. 2, *passim*), as is Christina's mother, Beatrix in the *Life*.

93 Ridyard, *The Royal Saints*, pp. 83–4.

94 *Vitae Edithae*, ed. Wilmart, ch. 16, pp. 76–7.

95 For an account and comparison of the Latin and Anglo-Norman lives, see Denis Bethell, 'The Lives of St Osyth of Essex and St Osyth of Aylesbury', *Analecta Bollandiana* 88 (1970), 75–127. Anglo-Norman and Latin texts are printed in 'An Anglo-French Life of St Osith', ed. Baker. For Osith's Hereford connections see Julia Barrow, 'A Twelfth-Century Bishop and Literary Patron: William de Vere', *Viator* 18 (1987), 175–89.

96 'An Anglo-French Life', ed. Baker, vv. 649–76, p. 40.

97 Jane Zatta, 'The *Vie Seinte Osith*: Hagiography and Politics in Anglo-Norman England', *Studies in Philology* 96 (1999), 367–93.

98 Zatta, 'Hagiography and Politics', pp. 373–4, 389; 'An Anglo-French Life,' ed. Baker, vv. 1,521–656.

99 'An Anglo-French Life', ed. Baker, vv. 425–75; Zatta, 'Hagiography and Politics', pp. 381–5.

100 Head, 'The Marriages of Christina Markyate' (Chapter 7, this volume, at p. 120). As Head notes, Christina's words have a liturgical flavour, but are not parallelled in standard liturgies for the coronation of virgins (p. 134, n. 20). Nor do they correspond to Anglo-Saxon formulae.

101 Theodore's *Penitential*, II.xii.14–15, I.xiv.5–7, I.xiv.7 (*Medieval Handbooks of Penance*, trans. John T. McNeill and Helena M. Gamer (New York, 1965), pp. 210, 196). As Head has argued, Christina's defence at her ecclesiastical hearing shows she thought herself to be vowed to Christ ('quod elegerim ab infancia castitatem et *voverim* Christo me permansuram virginem, *et feci coram testibus*', *Life*, p. 60, italics added).

102 Zatta, 'Hagiography and Politics', p. 386.

103 See D. H. Farmer, *The Oxford Dictionary of Saints*, 5th edn. (Oxford, 2003), for summary information about these figures and their documentation.

104 Venarde points out that only four of the twelve entries to convents noted by Orderic Vitalis are virgins, and that in the eleventh and twelfth centuries there is an increase

in the numbers of mature women making their own donations on entry rather than being oblated by their parents (Venarde, *Women's Monasticism*, pp. 98–9, 100–1).

105 For some rare cases of daughters being enclosed see Warren, *Anchorites and Their Patrons*, p. 63. Warren also cites the early fourteenth-century case of Beatrice Strong from Bishop John de Grandisson's register: her desire for solitude and perpetual continence was resisted when Grandisson heard that her old and sterile husband was incontinent. But he granted her a trial period of enclosure '*without suspending meanwhile all conjugal debts*' (p. 28, italics added).

106 Henrietta Leyser, *Hermits and the New Monasticism: A Study of Religious Communities in Western Europe, 1100–1150* (London, 1984).

107 'Life A' (1100 x 1120), *Saint Frideswide, Patron of Oxford*, trans. J. Blair (Oxford, 1988), pp. 29–39.

108 *Life and Miracles of St Modwenna*, ed. Bartlett, ch.11, pp. 32–4.

109 *AA.SS*, Aug I (1733), 173–5.

110 *Liber Eliensis*, ed. E. O. Blake, Camden Society, 3rd ser. (London, 1962), i, 11, p. 27.

111 Ibid., pp. 120–3; 221–34.

112 *AA.SS*, May III (1680), 477–97.

113 On the period 1080–*c.* 1170, see Venarde, *Women's Monasticism*, ch. 3 (esp. pp. 84–6). For Crabhouse, 'The Register of Crabhouse Nunnery', ed. Mary Bateson, *Norfolk Archaeology* 11 (1892), 1–71 (pp. 12–13).

114 For the manuscripts see Dean, *Anglo-Norman*, no. 563; Gaston Raynaud, 'Le Miracle de Sardenai', *Romania* 11 (1882), 519–37; and *Romania* 14 (1885), 82–93. Raynaud suggests that cedar wood could exude sap and produce 'une sorte de croûte' over the image in 'un espèce d'incarnation' (529), but the thematic relevance of an image entrusted to a recluse becoming embodied in a community is also significant here.

115 *Ancrene Wisse*, ed. Hasenfratz, pp. 270, ll. 921–2, 917.

116 Ibid., pp. 61, ll. 30–63, 67.

117 Thompson, *Women Religious*, p. 26. One of Godwyn's successors was a canon of St Paul's: Thompson suggests that the appointment of *magistri* without particular connection with Kilburn indicates less tight control of the priory (p. 63).

118 Leyser, *Medieval Women*, pp. 83, 87–8.

119 For hermitages as family property, see, e.g., Alcuin's inheritance of a hermitage from a kinsman who was a holy hermit, whose life he wrote (*Scriptores Rerum Merovingicarum*, ed. W. Levison vii. 81–141 (p. 81), (*Life of Willibrord*, ch. 1, trans. Talbot, pp. 3–22 (p. 3)).

120 *Life of Guthlac*, ed. Colgrave, chs. 50–3, pp. 154–6, 160–2, 168; Hollis, *Anglo-Saxon Women and the Church*, pp. 292–5.

121 Ibid., pp. 290–7.

122 The author tells us that he was anxious to provide a patron and the necessities of life for his successor, but subsequently narrates only arrangements with the archbishop concerning the annulment of Christina's marriage, although he does mention that the archbishop 'took her into his keeping' (*Life*, p. 113).

123 Caddington Manor (Cadendune) was held by St Paul's (ten hides) in the Hundred of Danais (Dacorum) (Hertfordshire Domesday, *VCH Herts*, i. 316, and see 281) and in Flitcham Hundred (two hides), both received from the same donor, Leofwine, before 1086 (*VCH Bedfs*. i. 229–30): Thompson, *Women Religious*, pp. 58–9. St Albans lost its reversion of land at Caddington to Nigel d'Albini after the Conquest (Williams, *History of the Abbey of St Alban*, p. 54).

124 Also *Gesta Abbatum*, i. 97.

125 For cases of servants or younger anchorites brought in to aid older recluses and eventually inheriting the cell, see Warren, *Anchorites and Their Patrons*, pp. 26, 34. L. Gougaud cites the cells of St Gall as inhabited continuously for over a hundred years by male and female recluses ('Étude sur la réclusion religieuse', *Revue Mabillon* 49 (1923), 77–102 (p. 80).

126 *Gesta Abbatum*, i. 184, 101 (Roger); 105 (Sigar).

127 Ibid., i. 97.

128 Ibid., i. 95–6; 205.

129 Thompson, *Women Religious*, p. 26.

130 *The Letters of Osbert of Clare, Prior of Westminster*, ed. E. W. Williamson (Oxford, 1929) no. 32, pp. 114–16: *Gesta Abbatum* i. 93, for Geoffrey's support of the feast.

131 *The Saint of London: The Life and Miracles of St Erkenwald*, ed. Gordon Whatley (Binghamton, NY, 1989), pp. 31–5.

132 *Early Charters of the Cathedral Church of St Paul, London*, ed. Marion Gibbs, Camden Society 3rd ser., lviii (London, 1939), no. 154, p. 120 ('Nulli autem ibi liceat mutare ordinem sanctimonialium quia super hac tenura nec clericis nec monachis aliquam facimus concessionem nisi sanctimonialibus tantum ibi commorantibus'); no. 155, p. 121 (petition to patrons for consent to the election of a prioress); no. 156, p. 121 (consecration of the Markyate church at Caddington by Alexander, bishop of Lincoln).

133 Ibid., no. 156, p. 122.

134 *Monasticon Anglicanum*, ed. Dugdale, iii. 365.

135 The charter stipulates that the virgins are to be locked in at night and only maidens are to be received, terms similar to those of Gilbert of Sempringham's provision for his initial group of young female recluses in 1131 as recounted (c. 1202) in his *vita* (Raymonde Foreville and Gillian Keir, ed. and trans. *The Book of St Gilbert*, OMT (Oxford, 1987), ch. 9, pp. 30–4).

136 *Gesta Abbatum*, i. 79.

137 *Gesta Abbatum*, i. 96 (Geoffrey's death): 'La custume de la commemoration de seint Alban soit gardé sicome il soleit estre, c'est asavoir que vous chauntrez de lui un jour en la symaigne', ed. Tony Hunt, 'Anglo-Norman Rules for the Priories of St Mary de Pré and Sopwell,' in *De Mot en mot: Aspects of Medieval Linguistics. Essays in Honour of William Rothwell*, ed. Stewart Gregory and D. A. Trotter (Cardiff, 1997), pp. 93–104 (p. 100).

138 *Gesta Abbatum*, i. 77.

139 Ibid., i. 201–4; Koopmans, 'The Conclusion', p. 696.

140 Eileen Power, *Medieval English Nunneries c. 1275–1535* (Cambridge, 1922), p. 244. See too David Knowles's dismissal of nuns and significant female religious in *The Monastic Order in England*, 2nd edn. (Cambridge, 1963) pp. 136–7, and for further discussion, Jocelyn Wogan-Browne, ' "Reading is good prayer": Recent Research on Female Reading Communities', *New Medieval Literatures* 5 (Oxford, 2002), pp. 229–97.

141 Thompson, *Women Religious*, pp. 39–42.

142 For the Anglo-Norman ordinances for the inmates of St Mary de Pré see Hunt, 'Anglo-Norman Rules', pp. 94–9.

143 *Gesta Abbatum*, i. 97–105.

144 Peter of Blois's epitome of the Guthlac *vita*, owned at St Albans in a manuscript partly copied by Matthew Paris, ejects Pega from her inheritance of Guthlac's cell by means of a story not otherwise known in which the devil disguises himself as Pega to tempt Guthlac to eat and Pega is forever banished from Guthlac's island by the saint to prevent further temptations (*Guthlac*, ed. Colgrave, pp. 22–4).

4

CHRISTINA OF MARKYATE AND
THE DOUBLE CROWN[1]

Samuel Fanous

The narrative skill of the author of *The Life of Christina of Markyate*, whoever he was, has been undervalued. This outstanding storyteller brought to life the account of Christina's experience in a highly dramatic narrative style that retains its power to startle and a vigour that implores the reader to respond to the text on the level of biography. In the absence of the customary prefatory discourse on the occasion of and circumstances behind the text's composition, the author's robust claims to authenticity, supported by the text's highly autobiographical flavour, have generally been accepted at face value.[2] Scholars have tended to follow Talbot's lead in discounting the significance of the text's patently hagiographic qualities, thereby discouraging the search for less obvious ones.[3] Yet beneath the text's literal surface there exists a fundamental bipartite structure deploying two closely related hagiographic traditions, in which experience is selected and grouped thematically. In the first, Christina's endeavours to escape her suitor, her parents and the ecclesiastical authorities, is closely modelled on the literature of the virgin martyrs. In the second (occupying the final two-thirds), her trials and privations in the anchorhold and the fruit of enclosure, *amicitia* with the hermit Roger and Abbot Geoffrey, and spiritual charisms, are patterned on the tradition of ascetic martyrdom.

I. Christina as virgin martyr

The theme of virgin martyrdom, the narrative mode of the first section – from Christina's betrothal to her flight – is announced, quite dramatically, from Christina's own lips on the eve of her attempted seduction when her fiancé, Burthred, enters her bedchamber and finds her dressed and sitting up. Christina welcomes him as a brother:

> She recounted to him in detail the story of St Cecilia and her husband Valerian, telling him how, at their death, they were accounted worthy to receive crowns of unsullied chastity from the hands of an angel. Not only this: but both they and many others after them had followed the path of martyrdom and thus, being crowned twice by the Lord, were

honoured both in heaven and on earth. 'Let us therefore', she exhorted him, 'follow their example, so that we may become their companions in eternal glory. Because if we suffer with them, we shall also reign with them.'

(*Life*, p. 51)[4]

While Christina ostensibly invokes the Cecilia legend to justify her desired chastity, she focuses on the maintenance of her virginity in the context of martyrdom and the rewards and honours of the virgin martyrs, including the virgin martyrs' double crown and their celestial reign.[5] This bold and powerful self-declaration, with its emphasis on the reciprocity of the double crown and eternal glory, serves as a marshalling device, signalling the mode of sanctity governing the first part of the *Life*.

Far from being a literal record of the ordeal of the martyrs, the narratives of the *passiones*, particularly those of the virgin martyrs, are highly stylized, in a pattern of binary opposition, characterized chiefly by a sense of heightened and distorted encounter designed to praise the heroine. Confrontation and combat are central themes.[6] The genre makes no allowance for neutrality: the *dramatis personae*, defined along moral axes and behaving largely according to stereotypes, are either for or against the virgin martyr.[7] Tension is writ into every event and encounter, no matter how mundane. The patterns and stages of the virgin martyr's ordeal are usually well structured and easily identified in a recognizable progression of events.[8] Before taking up her vocation, the virgin martyr renounces the world, its honours, privileges and pleasures, her heritage and social position. In the renunciation of her familial identity she redefines bonds of kinship based not on blood but on the radical claims of the Gospel. She rejects earthly suitors, transposing her sexuality onto her heavenly bridegroom. The maintenance of her faith, often enmeshed with and inseparable from her refusal to relinquish her virginity, signals a showdown with the authorities, beginning with the 'Match of Wills', which the authorities lose every time. Unable to make her abjure, they attempt to subjugate her physically, inflicting cruel and sadistic torture. Throughout the ordeal the virgin martyr is shielded partially or completely from pain by her guardian angel. She is summarily killed, sometimes with a single stroke of the sword. Each *vita* places differing emphases on every stage. Often, two themes may be inherent in a single narrative act or several stages may overlap, though in outline all the stages are fundamental to the virgin-martyr lives.

Aristocratic lineage

Many of the virgin-martyr *passiones* begin by cataloguing the saint's physical virtues, sometimes first citing her pedigree. She is usually aristocratic, sometimes even the king's daughter, at least of genteel background.[9] The details of Christina's birth and rank, announced in the very first words of the *Life*, are deployed within this convention of hagiographic nobility. Later, we are reminded that she came from an ancient and influential English family (*Life*, p. 83). This declaration of status is exemplified at the Gild Merchant where, according to local custom, her parents take the place of honour among the assembled nobility (*Life*, p. 49). Her family status is again invoked in the planning for her escape, when Christina is made to demur at the suggestion that she should flee accompanied by a young servant, since it was beneath her dignity that a nobleman's daughter should be found in the open countryside with a youth.

Beauty

Perhaps the most conspicuous characteristic of the virgin martyr is her superlative physical beauty.[10] Rather than concealing this and safeguarding her virginity, the demands of the narrative require the virgin to expose her beauty, thereby ensuring the unwanted attention of her suitors and initiating persecution and martyrdom. As the quality that gets her noticed, beauty can be regarded as the starting point of all her subsequent troubles and therefore a fundamental narrative ingredient.[11] Christina's comeliness and beauty, announced in the opening lines of the *Life*, are superlative, rendering her more lovable than all other women (*Life*, pp. 67–9). These qualities are described as commodities her parents were reluctant to lose, together with the dividends that would accrue thereby, such as attractive grandchildren. Some hagiographers frame the beauty *topos* in a romance context, wounding their suitors with the dart of the virgin's beauty. For example, when African sees Juliana, his heart is pierced with the arrows of love to desire her.[12] When Ranulf Flambard first saw the young Christina in her father's house, 'the bishop gazed intently at his beautiful daughter, and immediately Satan put it into his heart to desire her' (*Life*, p. 43). Just as the starting point for the virgin martyr's troubles is often traced to initial visual contact with her suitor-cum-persecutor, so Christina's hagiographer cites the genesis of her sustained persecution to this encounter with Flambard through a moral précis of the occasion: 'This was the beginning of all the frightful troubles that followed afterwards' (*Life*, p. 43).[13] The hyperbole of Flambard, the former king's deputy, coolly outwitted by the adolescent Christina (who escaped his advances by slipping out of the room and bolting the door shut from the outside), perfectly catches the spirit of the *passiones*, where the virgin martyrs consistently outwit and rebuke their enemies with steely courage. Depicted as a one-dimensional character and a repository of vice ('first a slave to lust and afterwards to malice', *Life*, p. 45), he seethes angrily at his failure to seduce the virgin and devises plots to corrupt her ('he was eaten up with resentment and counted all his power as nothing until he could avenge the insult he had suffered', *Life*, p. 43).[14] Curiously, no mention is made of Burthred's attraction to Christina or his interest in her beauty. As her suitor and spouse he should have most to say about her beauty. That he expresses not the slightest interest in this matter serves to caricature him into a weak, static figure, the agent of Flambard, whose primary function is to embody the threat to Christina's chastity and hence her religious vocation.

Intelligence

Like St Katherine, who defeated the fifty philosophers, many virgin martyrs possess uncommonly high levels of intelligence.[15] Christina too was acknowledged for her wisdom and intelligence. Her escape from Flambard's advances is prefaced by the rhetorical exclamation: 'Hear, then, how prudently she acted' (*Life*, p. 43). She also escapes her parents, whose 'wiles were outwitted at all points and served but to emphasize her invincible prudence' (*Life*, p. 49). When Christina is brought before Fredebertus, the prior of St Mary's, Huntingdon, and his canons, who cite no less an authority than St Paul against her in the attempt to convince her of the folly of her intentions to leave Burthred for a religious life, she professes ignorance of the Scriptures, but proceeds to quote Christ's own words from St Matthew on the propriety of leaving family for the sake of the Kingdom (Matt. 19.29).[16] She inverts the prior's argument – that many virgins perish while mothers are saved – by pointing out that if many virgins perish, so do many married women and that, moreover, salvation surely comes easier to virgins.[17] When he heard her answers, Fredebertus was astonished at her *prudencia* (*Life*, p. 63). After grilling her for a second time, he concedes defeat (*Life*, p. 65). When the wisest of the fifty philosophers heard Katherine's responses, he was *awundret of hire witti wordes* and, with the other philosophers, he similarly concedes defeat.[18]

Just as the virgin martyr's enemies are depicted as a repository of vice, she herself is presented as a paragon of virtues, pre-eminent among all women, as in the case of Eufrasia:

> Then her fame, wisdom and learning sprang throughout all the town, because she was adorned with virtues; many were attracted, so that they desired her in honourable marriage and spoke of it to her father.[19]

Christina, gifted and peerless, is a match for any virgin martyr:

> Christina was so conspicuous for such moral integrity, such comeliness and beauty, that all who knew her accounted her more loveable than all other women. Furthermore, she was so intelligent, so prudent in affairs, so efficient in carrying out her plans, that if she had given her mind to worldly pursuits she could have enriched and ennobled not only herself and her family but also her relatives (*Life*, pp. 67–9).

Renunciation

The virgin martyr is expected to respond to the lure of riches, though she rejects her family's wealth as an impediment to her vocation.[20] Undeterred, her parents tempt her with treasure while suitors offer her untold wealth to marry them.[21] Autti offers Christina his entire wealth, provided she marries Burthred (*Life*, p.

59). Fredebertus' suggestion that Christina's attempt to extricate herself from marriage to Burthred because she has a more wealthy suitor not only illustrates the attraction to wealth which a woman in Christina's position was expected to respond to, but allows her to express a fundamental *topos* in virgin-martyr lives – the transfer of her sexuality to a wealthier and more powerful heavenly bridegroom (*Life*, p. 63). Agnes is offered costly robes by the son of Sempronius, the prefect of Rome, and promised yet costlier ones, but the blessed Agnes despised his gifts, counting them no more than 'a reeking dunghill' (*reocendes meoxes*).[22] After his attempted seduction, Flambard 'came to Huntingdon, bringing with him silken garments and precious ornaments of all kinds. These he offered to the maiden; but she looked on them as dirt and despised them' (*Life*, p. 45).[23]

The virgin martyr's numerous qualities amplify the magnitude of her *renuntio* by illustrating what is at stake in her decision to give up everything in the pursuit of her vocation as the bride of Christ.[24] Her *renuntio* becomes an act of *imitatio Christi* exemplifying St Peter's remark to Christ on the cost of discipleship.[25] As the descendant of an ancient and influential family of nobles, Christina was expected to discharge her familial and communal duties, taking her proper place in a society founded upon a common understanding of its own conventions and values, in which the exercise of individual responsibility according to established notions was paramount. While monasticism was not without status, Autti's comment that Christina's desired monastic vocation would bring shame and dishonour upon the family (*Life*, p. 59) is designed to portray not only her *renuntio* as a rejection of her family in whom society was symbolically constituted by virtue of their nobility and pre-eminence, but also the difficulty of extricating herself from this patriarchal subculture and socio-economic nexus.[26] It is against this background that Christina's battle with the authorities takes place.

The naming of the martyr

The redefinition of familial bonds based on faith is articulated in the rejection of the martyr's personal names in favour of a generic one, 'Christian', expressing their collective identity. When in the *Life of St Alban*, the saint is asked 'What is your name?', he replies: 'Christianus sum'.[27] In the later recensions of the *Life of Alexis*, the saint replies to the same question that he is called *Chrestines*.[28] It is in the thick of her persecutions, when Christina feels alone and most abandoned, that the hagiographer avers that she who had been given the name Theodora at her christening deserved from henceforth her new name, Christina – a name belonging also to the fourth-century blood martyr, St Christina.

The Match of Wills

Having renounced her membership of her community, the virgin martyr embarks on the next stage of her *passio*, the testing, in which the authorities attempt to overturn her religious and sexual choices.[29] The testing consists of two stages: the psychological battle, fought largely in the verbal realm, the Match of Wills, and the physical battle, in which cruel and sadistic tortures are employed to break down the virgin's resistance.[30] To be sure, the virgin's will is tried throughout the physical contest right up to the point of her death and is graphically embodied in the tortures. In this sense the Match of Wills is subsumed into and continued in the physical contest. Yet the virgin's tortures begin only after the authorities roundly lose the Match of Wills. The contest is fought against incrementally higher representatives of society, often beginning with her father acting as a proto-representative of patriarchal power, followed by a suitor and finally the legal authorities.

After trying everything to force Lucy's submission, Paschasius the consul became tormented with bitter anguish because 'he was in no way able to deflect Christ's recruit from her firm resolution of virginity, neither by castigating her with the harsh reprimands nor by giving her over to the deceptive seduction of panders'.[31] Christina's hagiographer is highly conscious of the significance of framing the contest between her and her parents in the context of the Match of Wills: 'The more her parents became aware of her persistence in this frame of mind, the more they tried to break down her resistance' (*Life*, p. 47). Initially, Autti and Beatrix try to break down her resolve (*constantia*) through various benign means, including flattery, gifts and great promises (*Life*, p. 45). When these fail, they resort to reproaches, cajoling, threats, and afterwards to alcohol (*Life*, p. 47). In forcing her to act as cupbearer at the Gild Merchant, where, bare-limbed, she offers drinks to the nobility, her parents hoped that 'the compliments of the onlookers and the accumulation of little sips of wine would break her resolution' (*Life*, p. 49). Like the aptly named Aphrodisia, employed to effect Agatha's corruption, Christina's friend Melisen attempts to break down Christina's resolve over the course of an entire year 'by a continuous stream of flattery', but fails to extract a single word by way of consent (*Life*, pp. 45–7). Christina is brought before Fredebertus, ostensibly to hear his adjudication in the matter of her marriage to Burthred, though as Fredebertus openly admits in his admission of failure to Autti, he had tried unsuccessfully to break her will: 'We have tried our best to bend your daughter to your will [*ad voluntatem tuam*], but we have made no headway' (*Life*, p. 65). Having failed in every way to force her submission, Beatrix becomes obsessed with destroying Christina's will: *Et que non potuit filie victrix fieri* (*Life*, p. 74).[32]

Magic

In some cases, the virgin martyr's persecutors resort to magic and sorcery in the attempt to break down her will. St Christina's torturers recruit sorcerers to rouse asps in the attempt to force her to give up her virginity.[33] In a telling parallel, Christina's mother spends vast sums on old crones who use love potions and charms to drive her insane with impure desires. She also hires a Jewess to deploy strong tricks to harm Christina (*Life*, p. 75).

The stripping of the virgin

Before the Physical Match begins in earnest, the virgin is often stripped as the prelude to her ordeal. Juliana's father orders her to be stripped *sterotnaket* and beaten so cruelly that her flesh foams with blood.[34] In a direct hagiographic borrowing, Autti, *ira turbatus*, denudes Christina to send her out from his house into the night stripped naked (*Life*, p. 72). Autti's behaviour in stripping Christina is presented as a spontaneous action overflowing from his burning anger (*vehementer iratus*) and accords perfectly with Juliana's father's fury and the wrath of the authorities from virgin-martyr lives who angrily strip their prisoner as an expression of their failure to influence her will.

Detailed accounts of the stripping of the virgin martyr, with frequent focus on the whiteness or the delicateness of her limbs, have attracted much comment from the critics.[35] The stripped virgin is a highly complex image representing the profound contradiction of her innocence and beauty. Since her vocation is predicated on her virginal state, her enforced public nudity tests her resolve by placing her virginity in jeopardy. Ostensibly the stripped virgin is passive. Yet she is denuded precisely because she refuses to submit to the social ideal of marriage. In her nakedness, she becomes a figure of defiant resistance to male hegemony. The stripping is therefore a powerful statement of volition and resistance, culminating in the virgin's empowerment. In avoiding the snare of sexuality in this extremely vulnerable condition, the virgin has effectively won the battle for her sexual independence.[36] The stripped virgin martyr therefore symbolizes the failure of the authorities to enforce their will over her. They unwittingly humiliate themselves by conceding the paradox of their overwhelming powerlessness, despite marshalling all the resources of the state against the solitary virgin, literally stripped of every earthly protection, whose transcendent power frustrates worldly might.[37] The naked Christina about to be sent out into the night may seem an image of vulnerability, yet, as the hagiographer remarks, she preferred to be sent out, both naked and at night, for the sake of pursuing her religious vocation. Though through the intervention of a house guest she was not actually sent out of the house, Christina effectively defeats her father through her defiant readiness to go out into the night naked. When she attempts to leave the house the following morning her father retrieves her in a gesture which admits his failure and powerlessness over her in the Match of Wills.

Virgin martyr prepared to suffer

The virgin's refusal to relinquish her faith and virginity is met with threats of physical violence, which she declares herself ready to suffer.[38] When Fredebertus, the prior of St Mary's, Huntingdon, tests Christina's will, she offers to carry red-hot iron in her bare hands to prove the measure of her resolve (*Life*, p. 63). No one ever threatens to strike Christina with a sword, though in highly self-conscious language the hagiographer announces her willingness to be cut to pieces rather than relinquishing her virginity (*Life*, p. 71).[39]

The Physical Match

The authorities' failure to influence the virgin martyr's will, with all the immense power of the state at their disposal, represents a distortion of relationship between power and will.[40] When the bishop of Lincoln rules against Autti in the matter of his attempt to force Christina's marriage, Autti declares to her: ' … you are even made mistress over me' (*Life*, p. 65). This admission signals a modulation of the contest into the physical sphere where, incapable of impressing their will upon her volition, the authorities inscribe their anger on the virgin martyr's body. Far from stretching the bounds of credibility, the seemingly interminable tortures graphically demonstrate the authorities' impotence in the face of the virgin martyr's resolve. When Christina's parents realize they have failed to force their desires upon her will, they begin a short but intense campaign of torture against Christina. Immediately after Autti strips Christina, Beatrix commences on her tortures:

> From that day forward her mother, Beatrix, with God's permission but at the instigation of the devil, loosed all her fury on her own daughter, neglecting no sort of wicked artifice which might, in her opinion, destroy her integrity.
>
> (*Life*, p. 73)

Rather than describing these in detail, the hagiographer comments on the motivation for Christina's sufferings: 'But Beatrix, in her obstinacy, would put no term to her malice and as she could not break her daughter's will, tried to gain satisfaction from the shameful sufferings she inflicted on her' (*Life*, p. 75).[41] Forcibly ejecting Christina from a banquet, she pulls out her hair, beats her, and returns her to the banquet badly lacerated, an object of derision (*Life*, p. 75). Echoing the tortures of the virgin martyrs who were immersed in liquids of extreme temperature, Christina is plunged into cold water which blisters her excessively (*Life*, p. 55).[42] The effect of these tortures, particularly the enormous bruises and welts which were so severe as to leave behind permanent scars, could hardly commend Christina to a prospective suitor.

Characterization

In place of the *passiones*-persecuting judges and princes, the *Life* substitutes an ecclesiastical triumvirate, consisting of Flambard, cast as suitor-cum-persecutor, Robert Bloet, bishop of Lincoln, and Fredebertus, prior of St Mary's. When asked to dispute in the matter of Christina's betrothal to Burthred, Fredebertus initially rules in favour of Christina. On seeing Autti's anguish, he suggests that

Autti bribe Bloet: 'Are you not aware of his greed and vicious nature? Either of these would be sufficient; how much more when both are together!' (*Life*, p. 67).[43]

Sharing the pagan tyrant role, Autti is driven by an angry obsession to subjugate his daughter to his will, once he realizes that Christina will never freely consent to his plan (*Life*, p. 79). After stripping his daughter, he colludes with family and friends against Christina and, with his wife, abuses her. Beatrix, too, is shown venting her violent anger on Christina's body, drawing blood and hair, and leaving behind the permanent scars of her terrible wrath. Like Autti, she acts initially to deflower Christina, though when this fails, violence is motivated solely by obstinacy and malice (*Life*, p. 75).

The transformation noted earlier of Flambard to a persecuting prince-turned-suitor is particularly suitable, since it is the virgin martyr's suitor for whom the highest degree of diabolical motivation is usually reserved.[44] In a parallel characterization, Burthred is not simply motivated by the devil but takes on a diabolical appearance, appearing in her dream dressed in a black cape and lying face down in her path, ready to seize her as she passes in her white garments. Elsewhere, he *is* the devil. In a scene modelled directly on the dream of Perpetua on the night before her contest in the arena, in which she dreams that she fights the devil dressed as an Egyptian, Christina dreams the night before her contest with Burthred (in the bedroom scene where he attempted to take her by force and which ended in chase) of a devil with horrible appearance (*horribilem aspectu*) and blackened teeth running after her. On waking, she recognized the parallel: 'Truly in escaping him, I have escaped from the devil I saw last night' (*Life*, p. 53).[45]

The obvious conclusion of the genre's relentless duality leaves the virgin martyr ultimately in a solitary category, as family and friends turn against her.[46] In the same way, Christina's supporters turn against her, including Melisen, her closest friend (*Life*, pp. 45–7), and Sueno, her closest adviser (*Life*, p. 55). The virgin martyr's passion owes its ultimate rationale to the death of Christ, and in her complete rejection by her family, friends and society, she further enacts the *imitatio Christi*, a parallel Christina's hagiographer happily draws:

> Indeed, just as Christ was rejected by the Jews, afterwards denied by the prince of the apostles, Peter, who loved Him more than the rest, and was made obedient to His father even unto death, so this maiden was afflicted first by her parents, then abandoned by her only friend, Sueno.
>
> (*Life*, p. 57)

Alone and deserted, the virgin martyr pleads to her heavenly bridegroom for help, who answers with consolation and the promise of divine protection.[47] In the midst of her persecutions, Christina twice appeals to Christ for help and is twice comforted (*Life*, pp. 57, 75–9).

Divine protection

In a *topos* which draws its inspiration from the earliest *passiones*, where the martyrs were divinely shielded from pain in the moment of death,[48] the virgin martyr is safeguarded from pain and from the assaults on her virginity, by an angel or sometimes directly by Christ. A Jewess employed to harm Christina sees two persons dressed in white ceaselessly protecting her (*Life*, p. 75). In the Cecilia legend, the saint informed Valerian that her angel guarded her virginity and would slay anyone who attempted to deflower her.[49] When Burthred expresses his willingness to kill any other suitor should they attempt to take Christina, she replies, echoing Cecilia: 'Beware then of taking to yourself the spouse of Christ, lest in His anger He will slay you' (*Life*, p. 73). Christina's parents' attempt to marry her are thwarted by a fire which destroys all the preparations. Next, a raging fever prevents her from participating in the wedding. 'And yet with Christ guarding the vow which his spouse had made, the celebration of the wedding could no how be brought out' (*Life*, p. 55).

Of course, after all the parallels between Christina and the virgin martyrs have been drawn, one crucial difference remains. Whereas a martyr's death is the apparent *sine qua non* of every *passio*, Christina's battle with her parents ends not in death but in flight. And yet this difference is not as significant as it may seem. The protracted focus on the virgin martyr's suffering, by contrast to the summary treatment of her death, highlights her suffering as an essential ingredient in her story.[50] In any case, beheading is merely a convention of closure, as most virgin martyrs have a powerful afterlife.

Christina, too, is given a form of hagiographic closure. When confronted with the reported horrors of her torture, Ralph d'Escures, the archbishop of Canterbury, avers that if he heard Christina's mother's confession, he would impose on her the sentence of *homicidium* (*Life*, p. 85). Talbot's translation of *homicidium* as *manslaughter* is inadequate, not least since manslaughter is normally unpremeditated. In the context, *murder* better suits the meaning. Thus the hagiographer places in the mouth of the archbishop of Canterbury Christina's satisfaction of the criteria for martyrdom through her superhuman suffering, adding his own approval:

> And it should be borne in mind that as our blessed patron St Alban had her from the Lord as co-operator in building up and furthering his community on earth, so he had her afterwards as sharer of his eternal bliss in heaven.
>
> (*Life*, p. 127)

The saints' vocation was vital to their intercessory work. This is particularly true of martyrs and especially virgin martyrs, whose invocation was closely bound up with their passion. St Alban's *opera* was the intercession of a martyr, and his bliss can be understood as the martyr's palm and all the rewards, privileges and joys pertaining thereto. In confirming Christina as St Alban's *cooperatricem*, the hagiographer ascribes to her the vocation of a martyr, fulfilling an ambition first articulated in her invocation of St Cecilia.

The crowning of the virgin martyr

The coronation of the virgin martyr, though always implicit, is infrequently depicted. Moreover, the actual form of the crowning differs from life to life, as does the type and number of crowns.[51] In Ælfric's *Life of St Katherine*, Queen Augusta dreams she sees Katherine seated, surrounded by honourable men dressed in white and by holy virgins, one of whom places a heaven-sent golden crown on her head.[52] Christina, too, had a vision in which Christ approached her, wearing a crown of extraordinary beauty and divine workmanship, with two fillets hanging from either side of the crown (*Life*, p. 187). Earlier, Christina had found herself surrounded by three beautiful angels who placed on her head a crown of exceptional beauty and workmanship, *whiter than snow and brighter than the sun*. From either side of the crown reaching down hung two white fillets.[53] That Christina's crown is the virgin's crown is made obvious by its grant in answer to her doubts about her own virginity prior to her consecration. That it is also the martyr's crown can be deduced, not least, since usually the virgin martyrs (such as Ælfric's Katherine) receive a single crown for virginity and martyrdom, and since Christina's crowning is preceded by the grant of a cross by Christ in token of her afflictions, temptations and privations in her cell (*Life*, p. 107) and followed by a renewed round of diabolical warfare. The crowning episode frames Christina's experience around the achievement of the prize first articulated to Burthred in the bedroom scene, where she announced her desire to follow Cecilia, Valerian and all the virgin martyrs so that, like them, she might be *duplicter coronati*.

II. Christina as ascetic martyr[54]

Christina's hasty flight from her parents' house into the wilderness frames her eremitic experience with a spontaneity which argues against the idea of construction or appropriation. Yet her eremitic career is carefully constructed, beginning with the portrait of her mentor Roger the hermit, described as an old man, mature in wisdom. By virtue of his holy life he is considered as equal to the fathers of old. He is led to his cell by three angels, who meet him at Windsor on his return from Jerusalem. There he endures many sufferings. No one suffers more violent diabolical temptations or has more snares laid for them. 'Who could have been more cruel to his own flesh?', the hagiographer asks:

> He allowed himself no pleasure. His whole endeavour was to progress more and more in the service of God ... We have written these few words about our old man by way of preface, because we think that they

are pertinent to our story. The rest we pass over in silence, both because it is difficult to describe and because it is not necessary to tell here.

(*Life*, pp. 81–3)

Collectively, Roger's qualities form a summary of the ascetic virtues found in the constituent texts of the *Vitae Patrum*: the *Verba Seniorum*, Rufinus' *Historia mona-chorum*, Palladius' *Historia Lausiaca* and the *Lives* of SS Antony, Paul the Hermit and Hilarion,[55] an authoritative collection of lives and sayings of the early ascetic widely circulated in its own right and incorporated by Cassian in his *Conferences* and *Institutes*. In describing Roger as having equalled the fathers of old in *ascesis* and virtue, the hagiographer is invoking a celebrated tradition and locating Roger within it, presenting him as the embodiment – indeed the recon-stitution – of the tradition of ascetic martyrdom handed down from the great desert ascetics.[56] Into this ancient tradition of asceticism Christina is received and tutored in Roger's cell and it is in this tradition that she herself excels.

Voluptas

For all its apparent spontaneity, Christina's flight to Roger's cell in the wilderness draws on a tradition of secret flight to the desert in avoidance of arranged marriages, one of the most frequently recurring themes in desert literature.[57] Moreover, disguise is particularly common in the lives of women saints of this era, especially among those who flee from their homes dressed as men.[58] The saint flees not only marriage but also family, friends, neighbours, home, former life and even the world itself, often represented by public amusements and enter-tainments.[59] Symbolically, banquets signify the culmination of social ideals: the pleasures of meeting individuals, families, friends and neighbours; the celebra-tion of the fruitfulness of the earth through food and drink; the reaffirmation of social bonds and the maintenance of the social order, at the heart of which is fecundity exemplified by the ideal of marriage and the nuclear family.[60] This equation is forcefully illustrated in the *Life*, where, prior to her flight, Christina was taken by her parents and against her will …

> … to public banquets, where divers choice meats were followed by drinks of different kinds, where the alluring melodies of the singers were accompanied by the sounds of the zither and the harp, so that by listening to them her strength of mind might be sapped away and in this way she might finally be brought to take pleasure in the world.
>
> (*Life*, p. 49)

In Autti and Beatrix's world, partaking of the pleasures of the banquet are a discharge of social duty. In the lives of the desert fathers, the pleasures of the banquet represent *voluptas*: elaborately prepared food, wine and entertainment, such as singers and dancers. The saint's activities represent the antithesis of these frivolities: prayer, fasting weeping, chastity, solitude and self-denial. Christina's enforced participation in banquets therefore anticipates her flight.

The flesh and the devil

Having fought off the external enemy, represented by society, the desert fathers fled to the wilderness to do battle with the enemy within.[61] This was no metaphorical battle, waged in the stillness of quiet meditation, but a real, physical war fought in the arena of the monk's cell: first and foremost with the devil himself; second with one's flesh to overcome sexual temptation; and third with other natural desires. These causes of bodily temptation are each resisted in kind.[62]

The wars against Satan and the flesh are interconnected in that it is the devil who stirs up the saint's lust. This is illustrated in one of the set pieces of Western hagiography, where the devil assumes the shape of a voluptuous woman and enters St Antony's cell.[63] Such temptations are regarded as necessary and useful, and are even perceived as the natural state of the monk.[64] Thus, temptation simultaneously provides an opportunity for monks to practise *ascesis* and functions as a sign of sanctity. Paradoxically, the absence of temptation is perceived as evidence of sin.[65]

After the monk himself, the devil is often the most important character in the desert *vitae*. St Antony tells a novice in his charge: 'Behold you have become a monk. Stay here alone in order that you may be tempted by demons.'[66] Only the saints worthy in holiness do battle with the devil.[67] Conversely, lack of demonic intervention is evidence of spiritual immaturity, a point illustrated in *The Life of St Antony*, effectively the *vita prima* of desert spirituality, in which Antony's wars against Satan occupy a third of the *Life*.[68] Here, as in the corpus of desert literature, the devil is a physical character, wounding Antony and leaving him badly bruised and lacerated.[69] In the *Vitae Patrum* the devil is portrayed in very human terms, conversing with the saints and capable of anger, impatience, jealousy and other emotions.[70] He invades the fathers' cells with hoards of his demons. As the master of disguises, the devil assumes various shapes, sometimes appearing in the guise of man or boy, at other times inhabiting the body of a beast, frightening and assaulting the desert saints or chasing them as they emerge from their cells.[71] The devil uses every means possible to attack the desert monks: poverty, wealth, scorn, mockery, praise, flattery, health, illness, comfort and vexation.[72]

The devil plays a leading role in Christina's eremitic experience. No sooner does she enter her first cell than she attracts the attention of the devil. ' ... her reading and singing of the psalms by day and night were a torment to him. For although in her hiding-place she was hidden from men, she could never escape the notice of the demons' (*Life*, p. 99).[73] In a *topos* borrowed directly from the *Vitae Patrum*, they assume the shape of animals, appearing in her dreams as bulls with threatening horns and glaring eyes (*Life*, p. 99), and like the devils who suddenly penetrate Antony's cave in the form of lions, bears, asps and scorpions, they invade her cell assuming the shape of toads with big terrible eyes.[74] After Christina's coronation, the devil, enraged, embarked on a new campaign to terrorize her with horrible apparitions and 'unclean shapes' that haunted her for many years. Twice he attacks her by spreading slanderous rumours (*Life*, p. 173). When this fails, he employs 'every stratagem in bold and ruthless warfare' and assaults her with the spirit of blasphemy (*Life*, p. 131).

> But she would not listen. He attacked her, but was put to flight. He pressed her assaults, but was routed. Even so he would not be silenced; when put to flight, he would not disappear; when routed, he would not retreat. Taking new and more elaborate weapons of temptation, he assaulted the virgin all the more intensely, as his resentment grew to find a tender virgin more than a match for him.
>
> (*Life*, p. 131)

The devil waits till Christina is alone in the chapel to terrorize her with 'sordid apparitions' and 'harsh threats'. In his extreme anger, he attempts to frighten her by appearing as a headless body, because, the hagiographer adds, 'the devil had lost his head' (*Life*, p. 179).

Ascesis

The desert saints' battles are fought spiritually, in prayer, and physically, through various forms of ascesis, such as fasting, sleep deprivation and endurance of extreme heat or cold. By weakening their bodies, monks and nuns strengthen their spirits, a formula frequently repeated in the *Vitae Patrum*.[75] A life of ascesis also endows the monk with charisms, such as authority over animals, clairvoyance, exorcism and healing.[76] Monks very seldom cure illness among their ranks, believing it to be useful in taming the appetites, much as fasting and austerities. Its presence is frequently seen as a sign of divine favour.[77] Sometimes the greatest act of self-mortification in the desert is simply to stay in one's own cell. The desert cells were small, dark, often airless space. Athanasius described Antony's first cell as a tomb.[78] Hilarion could not stand upright in his cell, which was also described as a tomb.[79] Extreme ascesis of this kind fortifies the saint with power over the devil. After three years in prayer in a tomb, where he neither sat nor lay down nor even went outside, Sisinnius is deemed worthy of the 'gift against demons'.[80]

Christina's desert

For two years Christina endures Alfwen's cell in Flamstead, a room hardly large enough to house her body. Her second abode in Roger's hermitage is described in some detail. 'The space would not allow her to wear even the necessary clothing when she was cold' (*Life*, p. 103). The entrance is blocked by a log, too heavy for her to move. She sits on a hard stone, suffering terrible privations including cold, heat, hunger and thirst. She fasts daily and prays into the night. The airless enclosure becomes stifling hot. She hardly dares breathe for fear of being discovered (*Life*, p. 105). Her bowels contract and dry up through long fasts. Her burning thirst produces blood clots in her nostrils. She suffers a kind of paralysis, accompanied by inflammation of her cheeks, which nearly kills her. Here and elsewhere Christina's illnesses are described not as maladies (*infirmitas*) but as passions (*passiones*) (*Life*, p. 122), clearly invoking a tradition in which the sufferings of the hermits were equated with the passions of martyrs, earning them the martyr's crown.

'In this prison [*carcere*] therefore, Roger placed his happy companion,' says the hagiographer (*Life*, p. 103), a phrase evoking parallels between the cells of the hermits and the martyrs' prisons.[81] Entombed in their cells, the desert hermits acted out a kind of *imitatio Christi*. Christina's willingness to die in her cell (*Life*, p. 105) is mirrored in her inability to move and even breathe, a kind of death echoing the enclosure of the fathers in their desert tombs.

After Roger dies, Christina is forced to share a cell with another cleric, her 'evil genius', whom the devil uses to attack Christina. Overcome with concupiscence the cleric removes his clothes before Christina, and in an echo of the devil of fornication who fell at St Antony's feet declaring his intention, the cleric falls at Christina's feet and begs her to release him from his sexual torment.[82] Burning with lust, Christina fears her clothes will combust spontaneously. She overcomes sexual desire by 'long fastings, little food, and that only of raw herbs, a measure of water to drink, nights spent without sleep [and] harsh scourgings'.[83] She resists temptations violently, practising a severe form of ascesis which tears her flesh (*Life*, p. 115). The evil cleric reveals he is nothing more than an embodied devil, transforming himself into a wild, ugly, furry bear who blocks Christina's way into the monastery. Nothing can cool Christina's lust in his absence. She responds by kneeling in prayer, day and night, 'weeping, lamenting, begging to be free from temptation' (*Life*, p. 117). In all her temptations, Christina resists manfully (*viriliter*), displaying manly qualities (*virtute virili*) more frequently encountered among the monks of the Egyptian desert than Anglo-Norman nuns.

When Christina's temptations cease, she receives the spiritual gifts of healing, clairvoyance and the ability 'to penetrate the hidden things' of divine wisdom (*Life*, p. 189). Like St Antony, she foretells various events, including the arrival of guests.[84] Like St Antony, she is initially reluctant to perform her first miracle of physical healing but eventually relents, provided it is attributed to the merits of others (*Life*, p. 121).[85] The spiritual *amicitia* she enjoys with Abbot Geoffrey echoes the spiritual friendship is mirrored, for example, in earlier lives such as those of SS Paul and Thecla in expanded form. In the *Vitae Patrum* such friendships are normally preceded by periods of protracted asceticism; Antony meets the hermit Paul only at the end of Paul's life. Likewise, Christina's friendship with Geoffrey is presented as a charism arising from her protracted battles with, and victory over, the devil and her own flesh. Spiritual *amicitia*, together with her subsequent gift of prophecy, are the main themes of the final section of the *Life* and become her defining traits.[86]

In her flight from the village banquets which represent *luxuria* and *voluptas*, in her training by Roger who had equalled the fathers of old in virtue and holiness, in the extremely graphic description of the suffering that she endures in her cell as a kind of entombment, through her protracted warfare with the devil and his demons, through her severe sexual temptations and her fierce asceticism, consisting of fasting, physical suffering, heat and cold, eating raw herbs and uncooked foods, and sleeplessness, and in her subsequent gifts of healing and clairvoyance, and spiritual *amicitia* with Roger and Geoffrey, Christina's anchoritic experience presents unambiguously a composite portrait of the desert saint, transplanted and updated to twelfth-century Huntingdonshire.

The literary construction of martyrdom

The twin traditions of virgin and ascetic martyrdom were closely related in the Late Antique and Middle Ages. Practising martyrdom by asceticism, the monks were the natural successors of the tradition of blood martyrdom.[87] By the third century, the church fathers speak of a martyrdom of virginity, a martyrdom of the will, a martyrdom of resisting the spirit of fornication, and the daily martyrdom of ascesis.[88] The literary forms of blood and ascetic martyrdom share common themes and narrative structures – such as the perception of the desert as an arena; its limited size, prohibiting the saint and the devil from occupying it simultaneously; and the ceaseless war between the saint and the enemy – as well as a common lexicon of symbols. However, they vary in one crucial aspect: the *passio* is governed by diametrical opposition and binary structure, while the *vita* of the desert saint is marked by gradational opposition where sanctity is expressed incrementally and the life of the saint unfolds in linear fashion.[89] Accordingly, hagiographers who wished to portray their saints as martyrs generally assimilated them either to a spiritualized, bloodless martyrdom, by depicting their asceticism as 'worthy' of martyrdom, or to blood martyrdom, by presenting the saints' conflicts with their enemies in terms designed to recall the trials and confrontations of the blood martyrs.[90] While hagiographers generally avoid mixing both types of martyrdom in a single *vita*, a composite or syncretic sanctity is more common in Merovingian hagiography.[91] In Venantius Fortunatus' *vitae*, the saints' experiences recall the sufferings of the blood martyrs: possessed of unshakable faith, they resolutely oppose heretics, unbelievers and obdurate and disloyal clerics who fail to uphold the doctrines of the church. While Fortunatus also describes his saints as bloodless, ascetic martyrs (who as bishops never experience anything like the fierce asceticism of the desert) fighting a battle to tame their bodily passions, this is primarily a rhetorical device or in any case always subordinate to the main theme of blood martyrdom.[92] *Topoi* from both traditions are woven together in Fortunatus' *Life of St Radegund* whose chilhood yearnings for martyrdom are echoed in adulthood by corporal mortifications. Twice fleeing her suitor-turned-husband, she underwent periodic enclosure, eventually founding a women's religious community.[93] In this regard, Christina's hagiographer is truly exceptional in deploying two fundamentally different forms of sanctity, giving each equal weight, and uniting these seamlessly in successive narrative sequences.

Kitchen characterises Fortunatus' lives styled on blood martyr literature as those which turn on a 'religious issue', where the hero faces the possibility of suffering, and where the conflict is highly polarized or irreconcilable.[94] Each of these qualities is present in the first part of the *Life*. By presenting Christina's parents, family and clergy as greedy, irreligious and worldly, the hagiographer transforms her virginity and vocation into an issue of purely religious dimensions. By placing in Christina's mouth the willingness to undergo ordeal by fire and death by the sword, and in graphically illustrating her punishments for refusing to marry Burthred, Christina's suffering is transmuted into the persecution of the martyrs and her vow of virginity into the martyrs' profession of faith. Finally, by creating a climate of exaggerated hostility between Christina and her parents, family, friends, priests, bishops (indeed almost the entire *dramatis personae*), the *Life* recreates the central defining characteristic of martyr literature in which saint and society are irreconcilably opposed and from which there can be no peaceable exit.

St Albans: monastic library and cult

Underpinning the construction of Christina's sanctity in the twin moulds of the virgin martyrs and ascetic martyrs are the very texts which preserved and passed on these traditions. The monastic library of St Albans was one of the finest in medieval England and a major centre of scholarship throughout the Middle Ages. The scale and range of its holdings are recoverable.[95] They include a number of saints' lives,[96] particularly of blood (St Alban, *The Martyrology*, etc.) and bloodless (SS. Martin, Cuthbert, etc.) martyrs, as well as Italo-Greek saints' lives,[97] including a copy of Cassian's *Collations*, incorporating material from the *Vitae Patrum*. Moreover, the Abbey possessed a commentary by Fortunatus, and it is possible that in common with other monastic libraries, such as Holme St Benets and Glastonbury, it owned copies of his hagiographies which circulated in Britain.[98] Given the abbey's Anglo-Norman connections in the eleventh and twelfth centuries, it is likely that Christina's hagiographer was at least familiar with the Merovingian tradition of syncretic sanctity.

To these literary influences must be added the culture of martyrdom which flourished at the Abbey of St Albans and which undoubtedly contributed to the invention of Christina's sanctity in terms of martyrdom. The abbey had been built on the very site of the martyrdom of St Alban, whose shrine was rebuilt by Christina's friend and patron, Geoffrey, in her lifetime. An altar dedicated to 'Ste Marie et Ignatii' provides further evidence of the cult of martyrdom at St Albans.[99] Geoffrey held a special devotion to the virgin martyr St Katherine, having written a *Ludus Sanctae Catherinae* while master of Dunstable school for the children to perform, and much later, a treatise of her miracles.[100] The large number of virgin martyrs commemorated in the calendar of the St Albans

Psalter, whose patron it appears Geoffrey was, provides further evidence of his devotion to St Katherine and her circle. It seems likely therefore that the martyr theme in the *Life* represents not only St Albans' flourishing martyrdom culture, but also Geoffrey's personal piety and influence over the circumstances of its composition.

A new St Albans' martyr would undoubtedly bring honour and prestige to the monastic house, assuming her new role without dislodging the established saints. This is nicely illustrated by Bishop Germanus, who, according to Bede, ordered the tomb of St Alban to be opened so that he might place in it relics from the apostles and the martyrs.[101] In parallel with this physical re-arrangement of saintly relics, the *Life* proposes the expansion of St Alban's intercessory vocation to accommodate his new helpmate, Christina, now sharing in Alban's joy (*Life*, p. 127). And though the abbey might claim Christina for its own, a recurring theme in the *Life*, the hagiographer's intention in promoting Christina's sanctity was at least as much by way of example as for direct gain to the abbey. At the end of *Hali Meðhead*, the author commends SS Katherine, Margaret, Agnes, Juliana, Lucy and Cecilia to his reader as exemplars to fortify virginity.[102] Might not the promotion of the virgin martyrs as examples to putative virgins lie behind the presentation of Christina as a virgin martyr to generations of Markyate nuns? In the *Life* of their founder they could read the story of a holy woman who, like the martyrs and desert ascetics, had endured terrible sufferings to maintain her virginity and faith, becoming a new Alban, a new Cecilia, a new Antony, granting thereby comfort and fortitude in the maintenance of their vows.

History or pious fiction?

The ability to deploy evenly and effectively a single form of sanctity throughout an entire *vita*, with 'a vigour and economy' that galvanizes readers' attention on the literal plane, is a feat achieved by few contemporary hagiographers. The author of Christina's *Life* went one further, integrating two forms of related sanctity equally, consistently and seamlessly, without taxing Talbot's ability or our own to apprehend the text almost literally.

Yet narrative skill is no index of biographical accuracy in any genre. That we have allowed this authorial quality to govern our reading of the *Life* is evidence both of literary conditioning and our historicizing priorities. It is ironic that the latter two of Christina's hagiographer's three aims – to teach, to delight and to praise his subject – have prevented modern readers from searching for patterns of meaning in the text. In substituting the catechetic imperative of saints' lives with a historic one, we have inverted a fundamental axiom of medieval hagiography: that historical data is in almost every case inferior to the virtues illustrated in the life of the saint. Thus we have assigned Christina to the canon of history on the basis of a text designed to project her into the canon of saints.

Perhaps a way out of the biographical dilemma is to regard the *Life* as a testament to what was possible within the convention of medieval biography, albeit at its outer reaches. Through sheer narrative skill, an accomplished author could exploit the catechetic and panegyric requirements of saints' lives, using these to construct a life so compelling that it could inspire imitation of its virtues among contemporaries and admiration for its 'realism' among successive generations of readers.

Notes

1   I am grateful to Henrietta Leyser and Jocelyn Wogan-Browne for their abiding encouragement, generous advice, and perceptive readings of earlier versions of this chapter.

2   For evidence of the hagiographer's close relationship with Christina, see *Life*, pp. 6–7. Jocelyn Wogan-Browne: 'The biographer is too close to Christina and her circle to restructure events in ways unacceptable to his audience' ('Saints' Lives and the Female Reader', *Forum for Modern Language Studies* 4 (1991), 314–32). For Thomas Head, the events in the *Life* are 'an accurate reflection of Christina's lived experience' ('The Marriages of Christina of Markyate', Chapter 7, this volume). C. R. Dodwell was convinced that the *Life* 'unquestionably contains a substantial core of historical truth' (Pächt, pp. 136–7).

3   Talbot writes: 'The desire to show the reader that Christina possessed all the marks of sanctity is no doubt present, but this purpose is not flagrant, and as a result one is not plagued with a series of incredible occurrences calculated to tax the imagination ... the story soon comes down to earth and proceeds to narrate, with admirable conciseness and detail, the events, far from miraculous, which led Christina to embark on the religious life ... Indeed, the narrative is refreshingly unconventional, and it is only towards the end that any emphasis is laid on the unusual events in Christina's life' (pp. 30–1). While acknowledging Christina's 'marks of sanctity', Talbot purposefully ignores them, together with the miraculous aspects of her story. Only Ruth Morse (*Truth and Convention: Rhetoric, Representation, and Reality* (Cambridge, 1991), pp. 149–51) and Neil Cartlidge (Chapter 5, this volume) have drawn attention to the problem of truth vs. convention in the *Life*.

4   All translations, except from the *Life*, are my own.

5   For the argument that the virgin martyrs' lives served as inspiration and literal examples for rebellious women, see Wogan-Browne, 'Saints' Lives'. For the Cecilia legend, see *Passio Sanctae Caeciliae*, in Hippolyte Delehaye, '*Etude sur le légendier romain: les saints de novembre et de décembre*', *Subsidia Hagiographica* 23 (Brussels, 1936), pp. 77–96; on the development of the legend, see Sherry Reames, 'The Cecilia Legend as Chaucer Inherited it and Retold it: The Disappearance of an Augustinian Ideal', *Speculum* 55 (1980), 38–57.

6   Cf. the early Middle English *Seinte Marherete þe Meiden ant Martyr*, ed. Frances M. Mack, EETS OS 193 (1934), p. 2 (hereafter *Marherete*), where the martyrs are described as *icudde kempen* ('seasoned fighters').

7   Charles Altman, 'Two Types of Opposition and the Structure of Latin Saints' Lives,' *Medievalia et Humanistica* 6, ed. Paul Clogan (Cambridge, 1975), 1–11; Alison Goddard Elliott, *Roads to Paradise: Reading the Lives of the Early Saints* (Hanover, NH, 1987), p. 13; Rosemary Woolf, 'Saints' Lives', in *Art and Doctrine: Essays on Medieval English Literature*, ed. Heather O'Donoghue (London, 1986), pp. 219–44 (p. 225), first published in *Continuations and Beginnings. Studies in Old English Literature*, ed. E. G. Stanley (Edinburgh, 1966), 37–65; Jocelyn Wogan-Browne, *Virgin Lives and Holy Deaths: Two Exemplary Biographies for Anglo-Norman Women*, trans. Jocelyn Wogan-Browne and Glyn S. Burgess (London, 1996), p. xxix.

8 For various classifications of the themes in virgin-martyr narrative see, for example, Thomas J. Heffernan, *Sacred Biography: Saints and their Biographers in the Middle Ages* (Oxford, 1988), pp. 185–230; Wogan-Browne, *Saints' Lives*, pp. 92–106, 314–22; Karen Winstead, *Virgin Martyrs: Legends of Sainthood in Late Medieval England* (Ithaca, 1997), pp. 5–10; Eamon Duffy, *Stripping of the Altars: Traditional Religion in England 1400–1580* (New Haven, 1992), pp. 172–3, Dyan Elliott, *Spiritual Marriage: Sexual Abstinence in Medieval Wedlock* (Princeton, 1993), pp. 173–4. More generally, see Hippolyte Delehaye, '*Les Passions des martyrs et les genres littéraires*', Subsidia hagiographica 20 (Brussels, 1921; rpt. 1996).

9 Where hagiographers generally had few precise facts to work from, they ennobled their subjects through constructed pedigrees, frequently inventing a direct royal lineage (André Vauchez, *La sainteté en occident aux derniers siècles du moyen âge, d'après les procès de canonisation et les documents hagiographiques*, Bibliothèque des Études françaises d'Athèns et de Rome 241 (Rome, 1981), pp. 209–15). In Ælfric's *Saints' Lives* and in the Katherine Group lives, all the virgin martyrs are described as either noble or royal (*Ælfric's Saints*, i. 82, ii.356, i. 170, 24, 26, 186; *Marherete*, p. 4; *Þe Lifade ant Passiun of Seinte Iuliene*, ed. S. R. T. O. d'Ardenne, EETS OS 248 (1961), p. 7 (hereafter *Iuliene*); *Seinte Katerine*, ed. S. R. T. O. d'Ardenne and E. J. Dobson, EETS SS 7 (1981), p. 6 (hereafter *Katerine*)). References to the virgin martyrs in this chapter are from Anglo-Saxon, Anglo-Norman and the closely related thirteenth-century Katherine Group. While Christina's household and network of contacts were largely Anglo-Saxon (even the hermit Roger, whose name suggests Norman provenance, called Christina *myn sunendaege dohter* (*Life*, p. 106)), she was clearly at home in Anglo-Norman circles, witness her friendship with Abbot Geoffrey, the existence of the Anglo-Norman Alexis legend in the St Albans Psalter which is closely associated with Christina, and the possibility of her joining the monasteries of Fontevrault and Marcigny. On the circulation of Anglo-Saxon saints' lives well after the Conquest, see Joyce Hill, 'The Dissemination of *Ælfric's Lives of Saints*: A Preliminary Survey', in *Holy Men and Holy Women: Old English Prose Saints Lives and their Contexts*, ed. Paul E. Szarmach (Albany, NY, 1996), pp. 235–60. For the texts of the Latin lives, see Agape, Irene and Chione (*AA.SS* April I, 245–50); Agatha (*AA.SS*, February I, 596–656); Agnes (*AA.SS*, January II, 530–63); Katherine (*Katerine*); Lucy (Augustin Beaugrande, *Sainte Lucie Vierge et martyre de Syracuse (Paris, 1882)*), Margaret (*AA.SS*, July V, 30–1).

10 E.g., see *Ælfric's Lives*, i.32, 170; *Das altenglische Martyrologium*, ed. Günter Kotzor, 2 vols. (Munich, 1981), 25 June, ii. 132–3; *Iuliene*, p. 5. See *Marherete*, p. 6; *Katerine*, pp. 4, 18; *Virgin Lives*, vv. 595–626.

11 For graphic representations of this axiom, see the story of Margaret (*Marherete*, p. 6).

12 *Iuliene*, p. 5. Cf. *Das altenglische Martyrologium*, ed. Kotzor, 3 April, ii. 49–50.

13 The moral is further enhanced by the framing of this incident immediately after the account of Christina's vow of virginity at St Albans where that night, as the others in her company gave themselves up to revelry and amusements, she prayed: 'Lord ... Thou hast destroyed them that go a-whoring from Thee'. On the very following morning, the day of Flambard's attempted seduction, Christina confirmed her vow at the church in Shillington, praying for 'purity and inviolable virginity' (*Life*, p. 41).

14 On Flambard's alleged licentiousness, see R. W. Southern, 'Ranulf Flambard', in his *Medieval Humanism and Other Studies* (Oxford, 1970), 183–205; J. O. Prestwich, 'The Career of Ranulf Flambard', in *Anglo-Norman Durham, 1093–1193*, ed. David Rollason, Margaret Harvey and Michael Prestwich (Woodbridge, 1994), pp. 299–310.

15 For example, Eugenia is educated in *woruld-wysdome*: Greek philosophy and Latin, turning later to the study of St Paul (*Ælfric's Lives*, i. 26, 194. cf. Agatha, i. 26, 194, and Eufrasia, ii. 236). On the Katherine tradition, see Katherine J. Lewis, *The Cult of St Katherine of Alexandria in Late Medieval England* (Woodbridge, 2000).

16 On the education of well-born women, see Bella Millett, 'Women in No Man's Land: English Recluses and the Development of Vernacular Literature in the Twelfth and Thirteenth Centuries', *Women and Literature in Britain, 1150–1500*, ed. Carol M. Meale (Cambridge, 1993), pp. 86–103.

17 When Quintianus asks Agatha why she, a noblewoman, behaves like a servant, she replies that servitude to Christ is nobility. To his rhetorical question – has she no nobility since she does not despise Christ's servitude? – she points out that his nobility turns to shameful bondage, making him the servant of sin and idols (*Ælfric's Lives*, i. 98).

18 *Katerine*, p. 66.

19 *Ælfric's Lives*, ii. 336.

20 See, for example, the responses of Katherine, Eugenia and Lucy (*Katerine*, p. 6; *Ælfric's Lives*, i. 26–7, 212).

21 If Juliana marries Eleusius, she will be the wife of the Reeve of Rome and the lady of the city, *ant of alle þe londes þe þer-to liggeð*, no mean advantage as her father reminds her. Her suitor is called Eleusium *þe riche* (*Iuliene*, p. 15). Margaret's suitor, Olibrius, offers her all *al þet ich i world hah ant I wald habbe* (*Marherete*, p. 10).

22 *Ælfric's Lives*, i. 170. Cf Agatha, i. 196–8.

23 On the significance of this gift, see R. I. Moore, Chapter 8 this volume.

24 Rejection of one's family for the sake of the Kingdom is a recurring theme in the gospels (Matt. 10:34–8, 19:29 Mark 3:33–5; Luke 14:26) as well as early martyr literature (*Passio sanctarum Perpetuae et Felicitatis, Acts of the Christian Martyrs*, ed. and trans. Herbert Musurillo (Oxford, 1972), p. 108). As we shall see, this theme is particularly germane to the desert saints who often struggle to escape by flight, not only their nuclear families but also the social idea of *familia*.

25 Matt. 12:48–50, Mark 10:29–30, Luke 18:29–30. A monk who councils Eufrasia regarding her intention to flee her father's house for the cloister, after she had been promised in marriage without her consent, actually quotes very similar advice (*Ælfric's Lives*, ii. 242). cf. Luke 14:26.

26 These sentiments are perfectly summarized by the virgin Eugenia in a speech to her parents: 'And ic for cristes lufe forlæt eow ealle and middan-eardlice lustas swa swa meox forseah' (*Ælfric's Lives*, i. 38). ('And I for Christ's love, abandoned you all, and despised as dung the lusts of the world.')

27 Bede and Ælfric (*ic cristen eom*) incorporate this incident (*Historia Ecclesiastica*, ed. and trans. B. Colgrave and R. A. B. Mynors, OMT (Oxford, 1969), p. 30; *Ælfric's Lives*, i. 417). The *topos* is found in the *passiones* of Carpus ('My first and most distinctive name is Christian, but if you seek to know my name in the world, it is Carpus'), Sanctus (who responds to all questions with 'Christianus sum'), Pamphylia (who even claims a pedigree from Nazareth) and Dasius (*Acts of the Christian Martyrs*, ed. Musurillo, pp. 22, 276, 68–9, 188–9). Cf. Perpetua's reply to her father: 'ego aliud me uocari nisi quod sum, Christiana', p. 108) ('I cannot be called anything other that what I am, a Christian').

28 Elliott, *Roads to Paradise*, p. 21, n. 21.

29 In *Ælfric's Lives*, Eugenia and Basillia are martyred *for hyre mæðhade* (i.30, 46). In *de Virginitate*, Paschasius tortures Lucy to deflect her from her choice of virginity (pp. 427–8). The attempt to deflower Christina after Autti and Beatrix have lost the Match of Wills in order to consummate marriage and therefore prevent her from pursuing a religious vocation echoes the persecuting tyrants' attempts to deflower the virgin martyrs in the mistaken assumption that their power derives from virginity (see *Ælfric's Lives*, i. 30, 214).

30 The dialectic–physical phases of the contest have been noted by others (e.g. Altman, 'Two Types of Opposition', p. 2).

31 'Christi tiruncula nec sermonum severitate castigata nec lenonum fallaci lenocinio tradita a rigido virginitatis', Aldhelm, *De Virginitate*, 42, ed. Rudolph Ehwald, *Aldhelmi Opera Omnia, MGH AA* 15 (Berlin, 1919), p. 294. Cf. Aldhelm's Agatha, who becomes harder than iron in the face of the tortures (p. 293). When Aphrodosia attempts to corrupt Agatha with fair words into submitting to sexual pleasure, Agatha declares herself incorruptible on account of her *fæstræde geþanc* (steadfast will) grounded on immutability (*Ælfric's Lives*, i. 197).

32 While Jocelyn Wogan-Browne's assertion ('Saints' Lives', p. 321) that Christina's parents 'care less for her assent than for her technical violation' is ultimately true, it is important to observe that initially it is Christina's will which all parties attempt first to influence. Only when they fail in the Match of Wills do her parents resort to her attempted deflowering. On the other hand, the submission of the virgin martyr's will is only one stated goal of tortures in this genre. In numerous *passiones*, sexual subjugation is the concomitant corollary to recantation, as in the *Life*.

33 *De Virginitate*, ed. Ehwald, *Aldhelmi Opera Omnia*, p. 301. Eugenia's parents use witches and sorcerers to discover her whereabouts (*Ælfric's Lives*, i. 31). Cf. Justinia (*De Virginitate*, ed. Ehwald, *Aldhelmi Opera Omnia*, p. 295) and Agatha (*Ælfric's Lives*, i. 216).

34 *Iuliene*, pp. 14–15.

35 See, for example, Suzanne Kappeler, *The Pornography of Representation* (Cambridge, 1986); Kathryn Gravdal, *Ravishing Maidens: Writing Rape in Medieval French Literature and Law* (Philadelphia, 1991); Marina Warner, *Alone of All Her Sex: The Myth and Cult of the Virgin Mary* (London, 1990), p. 71.

36 Heffernan, *Sacred Biography*, pp. 278–81.

37 Sarah Salih reaches a similar conclusion independently ('Performing Virginity: Sex and Violence in the Katherine Group', in *Constructions of Widowhood and Virginity in the Middle Ages*, ed. Cindy L. Carlson and Angela Jane Weisl (New York, 1999), pp. 95–112).

38 Juliana speaks of her willingness to be burned alive; Agatha happily rolls naked on burning coals to prove her resolve (*Iuliene*, p. 11, *Ælfric's Lives*, i. 204).

39 Cf. Margery Kempe's application of this convention (*Book*, ed. Meech and Allen, ch. 14 and p. 131).

40 Maxentius becomes increasingly crazed and ferocious, and his later speeches show his world unravelling in the improper relations between his will and power: 'I am a serf and no emperor' (*Virgin Lives*, trans. Wogan-Browne and Burgess, v. 2390).

41 While the virgin martyr's mother is not usually the torturer, Beatrix acts in the name of the patriarchal family.

42 *Iuliene*, p. 61.

43 Fredebertus then joins Autti's coterie which secretly plots to bribe Bloet (*Life*, pp. 67–9).

44 Olibrius, Eleusius and Maxentius are all descended from the devil (*Marherete*, p. 6; *Iuliene*, p. 49; *Katerine*, p. 40). Katherine's torturers are the devil's slaves (*Katerine*, p. 110), as is Quintianus (*Ælfric's Lives*, i. 196), while Juliana's torturers become the devil's limbs (*Iuliene*, pp. 51, 23).

45 ' … et experrecta sum. Et intellexi me non ad bestias, sed contra diabolum esse pugnaturam' (*Acts of the Christian Martyrs*, ed. Musurillo, pp. 118–19). ('I awoke. I realized that it was not with wild animals that I would fight but with the Devil.')

46 In a passage which recalls Christina's ejection from her house by her father, Margaret, too, laments to Christ her solitude and her betrayal by her own family:

> Min ahne flesliche feader dude ant draf me awei, his anleþi dohter, ant mine freond aren me for þi luue, Lauerd, famen ant feondes. (My own natural father rejected me and drove me away, his only daughter, and my friends are my enemies and hostile towards me because of your love, Lord.)
>
> (*Marherete*, p. 28; cf. *Iuliene*, p. 27)

47 See, for example, Juliana's prayer (*Iuliene*, p. 28).

48 *Acts of the Christian Martyrs*, ed. Musurillo, pp. 122–4.

49 *Ælfric's Lives*, ii. 358.

50 Eugenia: 'Þa com se cwællere. on cristes akenned-nysse dæge/ asend fram þam casere. and he þæt mæden acwealde. heo wear gemartyrod' (*Ælfric's Lives*, i. 48.) ('Then came the executioner on the day of Christ's birth, sent from the emperor, and he killed the maiden; and so she was martyred'.) Cf. Agnes and Lucy (ibid., i. 185, 219) and Juliana (*Iuliene*, p. 69).

51 Relying on the traditional language of crowns and garlands, Aldhelm metaphorically represents the ideal, e.g. in Chionia, Irene and Agape; Eulalia; and Anatolia (*De Virginitate*, ed. Ehwald, *Aldhelmi Opera Omnia*, pp. 307, 300, 310). In *Marherete* (p. 26) the heroine describes Christ as the virgins' joy and martyrs' crown.

52 *Ælfric's Lives*, i. 82.

53 Though it might reasonably be assumed that the virgin is crowned in the afterlife, some virgin martyrs, such as Cecilia herself, were crowned on earth. Ælfric relates the story of the virgins Julian and Basilissa, who were forced into marriage but agreed to live chastely. Two saints appeared at their bedside, with a crown for each (*Ælfric's Lives*, i. 90–114).

54 I am grateful to Sister Benedicta Ward, who first suggested to me the existence of parallels between Christina and the desert fathers.

55 *Verba Seniorum*, *PL* 73, cols. 855–1022; Rufinus, *Historia monachorum sive de Vita Sanctorum Patrum*, ed. Eva Schulz-Flügel, Patristische Texte und Studien 34 (Berlin, 1990); *Die Lateneinische Übersetzung der Historia Lausiaca des Palladius*, ed. Adelheid Wellhausen, Patristische Texte und Studien 51 (Berlin, 2003); Athanasius, trans. Evagrius, *Vita Antonii*, *PL* 73, cols. 125–70; Jerome, *Vita Pauli*, *Vita Hilarionis*, *PL* 23, cols. 17–28, 29–54. I am grateful to Peter Jackson for this bibliography of the *Vitae Patrum*. Translations in: [*Verba Seniorum*] *Sayings of the Desert Fathers*, trans. Benedicta Ward (London, 2003); [*Vita Antonii*, *Vita Pauli* and *Vita Hilarionis*] *Early Christian Lives*, trans. Carolinne White (London, 1998). There is no translation of Rufinus' *Historia monachorum*, though the Greek text underlying it (and differing significantly) is translated in *The Lives of the Desert Fathers*, trans. Norman Russell (Kalamazoo, MI, 1980). Similarly the Greek *Historia Lausiaca* is translated in Palladius: *The Lausiac History*, trans. Robert T. Meyer, Ancient Christian Writers 34 (London, 1965). On the early ascetics generally, see Philip Rousseau, *Ascetics, Authority, and the Church in the Age of Jerome and Cassian* (Oxford, 1978).

56 Felix's *Life of St Guthlac*, ed. and trans. B. Colgrave (Cambridge, 1956), consciously draws on the *Vita Antonii*, comparing Guthlac with Antony, Arsenius and Macarius (p. 87). In his *Dialogues*, Gregory styles the lives of Italian ascetics after those of the desert monks and hermits, locating them within the Eastern tradition to demonstrate that the West was capable of producing saints every bit as venerable as the East. Jerome commends the Old Testament prophets to Paulinus: Epistula 58.5, *Epistulae*, ed. I. Hilberg, 3 vols., CSEL 54–56 (1910–18), i. 533–5.

57 See, for example, the story of Amoun, in *Historia Monachorum*, 23, ed. Schulz-Flügel, pp. 359–61. The *topos* applies equally to women: Eugenia, Euphraxia and Eufrasia.

58 Elliott, *Roads to Paradise*, p. 109.

59 Elliott, *Roads to Paradise*, pp. 85–102. Philemon, the flute player turned monk, had been famous on account of his debaucheries (*Historia Monachorum*, 19, ed. Schulz-Flügel, p. 351).

60 The banquets are often the saints' own wedding feasts which they flee, adding greater poignancy to the idea of banquet as *voluptas*, which in this case is the prelude to nuptial consummation and hence the creation of a new family.

61 As St Antony said: 'Qui sedet in solitudine, et quiescit, a tribus bellis eripitur; id est, auditus, locutionis, et visus; et contra unum tantummodo habebit, pugnam, id est, cordis' (*Verba Seniorum*, 2.2, *PL* 73, col. 858) ('Whoever sits in solitude and is quiet has escaped three wars: hearing, speaking, seeing: yet against one thing he continually battles: that is, his heart').

62 *Verba Seniorum*, 5.1, *PL* 73, col. 874.

63 *Vita Antonii*, 4, *PL* 73, col. 129. The *topos* recurs in the *Vitae Patrum*, eg. *Historia Monachorum*, 15, ed. Schulz-Flügel, p. 335; *Verba Seniorum* 5.36, *PL* 73, col. 883.

64 'Sic debet nudus esse monachus ab omnia materia saeculari, et crucifigere se adversus tentatinem atque certamina mundi' (*Verba Seniorum*, 6.16, *PL* 73, col. 891) ('The monk should be stripped naked of everything and crucified by temptation and combat with the world.') A monk who claimed to be at peace was told by his elder to pray that God would stir up a new war in him (7.8, *PL* 73, col. 894).

65 'Si cogitationes non habes, spem non habes; quoniam si cogitationes non habes, opera habes' (ibid., 5.5, col. 875) ('If you have lustful thoughts, you have no hope; if you do not have lustful thoughts, it is because you are sinning.'). For the extremes to which some monks went to avoid sexual temptation, see *Historia Lausiaca*, 11.5, ed. Wellhausen, p. 518. An abbot tells his young charge that even after a lifetime of ascesis, he is plagued by lust and that this is necessary to acquire perfection; *Verba Seniorum* 5.13, *PL* 73, col. 876.

66 'Ecce, quia iam monachus effectus es, solus mane, ut possis etiam daemons experiri', (*Historica Lausiaca*, 22.17, ed. Wellhausen, p. 570). cf. Jerome, *Life of Hilarion*, 5, *PL* 73, col. 51.

67 *Verba Seniorum*, *PL* 73, cols. 874–5.

68 On Antony's enormous importance to successive hagiographers, see B. P. Kurtz, 'From St Antony to St Guthlac: A Study in Biography', *University of California Publications in Modern Philology* 12 (1925–6), 103–46.

69 *Vita Antonii*, 7, *PL* 73, col. 151. The devils' blows nearly kill John of Lycopolis (*Historia Monachorum*, 1, ed. Schulz-Flügel, p. 266; cf. 11 (p. 330).

70 For example, *Historica Lausiaca*, 18.8, 23–4, ed. Wellhausen, pp. 542–5.

71 Ibid., 16.4, 19.9, pp. 526–7, 554–5.

72 *Verba Seniorum*, 7.16, *PL* 73, cols. 895–6.

73 Guthlac's severe temptations become the primary focus of the author of his story in *The Vercelli Homilies* ed. D. G. Scragg, EETS OS 300 (1992), pp. 383–92. See Rosemary Woolf, 'The Devil in Old English Poetry', in Art and Doctrine, ed. Heather O'Donoghue (London, 1986), 1–14; and Henry Mayr-Harting, *The Coming of Christianity to Anglo-Saxon England*, 3rd edn. (London, 1991), pp. 220–39.

74 *Vita Antonii*, 8, *PL* 73, col. 152.

75 Ibid., col. 131. Cf. 2 Cor. 12:10. See further *Verba Seniorum*, 5.31, *PL* 73, cols. 881–2; *Historia Monachorum*, 3.27–8, ed. Schulz-Flügel, p. 261 and *Verba Seniorum*, 10.17, *PL* 73, col. 915. Ambrose, Jerome and the other church fathers drew a strong and direct relationship between fasting and chastity (Ambrose, *Liber de Paradios*, 14, *PL* 14, 311; Jerome, *Epistola* 54, CSEL 54, pp. 466–85 (574–6)). For sleeplessness, see *Vita Antonii*, 6, *PL* 73 cols. 130–1; *Verba Seniorum*, 4.5, *PL* 73, col. 865; *Historia Lausiaca*, 48.2, ed. Wellhausen, pp. 656–7; *Historia Monachorum*, ed. Schulz-Flügel, 10 (p. 324), 27 (p. 364), 7 (pp. 288–9).

76 *Historia Lausiaca*, 42, ed. Wellhausen, p. 636.

77 *Verba Seniorum*, 7.17, *PL* 73, col. 896.

78 *Vita Antonii*, 7–8, *PL* 73, cols. 151–2.

79 Jerome, *Vita Hilarionis*, 9, *PL* 23, col. 52. On the monks' perception of the desert as a place of burial, see Antoine Guillaumont, 'La conception du désert chez les moines d'Egypte', *Revue de l'Histoire des Religions*, 188 (1975), 3–21.

80 *Historia Lausiaca*, 49.1, ed. Wellhausen, pp. 658–9. The stories of monks who stayed in their cells for many years were cited as example by other monks (*Historia Lausiaca*, 58.2, ed. Wellhausen, p. 669.)

81 Jean Leclercq, 'Le cloître est-il une prison?', *Revue d'ascetique et de mystique* 47 (1971), 407–20; Ann K. Warren, *Anchorites and Their Patrons in Medieval England* (Berkeley, 1985), p. 93.

82 *Vita Antonii*, 6, *PL* 73, cols. 150–1.

83 Cf. Sarah, who was attacked by the demon of lust for thirteen years. She prayed not for release from temptation but for strength to fight (*Verba Seniorum*, 5.10, *PL* 73, col. 876). Candidia fasted and practised sleep deprivation (*Historica Lausiaca*, 57.3, ed. Wellhausen, p. 688).

84 *Vita Antonii*, 31, 34, *PL* 73, cols. 151–2, 154.

85 Ibid., 30, col. 152.

86 See Rachel Koopmans's chapter in this volume on her clairvoyance (Chapter 9). As a charism of asceticism, prophecy was expected of hermits. See Henry Mayr-Harting, 'Functions of a Twelfth-century Recluse', *History* 60 (1975), 337–52. Sueno and Roger also have the gift (*Life*, pp. 97, 101).

87 Edward E. Malone, *The Monk and the Martyr: The Monk as Successor of the Martyr*, Catholic University of America, Studies in Christian Antiquity 12 (Washington, D.C., 1950). Athanasius' description of St Antony returning from encouraging the zeal of the martyrs at their trials in the law courts of Alexandria to his cell, 'where daily he was a martyr to his conscience', neatly summarizes the overlap between the martyrs of the Roman persecutions and their successors, the desert monks and nuns (*Vita Antonii*, 47, *PL* 73, col. 147).

88 Edward E. Malone, 'The Monk and the Martyr', in *Antonius Magnus eremita 356–1956*, ed. Basilius Steidle (Rome, 1956), pp. 201–28 (p. 201). Owen Chadwick, *Western Asceticism* (Philadelphia, 1958), pp. 20ff.

89 Altman, 'Two Types of Opposition', p. 3

90 Delehaye, *Sanctus*, pp. 109–14, 132–76.

91 In the *Vita Martini*, one of the most influential lives of the Middle Ages, Sulpicius Severus presents St Martin of Tours primarily as a bloodless martyr but also assimilates him to the blood martyrs, styling, for example, his brief but fundamental encounter with the Emperor Julian self-consciously after the pattern of the soldier-martyr's acts and legends (C. Stancliffe, *St Martin and His Hagiographer: History and Miracle in Sulpicius Severus* (Oxford, 1983), pp. 141–2, 147; see also her discussion on literary stylization in the *Vita Martini*, pp. 186–202).

92 John Kitchen, *Saints' Lives and the Rhetoric of Gender: Male and Female in Merovingian Hagiography* (New York, 1998), pp. 50–3.

93 *Vita Radegundis*, *AA.SS* Aug. III (1737), 67–83; for translation see *Sainted Women of the Dark Ages*, ed. Jo Ann McNamara, John E. Halborg and E. Gordon Whatley (Durham, N.C., 1992)). In an illustrated *Life of Radegund* (Poitiers, Bibl. Mun. MS 250), she is depicted in a manner reminiscent of Christina in the initial to Psalm 105 of the St Albans Psalter (see M. E. Carrasco, 'Spirituality in Context: the Romanesque illustrated Life of St. Radegund of Poitiers (Poitiers, Bibl. Mun. MS 250)', *Art Bulletin* 72 (1990), 414–35). Radegund appears in the St Albans Psalter litany. Hildebert of Lavardin, Abbot Geoffrey's supposed teacher at Le Mans, composed her life anew (*Vita Radegundis*, *PL* 171, cols. 967–88). I owe this reference to Jane Geddes.

94 Kitchen, *Saints' Lives*, p. 52.

95 *Corpus of British Medieval Library Catalogues: English Benedictine Libraries*, ed. R. Sharpe *et al.* (London, 1996). The fullest account of the library at St Albans is *Manuscripts from St Albans Abbey 1066–1235*, ed. R. M. Thomson, 2 vols. (Woodbridge, 1982).

96 *Corpus of … Libraries*, ed. Sharpe *et al.*, Nos 41 and 43. On the circulation of the *Vitae Patrum*, see Peter Jackson, 'The *Vitas Patrum* in Eleventh-Century Worcester', in

England in the Eleventh Century, ed. Carol Hicks (Stamford, 1992), pp. 119–34. The *Vitae Patrum* itself wholly or through its various parts figures frequently in surviving book-lists, for example at Bath, Worcester and Peterborough (Helmut Gneuss, *Handlist of Anglo-Saxon Manuscripts: A List of Manuscripts and Manuscript Fragments Written or Owned in England up to 1100*, Medieval and Renaissance Texts and Studies 241 (Arizona, 2001), Nos. 103, 281e, 311, 359e*, 389e, 761e, 808e; Richard Gameson, *The Manuscripts of Early Norman England (c. 1066–1130)* (Oxford, 1999), No. 407; Michael Lapidge, 'Surviving booklists from Anglo-Saxon England', in *Learning and Literature in Anglo-Saxon England: Studies Presented to Peter Clomoes on the Occasion of his Sixty-Fifth Birthday*, ed. Michael Lapidge and Helmut Gneuss (Cambridge, 1985), pp. 33–89 (59–61). See also in the same volume J. E. Cross, 'On the Library of the Old English Martyrologist', pp. 227–47).

97 *Manuscripts*, ed. Thomson, 1.39.
98 *Corpus of … Libraries*, ed. Sharpe *et al.*, p. 255.
99 *Gesta Abbatum*, i. 147.
100 Ibid., i. 73.
101 *Historia Ecclesiastica*, ed. and trans. Colgrave and Mynors, p. 58.
102 *Hali Meðhead*, in *Medieval English Prose*, ed. Bella Millett and Jocelyn Wogan-Browne (Oxford, 1990), p. 40. Similarly, the lives of Katherine, Margaret and Juliana are included in *Ancrene Wisse* to serve the anchorites as models in the preservation of their virginity. Likewise, Aelred's letter *De Virginitate* commends the virgin martyrs to women religious.

5

THE UNKNOWN PILGRIM

Drama and romance in the
Life of Christina of Markyate[1]

Neil Cartlidge

In all the excitement surrounding Christina of Markyate's recent rise to the moderate heights of academic stardom and a level of celebrity only made possible by C. H. Talbot's pioneering first printed edition of the *Life of Christina of Markyate* in 1959, the *Life* itself increasingly seems to be a casualty of her success. It is Christina's own remarkable historicity that seems to appeal to students and teachers alike, the seeming immediacy of her presence and personality in the milieu of twelfth-century St Albans. To that historicity the *Life* itself is often adduced merely as a witness, an inert and not always very cooperative testimony to the existence of an extraordinary individual, and not, as it deserves to be, as a text that is extraordinary in its own right – and of which Christina's charisma is only a product, and not (in any sense that can be proved) the cause.[2] In operation here is a variety of what literary theorists call the 'biographical fallacy', the notion that texts are only meaningful in relation to the people who produced or inspired them – an assumption that often results in all too comfortable conclusions about how discourses are constructed and how they should be read. As Christina's presence in source-books, anthologies and university courses becomes more and more assured, her individuality seems ever more independent of her biography, to the point that there even seems to be a tendency now to read her as, in some sense, the victim of her own written *Life* – a living female 'experience' contained and enclosed by the dead, patriarchal 'auctoritee' of the written word.[3] It does not help that the Christina who has recently acquired such a presence in the historical landscape apparently speaks perfect English, the English of Talbot's translation – which is all too often the only means by which her 'personality' is accessed – rather than the often awkward or damaged Latin of Talbot's necessarily tentative edition. Whether or not Christina's character was really as remarkable as the author of her *Life* thought it was – and that is not a question that we will ever be in a position to judge – we need to pay more attention to the play of language and imagination that makes the *Life* itself, even in the slightly blurred form in which we have it, the real star of the show.

Talbot himself was quite clear about the special qualities of the text. In the introduction to his edition he made an attempt to define its peculiarities of style and content, though unfortunately only in ways that have tended to foster just the tendencies that I have described. 'One of the more pleasant aspects of the Life of Christina', he declared, 'is its comparative freedom from the miraculous elements which invariably creep into hagiographical literature' (pp. 30–1) – a formulation by which, without actually saying anything inaccurate about the text in front of him, he succeeds in communicating a historian's disdain for the verminously fantastic motifs of medieval hagiography. There are no dragons in Christina's *Life*, certainly, and to that extent Talbot's emphasis is quite fair; but his suggestion that the *Life* does not 'tax the imagination', as he puts it, is at least misleading. It is not true to say that Christina's biographer 'contents himself with the bare facts which he describes as simply and objectively as he can': instead, he constantly shapes the events of her life by reference to imaginative models drawn from other texts, often in ways that are quite explicit. At the same time, Talbot's assumption that the *Life* was designed 'to give us a complete picture of a woman, highly strung but not hysterical, overcoming her physical disabilities and finding her equilibrium in a life of prayer and contemplation' (p. 33) sounds a little too much like a publisher's book-jacket blurb, and it clearly outruns the evidence. His conclusion that Christina was 'a well-balanced and integrated person' seems an over-ambitious interpretation even of the story told by her *Life*, let alone of the historical evidence; and his idea that the more extraordinary events in the text, such as the headless body at the entrance to the church, or the mysterious vanishing pilgrim, reflect a 'spirit of simplicity' that 'must be accepted' by the modern reader, is quaintly uncritical.[4] Even so, the general direction of his remarks – his emphasis on the impression of realism that the text creates and on its relative lack of dependence on conventionally melodramatic hagiographical motifs – does accurately record something of the uniqueness, the originality and the independence of mind that the *Life of Christina of Markyate* certainly possesses.

What Talbot failed to recognize is that the *Life*'s failure to engage in any 'medieval extravaganza' of piety is a function, not of good taste, but of effi-ciency of purpose. It employs unrealistic motifs not, as is usually the case in medieval hagiography, in order to assert what might be called the authority of wonder – the divine and saintly prerogative of disobeying the usual rules of nature[5] – but in order to develop a complex and highly coherent thematic commentary on the meaning of Christina's existence. Medieval hagiography typically depicts wonders that are excessive – often the more so the better.[6] The St Albans biographer, by contrast, introduces uncanny events into his story only when they also happen to be apt reflections of what he chooses to define as key themes in Christina's life. From this point of view, the realistic qualities of *The Life of Christina of Markyate* have more to do with narrative economy than with evidentiary value – to have multiplied Christina's miracles would have been to dilute the interpretative gloss that the biographer was trying to develop. Even so, his respect for realism rather than miraculous extravagance clearly also supports his purpose, if only in that it encourages the perception that the serendipities of

Christina's life-story are not of his construction, but merely events that happen to come from God. In other words, his 'realism' – like the realism of nineteenth-century novelists – is a way of denying or minimizing the author's demiurgic role in the universe of the story being told; and indeed one cannot help but suspect that the current preference for the 'real' Christina over the narrated one is in some ways analogous to the difficulties many students of literature find in treating characters like Dorothea Brooke or Etienne Lantier (in *Middlemarch* and *Germinal* respectively) as authorial constructions (rather than as real people with motivations beyond the novelist's knowledge). Yet realism even of this kind is as much an effect of style and narrative technique as of observation and empathy.[7] The impression of relatively sober facticity that Christina's *Life* creates is just as much a product of the author's manipulation of the 'reality' of events as the hagiographical wonders and monsters whose absence from this particular text Talbot was so ready to celebrate.

Take, for example, the case of Christina's mysterious vanishing pilgrim (Talbot, *Life*, pp. 182–8) – an incident that tends to be discussed only cursorily in modern studies of her *Life*, and perhaps precisely because it combines mundane detail and rapturous fantasy in a way that baffles narrowly realist approaches to the text. Initially, at least, the account of the pilgrim's arrival certainly seems dryly circumstantial. 'Contigit aliquando' ('it happened once'), begins the author, using the impersonal construction and the indefinite temporal adverb with the vague specificity of a casual anecdote; and he goes on to introduce us to a 'peregrinum quemdam, ignotum quidem' ('some pilgrim, quite unknown') – a markedly vague description implying that he has no clues to the stranger's identity, even though it is quite clear from his surmises a few pages later that he knows quite well how important he is. Yet, having located the pilgrim in Christina's everyday existence in this apparently artless fashion, the author then starts to draw attention to precisely those features of his tale that are not accidental – to develop, that is, an increasingly conspicuous commentary on the purposes implicit in these events. The circumstantial quality of this account is challenged and counterpointed, even within the narrative, by the author's establishment of a register of suggestion that works only to betray just how contrived his illusion of realism actually is. Talbot's translation tells us that the stranger left a 'a deep impression' on Christina's memory, but this formulation is less suggestive than the Latin itself: for the phrase 'quale-cumque … insigne' (literally 'some kind of emblem' or 'sign') not only emphasizes Christina's subjectivity by using an image that is explicitly semiotic, but also suggests the language of typology – the method of exegesis funda-mental to the medieval interpretation of scripture.[8] As such, it clearly prompts the *Life*'s reader to recognize that Christina's pilgrim has a symbolic signifi-cance, to see him as a type of Christ, in just the same way that she or he would recognize the characters and events of the Old Testament as types or 'signs' of the New.[9] It is not just in the general sense of being a stranger and an alien on earth that Christ is the natural point of reference for the *Life*'s figure of the pilgrim, but also in the specific sense of being the unrecognized Pilgrim (*peregrinus*: Luke 24:18) who encounters the apostles on the road to Emmaus. Some evidence for Christina's particular engagement with this event can be found in the St Albans Psalter, the richly illuminated manuscript possibly used by Christina, and conceivably adapted for her use.[10] This contains three pictures of scenes from the Emmaus story; and these are placed significantly apart from the main body of forty full-page illustrations, after the Psalter's copy of the Old French *Chanson de St Alexis*, rather than before it with the rest.[11] As Otto Pächt argued, these images can be interpreted as a kind of commentary on the *Life of St Alexis*, the saint whose unnoticed return to his grieving family makes him another type of the *peregrinus ignotus*;[12] but they also associate themselves equally forcibly with the tale told in Christina's *Life*.[13] Indeed it might even be argued that the apostles' encounter with Christ is much more closely paralleled by Christina's encounter with the pilgrim than by anything in the *Life of St Alexis*, for it is only in these two accounts that a ceremonious meal is shared and in which the pilgrim subsequently makes a dramatic disappearance (rather than dies, as in the *Chanson de St Alexis*). At the same time, while the 'qualecumque ... insigne' that the pilgrim creates should probably be read both as the mark he leaves on Christina's memory and as a referential sign within the text, it can also be interpreted as a sign of the referentiality *of* the text. What is highlighted here is not just *that* the pilgrim is significant, but *how* he comes to signify. That is: Christina's *Life* deliberately draws attention to the processes by which it calls on a deeper pattern of meanings, as well as to those meanings themselves – even within a narrative of events that is apparently matter-of-fact. The peculiar effect of immediacy that this passage creates is therefore a function not of its plain realism nor of its artful suggestiveness, but of the way in which it self-consciously holds these contradictory qualities in tension.

The essence of this technique is its boldness – and the biographer's stylization of Christina's encounter with the pilgrim is bold to the point of profanity. He explicitly reads Christina's attention to her guest as a reflection of Mary of Bethany's paradigmatic devotion to Christ:

> ... humanitatis officio cibum eciam illum cogit sumere. Discumbit ipse: illa cum sorore .M. dulce parat edulium. Cristina tamen attencius assidet viro: Margareta laboriosus circa necessaria discurrit; ita ut aliam Mariam, aliam videres et Martham, si Ihesum discumbentem daretur conspicere. Itaque mensa parata, ori panis apponitur et quasi cibum sumere videbatur: sed si adesses plus gustantem eum adverteres, quam edentem. (... she pressed him to share in the meal, as a courtesy/celebration/rite of humanity. He sat down, while she and her sister Margaret prepared a pleasant meal. Christina, however, attended more assiduously to the man, as Margaret ran about more busily on account of the things that needed to be done, so that in this way you might have seen another Mary and another Martha, if you had been able to look at

Jesus sitting [with them]. And so, once the meal was ready, he put bread to his mouth, but if you had been present you would have noticed that he tasted rather than ate.)

(*Life*, pp. 182–4)

The phrase *humanitatis officio*, which Talbot translates a little too elegantly as 'with kindly hospitality', implicitly suggests a comparison with the *divinitatis officio cibum* – the meal that is also the sacred *office* of the Mass. This impression is supported by the pilgrim's mere appearance of eating, for this peculiarity not only underlines his divine identity, but also recalls the magical and paradoxical qualities of the Eucharist. The *Life* also verbally underlines its self-identification with the gospels' account of the meal at Bethany: Margaret 'was busy running about on account of what had to be served' ('laboriosus *circa* necessaria discurrit') in much the same way that Martha 'busily ran about on account of the serving [of the meal]' ('satagebat *circa* frequens ministerium') in Luke 10:40; while the word 'necessaria' here clearly recalls the 'unum ... necessarium' ('the one needful thing') of Luke 10:42. The influence of John 12:2 is perhaps discernible in the *Life*'s double use of the verb 'discumbere', 'to sit down'. Yet the appropriation of the role of Mary by Christina, together with all the connotations of that role, is also explicitly presented by her biographer as a deliberate act of interpretation – 'si ... daretur conspicere' ('if it were granted to see'), 'si adesses' ('if you had been present'); so that, while this passage is clearly designed to create a sense of wonder, it is the wonder not of improbable facts (such as the dragons or other 'miraculous elements which invariably creep into hagiographical literature') but of conscious hypothesis, of an imagination observed in action. The marvellous events in Christina's *Life* are always what might be called conditional marvels – contingent, that is, on the way in which they are perceived and interpreted. What makes them marvellous is their serendipitous fitness, their extraordinary susceptibility to reading in terms of patterns already existing in a range of cultural models. In other words, Christina's life, in her biographer's eyes, was miraculous not because extraordinary things often happened, but because events that are in most cases fairly ordinary occurred in ways that expressed her sense of vocation in extraordinarily resonant ways. The meal with the pilgrim, which in itself is nothing supernatural, is only worthy of narration because of its remarkable readiness to adapt itself to the gloss which the narrator chooses to apply to it.

This may seem like a back-handed way of admitting the imaginative power of Christina's story, but what lies behind the unusual hagio-biographical technique that I am trying to define is something fundamental to her biographer's sensibility. This particular narrative mechanism seems to me to depend, like so much in his thinking, on what could be described as the reversed polarity of late medieval religious symbolism. What I mean by this is that, for Christina, as for more and more people as the Middle Ages progressed, it was not so much that symbols imitate or impersonate the truth as that the truth, characteristically, appropriates symbols.[14] To read the pilgrim simply as a symbol of Christ – as an unreal equivalent to the real – is to read against the grain of the text, which actually insists on the reality of Christ within the symbol – the presence of the real, in this sense, dissolving the extrinsic irreality of the symbol. This attitude of mind is fundamentally different from the mentality expressed in the conventional scholastic tradition of scriptural exegesis, for it emphasizes the effect of symbols as experiences, rediscovering the immediacy of images and stories that traditional exegesis tends to reduce in the end to a mere currency, an endless circulation of ideological equivalences. So it is that late medieval religious literature, particularly in the so-called 'mystical' tradition of which the *Life of Christina of Markyate* was in several respects a pioneer, often insists on the literal re-enactment of events in the cycle of Christian narrative, to a degree of engagement that many modern readers find disturbing. Perhaps the most famous example of this is Margery Kempe's imagined presence at the Crucifixion, when she characteristically expends her tears, not as a passive observer of the scene, but as an intrusive participator within it, talking to the other people present and actively helping them.[15] This is a textual moment clearly anticipated by Christina's usurpation of Mary's role during the meal at Bethany, although the appropriation of scriptural data as if they were remembered experiences in this way might be regarded as one of the definitional features of mysticism in general. As Alois Haas puts it, 'a mystic is one who is able to experience and get to know God in a peculiarly intense way.'[16] Yet the explanation for the development of such a sensibility, at least in the particular case of the *Life of Christina of Markyate*, might also be sought in terms of another referential system that might be said to have arisen out of the exegetical tradition during the Middle Ages, a tradition that nevertheless stands in a distinct contrast with it – and that is the tradition of dramatic performance.

Much of what I have just said could be recast in explicitly dramatic terms. What I am arguing is that, in terms of the way Christina's biography is constructed, the pilgrim is a part played by Christ; that Christina, her sister and her guest literally re-enact the meal at Bethany; that the language of hypothesis ('si ... daretur conspicere', 'si adesses', *Life*, 182–4) is also the language of dramatic ambition – 'as if' what is performed is real. It is a sense of drama, as a means of connecting symbols with reality, that enables Christina's biographer to insist simultaneously on the actuality of the events in her life and on the significances that they disguise. It is therefore as much in a dramatic sense as in a rhetorical one that Christina's pilgrim can be described as a *figure* of Christ – since in some of the earliest surviving dramatic texts 'figura' is the word used to denote a role, the higher reality to which the actor's presence within the play only refers. For example in the *Mystère d'Adam*, God is referred to simply as the 'Figura' – not as the 'role' of God, that is, but simply as The Role.[17] This is why the physicality of the pilgrim is a deliberate theme in the biographer's account of Christina's feelings about him: his beautiful face, fine beard and grave deportment ('vultus venustatem, decorem barbe, maturitatem habitus') substantiate

Christ's presence in the symbol – they enforce the notion that the 'peregrinus ignotus' is not just an image or an idea, but a tangible presence, a role fully inhabited by Christ, in just the same way that an actor literally embodies the part that he plays. Indeed, what finally forces the narrative out of its generally realistic framework – asking us unequivocally to 'tax the imagination' – is precisely this obsessive interest in the immediate tangibility of Christ's presence; for as the sick Christina is depicted lying listening to the hours of the Christmas vigil, so the narrative gradually becomes more and more fevered, binding the liturgical verses into a crescendo of insistence on Christ's actual imminence:

> Cumque decumbenti virgini horas vigilie dominice psallerent: audit inter cetera totaque mente concipit, versiculum hore none, speciale scilicet singularis illius festi gaudium: *Hodie scietis quia veniet Dominus, et mane videbitis gloriam eius.* Cuius versiculi percepto sensu tanto spirituali gestivit gaudio, ut in residuo die vel in subsequenti nocte vix ab eius corde huiusmodi meditationes exciderent. O qua hora veniet Dominus? O quomodo veniet? Quis videbit venientem? Quis eius glorie visionem dignabitur? Qualis quantave illa erit gloria? Qualem quantumve gaudium erit intuentibus? (And while they were chanting the hours of the Christmas vigil to the virgin [Christina] as she lay there, she heard among the other [versicles], the versicle of the hour of None (the special delight, that is, of that unique feast) and understood it with her whole mind: 'Today you will know that the Lord will come and tomorrow you will see his glory'. Having realized the significance of this verse, she was filled with yearning of such spiritual joy that for the rest of the day and the following night contemplations of this kind scarcely left her heart: O at what hour will the Lord come? O how will he come? Who will see him arriving? Who will deserve a vision of his glory? How great and in what form will his glory seem? How great and in what form will be the joy of those seeing it?)

> (*Life*, p. 184)

The sense of the real within the ritual – the notion that Christ's birth is being celebrated for the first time, as it were, and not as a repetition that looks back to an earlier point of time – leads Christina from recovery, through exhilaration and into rapture. Borne out of her body and into the church of St Albans, she sees a 'person' sitting in the middle of the choir, watching the monks approvingly – a figure of transcendent beauty, wearing a crown with a golden cross. 'Persona' happens to be the usual word in Latin for a role in a drama, so that the *Life* might be taken at this point to suggest that the person of the pilgrim was like a part played in a drama enacted in Christina's mind.[18] The word that the biographer uses for the person's dress and appearance is 'species' – literally 'appearance', but also, in a dramatic context 'costume', a sense that gives added force to his wordplay on the emotional effect of the imagined stranger's 'species':

'Hac specie refulserat persona illa cuius species admirabilis est enim speciosus pre filiis hominum' (*Life*, p. 186). ('in this guise [*species*] shone the *persona*, whose marvellous appearance [*species*] is indeed more beautiful [*speciosus*] than that of the sons of men.')[19]

It might seem a roundabout way of explaining the effect of immediacy created by Christina's biography to refer to medieval ideas about drama, but in fact the materials for establishing a chain of connection between contemporary dramatic texts and Christina's *Life* lie readily to hand in the St Albans Psalter – though in fact it is the shared sensibility, the shared sense of a continuity of symbol and experience through the conscious playing out of roles, that I want to emphasize here, rather than any detailed indebtedness to any particular text or texts. As Pächt has shown, the depiction of the Emmaus story in twelfth-century images was possibly directly influenced by the dramatic tradition of 'Peregrinus' plays (the term used by Karl Young for plays on the Emmaus theme).[20] 'In one way or another,' says Pächt, 'it is the impersonation of the Peregrinus of the mystery plays and not the Jesus of the Gospel text which is reflected in all these twelfth-century representations. [...] The *mise en scène* may vary, but what is recorded in the miniatures [of this period] is always a stage setting.'[21] His evidence lies in the similarities between the way in which the Pilgrim's costume is described in the play-texts and the way in which it is depicted in the Psalter's illustrations. Although Christina's *Life* lacks any specific account of her pilgrim's costume – it is hardly necessary in the context – the very possibility that the St Albans artist automatically turned to the drama for his pictorial models makes it natural to assume that Christina's biographer was thinking in terms of models of a similar kind. Their influence on the construction of her *Life* is perhaps discernible in the way that Christina's encounter with the pilgrim is staged in the church itself (as these early dramas would have been) – and indeed staged twice over: that is, once in her vision of the *persona* sitting in the choir and then again in the 'real' pilgrim's disappearance from the church. This second incident is clearly a refiguration of Christ's Ascension, but it has something of the makeshift quality of the plays' own depiction of the Ascension, in which the actor playing Christ often simply removes himself to another part of the church;[22] as well as something of the same sense of occasion as a dramatic event might have possessed, a feeling captured in the biographer's account of the excited gathering of expectant people waiting outside the church to meet the pilgrim as he comes out.[23]

The plays' influence, I suggest, is even more pronounced in the particular language and logic of Christina's *Life*. As her biographer himself analyses the matter: 'Qui enim in nocte in tanto scemate apparuit, qualis videndus est in gloria quoquo modo innotuit' (*Life*, p. 88). ('He [that is, the divine presence playing the part of the pilgrim] who appeared in the night in such a costume/representation indeed showed in some sort of way how he will appear in glory.') *Schema* can mean 'appearance' in a general sense: it also denotes not just clothes (particularly clerical dress), but also representation or performance ('inductio, representatio').[24] The use of such a word so closely associated in several senses with the register of dramatic language is surely deliberate; and the biographer himself takes care that we note the suggestiveness of his language with the emphasis-cum-qualification, 'quoquo modo' – 'in some particular way'. The sheer accumulation of words and phrases dealing with representation and interpretation, not just in this sentence (such as 'apparuit', 'qualis videndus'), but also in the whole account of the pilgrim's presence in Christina's life, recalls the language used in the stage-directions of medieval plays. The Fleury Peregrinus play, for example, describes itself as the 'similitudinem Dominici Apparicionis in specie Peregrini' ('the likeness of the divine apparition in the guise of a pilgrim'), self-consciously drawing attention to its own representationalism with a threefold emphasis on appearance ('similitudo ... apparicio ... species').[25] The *Carmina Burana* Peregrinus play calls itself an 'exemplum apparitionis Domini discipulis suis iuxta castellum Emmaus, ubi illis apparuit in more peregrini et tacuit videns, quid loquerentur et tractarent' ('an *exemplum* of the appearance of the Lord to his disciples at the castle of Emmaus, where he appeared to them in the guise of a pilgrim and silently observed what they said and did'), a description that not only also insists on the play's parabolic quality (as an 'exemplum'), but also emphasizes dumb-show in a way that recalls Christina's biographer's formulation of the mysterious pilgrim's token performance of the act of eating.[26] The *Life* seems to absorb both the language and the element of anxiety about representation implicit in such texts and restate them, not just in a different generic form (the biography), but also in much more direct and explicit terms, for this passage modulates from the qualified identification of the pilgrim as 'videndus ... in gloria' – 'one who will be seen in glory' – into an aggressive defence of the very process of such imaginative refiguration. The biographer's interpretation of the pilgrim's significance to Christina's life amounts not just to a justification of representationalism such as the contemporary play-texts only hint at, but also to an object lesson in the 'reversed polarity' of symbolism that, as I have suggested, came to be typical of medieval 'mysticism'.

It is with the language of St Paul that this defence begins:

Hec namque in presenti nobis est illi gloria, qui de illa non nisi per speculum videmus [I Corinthians 13:12]. Unde caliginem Deus inhabitare dicitur [II Paralipomenon 6:1], non quod caliginem inhabitet, sed quia lux sua pre immensitate nos corporis graves pondere hebetare videtur. In die vero sub peregrini, sed maturioris viri specie videre voluit, quia qualiter ... [lacuna of four lines in MS] ... perfudit. (For this is glory for us in the present, since we may not see any of it except through a glass darkly. For this reason God is said to inhabit a cloud not because cloud is his habitation, but because his light in its immensity deadens our senses, heavy as we are in the weight of our bodies. On that day [i.e. Christmas] he wished to appear in the guise of a fully grown man [as opposed to an infant, as one might expect at the

Nativity], since in this way … [here there is a lacuna in the manuscript] … [he/she/it] infused.

(*Life*, p. 188)

Talbot refers at this point to the pseudo-Dionysian *De mystica theologia*, and reasonably so, since this text was undoubtedly the fountainhead for medieval mystical theology, but there is in fact no particular need for the passage quoted here to be understood in terms outside those of the *Life* itself, since all the issues it addresses have already been signalled in the course of the biographer's account of the pilgrim's effect on Christina. Here, he argues that truth is immanent in the sign, not obscured by it. Although we see 'through the glass darkly', the light that shines through is nevertheless contained within the sign, direct and undistorted. The glass – the pattern of symbolism through which we 'imagine' divinity – is not an obstacle, but a necessary shelter for the limited capacity of the human mind from the sheer brightness of the light of truth. Therefore, representation is not, by definition, unreal – not even a fiction that has validity as a form of reference. Representation is an image of the truth – and to that extent, it is true. As the biographer recognizes, this only raises questions about interpretation, and the relativity that characterizes human perceptions, but this barely seems to shake the confidence with which he insists on the right to read – and indeed to state for us – the play of symbols at work in Christina's *Life*. This confidence in the appropriation of symbols and in the validity of representation perhaps recalls the defence of iconography borrowed from Gregory's Letters and inserted into the St Albans Psalter between the *Chanson de St Alexis* and the three 'Peregrinus' miniatures, which, in this context, might be seen as an analogously considered defence of art and imagination in the cause of understanding God.[27] It is, at the very least, a long way from Erasmus's use of the same image of 'seeing through a glass darkly' in an attempt to mark the limits of the human capacity for comprehending the mystery of divinity, and thus of reasonable intellectual ambition.[28]

So self-conscious and distinctive is the concern with representationalism as a theme in the *Life of Christina of Markyate* – so far, indeed, from Talbot's 'spirit of simplicity' – that its sense of drama ought to be difficult to overlook. It is tempting to seek some explanation for this in what little we know about the circumstances in which it was written: and one is perhaps readily available in the strange parable of the power and danger of drama told in the *Gesta Abbatum* about Geoffrey of Maine (or of Le Mans), the special friend who looms so largely in Christina's *Life*.[29] According to this account, Geoffrey entered the monastery of St Albans only as an act of restitution. Working as a schoolmaster in Dunstable, he had borrowed some liturgical vestments from the abbey for a play of St Katherine, and when these vestments were burned in a fire at his house, he saw no other way to make a reparation, we are told, than by entering the monastery, making a sacrificial victim ('holocaustum') of himself, as it were, in exchange for the burning ('holocaustum') of the copes ('Nesciens igitur quomodo hoc damnum Deo et Sancto Albano restauraret, seipsum reddidit in holocaustum Deo, assumens habitum religionis in Domo Sancti Albanis').[30] This story happens to be the earliest record of any dramatic performance in England, and as such is often cited, but it is less often remarked quite how extraordinary the thinking lying behind this episode actually is. The logic seems to be that, as symbols, the burned copes were worth precisely what they symbolized, not what they were actually worth as objects: and, therefore, since there was nothing in the world with which they could be replaced, Geoffrey could only give up the world itself. It would be easy to read this as a parable against play-acting, but in a deeper sense it signifies precisely the opposite – that is, that in the business of approaching God there is no play-acting: every representation is real. What we see here is an exaggerated sense of the potency and significance of dramatic practice; and although the *Gesta Abbatum* rationalizes the episode into a banal aetiology for Geoffrey's attention to the state of the Abbey's vestments, it might be valid to assume that the distinctive mentality that lies behind this story is accurately associated with Geoffrey and that it is this same mentality that drives the interest in representation expressed in both the St Albans Psalter and the *Life of Christina of Markyate*. Indeed, even in the relatively dry and undemonstrative account of Geoffrey offered in the *Gesta Abbatum*, scattered evidence for such a sensibility can still be found. For example, Geoffrey's decision to distribute some of the material accumulated for the construction of his Abbey's new shrine to the poor is defended in terms that insist, like Christina's account of the pilgrim, on the immediacy of Christ's presence in the world, and particularly among the poor at the gate – that is, with reference to Christ's words in Matthew 25:40, 'what you do for the least of my people, you do for me.'[31] This is surely just the kind of justification that might naturally have occurred to someone imaginatively engaged either with the *Chanson de St Alexis* in the St Albans Psalter or – more to the point – with the story of Christina and the pilgrim in the context of her *Life*.

What I have been arguing for so far, I hope, amounts to a demonstration of the high degree of self-conscious literary artistry in Christina's *Life* – expressed not just through a deep engagement with such specific images as that of the 'peregrinus ignotus', but also in a general interest in the use of the imagination as a means of apprehending God – and indeed in the very concept of symbolism. The symbolic resonance of the unrecognized pilgrim possibly owes much to model of St Alexis' unrecognized return to the house of his father and even more to the story of Christ's encounter with the apostles at Emmaus, and perhaps specifically as it was depicted in the St Albans Psalter and in contemporary dramaturgy. Yet the net might be cast more widely than this. Just as the melodramatic possibilities of the St Alexis story were quickly recognized and reworked by secular romancers in the form of the tradition of stories about Guy of Warwick,[32] so the figure of the mysterious and charismatic outsider has a currency in twelfth-century vernacular narrative more generally.[33] Indeed the encounter with the itinerant or mendicant figure who turns out to be the hero disfigured or disguised is a scenario so often replayed in such texts that it might even be described as one of the leitmotifs of insular fiction in this period. In both *Gui de Warewic* and the *Roman de Horn*, for example, the protagonists memorably portray themselves as pilgrims;[34] in the Oxford *Folie Tristan* the hero pretends to be another kind of holy alien, the fool;[35] while in the Middle English *Sir Orfeo* – a text that possibly records something of a now lost twelfth-century *Lai d'Orfée* – Orfeo adopts the role of a travelling minstrel.[36] None of these texts pre-date the *Life of Christina of Markyate*, but some of them are little more than a few decades younger and they may well suggest something of the nature of the vernacular traditions that would have been current as Christina's biographer was writing. Again, though, it is the shared sensibility, the shared interest in the imaginative possibilities of the figure of the anonymous wanderer that I want to demonstrate here, rather than any specific lines of indebtedness. It is only conceivable – merely a possibility – that the story of Christina and the pilgrim was written with an awareness of some of the heroic *ignoti* to be found in Anglo-Norman romance.

As it happens, when the romances describe pilgrims, they tend to costume them in much the same way as the play-texts that Pächt assumed must have determined the depiction of the Peregrinus in the St Albans Psalter.[37] It would at least be difficult to deny that what made the staging of this particular motif so attractive to the romancers is likely also to justify, to some extent, its inclusion in Christina's biography. Not only do such scenes serve as preludes to recognition (*anagnorisis*) and resolution:[38] they also epitomize the way in which both hagiographical and romance narratives depend on the outward forms of social identity in order to create both emotional momentum and meaning.[39] With the re-establishment of identity comes the re-assertion of rights, hereditary, spousal or saintly – the feudal prerogatives of lords and kings like Horn and Orfeo, those of husbands such as Guy, Alexis and Orfeo; of lovers like Horn and Tristan; and of saints and para-saints like Alexis and Guy. All of these wanderers are in some sense returning home, as the reader already knows, but this knowledge is withheld from the other characters within the narrative, so that their ability to see through the disguise – to sense Odysseus' 'return', as it were – becomes a touchstone of their fidelity.[40] In the context of such narratives, it is hard not to read the account of the pilgrim's appearance in Christina's biography as a kind of imaginative dramatization of Christ's 'return' – an assertion of Christ's rights over her, that is, as Lord and King, and as the divine Husband of a woman vowed to be his *sponsa Christi*. As I have argued elsewhere, Christina's vow of chastity is depicted in the *Life* in such a way as to suggest that it is at least equivalent to a marital vow:[41] and from this perspective, the pilgrim might be seen not just as a parallel figure to St Alexis, coming home to be honoured but not fully recognized by his 'blessed and ever-grieving bride' ('sponsa beata, semper gemebunda', as she is labelled in the St Albans Psalter), but also as a figure of the heavenly bridegroom whose presence Christina can never ultimately enjoy on earth. The narrative thus allows Christ to play one of the characteristic roles of the role-playing lover of romance, in such a way as to prove and sanctify the heroine's loving fidelity.

Crucial to such a reading is that Christina, like Horn's beloved Rigmel, or Guy's Félice, does not entirely fail to sense the presence of her hero. She, like her female counterparts in romance, is emotionally attracted to the stranger in a way that only serves to demonstrate the existence of some sort of affective bond between them. This is expressed, as it is in the secular texts, by an emphasis on the pilgrim's incongruously impressive physical presence. In the *Roman de Horn*, for example, the paradox of the pilgrim who is a mendicant by status but not in manner – equivalent perhaps to Christina's *peregrinus ignotus sed reverendus* – is so often enunciated as to become almost a refrain. The narrator reports:

> En la sale est entré   li paumer pelerin.
> Escreppe ot e burdun   e un chapeau feutrin,
> Par mi çoe que povre iert   bien semblot de bon lin.

> (Into the hall came the palmer-pilgrim. He had a scrip, a long staff and a felt hat; and despite his poverty, he looked as if he were well-born.)
>
> (*Roman de Horn*, ll. 3, 682–4)

This impression is shared by Horn's rival for Rigmel's hand, King Modin, who notices the disguised hero's surprisingly healthy complexion ('char blanche e fresche la colur', l. 4,039) and who is prepared to swear to the apparent pilgrim's noble ancestry ('ja mar me crerez mais, s'il n'est ned de bon lin', l. 4,063), despite his professed poverty. Rigmel herself is struck by Horn's 'char blanche e … visage cler' (l. 4,195) and even though she cannot bring herself to imagine that the man before her is her lost beloved, she is so deeply moved by his presence, and by the very possibility that he might be a messenger from him, that she almost faints (ll. 4,215–18, 4,218a).[42] Guy's betrothed Félice is similarly affected by the appearance of the strange pilgrim among the poor men at her gates; and she expresses her pity for the mendicant that Guy has become by sharing her meal with him:

> La cuntesse l'ad esgardé;
> Pur ço qu'il ert plus mesaisé,
> De li l'en prist mult grant pité,
> De chascun mes qu'ele ad mangé
> Li ad ele cel jur enveié …

> (The countess looked at him: because he was suffering hardship she took pity on him, sending every meal that she took that day to him.)
>
> (*Gui de Warewic*, ll. 11,399–403)

Christina's sense of the stranger's importance is similarly powerful and irrational: as she talks to the *peregrinus* for the first time she feels a divine fervour ('fervorem illa senciens divinum', *Life*, p. 182) and she realizes that the man before her far surpasses either men or the ordinary rewards of men ('aut homines aut hominum commune meritum') – an odd formulation that is perhaps riddlingly suggestive of Christ's transcendance of death, the 'commune meritum' of Adam's descendants. Christina's biographer is even prepared to inject an element of suppressed eroticism into his account of her feelings for the angelic stranger: not only does she admire his physical appearance, she and her sister are only prevented from begging him to stay with them by their 'virginal sense of shame' ('virginalis ... pudor', *Life*, p. 184). This combination of allusive wordplay with what is at least a teasing awareness of the operations of sexual chemistry is much more in tune with the methods and motifs of secular romance than it is even with what is the obvious religious model for Christina's encounter with the pilgrim, the *Chanson de St Alexis*: for while texts like the Oxford *Folie Tristan* are so highly charged precisely because they flirt so deliberately with the possibility of recognition, the *Chanson de St Alexis* explicitly denies that the saint's family ever came close to guessing the identity of the stranger under the stairs – 'Par nule guise unces ne l'aviserent' (l. 238). It might be argued that Alexis' father, Eufemien, must at some subconscious level recognize his son in the poor man who begs for a bed in the name of his lost son ('empur tun filz dunt tu as del dolur', l. 219), but the narrator himself chooses not to explore the dramatic possibilities of the saint's recognition before his death, even at the level of suggestion. The *Life of Christina of Markyate*, by contrast, shows us its heroine tentatively coming to an understanding of the stranger's real identity, in this way proving both her delicacy of feeling and, in a sense, her love for him, in a fashion that fully deserves to be called romantic.

If the arrival of the pilgrim and Christina's gradual movement towards recognizing him can be seen to be paralleled by some of the disguise-scenes in secular Anglo-Norman romance, so there is also at least one model in vernacular narrative for the pilgrim's strange disappearance: and this is to be found in the *Roman de Waldef*.[43] Here the palmer's role is essentially prophetic: at this point in the story, Waldef's son Guiac has just supplanted the German Emperor (a character perhaps significantly called Alexis) and in the course of a feast celebrating his election expresses a policy of hubristic expansionism – his ambition to conquer not just Greece, Rome and the Holy Land, but also the angelic hosts of the Earthly Paradise. It is at this moment that a pilgrim suddenly appears in the hall and approaches the dais:

> Chapel avoit e esclavine,
> Qui plus iert blanc que peil d'ermine,
> Beals vis avoit e culuré,
> La barbe ot longe e tute blanche,

Plus ke n'est nois desus la branche,
Larges vis avoit, les euls clers,
Par semblant resembloit mult fiers,
Es sa mein tenoit un burdun ...

(He had a hat and a pilgrim's cape whiter than ermine; a beautiful, high-coloured complexion; a long beard, totally white, whiter than snow on the branch; a generous face; clear eyes; an appearance of great inner strength; and a pilgrim's staff in his hand.)

(*Waldef*, ll. 20,693–701)

Guiac's visitor recalls the Peregrinus of the Emmaus illustrations in the St Albans Psalter, not just in the particular details of his costume, but also in the general effect of his beauty. His beautiful high-coloured complexion, 'generous' expression, 'clear' eyes and beard suggest not just the distinctive stylization of human faces in the Psalter, but also the 'beautiful features, elegant beard and mature deportment' ('vultus venustatem, decorem barbe, maturitatem habitus', *Life*, p. 184) of Christina's Peregrinus. Such comparisons only extend so far – *Waldef*'s 'pelerin' is said to be an old man, for example, while no explicit reference is made to the age of the 'peregrinus' in the *Life*: but it is striking, nevertheless, that both texts employ the characteristic costume of the pilgrim for the same dramatic purpose – that is, of underlining the stranger's awesome and mysterious authority. All of Guiac's vassals and servants ('tuit li conte e li barun ... tuit li sergant qui servirent') instinctively recognize the wanderer's power, automatically making way for him as he walks through the hall; while the new emperor not only allows him to speak, but is strangely unable to make any reply to what he hears. It is as if they sense the presence among them of an angelic visitor, in much the same way that Christina and her sister are aware of the superhuman qualities of the beautiful stranger who comes to them ('ut angelum non hominem se pre se sentiret habere', *Life*, p. 184). Having delivered his message, *Waldef*'s heavenly emissary walks out of the hall and is never seen again: no one knew what became of him; as the poet puts it, 'Nus ne sot plus que il devint' (l. 20,804). This disappearance seems unremarkable in itself, but the *Waldef*-poet subsequently attempts to make it remarkable in much the same rather prosaic way that Christina's biographer emphasizes the peculiar circumstances of her pilgrim's disappearance from the church. The Emperor sends out all the retainers he has ('Tuit li sergant ke ço oïrent', *Waldef*, l. 20,823) to seek the missing pilgrim, but although they look everywhere ('Quistrent le sus, quistrent le jus', *Waldef*, l. 20,825), they fail to find him – which the text clearly invites us to think is something almost inexplicable. Of the two disappearances, Christina's pilgrim's disappearance from a locked church is rather more difficult to believe than *Waldef*'s pilgrim's disappearance into the countryside. Yet, by insisting on circumstantial details in order to stress the wonderful aspects of the pilgrims' exits, both texts manage to make both events more mundane and less dramatic than one might expect either of romance or of hagiography. In both cases, the authors seem to be relying on the principle that a marvel is only marvellous as long as it is located in a context that is believably 'normal' – a limited form of literary realism in which the relatively few fantastic elements of the narrative are supported and emphasized by the contingency of a distinctly everyday world.

The presence of the figure of the mysterious Pilgrim in the *Life* is justified there by the ready availability of an interpretative gloss in the Gospel depiction of Christ-as-Pilgrim on the Road to Emmaus, and perhaps, for the *Life*'s first audience, by the possibility of drawing connections with the iconography of the St Albans Psalter. For the author of *Waldef*, by contrast, as for vernacular romancers more generally, the figure of the pilgrim seems to have had a compelling fascination that is not entirely proportionate. It is so over-determined dramatically as to suggest that, perhaps even before Christina's biographer was writing, and certainly not long afterwards, the figure of the pilgrim had acquired some of the mythical resonances of a literary archetype. Guiac's reaction to the disasters that befall him in the wake of the mysterious pilgrim's visit prompt him to become an anonymous pilgrim himself, exchanging clothes with a poor man outside his city in a pathetic scene that is repeated with variations over and over again in the corpus of romance.[44] Whether or not Christina's biographer and his readers had already been sensitized to the figure of the unknown pilgrim by their familiarity with the recurrence of such pilgrims in vernacular narrative is impossible to prove; and the mutual interaction between medieval romance and hagiography is in any case too complex for patterns of influence to be so narrowly defined. But it seems to me reasonable to assume that the St Albans biographer's exploration of the thematic and dramatic possibilities opened up for him by the figure of the *peregrinus ignotus* at least marks a stage in the development of this figure into a narrative stereotype, and possibly explains to some extent how it came to be so suggestive in the first place.

So, to conclude: the individuality that makes the *Life of Christina of Markyate* such an extraordinary text is in the first place an imaginative individuality – an individuality that might reflect, but is in no way equivalent to, the individuality of the woman whose special qualities it is designed to depict. This is not the same as imaginative *originality*, for the raw material of its author's imagination can be identified not just in the iconography of the St Albans Psalter and its text of the *Chanson de St Alexis*, but also in contemporary dramatic and narrative texts more generally. The terms in which her biographer chose to imagine her *Life* seem so little at odds with the more 'realistic aspects' of the narrative only because they are so thoroughly and coherently adapted to his thematic concerns. Even if the pilgrim's role in the *Life* is perhaps one of its more melodramatic, even 'extravagant' elements – and it is certainly intended to evoke wonder – its place in the text is nevertheless secured by the author's provision of a number of different interpretative contexts in which it might be read. The pilgrim's arrival and disappearance is depicted in such a way as to draw on its resonances not just with the Gospel story of Christ at Emmaus and with the story of the unrecognized return and death of St Alexis, but also with secular dramas and romances which increasingly tended to stylize the role of the unidentified pilgrim. Not only do such resonances underline the association of Christina's pilgrim with the heavenly bridegroom whose rights over her the text repeatedly asserts: the text also draws attention to its own symbolic practice so markedly as to make us, as readers, acutely aware that Christina's struggle for independence necessarily also involves a struggle for the very resources of self-definition. From this point of view, the tendency to move generically outwards into the realms of drama and romance should be seen, less as a deliberate transgression of the limits of hagiography, than as a measure of its ambition, exploiting and laying claim to whatever images and ideas it needs for its purposes. At the same time, it frequently points out the mechanisms of its own staging in a such a way as to remind us that it is a fundamentally expressionistic text. It presents itself, in other words, only as an attempt to convey something of Christina's spiritual power, using whatever materials lie at hand in order to do so, but without ever claiming any final impartiality or completeness. It is ironic that such a work that makes so little attempt to conceal either its methods or its sources should so often have been seen as refreshingly and directly 'realistic'.

Notes

1   I am grateful to the Alexander von Humboldt Stiftung, the Seminar für Lateinische Philologie des Mittelalters in the University of Freiburg and University College Dublin for making it possible for me to take research-leave in Freiburg during 2002–3.

2   See, for example, Koopmans, 'The Conclusion', p. 698: 'The incomplete *Vita* therefore provides a glimpse not only into the early career of a medieval woman but also of the complex of forces governing the production of a *Vita* in a twelfth-century religious community.'

3   See, for example, Margaret Hostetler, 'Designing Religious Women: Privacy and Exposure in the *Life of Christina of Markyate* and *Ancrene Wisse*', *Medievalia* 22 (1999) 201–31.

4   Talbot's influence is perceptible in other accounts of the *Life*. Sharon K. Elkins, for example, acknowledges that the text 'blends perception and reality', but still insists that the monk who wrote it was 'intending to be reliable' – an argument both unprovable and circular (*Holy Women*, pp. 27–8). Similarly, Thomas Head points out the possibility of a gap between fact and fiction in Christina's *Life*, but without any hint that identifying it might be difficult: 'I would distinguish between the actions described in the text, which I take to be an accurate reflection of Christina's lived experience, and the description of those actions, whose language provides an entry into the mind of her male hagiographer' (see p. 117).

5   As R. W. Southern put it, 'the miracle was an argument from which there was no appeal'. See Southern, *The Making of the Middle Ages* (London, 1953; rpt. 1993), p. 242.

6   Cf. Hippolyte Delehaye, *Les Légendes Hagiographiques*, 4th edn. (Brussels, 1955), p. 49.

7 See, for example, Erich Auerbach's remarks on Zola's *Germinal* in *Mimesis: dargestellte Wirklichkeit in der abendländischen Literatur*, 10th edn. (Tübingen and Basel, 2001), pp. 472–8.

8 See J. F. Niermeyer and C. Van de Kieft, *Mediae Latinitatis Lexicon Minus*, revised by J. W. J. Burgers, 2 vols. (Leiden and Darmstadt, 2002), *s.v.* 'insigne'.

9 For a classic exposition of typological exegesis, see Ælfric's 'Preface to Genesis', *A Guide to Old English*, ed. Bruce Mitchell and Fred C. Robinson 5th edn. (Oxford, 1992), pp. 190–5.

10 Kristine Haney has recently summarized the evidence for the relationship between Christina and the Psalter. She cautiously emphasizes that the Psalter is a 'composite book': and while she accepts that the quire containing the *Chanson de Saint Alexis*, the extract from St Gregory, the Emmaus illustrations and the picture of David as psalmist may have been designed for Christina, she sees nothing in the pictorial design of the Psalter itself that would have been exclusively of interest to her. See *The St Albans Psalter: An Anglo-Norman Song of Faith* (New York, 2002), pp. 334–9.

11 *La Vie de Saint Alexis*, ed. Maurizio Perugi, Textes littéraires français (Geneva, 2000).

12 Otto Pächt, in Pächt, p. 78: 'As a kind of *imitatio Christi Peregrini* the peregrination of Alexis, the 'homo Dei', associates itself forcibly with the Emmaus story which is meant as its prefiguration. The Emmaus miniatures have to be read as a kind of pictured gloss on Alexis, and by their separate treatment and interpolation immediately after the Alexis song underline the fact that they belong both to the life of Christ and to the Alexis theme.'

13 Cf. Holdsworth, 'Christina of Markyate', p. 192.

14 Cf. Head, Chapter 7, this volume.

15 *The Book of Margery Kempe*, ed. S. B. Meech and H. E Allen, EETS OS 212 (London, 1940), p. 195. Cf. Margery's involvement with the Flight from Egypt, when she helps the Virgin Mary by arranging accommodation for her on her journey ('day by day, purueyng hir herborw', p. 19).

16 Alois Haas, 'Die Sprache der Mystiker', in his *Geistliches Mittelalter* (Fribourg [Switzerland], 1984), pp. 185–91, at p. 185: 'Der Mystiker ist einer, der Gott in besonders intensiver Weise erfahren und kennenlernen darf.'

17 *Le Mystère d'Adam: (Ordo representacionis Ade)*, ed. Paul Aebischer, Textes littéraires français (Geneva and Paris, 1963, rpt. 1964); *Medieval Drama*, ed. David Bevington (Boston, 1975), pp. 78–121.

18 See, for example, Karl Young, *The Drama of the Medieval Church*, 2 vols. (Oxford, 1933; reprint 1962), ii. 212: 'Ad quem [ludum] iste persone sunt necessarie … '. The usage survives into a modern English context in the phrase *dramatis personae*.

19 As Talbot points out, there is an allusion here to Psalm 44:3: 'speciosus forma prae filiis hominum'. The oft-quoted incipit to this Psalm, 'Eructavit cor meum verbum bonum', perhaps implicitly underwrites the motif of Christina's rapture.

20 Young, i. 451.

21 Pächt, pp. 74–5. This formulation could perhaps be reversed: that is, the realism of the Psalter's depictions of the pilgrim is not so much an imitation of dramatic costume as a reflection of the fact that in this respect the drama itself was relatively realistic. As Auerbach puts it (p. 153): 'Das Alltäglich-Realistische ist also ein wesentliches Element der mittelalterlich-christlichen Kunst und besonders des christlichen dramatischen Spiels.'

22 Young, i. 483–4.

23 The strangely banal tone of the *Life*'s account of the pilgrim's disappearance is best illustrated in the disproportionate attention given to the key of the church: 'Mirata virgo ubi sit clavis ianue quasi commota requirit. Ecce ait, cui talis erat cura tradita' (*Life*, p. 188) ('Christina, wondering [at the nuns' failure to find the pilgrim] and seemingly upset, asked where the key was. 'Here it is', said the nun who had charge of it.)

24 Niermeyer, *s.v.* 'schema': 'look, appearance, attire, dress ... especially with reference to religious apparel'; Charles Du Fresne, Sieur Du Cange, *Glossarium Mediae et Infimae Latinitatis* (1883–87: reprint Graz, 1954), *s.v.* 'scema', sense 4, 'induction, repræsentatio'.

25 Young, i. 471.

26 *Carmina Burana: Die Lieder der Benediktbeurer Handschrift: Zweisprachige Ausgabe*, ed. A. Hilka, O. Schumann and B. Bischoff, trans. C. Fisher and H. Kuhn (Munich, 1979), no. 26*, pp. 826–32, at p. 826; Young, i. 463.

27 See Pächt, p. 138.

28 *De libero arbitrio* (*A Discussion of Free Will*), trans. Peter Macardle and Clarence H. Miller, in *Collected Works of Erasmus*, lxxvi, ed. Charles Trinkaus (Toronto, Buffalo and London, 1999), p. 9; see also Johann Huizinga, *Erasmus and the Age of the Reformation*, trans. from the Dutch by F. Hopman (New York, 1957; rpt. Mineola, NY, 2001), p. 164.

29 *Gesta Abbatum*, i. 73.

30 Lawrence M. Clopper chooses to interpret the 'ludus de sancta Katerina – quem "miracula" vulgariter appellamus' as a 'a raucous celebration by choirboys ... that was to have taken place on the eve of the feast of Saint Catherine.' His only support for this assertion is the observation that the *Gesta Abbatum*'s word *miracula* could have pejorative connotations in medieval Latin; which hardly amounts to compelling (or even relevant) evidence in this particular case. See *Drama, Play and Game: English Festive Culture in the Medieval and Early Modern Period* (Chicago and London, 2001), p. 128; also pp. 69–78.

31 *Gesta Abbatum*, i. 82.

32 See my *Medieval Marriage: Literary Approaches 1100–1300* (Cambridge, 1997), pp. 99–106.

33 The dramatic impact of the figure of the pilgrim/exile is undoubtedly reinforced by the fact that pilgrimage/exile is a recurrent image of the human condition in medieval thought. See Gerhard B. Ladner, '*Homo Viator*: Mediaeval Ideas on Alienation and Order,' *Speculum* 42 (1967) 233–59; Charles Dahlberg, *The Literature of Unlikeness* (Hanover and London, 1988); Hans-Henning Kortüm, '*Advena sum apud te et peregrinus*: Fremdheit als Strukturelement mittelalterlicher *conditio humana*,' in *Exil, Fremdheit und Ausgrenzung in Mittelalter und früher Neuzeit*, ed. Andreas Bihrer, Sven Limbeck and Paul Gerhard Schmidt (Würzburg, 2000), pp. 115–35. Even so, it is specifically the effect of the pilgrim/exile as a figure viewed from outside (whether or not the audience already knows his identity) that I want to focus on here, since it is from this perspective that Christina's pilgrim seems to have so much in common with the 'pilgrims' of vernacular romance.

34 *The Romance of Horn, by Thomas*, ed. Mildred K. Pope, 2 vols., ANTS 9–10 (Oxford, 1955), revised and completed T. B. W. Reid, ibid., 12–13 (Oxford, 1964). *Gui de Warewic*, ed. Alfred Ewert, Classiques français du moyen âge, 2 vols. (Paris, 1932–33). All subsequent references to these works are from these editions, cited in the text by line number.

35 *La Folie Tristan d'Oxford*, ed. E. Hoepffner (Paris, 1943). The *Folie Tristan d'Oxford* and the *Roman de Horn* are both translated by Judith Weiss in *The Birth of Romance: An Anthology: Four Twelfth-Century Anglo-Norman Romances* (London, 1992).

36 *Sir Orfeo*, ed. A. J. Bliss, 2nd edn. (1966; rpt. Oxford, 1971). On the evidence for a lost Anglo-Norman lay of Orpheus, see Bliss, pp. xxxi–xxxii; Marie-Thérèse Brouland, *Sir Orfeo: Le Substrat celtique du lai breton anglais* (Paris, 1990), pp. 40–1.

37 See, for example, the *Roman de Horn*, ll. 3,971–82, which mentions among other things the pilgrim's 'esclavine' (hooded cape), 'chauces d'osterin' (leggings), 'burdun' (long staff), 'paulme' (palm) and 'chapel feutrin' (felt hat).

38 On anagnorisis, see Terence Cave, *Recognitions: a study in poetics* (Oxford, 1988).

39 See Morgan Dickson, 'Verbal and Visual Disguise: Society and Identity in Some Twelfth-Century Texts,' in *Medieval Insular Romance: Translation and Innovation*, ed. Judith Weiss, Jennifer Fellows and Morgan Dickson (Cambridge, 2000), pp. 41–54. Dickson also discusses the significance of disguise in the *Gesta Herewardi*, ed. T. D. Hardy and C. T. Martin, in Geoffrey Gaimar, *L'Estoire des Engles*, Rolls Series 91 (London, 1888–89), i. 339–404; partial trans. by Michael Swanton in Stephen Knight and Thomas H. Ohlgren, *Robin Hood and Other Outlaw Tales* (Kalamazoo, 1997), pp. 638–67; and in *Ipomedon*, ed. A. J. Holden (Paris, 1979). On the *Gesta Herewardi*, and other exiled heroes in Latin narrative (Ruodlieb, Waltharius, Apollonius, Harold), see Paul Gerhard Schmidt, 'Der Held im Exil: Ruodlieb und Hereward,' in Bihrer, Limbeck and Schmidt, pp. 233–45.

40 This is illustrated most obviously by Tristan's dog, Husdent, who recognizes his master with a certainty that Isolt herself lacks, as Tristan then reproachfully points out (*Folie Tristan d'Oxford*, ll. 907–42). This motif is also clearly Odyssean.

41 *Life*, p. 40; Cartlidge, *Medieval Marriage*, pp. 106–17, esp. p. 107; and Head, Chapter 7, this volume.

42 As Dickson points out (p. 46), 'she cannot believe that the stranger before her is Horn, yet she faints for love "quant l'ot esgardé" ("when she looked at him", line 4,220).'

43 *Le Roman de Waldef; (Cod. Bodmer 168)*, ed. A. J. Holden, Bibliotheca Bodmeriana: Textes 5 (Cologny-Geneva, 1984). All subsequent references are from this edition, cited by line number. For critical assessment, see Rosalind Field's two essays, '*Waldef* and the Matter of/with England', in *Medieval Insular Romance*, ed. Weiss, Fellows and Dickson, pp. 25–39, and 'The King Over the Water: Exile-and-Return in Insular Tradition', in *Cultural Encounters in the Romance of Medieval England*, ed. Corinne J. Saunders (Cambridge, forthcoming).

44 *Waldef*, ll. 22,061–108. Cf. e.g. *Horn*, l. 3,949; 'Robin Hood and the Beggar I', ed. F. J. Child, *The English and Scottish Popular Ballads*, 5 vols. (Boston, New York and London, 1882–98; rpt New York, 1962), no. 133, iii. 155–8, str. 15.

6

THE LOVES OF CHRISTINA
OF MARKYATE[1]

C. Stephen Jaeger

The twelfth century marks a watershed in the ethics of passion and sexuality in the West. Hellenic, Roman and Christian traditions developed philosophies of love which consigned sexual desire to the lowest level of philosophical and social ideals. For Hellenic and Roman thought on love and friendship, love as a social ideal had its fulfilment in the development of character, virtue and self-control, or, in Platonic philosophy, in addition to its positive social functions, in a cognitive process fuelled by desire and fulfilled in vision of the archetypal forms. The idealism of love presupposed the restraint, the control, in some cases the renunciation of sexuality.[2]

Prior to the twelfth century no strain of Western thought had incorporated the sexual act and sexual passion into an idealism of love. And yet this was precisely the conceptual *tour de force* of twelfth-century thought on the experience of love: to incorporate the act of love itself and the adventures surrounding it into the idealism of love. In a variety of twelfth-century works we find physical passion built into an idealism of love. The chaplain of the French King Louis VII can open his work *De amore* (c. 1185) with the much quoted definition: 'Love is a certain inward suffering [*passio*] … It makes a man desire before all else the embraces of the other sex, and to achieve the utter fulfilment of the commands of love in the other's embrace by their common desire.' And yet only a few pages later he can claim that love gives 'nobility of manners', humility, generosity and chastity (meaning monogamous love). And he exclaims: 'What a remarkable thing is love, for it invests a man with such shining virtues … '[3] While individual voices in Andreas' work give expression to this connection of sexual fulfilment (all the commandments of love) and virtue, the work is notoriously shot through with ironies and contradictions.[4] The apparently full renunciation of 'courtly love' in Book Three of his tract would seem to reverse all that was said in the first two books. And yet the ideas propounded in the sections retracted have documentary value as sentiments in the air that it seemed worth the author's while to formulate, if only to retract and warn against. But the two statements quoted can claim a kind of consistency as words of the author himself, not speeches placed in the mouths of imaginary participants in love dialogues. They imply clearly that there is no contradiction between the virtue-giving force of *amor* and sexual fulfilment. The connection implied between virtue and sexual gratification can at least stand as one sentiment stated strongly in the early part of the work, which seemed worthwhile to Andreas to set up for later rejection.

We find that sentiment in a far less equivocal form in the set of love letters, anonymously transmitted, called *Epistolae duorum amantium*. While there is controversy about their authorship, I take a dating in the early twelfth century and the ascription to Heloise and Abelard as the most probable explanation of their provenance.[5] The letters combine a Ciceronian love-idealism (virtue is the source of genuine love; love aiming at wealth and rank is ignoble) with a frank and passionate sensuality that would either have shocked or amused Cicero, or both.[6] They have this in common with the personal letters of Heloise to Abelard.

Writing some twenty years after the end of their affair, Heloise asserts a love which she calls 'pure' in spite of its sensuality. The judgement of men that sex is wicked when not sanctified by marriage is, she suggests, shallow and false: 'Men call me chaste; they do not know the hypocrite I am. They consider purity of the flesh a virtue, though virtue belongs not to the body but to the soul.'[7] This subversive claim frees the body from moral scrutiny. The soul, not the body, is the locus of innocence and sin. Heloise knows how false the appearance of a respectable life as abbess is and how her inner life violates the values of those who judge her. The same attitude condemned the sins of the flesh she committed with Abelard in her youth. But she knows: her 'fornication' as Abelard's mistress was without sin, while her chastity as abbess is hypocrisy. She has neither regret nor repentance for her earlier love: 'The pleasures of lovers which we shared have been too sweet – they cannot displease me ... '[8] Her bitterness and 'ancient lament against God' are aimed at two events: their marriage and Abelard's castration, not their love affair. Marriage was more sinful than concubinage. God himself signalled his agreement with Heloise:

> While we enjoyed the pleasures of an uneasy love and abandoned ourselves to fornication ... we were spared God's severity. But when we ... atoned for the shame of fornication by an honourable marriage, then the Lord in his anger laid his hand heavily upon us, and would not permit a chaste union though he had long tolerated one which was unchaste.[9]

She clearly imagines that God has his priorities right. Heloise's sentiments sanction a genuine, inward love of the soul for a man, which aims at no material or social gain, at the same time as they reject marriage, the institution made to sanction love. She becomes one of the great heroines of the amatory life, a tragic figure whose love-tragedy exalts her.[10] A romantic pathos develops around this strain of love. The facing of love trials, separation, testing, jealousy, shapes a mechanism of exaltation for lovers. This developing mentality sets noble love above social institutions and legal bonds like marriage or fidelity to feudal lord. Passion becomes a testing ground for nobility of soul.

Samuel Fanous has shown in his contribution to the present volume how indebted the *Life of Christina* is to the traditions of Christian hagiography. The present chapter complements that of Fanous by stressing its unconventional elements. The argument is that the *Life of Christina* is also one of the major statements from the twelfth century of a daring and entirely innovative attitude towards the role of passion in the life of virtue. It makes passionate love into a testing ground of human worth and a means of inculcating virtue. Passion creates and shows forth an elitism of the soul. This study identifies the innovative 'romantic' aspects of the *Life of Christina* and sets them against the background of the love-idealism developing in the course of the twelfth century, both in religious communities and in courtly society.[11] The *Life of Christina* is a defining moment in the historical development of passionate love. Its treatment of erotic desire is unique and problematic within the conventions of hagiography.[12] Christina deserves a place alongside the representative figures of the amatory life in the twelfth century as a transitional figure between the hero of the erotic agon, Robert of Arbrissel, and the heroines of passionate love like Heloise and Isolde.

The story of Christina of Markyate has played a marginal role in discussions of marriage and spiritual friendship in the period.[13] Yet it is particularly rich in what it teaches us about marriage law and practice,[14] spiritual friendship, visions and miracles, and also about sex, rape, desire, love, passion and a woman's psychological response to them. It is still chaste love, but passion and sexual desire, male and female, are the big forces placed in opposition to chaste love, which remains chaste by the skin of its teeth.

The unfinished *Life of Christina* is structured as a series of relationships with men, which rise from rape and seduction to a deep spiritual love. They involve five men. Ranulf, bishop of Durham, tries unsuccessfully to seduce, then to rape her (*Life*, pp. 41–5). A young nobleman named Burthred, egged on by the vengeful bishop, then by Christina's own family, marries her, but never consummates the marriage and after intricate plots and counterplots agrees to an annulment (*Life*, pp. 45–77). She then lives for several years with a hermit, Roger of Markyate, in a secret spiritual love relationship (*Life*, pp. 81–113). After his death she is in the care of a 'certain cleric', a man so powerful in both religious and secular life that the writer cannot divulge his name. He loves her and is loved by her passionately (*Life*, pp. 115–19). Finally she forms a loving friendship with Abbot Geoffrey of St Albans and becomes his spiritual guide and educator (*Life*, pp. 135–93).

The writer's intention was clearly to narrate a series of 'love stories', all in some sense controversial, problematic and troubled, but of rising spiritual value.[15] More than Christina, who remains constant in her vow of virginity and more or less constant in her exclusive espousal to Christ, it is her 'lovers' who illustrate stages of love. But Christina herself has a powerful capacity to experience human passion.[16] The conflict between spiritual and carnal passion is at the core of the work, and her commitment to virginity must maintain itself against a character and psyche strongly oriented to the erotic.[17]

The narrative art of the writer is our point of departure. I have used the word 'romantic' to describe the trend in erotic thinking developing in the twelfth century. It also describes a genre of narrative that originates in that age. We see the romance-making imagination powerfully at work in the *Life of Christina*, especially evident in the staging of some of the scenes. There is for instance the striking episode of Christina and Roger, the hermit of Markyate, 'falling in love' with each other. After long refusing to become her spiritual adviser, Roger is gradually won over by Christina's good reputation, though he still resists seeing and talking to her. But one day they meet by chance:

> It happened in this way. The virgin of God lay prostrate in the old man's chapel, with her face turned to the ground. The man of God stepped over her with his face averted in order not to see her. But as he passed by he looked over his shoulder to see how modestly the hand-maid of Christ had composed herself for prayer ... Yet she, at the same instant, glanced upwards to appraise the bearing and deportment of the old man, for in these she considered that some trace of his great holiness was apparent. And so they saw each other, not by design and yet not by chance.
>
> (*Life*, p. 101)

The half-licit meeting 'kindles a fire' in their spirit, which 'burned in each one of them' and 'cast its sparks into their hearts by the grace of the mutual glance'; it stimulates 'heavenly desire' which creates a new life together in the very close quarters of Roger's hermitage (*Life*, p. 103).

The scene has elements of the beginnings of romantic love: a half-intentional, furtive glance of lovers in some sense meant for each other, is the beginning of a fiery love – but all of it is transferred above human passion into ethereal. The physical posturing, the composition and staging, are remarkable: Christina, supine in prayer, arches her back as the old man steps over her, himself looking back as he does so. In both, the reluctance is visually realized by directing the momentarily ungoverned glance over the shoulder. The double-arching – the man higher, the woman lower – creates both harmonic, symmetrical composition, and tension – the forced posture of the heads. The unnatural physical pose is answered by the moral posturing: the old man's glance seeks only 'to see how modestly the handmaid of Christ had composed herself for prayer', and the maiden's glance intends 'to appraise the bearing and deportment of the old man', in which his holiness is visible. Furtive lovers' glances, the stuff of romantic first meetings, are moralized. The scene is perhaps best described as 'exquisite'; it wants to appear spontaneous, but is obviously artificial, 'thought out' (*exquisitus*), concocted for a narrative and moral effect. The emotions and motivations are good and pure beyond human nature, but the artifice is so evident that 'sublime' overstates it. They are like actors in some Enlightenment drama of virtue. Watteau could have made good use of the composition, with costumes and scenery appropriately changed, to depict a flirtation between some courtly shepherd and a coy shepherdess.

The romance-making imagination is also at work in a scene in which Christina flees her parents' house, where she is virtually held prisoner. They want to force her to have sex with her husband, Burthred, and so legitimize the marriage by consummating it. She has steadfastly refused and prefers to flee than to face further coercion. The escape is the result of careful intriguing and planning on the part of the archbishop of Canterbury, the hermit Edwin, and Edwin's servant, who conspire to rescue Christina and to provide refuge in Roger's hermitage. The servant gets a chance to speak to the closely guarded Christina, and the words he whispers to her are: 'Would that I might have you outside the city' (*Life*, p. 86).[18] Christina 'blushed and was embarrassed' at these words, but not for the obvious reason that they sound like the prelude to a love confession and the invitation to a tryst ('I need to talk to you privately' would have served the practical purpose better), but rather for 'exquisite' reasons: the narrator explains that she blushed because the servant was non-noble and she feared detection. None the less she gives him elaborate instructions for a meeting:

> 'Go and tell your master to prepare two horses, one for me and one for you, at a precise time', and she fixed the day of the week. 'As soon as Aurora appears,[19] wait for me with the horses in that field over there': and she pointed to the spot with her finger. 'I will come to you there … When the horse is ready you will recognize me by this sign. I will place my right hand to my forehead with only the forefinger raised.'
>
> (*Life*, pp. 87–9)

Christina comes on the appointed day at dawn, and strides 'towards the river, carefully scanning the meadow to see if her companion[20] were there' (*Life*, p. 89). No companion, no horses, and Christina must wait out a whole day, hidden in her aunt's house. The secret arrangements are not working. She is anxious, fears detection, and holds a nervous vigil: she 'scanned the meadow'; she waited anxiously 'with her eyes fixed all the time on the meadow beyond the river'; 'scanning the meadow beyond the river once more and not seeing the man she longed for, she turned her steps homeward' (*Life*, pp. 89–91). The next morning she disguises herself as a man and heads for the assigned spot 'swathed in a long cloak that reached to her heels' (*Life*, p. 91), and after a final leave-taking from her sister, she 'turned her steps towards the meadow' (*Life*, p. 93), where at long last she meets her companion with the horses. She puts on 'manly courage' to match her garb, and 'jumping on the horse as if she were a youth and setting spurs to his flanks, she said to the servant: "Follow me at a distance: for I fear that if you ride with me and we are caught, they will kill you."' (*Life*, p. 93).

The scene is swashbuckling and romantic: a furtively arranged meeting, horses at dawn, a secret sign of recognition, a disguise, a dramatic, unexplained delay, an agile leap into the saddle, a desperate race to safety where the 'beloved' waits, life, love and freedom hanging in the balance. This scene also wants a painter from the eighteenth or early nineteenth century to do justice to its romantic staging, and no doubt the long cape streaming out behind the disguised fleeing maiden would provide a good effect.

Besides being swashbuckling and romantic, the scene is also completely superfluous. It adds nothing to the story of Christina's sanctity, miracles and visions, nor of her close relations with Christ. It could have been replaced by a brief, sober report ('Christina escaped her parents with the help of Edwin's servant'). And yet it is one of the longest sustained scenes in the work, taking up five pages in the printed version. It was included as far as I can see because the writer had a conception of Christina's life that he wanted to dramatize. This is not to exclude the possibility that the scene actually happened very much as described, but much of it and of the *Life* in general shows literary modelling, is formulated by a writer with a keen sense of romance, of drama and of narrative staging. Especially striking (besides the formulations discussed in notes 16–18 below) is the dramatic and sentimental framing of anxiety in the landscape, 'her eyes scanned the meadow beyond the river', thrice repeated like a fairy-tale motif.

I have, again, used the term 'romantic' loosely to describe a certain atmosphere of love stories more common in the nineteenth than in the twelfth century. But in the years immediately following the composition of the *Life of Christina*, a new form of narrative, called for the first time *roman*, was in its youth and was highly popular in France, England and Germany. There are elements in the *Life of Christina* that bear comparison with 'Romance' in the stricter sense. For instance, the motif of trickery and cunning. Christina escapes the wooing of Bishop Ranulf of Durham by a clever ruse. The lascivious bishop has trapped her in his bedchamber and will not take no for an answer. Christina faces an intricate dilemma, like Lancelot compelled against his will to sleep with the *damsel avenant*,[21] like Sir Gawain beset by Lady Bertilak; and like Lancelot and Gawain, Christina reacts with a series of questions that have the character of a narrated inner monologue:

> What was the poor girl to do in such straits? Should she call her parents? They had already gone to bed. To consent was out of the question: but openly resist she dared not because if she openly resisted him, she would certainly be overcome by force.
>
> (*Life*, p. 43)

She quickly conceives a ruse. Seeing that the door is not bolted, she asks permission to bolt it, pretending to give in to him: 'we should take precautions that no man should catch us in this act' (*Life*, p. 43). He agrees, after receiving an oath that she will not deceive him. She flees, bolts the door from outside, and runs home, leaving the bishop to seethe in revenge plots. The girl is 'prudent' and the seducer 'deceived' (*illusus*).

Deceit becomes a standard weapon in the defence of her virginity. The escape from her parents' house with horses at dawn is the culmination of her counterplots, and the scene ends a series of ruses in which she matches wits with her persecutors to protect her vow and her virginal 'marriage' to Christ. Of course, Christina is aided also by moral will and divine help, but clearly the narrator structured the early episodes of the defence of her vow against seduction and marriage as a series of plots and counterplots, of clever deceptions thwarted by yet more clever ones.[22]

The scenes bear comparison with the romance of Tristan and Isolde, where the episodes after the onset of love involve holding the husband at bay through clever deceptions and thwarting attempts at exposing the love affair by cunning. As in the Tristan romance, the issue is not whether or not to marry – she marries Burthred – but how to maintain a higher obligation to love in spite of the forces opposing it, among them marriage.

Christina is also aided throughout by her true lover and spouse, Christ, and this division of life into spiritual, exalting love and degrading physical/social attachment is one of the basic tensions the *Life* shares with the Tristan romance. Marriage, the husband, the parents and their helpers are powerfully in conflict with the wishes of the protagonist, which take on in the eyes of the antagonists the aspect of secret and forbidden alliances. The private and personal attachment to Christ is set above the worldly plans and ambitions of the family, and so the story divides into a corporal and a spiritual level of amatory and erotic attachment. Both the *Life* and the Tristan romance have in common the subordinating of the marriage tie to higher spiritual obligations. In both, the 'lover' or lovers are aided by Christ in thwarting the claims of the worldly attachment. And in both there is a radical reversal of the values of public and private. Christina's public relations – with her family, husband, with various advisers, bishops and archbishops – are negative, inimical to her spiritual vow. The legal rights of parents and marriage are invoked against the heroine with accurate use of contemporary legal practice.[23] But marriage, the law, the arrangements that structure civil society, are relegated to a lower order of experience; their representatives are dubious, immoral, their claim to legitimacy so undermined that Christina has licence to deceive – by way of protecting her higher, spiritual obligations. Again, the similarity to the Tristan romance is evident. Christina is admirable for the false oath she swears to Bishop Ranulf that she will return and slake his lust, as is Isolde in the false oaths made to her husband, King Mark.

Christina's true 'loves' all have the character of private, personal, individual arrangements made in secret, maintained secretly (except Geoffrey), and all of them are threatened by the evil tongues who want to force the private realm into public scrutiny and paint it in the worst light. The 'lovers' are beset by envious detractors eager to blame, discredit and bring disgrace upon the protagonists – a motif common in courtly romance but unusual in saints' lives. From the very outset the men who love Christina spiritually are accused by unnamed malicious persons of carnal motives. The first thing we learn about her early spiritual adviser, the cleric Sueno, is that he is accused of vile sexual practices. 'Someone' claims that he 'was still so stimulated by lust that unless he were prevented by the greater power of God he would without any shame lie with any ugly and mis-shapen leper' (*Life*, p. 39). And so it goes throughout. The narrative is infected with the fear of shame and the threat of disgrace.[24]

This is an atmosphere different from that of any conventional female saint's life prior to the twelfth century. Of course, the early Christian female saint and martyr faces temptations and the sexual advances of Roman wooers, but she wards them off valiantly; the innocence of the Christian life remains inviolable. But Christina's tempters are participants in the Christian life and, with the exception of her husband, Burthred, its institutional representatives. In the *Life of Christina* the narrator's consciousness is unusually tuned to sexual disgrace. He senses that Christina's mode of feeling and loving, and that which she inspires in men, is highly open to misunderstanding and attack; otherwise it would not need such justification. But most striking is that Christina herself is infected with doubt of her own innocence. This becomes clear when she must examine her own conscience before her monastic profession, and she finds it not clear:

> Inwardly she was much troubled, not knowing what she should do, nor what she should say, when the bishop inquired during the ceremony of consecration about her virginity. For she was mindful of the thoughts and stings of the flesh with which she had been troubled, and even though she was not conscious of having fallen either in deed or in desire, she was chary of asserting that she had escaped unscathed.
>
> (*Life*, p. 127)

It would take some intricate defining to eliminate her nearly ungovernable desire for the unnamed cleric from the category 'fallen in desire'. While the hagiographer always has the trump card of Christ, the judge of innocence, he does not play it. He allows the uncertainty to hover over a life troubled by inner and outer accusations of sexual fault – and only in the end rescues her sanctity. The narrative consciousness of the *Life* has passed beyond the threshold of inno-cence which hedged earlier saints' lives. The narrative suggests – wants to suggest – that the awareness of sensuality and the successful facing of malice and misunderstanding in spiritual love are part of the pattern of sanctity.

In the centre of the work and central to the theme of passionate desire is the episode of the mutual love of Christina and the unnamed wealthy and powerful cleric. After the death of Roger, she is placed in the charge of this man, and at first the love they feel for each other is strictly 'chaste and spiritual' (*castum et spiritualem amorem*; *Life*, p. 114). But then the man's resistance is overwhelmed by the devil, who attacks him with 'fiery darts'. Christina herself is assailed with 'incitements to pleasure' and with 'impure thoughts', but resists for the time being. 'Insane with desire', he even appeared before her naked and 'behaved in so scandalous a manner that I cannot make it known, lest I pollute the wax by writing it' (*Life*, p. 115). Christina's reproaches and admonishments can recall him temporarily to his senses. But even while she does so, she conceals the same fierce desire that is tearing at her:

> ... though she herself was struggling with this wretched passion [*incendio miserabili*], she wisely pretended that she was untouched by it ... She used to be so inwardly inflamed that she thought the clothes which clung to her body might be set on fire. Had this occurred while she was in his presence, the maiden might well have been unable to control herself.
>
> (*Life*, pp. 115–17)

She can control the 'desires of her flesh' only by extraordinary asceticism, fasting, waking, scourging and 'trials which tore and tamed her lascivious body' (*Life*, p. 115). She falls seriously ill after receiving a vision of her lover as a monstrous bear blocking her way into the monastery. The man himself is cooled by a warning visitation from three saints, John the evangelist, Benedict, the founder of his order, and Mary Magdalen. Their threats and warnings prevail over his passion, and he is cured. But Christina herself is still tortured and nothing could cool the 'fever' (*estus*) of her longing. Finally she retreats to the wilderness, where, still lashed by desire, she receives an 'unheard of act of grace' which frees her from this torment. Christ himself came to her in the guise of a small child. He was taken into the arms of his 'sorely tried spouse' who for an entire day not only saw but also felt his presence. The redeeming moment and the rise to a higher stage of loving comes in an ecstatic embrace of Christina and Christ:

> So the maiden ... pressed him to her bosom. And with immeasurable delight she held him at one moment to her virginal breast, at another she felt his presence within her even through the barrier of her flesh. Who shall describe the abounding sweetness with which the servant was filled by this condescension of her creator? From that moment on the fire of lust [*libidinis ardor*] was so completely extinguished that never afterwards could it be revived.
>
> (*Life*, p. 119)

We should be slow to pass over the ambiguities of the scene by reducing it to an unequivocal meaning: the experience is not distinct but layered. On the surface certainly it is the experience of maternity: she cradles the Christ child in her arms and at her breast for a full day, but the narrator's formulation carefully divides it, twice, into two experiences: once, the maternal embrace (*nunc ... tenebat ... in suo sinu*), and a second time, Christ's presence inside her (*nunc intra se ... apprehendebat intuitu*). That is the one division into a two-fold experience. The other divides the internal sensation into two: 1) she felt Christ inside herself (*intra se*); and 2) she felt him 'nay rather' through the barrier of the flesh (*immo per ipsam cratam pectoris*).[25] This second distinction is only necessary if the writer wants to stress penetration: not only was Christ there, but also he passed through her very flesh to get there. I would suggest that this division refers to two stages, the two highpoints, of female sexual experience: intercourse and child bearing; bearing the child (*intra se*) and receiving its presence (*per ipsam cratam* ...). The emotional response is ecstatic: 'immeasurable delight' and 'abounding sweetness'.

The effect of this act of grace is that she is cured of her lust for the cleric. Christ's presence in her body provides the cleansing flame,[26] and Christina's bliss responds to both the spiritual and the physical presence of divinity, and the physical is stressed (*non modo sensibilis, sed eciam visibilis*). But did the cure of carnality need to be so carnal? Christina's consoler would seem to be fighting physical fire with spiritual – which, however, is experienced as physical, the feeling of Christ, man and child, bridegroom and foetus, within her body. The writer clearly had a purpose in extinguishing his heroine's physical passion by a higher ecstasy also experienced as physical. The idea is not to reject passion and intercourse, but to posit a passion so deeply, inwardly and ultimately satisfying that it ends the demon-inspired, earthly kind.

This strange drama of passion exorcised by passion is a pure example of the fundamental paradox and mystery of passionate love affirmed: the sexual is incorporated into a higher, purer kind of love by the deifying of human desires. One may wonder whether this 'solution' is anything other than mystification and conceptual sleight of hand, whether there is any psychology of the overcoming of tormenting desire through spiritual–carnal ecstasy. Garden-variety ascetic discipline is real, empirically realizable, and effective in the economy of self-control. But Christina's sexual experience to end all sexual experiences is a confection of a romantic imagination that solves real human problems by ecstasies beyond human experience. But whether the 'cure' envisioned in the *Life* is practically realizable or not, it involves a radical upgrading of sexual experience, its translation into the spiritual.[27]

The mutual love of Christina and Abbot Geoffrey is the highpoint of the narrative, as received (it breaks off while describing their relations). But to understand its place in the structure of the narrative, it is important to see the development which preceded it. The quality of love relations rises in a steady curve throughout the narrative. The rises mark stages in a process of spiritual development, a process of education if you will. Christina has a series of spiritual mentors, beginning with her early friend Sueno, who encourages her vow of virginity and instructs her in the virtues and trials it will bring her (*Life*, p. 37).

Her relations with the hermit Roger are characterized by mutual love and mutual instruction and guidance, and the two (love and instruction) go together: 'Through their dwelling together and encouraging each other to strive after higher things their holy affection grew day by day ... And so their great progress induced them to dwell together' (*Life*, p. 103). The teaching is not one-sided, but mutual, as is the love.

It is different with Geoffrey of St Albans. Christina is his spiritual mentor. He is a 'noble and powerful person', 'a man of great spirit' (*magnanimus*, *Life*, pp. 134–5). But no sooner does he appear on the scene, than his judgment as abbot is called in question. Christina receives a vision admonishing her to correct a plan that the abbot is considering – before he has confided it to anyone. With the help of supernatural visitations, Christina bends his arrogance and persuades him to abandon his 'evil course' (we never find out what it was). And from this time on, Geoffrey 'heard her admonitions, accepted her advice, consulted her in doubts, avoided evil, bore her reproaches' (*Life*, p. 139). Seeing him so improved and now 'bent on doing good', Christina 'cherished him with great affection and loved him with a wonderful but pure love' ('multo eum excoluit affectu. miroque sed sincero dilexit amore', *Life*, pp. 138–9). This marks the course of their love: Christina is the warden of his behaviour. She 'reproves him harshly' when he has sinned (*Life*, p. 141). She cures him when sick and wards off dangers and temptations. She prays for him when she sees 'that he was making every effort to become more spiritual' (' ... ad superna eum toto senciebat tendere conatu', *Life*, pp. 142–5). A major thread of the narrative until the end is the spiritual development of Geoffrey with Christina's guidance. 'She strove to enrich [Geoffrey] in virtue' ('Desudat illa virum accumulare virtutibus') (*Life*, pp. 154–5).

The narrator framed one incident of spiritual correction in another peculiar and completely unconventional drama. Abbot Geoffrey is called to Rome. Having determined that he must make the arduous trip, which he resisted and which Christina disapproves of, he comes to his spiritual guide and requests two undergarments (*interulas*), 'not for pleasure', the biographer assures us, 'but to mitigate the hardship' of the journey. Christina hesitated and finally deflected the request by giving the desired garments to the poor when this line of response was approved by a voice from heaven, which evidently did not consider the issue beneath its dignity (*Life*, pp. 160–3). Again, we have an incident which is designed to show Geoffrey's limited judgement and his need for guidance from Christina. But the incident poses intricate problems of interpretation. The passage leaves open the question, 'whose undergarments?' They may have been clothing that Christina made, as she made other garments (see the contribution of Jane Geddes, Chapter 12 this volume), that is, new and available for anyone's use. Or they may have been Christina's own *interulae*, already worn and dearer to Geoffrey for their intimate contact with Christina's body. Two considerations argue for the more sober reading: first, a common-sensical reluctance to entertain the stranger of the two readings, which may make the scene appear like some sort of fetishism on Geoffrey's part; and, second, the formulation of the heavenly voice, ' ... interulas, quas ad laboris sui levamen preparasti ... ' (*Life*, p. 160), ' ... the undergarments which you have prepared to lighten his suffering ... [my translation]' Christina has made, or at least 'prepared', the garments. Nothing indicates directly that she has worn them. (But also nothing indicates that she has not.)

But other considerations argue for the more problematic reading. First, Geoffrey assures Christina that he makes this request, *non ad voluptatem sed ad laboris relevandum sudorem*. Talbot translates: 'not for pleasure', though 'pleasure' does not quite convey the voluptuarial quality which is dominant in *voluptas*. A sober request for new undergarments would not seem to require such a qualification. Second, the fuss made over the request does seem excessive if we are to accept the sober reading. A clearly embarrassed Geoffrey is himself uncertain about his petition. He excuses himself (*non ad voluptatem*) and asks Christina to consult God's will on the matter. Christina does. Her prayers, which continue day and night, are finally answered with the heavenly voice assuring Christina that Geoffrey is well enough protected by Christ's care, and she should give the garments to the poor. So much is at stake in the issue that it takes heavenly guidance to resolve it. Third, the highly emotional charge placed on the request: Christina prays for guidance 'with her countenance bathed in tears, her heart torn by sighs'. Upon receiving the angelic advice, 'she turned her tears into joy ... ' (*Life*, p. 163). However we choose to clarify the ambiguity of the passage, I think we must see the two undergarments as love tokens. That would explain the emotional charge, the embarrassment of both parties, and the heavenly refusal. It also situates Geoffrey's reaction to his own request (*non ad voluptatem*) as a parallel to the other frequent assurances in the *Life* that what might look sexual and dubious to unspiritual observers is a higher form of spiritual devotion.

I believe we come closest to understanding the implications of this obscure episode if we see Christina's *interulae* as a parallel to contact relics. There is an illuminating incident in the *Life of Saint Wilfrid*, a seventh century bishop of Northumbria, by Eadmer of Canterbury (d. 1124), friend, advisor and biographer of Anselm of Canterbury. Wilfrid arranges for the distribution of his clothes after his death. A priest is entrusted with Wilfrid's undergarment (*interula*) which was to be given to an unnamed abbess. The garment 'drips with the sweat of his most sacred body'. A certain woman, racked with paralysis, asks insistently to be permitted to touch the garment. She is found unworthy, however, but the undergarment is dipped in water; she drinks the water, and is cured.[28] So here an undergarment is charged with miraculous powers because it has touched the body of the saint and become saturated with his sweat. It is the closeness to 'the most holy body', its absorption of his very bodily exhalations, that gives it healing power. I suspect that we are on firm ground in seeing the episode in Christina's life as a parallel. (The proximity of the *Vita Wilfridi* in time and cultural orbit to Christina's *Life* suggests there may even have been a recognizable resonance between the two episodes.) If she had not herself worn the garments, then their power to comfort would be far less. The warding off of low suspicions (*non ad voluptatem*) is necessary here as so often in the *vita*, because the love of Geoffrey for Christina is expressed in an intimate love-token. It may offer a parallel also to less spiritual love tokens like the standard belt and ring of courtly romance, or the *girdel* of Lady Bertilak in *Sir Gawain*.

If we are correct in seeing in the undergarments a merging of a contact relic with a love-token, then the incident underscores once again the role of the erotic in the drama of Christina's life. The talismanic garment could not have been a sleeve or scarf. Its 'comforting' force grew greater the more intimate it was, the closer it had touched Christina's body. We might take Geoffrey's request as a form of love folly. That at least would explain why its sub-burlesque character is treated with such high moral seriousness by both Christina and whatever heavenly voice responded to her prayers. There is a dawning sense implied in this incident that abasement in love brings exaltation to those who suffer it, as it did to Lancelot and to Gawain.

In fear of another impending journey, Christina prays so intensely for Geoffrey's safety that she has an ecstatic vision. She stands before Christ, embracing Geoffrey: 'she saw him, whom she loved above all others, encircled with her arms and held closely to her breast' (*Life*, p. 169). Later she receives word from heaven that Geoffrey will be 'enlightened with eternal light', as she had prayed, and this brings her 'to examine more closely in the depths of her heart whether anyone can love another more than herself' (*Life*, p. 181).

The high point of the scenes of intensifying devotion is a kind of spiritual love-death, at least the positing of it, and this is also perhaps the high point, at least the point of highest moral drama, of the *Life*. God himself asks Christina if she would like Geoffrey to die for his sake. Her answer: yes, she would; in fact she would be more than willing to do the deed herself. Her love for Geoffrey is more spiritual than Abraham's for Isaac, she argues, therefore she can 'sacrifice' her friend in the name of higher love: 'the kind of love that binds me to him, Thou alone understandest. For what death is more glorious than that which is accepted out of love for the Creator?' (*Life*, p. 181). The episode is perplexing and mysterious, but it seems as if the writer wanted to represent an extravagant act of spiritual love, a much more serious kind of *amor fol* or a spiritual *liebestod* inflicted on the lover by the beloved, once the highest level of loving is attained: fulfilment of love in death, death inflicted by the one who loves most. There is a peculiar play on the love great enough to lay down your life for a friend. Possibly the scene suggests there is after all one love greater: the willingness to take the life of the beloved for the sake of his redemption.

The structuring idea of Christina's friendship with Geoffrey is that the love reaches ever higher stages, consistent with the abbot's rise in spirituality through Christina's efforts to improve him. It is rich in reverberations with courtly love themes. The reward of love is given in accordance with the man's improvement. The woman becomes the moral force which 'educates' him and assures him of God's favour.

The *Life of Christina* is a kind of summa of erotic–spiritual love; it might be justly called *scala amoris* or *de gradibus amoris*. It shows the rise from earthly to spiritual, a progression from the lowest to the highest forms of loving. Each love relationship has the character of a *speculum* of a certain kind of love. Like Bernard's *Steps of*

Pride and Humility it begins with negative examples and ends with positive. The lovers move from carnality (Bishop Ranulf) to utility (Burthred), to two stages in the conquest of the body (Roger, fierce asceticism; the unnamed cleric, sensual overcome by spiritual desire), to a purely spiritual love based on moral improvement (Geoffrey). Seen in terms of its narrative structure, the really hard question the *Life* poses is, what idea justified the placement of the unnamed cleric so high in this hierarchy of loving? The episode represents a love so sensual that the desire-torn woman fears her clothes will catch fire, a hunger so intense that only the experience of Christ pressed 'to her bosom' and the 'immeasurable delight' of 'feeling his presence within her or rather through the barrier of the flesh' can quench it (*Life*, p. 119). This love experience finds its place in the narrative sequence between Roger, the ascetic hermit, and Geoffrey, the abbot. Important is the transitional moment, the rise from earthly to heavenly love. It is mediated still by the body, whose experience of desire and fulfilment provides the dynamics of rise. It is an extraordinarily bold affirmation of human erotic experience, at least as bold as Bernard's eroticizing the relations of the soul to Christ in his reading of the *Song of Songs*. It anticipates the moment in the *Divine Comedy* when Dante's earthly beloved Beatrice guides him from Purgatory into Paradise. But the comparison only shows how much more powerful the erotic side of love was for the English recluse-saint than for the Florentine poet.

Notes

An earlier version of this chapter was published as C. Stephen Jaeger, 'The Loves of Christina of Markyate', in *Ennobling Love: In Search of a Lost Sensibility* (Philadelphia, 1999), pp. 174–83.

1   The chapter title is both indebted to and set against Thomas Head's useful article, 'The Marriages of Christina of Markyate', now revised for this volume, which did not pose 'the marriages' as the thematic dominant, so much as just an important theme. Answering with 'the loves' is not meant polemically, though I see love as a structuring element of the *Life* much more than marriage.

2   See Michel Foucault, *The History of Sexuality*, esp. vols. 2 and 3 (New York, 1988–90); Peter Brown, *The Body and Society: Men, Women and Sexual Renunciation in Early Christianity* (New York, 1988); Dyan Elliott, *Spiritual Marriage: Sexual Abstinence in Medieval Wedlock* (Princeton, 1993); Jaeger, *Ennobling Love.*

3   *Andreas Capellanus on Love*, ed. and trans. P. G. Walsh (London, 1982), p. 33 (*De amore*, Bk. 1, ch. 1) and p. 39 (Bk. 1, ch. 4).

4   See esp. Alfred Karnein, *De amore in volkssprachlicher Literatur: Untersuchungen zur Andreas-Capellanus Rezeption in Mittelalter und Renaissance* (Heidelberg, 1985), and his various studies of Andreas in the collection of his essays, *Amor est Passio: Untersuchungen zum nicht-höfischen Liebesdiskurs im Mittelalter*, ed. Friedrich Wolfzettel (Trieste, 1997). This collection of studies is of extraordinary importance but has not received the attention due to it.

5   Ewald Könsgen, *Epistolae duorum amantium: Briefe Abaelards und Heloises?* (Leiden, 1976). The study by Constant J. Mews, *The Lost Love Letters of Abelard and Heloise* (New York, 1999), offers a case for the authorship of Heloise and Abelard which is strong but not conclusive. My treatment of the letters in *Ennobling Love* (pp. 160–4) is based on a pre-

critical acceptance of Mews's claims, which I now regret. Peter von Moos analyses the letters within the traditions of medieval love letters and suggests a product of the four-teenth century with influence of humanism and *dolce stil nuovo*: 'Die *Epistolae duorum amantium* und die säkulare Religion der Liebe: Methodenkritische Vorüberlegungen zu einem einmaligen Werk mittellateinischer Briefliteratur', *Studi Medievali* 3rd ser., 44 (2003), 1–115. Von Moos's hypothetical siting of the letters in the fourteenth century is highly improbable. His conviction that the ascription to Heloise and Abelard can be easily overturned has not proven justified. An article I wrote in 2000 is currently languishing at Notre Dame University Press, due to appear in autumn 2004: 'The *Epistolae duorum amantium* and the Ascription to Heloise and Abelard,' *Voices in Dialogue: New Problems in Reading Women's Cultural History*, ed. Linda Olson and Katherine Kerby-Fulton. It strengthens the arguments for the authorship of Heloise and Abelard.

6 See Jaeger, *Ennobling Love*, pp. 160–4.

7 *The Letters of Abelard and Heloise*, trans. Betty Radice, rev. M. T. Clanchy (London, 2003), p. 69.

8 Ibid., p. 68.

9 Ibid., pp. 65–6.

10 See the study by Peter Dronke, *Abelard and Heloise in Medieval Testimonies* (Glasgow, 1976).

11 I would exclude from these parallel areas what has been called the 'Ovidian subcul-ture' of the twelfth century. The frank sensuality of the Paris student milieu and of many of the love poems of the *Carmina Burana* tends to have an atmosphere of ribaldry quite remote from the moral seriousness of Heloise's letters or the romance of Tristan and Isold.

12 See Renna, 'Virginity'; also Barbara Newman, 'La mystique courtoise: Thirteenth-Century Beguines and the Art of Love', ch. 5 of her *From Virile Woman to Woman Christ: Studies in Medieval Religion and Literature* (Philadelphia, 1995), 137–67.

13 See Raymond J. Cormier, *One Heart, One Mind: The Rebirth of Virgil's Hero in Medieval French Romance* (University, Miss., 1972), introduction, pp. 71–5 on Christina. I have also learned much from the article by Ruth Mazzo Karras, 'Friendship and Love in the Lives of two Twelfth-Century Saints', *Journal of Medieval History* 14 (1988), 305–20. Robert Hanning's reading of the *Life* is still interesting for the topic of indi-viduality: *The Individual in Twelfth-Century Romance* (New Haven, 1977). Also analysing Christina's marriages: Carol Symes, *Aspects of Marriage and Sexuality in the Miracle Literature of Twelfth-Century England* (M. Litt. Thesis, Oxford University, 1990); and Christopher N. L. Brooke, *The Medieval Idea of Marriage* (Oxford, 1989).

14 Holdsworth, 'Christina of Markyate'.

15 See Thomas Renna, 'Virginity in the *Life* of Christina of Markyate and Aelred of Rievaulx's Rule', *American Benedictine Review* 36 (1985), 79–92. He also sees a progres-sion in the male figures (p. 87).

16 Karras's commentary, 'Friendship and Love', pp. 315–17, is especially insightful on this point.

17 See Renna, 'Virginity in the *Life* of Christina'.

18 'Utinam tenuissem te extra civitatem.' Talbot weakens the formulation in his transla-tion: 'I wish I could have you with me outside the town.' There is tremulous anxiety in the past perfect of the subjunctive (*tenuissem*), not renderable in English: that I 'might have had' you. It implies, 'I know what an impossible request this is.' Also, why *tenere* instead of the sober and unambiguous *loqui*? The writer wanted to imply a lover's whispered hopes, not a servant's directions.

19 Talbot translates, 'When dawn is breaking'. The writer's *Apparente aurora* (*Life*, p. 86) is poetic language, however. The biographer wants allure in his formulations, at least in this episode. *Prima luce* would have been the more literal formulation.

20 Talbot renders *sodalis* as 'accomplice', though this word, too, participates in the ambiguity of the scene, meaning both 'conspirator' and 'companion'.

21 Chrétien, *Le Chevalier de la charette*, ed. Mario Roques (Paris, 1952), ll. 941ff.

22 Her parents try to weaken her resolve with worldly allurements, but she matches them wit for wit, 'deceiving their cunning' [*illorum delusa calliditas*], and heightening her 'invincible prudence' (p. 49); they encourage her to drink wine, but she resists, and thus 'her parents had been outwitted in this' [*in hoc illusi*] (pp. 50–1); they send Christina's husband into her room at night to consummate the marriage by force if necessary, and she talks him into a chaste marriage, which the parents regard as just another of 'her deceitful tricks' [*ambagibus fallentis*] (pp. 50–1). Repeatedly, the parents' efforts to have the marriage consummated take the structure of plot and counterplot; they lay *insidias* and *laqueos* (p. 54), which Christina foresees, thwarts, eludes, repeatedly showing herself 'intelligent, prudent in affairs, efficient in carrying out her plans' [*acumen in sensu ... providencia in gerendis ... efficacia in deliberatis*] (pp. 67–8). The parents plot secretly in *clandestina conventicula*, and Christina calculates 'how she could counter any plots they might make against her' (pp. 68–9). The series of plots and counterplots ends when the husband, Burthred, again finding himself 'deceived' – *homo delusus abscessit* (p. 94) – finally vows to give up such attempts and ultimately allows the annulment of the marriage.

23 This is the insight of Symes, *Aspects of Marriage and Sexuality*, pp. 44–57, and Head, 'The Marriages'; see also Brooke, *The Medieval Idea of Marriage*.

24 Christina and Roger conceal the fact that they are living together, 'for they feared scandal to their inferiors and the fury of those who were persecuting the handmaid of Christ' (*Life*, p. 103). Late in the story the devil is so frustrated by Christina's virtue that he plots to break her steadfastness by creating false rumours and spreading abroad unheard-of and incredible slanders through the bitter tongues of his agents (*Life*, p. 131). She is accused of 'every imaginable evil' but her faith keeps her safe from the 'malice' of 'perverse minds'. Also in her love for Abbot Geoffrey she is persecuted 'with gossip, poisonous detractions, barbed words'. Some of her detractors 'spread the rumour that she was attracted to the abbot by earthly love' (*Life*, p. 173).

25 Talbot renders *immo* as 'even'. But it has adversitive force: *per ipsam cratam* is not an intensification of *intra se* ('even through the barrier'), but rather a separate level of the experience: 'nay rather, through the very gridwork of the breast'. Talbot gives *cratam*, but I can't find *crata* as a first declension noun and would expect *cratem*, from *cratis*, third declension.

26 See Karras's reading of the scene, 'Friendship and Love', pp. 315–16.

27 Anyone sceptical of this reading of Christina's cured sensuality need only compare it to the far more extravagant examples of Christ experienced sensually in contemporary and later mysticism. Rupert of Deutz receives understanding of the Gospel of Matthew by a kiss of Christ which pleases Christ so much that He opens his mouth *ut profundius oscularer* (Comm. in Matth., Bk. 12, 741–62; ed. Haacke, CCCM 29, pp. 382–3 (*PL* 168, 1601). Agnes Blannbekin, the Viennese beguine, is famous for a vision in which she witnesses the circumcision of the baby Jesus, then is given the foreskin, which she eats (as if it were a host) and has a rapturous experience (*Agnes Blannbekin, Viennese Beguine: Life and Revelations*, trans. Ulrike Wiethaus (Woodbridge, 2002)). Cf. Hadewijch (Vision 7), Mechthild of Magdeburg ('Das *Fliessende Licht der Gottheit*, ed. Hans Neumann and Gisela Vollmann-Prose (Munich, 1990), I.44), Angela of Foligno (*Il Libro della Beata Angela da Foligno*, ed. Thier Ludger and Abele Calufetti (Rome, 1985), ch. 7c), Catherine of Siena, and Margery Kempe *(Book of Margery Kempe*, ed. S. B. Meech and H. E. Allen, EETS OS 212 (1940), chs. 35–6). Already in Jerome, letter 384 to Eustochium, *de virginitate servanda* featured a curiously explicit passage in which a cento of the *Song of Songs* describes the virgin's relations with Christ: 'Let the secrecy of your bedchamber always guard you and let the Bridegroom always sport

with you within…. When sleep oppresses you, He will come behind the wall and put his hand through the hole and will touch your belly (*venter*), and, all aquiver (*tremefacta*) you will rise and say, "I am wounded with love".'

28 *Vita Sancti Wilfridi Auctore Edmero – The Life of Saint Wilfrid by Edmer: An Edition with Translation, Historical Introduction and Commentary*, ed. Bernard J. Muir and Andrew J. Turner (Exeter, 1998), pp. 138–9 (ch. 59, para. 111): 'Unde interulam eius sanctissimi corporis sudore sepe madentem cuidam religiose abbatisse deferendam minister accepit, quam mulier quedam paralysi dissoluta, ut tangere mereretur, obnixe rogavit. Sed hec quidem ipsam vestem tangere non meruit, verum aquam, ubi eadem vestis intincta fuit, in potum accepit, ilicoque sanata est' (*PL* 159, col. 749 (ch. 62)).

7

THE MARRIAGES OF
CHRISTINA OF MARKYATE

Thomas Head

Medieval Christians often described their religious experience with startling immediacy. This remains one of the most striking – even disturbing – aspects of their
religion for a modern audience. In many cases, of course, the language used to
register the tangible presence of the holy in the everyday environment was
repeated by author after author. Take, for example, the phrase *sponsa* or *sponsus
Christi*. Beginning in the literature of late antiquity, writers referred to monks, nuns,
hermits and anchoresses as brides of Christ with such frequency that the expression now seems almost hackneyed. Such images are quite rightly treated as *topoi* by
scholars. Focusing solely on the stock character of these images, however, suggests
that they had a literary life of their own almost unconnected to the lives of real
people. It obscures the light such imagery can throw on the rich texture of the
lived experience of medieval Christians. For being a 'bride of Christ' was not *like*
marriage to Christ, it *was* marriage to Christ. In this essay I wish to explore the
marital relationship as it existed between a twelfth-century woman, known to us as
Christina of Markyate, and her saviour. By doing so I hope not only to illuminate
her life and the text which records it, but to suggest something about the function
of medieval religious imagery and its relationship to a social context.

Sometime in the 1160s, a monk of St Albans composed an account of the life
of this woman with whom he had been personally acquainted. Born into a
family of the Anglo-Saxon elite during the early years of the century and chris-
tened Theodora, she had decided at a young age to dedicate herself to the
religious life and so had vowed herself to virginity. Her parents, however, had
determined that she should be married to a man from their district named
Burthred. Their attempts to force their daughter into such a socially suitable
match proved unsuccessful. Theodora eventually escaped the control of both her
family and her putative secular spouse through a campaign which involved both
court actions and outright deception. Thereafter she lived as a religious recluse,
that is as a *sponsa Christi* in the language of the hagiographer. She spent time at
several hermitages, first in the vicinity of her hometown of Huntingdon and
then near the Abbey of St Albans. There, at the insistence of Abbot Geoffrey,
she was formally consecrated as a virgin in a ceremony which was compared to a
wedding. Still later, the abbot appointed the former anchoress – now known as

Christina, a name which reflected her intimate personal relationship with her true spouse – to be prioress of a newly founded convent at Markyate.

Over the course of her struggles to avoid a secular marriage and enter instead into a spiritual one, this young Anglo-Saxon woman had exhibited a virtuoso ability to use and to transform the traditional symbols and rituals both of marriage and of the religious life. She conceived of her marriage to Christ, and thus her religious vocation, in extraordinarily concrete terms. Being the bride of Christ was not a metaphorical expression of her spiritual intimacy with her saviour, rather it was a contractual relationship involving mutual privileges and obligations which bound her to him, and him to her.

To speak of Christina's own experience and conceptions is to raise one of the vexed problems presented by any hagiographic source, namely the relationship between the text and the lived experience of its subject. In discussing this work Ruth Mazo Karras has been careful to note that 'When this paper speaks of "Christina," then, it means Christina as a subject of the *vita*, rather than Christina the historical individual.'[1] Certainly the language of the *Life of Christina of Markyate* is that of the monk of St Albans. It tells us little or nothing of Christina's self-understanding. That monk, however, had conversed with the nun and the details which he provides concerning her life bespeak a thorough and accurate knowledge of its events.[2] Thus I would distinguish between the actions described in the text, which I take to be an accurate reflection of Christina's lived experience, and the description of those actions, whose language provides an entry into the mind of her male hagiographer.

It is hardly surprising or unusual that the monk of St Albans chose numerous times to term Christina a *sponsa Christi* (*Life*, pp. 54, 68, 72 and 78). His heroine's struggle to avoid a secular marriage in favour of the vow made to her spiritual spouse was one of his central concerns, occupying fully a third of the extant text. Moreover, writers throughout the Middle Ages employed nuptial metaphors to describe the relationship between individuals in the religious life, both male and female, and God. Perhaps the most famous exploration of this image in the twelfth century, Bernard of Clairvaux's *Sermons on the Song of Songs*, portrayed the love which existed between a male monk and Christ in terms of the lovers described, supposedly, by Solomon. Although Bernard's work betrayed the developing interest in affective emotions, he transformed the highly physical and even erotic images of the biblical text into a contemplative relationship where physical desire played little part.

As medieval clerics tended to define women in terms of their relationships to men, nuptial imagery provided a particularly useful means of discussing religious women who were not otherwise linked to a man in marriage. Indeed, in pre-Conquest England male clerics specifically applied the marriage motif only to women, never to themselves.[3] Women, for their part, often embodied these ideals in their own lives and experience. Hildegard of Bingen, for example, had the nuns of her convent dress in nuptial garb for their monastic profession in order to demonstrate their status as brides of Christ.[4]

The use made of marriage as a means of describing a relationship to Christ in the *Life of Christina of Markyate* differs sharply both from the spiritualized nuptial imagery of the Cistercian tradition and from the extremely sensual unions of female visionaries in the later Middle Ages. The monk of St Albans considered marriage, to Christ as much as to human beings, to be a juridical or contractual relationship rather than a metaphor. The use of the term *sponsa Christi* was thus of a different order from those works which modelled the marriage of humans to Christ on language derived from the Song of Songs. Whereas the monk of St Albans never cited that biblical text, even indirectly, he frequently used the legal and liturgical language of contemporary marriage practice. While medieval marriage rituals themselves, like all Christian liturgies, used much biblically inspired language, it is interesting to note that no such ritual employed language from the Song of Songs.[5]

Christina did not flee an earthly marriage in order to seek marriage to Christ, as did such late medieval women as Dorothy of Montau and Margery Kempe. Her marriage to Christ instead served as the basis for a court action designed to annul an earthly marriage which had been contracted subsequent to her vow of virginity. This use of the nuptial theme is so different from the usual *topoi* that Thomas Renna has commented: 'The theme of the virgin as *sponsa Christi* is not particularly emphasized in ... the *Life* of Christina.'[6] This surprising observation was made despite the fact that the hagiographer used that phrase numerous times to describe his heroine. The observation could only be true in so far as the commonly understood motifs of the marriage to Christ were not employed by the monk of St Albans. Actual marriage to Christ was absolutely central to Christina's own experience and to the hagiographer's description of that experience.

To understand the life of Christina of Markyate – both her own experience and the text which recorded that experience – it is crucial to realize that Christina's marriage to Christ was not a disembodied or mystical metaphor for her relationship to the saviour, but an ongoing union which was both concrete and juridical. Christina and her hagiographer seem to have understood that relationship in terms which directly paralleled contemporary legal and sacramental definitions of marriage. Those definitions were undergoing change in twelfth-century England, and in Europe more generally. Furthermore, it seems that Christina was able to exploit such an understanding of her vowed relationship to Christ in order to thwart the desires of her parents and to avoid subjugation to a man in an ordinary marriage. An analysis of the description of Christina's actions provided by the monk of St Albans, and an attempt to place those actions within the context of changing understandings of marriage, will help to show how at least one medieval religious woman was able to experience her status as a 'bride of Christ' not as an ontological status or visionary state, but as a continuing personal and legal relationship which empowered her to pursue the course in life which she deemed most desirable.

Let us turn first to an examination of the vow which Christina, then named Theodora, made as a young adult to link herself to Christ. When Christina was in her teens, her parents, Autti and Beatrix, brought their religiously precocious child to the Abbey of St Albans, which was located not far from their hometown of Huntingdon. They intended to seek the protection of the saint whose relics were interred there for their daughter on the celebration of her birthday. Impressed by the example of the monks, Christina used her fingernail to mark the door to the church with the sign of the cross. The next day, while staying in Shillington on the homeward journey, she attended mass, presumably in the village church. After the reading of the gospel, she approached the altar and placed a *denarius* in the hands of the priest. As she did so, she silently made the following vow: 'Lord God, merciful and almighty, accept my oblation through the hand of your priest. For I offer this *denarius* to you in handing over myself. I ask that you deem my purity to be worthy and that you confer on me the integrity of virginity through which you may renew the image of your son in me, who lives and reigns with you in the unity of the Holy Spirit God for ever and ever, Amen' (*Life*, p. 40).[7] On her return to Huntingdon she related her vow to Sueno, a local canon known for his holiness. He confirmed it, presumably with a blessing.

This episode reveals two differing sensibilities about how a Christian could form links to the supernatural world. Autti and Beatrix, members of the Anglo-Saxon nobility rooted in the piety of the early Middle Ages, sought to form a bond between their daughter and a saint whose relics rested in their region. Alban would act as a powerful *patronus* for the young woman. That logic of patronage stood at the root of the traditional cult of saints' relics. As a *patronus* the saint protected those people who had bound themselves to him or her either through an explicit oath of servitude or by means of some exchange of gifts and service. These 'servants' – who included the monastic community dedicated to the saint, the peasants who inhabited and worked that community's lands, and the pilgrims who came to the saint's shrine bearing gifts – had obligations to their patron. Frequently such obligations came to be ritualized, for the laity, as the donation of a token amount of money such as a *denarius*, the same coin used when a peasant swore fealty to an overlord. As pilgrims, Autti and Beatrix may well have made just such a payment during their visit to St Albans. Thus the laity became part of the *familia* of the saint. Like a lay lord, the saint was bound to provide protection to those who had entered into this relationship of gift-giving and service. This was not a symbolic relationship. The saint and the lay members of the *familia* had very real duties to perform. The concrete understanding of these obligations can be seen in countless stories included in *miracula* collections composed during the eleventh and twelfth centuries.[8]

Christina altered this traditional way of relating to the holy by making her oath of servitude and the concomitant payment of money directly to Christ rather than to a saint. The ability to enter into such a relationship of mutual exchange with the saviour, and not through the intercession of a saint, signalled a growing emphasis on the humanity of Christ. As such it serves as a powerful example of a new piety centred directly on Christ and the Virgin rather than on saintly intermediaries. Christina's relationship was, like that of Autti and Beatrix to St Alban, one of mutual exchange and service. This relationship, however, was modelled on the bond between husband and wife rather than those between serfs and lords.

As later events were to make clear, Christina intended her *votum* to be a very particular type of vow, that is, a promise to become married to Christ. In twelfth-century Latin such a promise was generally called a *desponsatio*, although the monk of St Albans did not use that term here. In current English usage we might call such a promise a betrothal, but the term lacked a specific definition.[9] While the explicit language of marriage was absent from this particular episode, the events themselves followed the form of contemporary betrothal or marriage rituals. Christina placed the first sign of her vow on the church door, the traditionally favoured location for betrothals. In such ceremonies the donation of a *denarius* served as a symbol of the dowry which was to be paid as part of the actual wedding rites. Thus, through her donation of a *denarius*, Christina declared her intention to marry Christ through a life of virginity lived apart from the world, rather than her intention to become part of the *familia* of a saintly intercessor while remaining in the world. The monastic hagiographer added several important details. He explicitly claimed that Christina had given her consent to her marriage to Christ and that a priest, namely Sueno, had confirmed the vow. It was these ritual actions – the indication of the vow at the church door, the payment of the symbolic dowry, the obtaining of a priestly blessing – which set Christina's vow apart from a simple vow of virginity and made it into a betrothal to Christ.[10] Christina's later actions and the hagiographer's descriptive language both imply that each understood the young woman to have been effectively betrothed to Christ from this moment.

While Christina was still in her teens, her beauty attracted the attentions of Ranulf Flambard. This Norman bishop of Durham, notorious for his dissolute life, attempted to seduce her. Frustrated by his failure, he prompted Burthred, a local youth of high social standing, to propose marriage. Christina publicly resisted the match on the grounds of her prior vow of virginity and implicit betrothal to Christ. The hagiographer expressed Christina's underlying lack of consent to this second betrothal through a magnificent use of chiasis: *Vellet nollet Christina Burthredus illam sibi desponsandam accepit* ('Burthred wished, and Christina denied, that she be taken as betrothed to him' (*Life*, p. 44)). Under extreme and even violent pressure from her family, however, she eventually submitted to a promise to marry this suitor (*Life*, p. 47). This *desponsatio* was made in a church and, as later references indicate, blessed by a priest also named Burthred, quite possibly a kinsman of the groom (*Life*, p. 109). Thus it was considered to be part of a sacramental marriage. Nevertheless the would-be hermitess was publicly considered betrothed by her parents and others, a fact which the monk of St Albans made clear with the following phrase: *Burthredus illam in coniugem sibi desponsavit* ('Burthred betrothed her in marriage to him' (*Life*, p. 46)). The position of affianced spouse was certainly at odds with Christina's vow of virginity and intention to follow the religious life, a dilemma captured by the hagiographer's use of the almost intentionally oxymoronic phrase *desponsata virgo* (*Life*, p. 46) to describe her condition.

Christina's betrothal to Burthred set in motion a chain of events which was virtually inexorable according to medieval custom and canon law.[11] Ecclesiastical authorities had long campaigned to bring marriage fully under their control and to place the nuptial ceremonies themselves in churches. An Anglo-Saxon legal treatise of the early eleventh century required the blessing of a mass-priest on a marriage.[12] Shortly after the Conquest, Archbishop Lanfranc not only repeated the requirement of an ecclesiastical blessing, but threatened those who did not obtain it with the sin of fornication.[13] The *desponsatio* had taken place in a church and would normally have been accompanied by an announcement of marriage banns. Autti, Beatrix and Burthred expected Christina to participate in a second liturgical ceremony which would have made her marriage formal and complete. Such a wedding celebration would have been followed by the blessing of the bridal bed and the sexual consummation of the union. A great many marriages, however, were still contracted in private, away from the church building and accompanying clerical supervision. Such clandestine marriages were simply consummated by sexual intercourse without clerical blessing. In either case, once a marriage was complete, it was considered indissoluble unless some impediment was subsequently discovered which would annul the original contract. There was, as we shall see, considerable debate in twelfth-century ecclesiastical circles as to whether a marriage was complete from the moment of betrothal or from the moment of consummation.

Christina considered her prior vow to Christ as just such an impediment to her contracted marriage to Burthred. Disdaining this *desponsatio* as invalid, she was kept in custody by her parents for over a year (*Life*, pp. 47–55). They denied her the chance to visit a local monastery, to visit with religiously-minded friends, to consult her spiritual advisor, and even to go to her favourite chapel, all in the hope that her resolve would weaken. One of the most interesting features of this hagiographic text is the remarkable variety of resources which it indicates were available to pious laypeople in a twelfth-century town. During this time, Autti and Beatrix planned a formal blessing of the marriage, even setting a date for the ceremony. Christina contracted, or perhaps feigned, a fever, and so the plans were put off. Her parents also urged Burthred to consummate the union by any necessary means, including resorting to rape. They even provided him with entrance to Christina's sleeping chamber for that purpose. She dissuaded him, first by telling religious stories and later by hiding under the hangings which draped the walls. In the eyes of the monastic hagiographer, the failure of these efforts was the result of divine intervention: 'Nevertheless, since Christ protected the vow of his bride, the celebration of the nuptials was in no way able to go forward' (*Life*, p. 54). Significantly this passage marked his first use of the term *sponsa Christi.* The harshness of twelfth-century life comes through in the almost casual brutality of Christina's parents, who regularly beat her and also doused her with alternating drafts of scalding and icy water in a self-serving attempt to dispel her fever.

One detail of this episode may provide a helpful clue about the relationship between Christina and her hagiographer. The young woman attempted to convince Burthred to practise a celibate marriage with her by narrating the story of St Cecilia. This was by no means the only example of a chaste married couple which she could have chosen.[14] Some years later, the scriptorium of St Albans prepared a psalter for Christina's use which included another such story, the *Life of St Alexis*.[15] Scholars have assumed that it was included in the codex because Christina's experiences reminded the monks of the story of Alexis.[16] This is precisely true in a way which has been ignored. The story of Alexis had been written in Old French and was imported to England by Norman clerics. The feast of Cecilia, on the other hand, had been commonly celebrated before the Conquest and several Anglo-Saxon homilies concerning her life survive. When Christina, a product of Anglo-Saxon culture, was faced with the prospect of sexual intercourse, she drew on the example of a story familiar to her from preaching she had heard as a child. Later, the monks of St Albans, products of the Norman cultural sphere, interpreted her story in terms familiar from their own background and so provided her with a copy of a vernacular text which may well have been incomprehensible to her. In similar fashion, her hagiographer described her birthday (6 November) as the feast of Leonard of Noblat, which had been imported by the Normans, rather than as the feast of the native Anglo-Saxon Winnocus, which had until recently been celebrated in England.[17] Such is the construction of sanctity. The saint models his or her behaviour on familiar patterns, while the hagiographer uses yet other models of sanctity in shaping a narrative which will itself serve as a new model of sanctity for later generations.

While Christina resisted all attempts to force consummation of her marriage, she was still publicly considered to be betrothed to Burthred, not a bride of Christ. News of her betrothal caused her counsellor Sueno to think her guilty of 'feminine inconstancy' and temporarily to abandon her cause (*Life*, p. 54). At this point in the narrative, neither betrothal – that is, neither Christina's *votum* to Christ nor the *desponsatio* to Burthred – had been consummated. Christina, the *desponsata virgo*, lived neither the life of a wife nor that of a recluse. The competing claims of the would-be hermitess and her family constituted a legal problem. Therefore the antagonists sought a legal solution.

Autti and Beatrix brought their recalcitrant daughter before Fredebertus, prior of the local college of canons, for correction. Autti confessed, 'I give testimony to my daughter that I and her mother have forced her into this marriage despite her reluctance and that she has agreed to this sacrament against her will' (*Life*, p. 58). He argued that she should nevertheless accept the marriage, for it was traditional to comply with parental authority. Moreover, her desire to practise the religious life was at odds with the ideals of the nobility to which she belonged. Despite Autti's frank admission of the use of force in exacting the betrothal, Fredebertus urged the young woman to accept it since it had been performed and blessed in a church 'according to ecclesiastical custom' (ibid.). After noting that the sacrament of marriage was indissoluble, the prior attempted to reconcile Christina with the thought that married women could be saved as well as virgins. While the prior did not accept the arguments of Autti, he still felt that there was sufficient cause to make Christina accept her betrothal to Burthred.

The young woman replied that a betrothal extracted against her will could not constitute a true sacrament. Moreover, she had earlier made a vow of virginity before witnesses and that to break that vow would be wicked: 'I would not be disobedient to my parents against the precept of the Lord if I were to free myself in order to fulfill my vow to Christ. I do this on the invitation of him whom you claim to be the voice in the Gospel' (*Life*, p. 62). The key to her legal argument was that only one of the two vows, and that the prior vow, was consensual and therefore valid. She then offered to vow never to accept a human marriage and even volunteered to have her testimony verified through the ordeal by fire. In the end Fredebertus suggested that Autti bring the case before Robert Bloet, bishop of Lincoln, who was scheduled to visit a nearby town. Autti and his fellow nobles felt that the bishop must rule in their favour, 'because the sacrament of marriage [*sacramentum coniugii*] had already been performed' (*Life*, p. 64). On first hearing the case, however, Robert said that 'there is no bishop under heaven who could force her into marriage, if she wishes to serve God and not another man according to her vow' (ibid.). The bishop thus seemed to have accepted Christina's reasoning, rather than that of Fredebertus. The following day, however, Robert reversed his judgement after Autti bribed him.

In the wake of this trial the hagiographer recorded three comments whose language reveals much about the attitude towards marriage of the participants in this drama. First, Christina's father stripped her of her garments, saying that 'If you want to have Christ, follow him naked' (*Life*, p. 72). Since that phrase was a play on a common twelfth-century image for the religious life, Autti was warning his daughter of the potentially severe economic consequences of her decision. He seems to have wished to convince her that Burthred was in fact a more desirable spouse than Christ. For him, marriage was largely a matter of exchanged gifts.[18] Next, Beatrix declared that she did not care who deflowered her daughter, so long as the deed – that is, the consummation of her marriage – was accomplished. She even paid elderly women (*vetulae*) in the community who practised a form of magic to use charms and potions in order to gain the desired end (*Life*, p. 74). For this Anglo-Saxon woman, any sexual union between Burthred and Christina would have settled the contested matter. At length Fredebertus reversed his earlier position and couselled Autti not to resist the 'judgement of God', but to respect Christina as the *sponsa Christi* (*Life*, p. 78). In Fredebertus' view marriage was not so much a matter of gift-giving or sexual intercourse, but the result of a vow given with full consent.

The failure to win respite from the ecclesiastical courts prompted Christina to consider flight, a common recourse among those who failed to gain a favourable judgement in marriage cases. Edwin, a hermit who lived near Huntingdon, attempted to persuade his cousin, a more widely-famed hermit named Roger, to offer refuge to the beleaguered woman. On hearing the story, Roger refused, saying 'Have you come here in order to teach me how to dissolve marriages?' (*Life*, p. 82). Rebuffed, Edwin sought advice from Ralph d'Escures, archbishop of Canterbury. Ralph ruled in Christina's favour and stated that he would impose a penance equal to that for manslaughter on those who had forced her into a betrothal (*Life*, p. 85). Heartened, Edwin arranged for Christina to escape and live with a female recluse named Alfwen.

Eventually Roger became convinced of the sincerity of Christina's vow, as she was conducting her life as a bride of Christ in the company of Alfwen. Roger therefore agreed to house her as his pupil, but only in secret. Christina then moved to his hermitage, thus entering the circle of St Albans. The next segment of the *Life* was devoted primarily to her career as an ascetic and a visionary. The official dissolution of her betrothal to Burthred, however, was still important, for Christina and Roger 'had a fear ... lest Christina, having by some chance been discovered with him, be taken away on the authority of the bishop [Robert Bloet] and be handed over to the wishes of her husband' (*Life*, p. 106).[19] After a while, Christ appeared to her and reassured her that all would be well. Shortly thereafter, Burthred appeared at Roger's hermitage. The young man was now willing to release any claim on his putative spouse, since the Virgin Mary had appeared to him several nights before. Not trusting Burthred, Roger demanded that the young man return with witnesses and repeat his willingness to release Christina. Burthred complied in a ritual handshake whose witnesses included the priest who had blessed the original betrothal (*Life*, p. 109). Shortly thereafter Thurstan, archbishop of York, agreed to annul that betrothal, to confirm Christina's vow of virginity, and to permit Burthred to marry another woman (*Life*, p. 113). This decision marked an end to the court battle and removed all possible impediments from Christina's pursuit of the religious life.

The story of Christina's conflicting betrothals did not culminate, however, for some time. After Roger's death, she became established as an independent recluse, eventually becoming a spiritual advisor to Geoffrey, abbot of nearby St Albans. She was an independent woman living within the orbit, but not under the control, of a male monastic community:

> [Christina] lived in the hermitage which we know for a long time before she received a blessed sign of her virginal humility and humble virginity from the bishop. She was encouraged, both by many very wise and religious persons and by her own relations and friends, to place her neck under the yoke and to confirm the vow of her soul by the dignity of consecration. [They said] that it was fitting that, having promised to be a spouse of Christ, she should be marked through a

wedding to Christ. She put off the decision, having some uncertainty as to whether she would remain in that place, the more so because she had once decided to retire to some distant land where some unknown city might provide her a hiding place to be with Christ. At length, divinely inspired and persuaded by the frequent supplications and sweet humility of the above-mentioned abbot, she gave her consent to their suggestions. Thus on the feast of St Matthew, who is described as the first consecrator of virgins, the virgin was consecrated to Christ by Alexander, bishop of Lincoln.

(*Life*, pp. 144–6)

The long period which had intervened between Christina's original vow of virginity and this consecration was by no means unusual. The word used here for Christina's consecration ceremonies, *sponsalia*, had earlier been used for her blessed betrothal to Burthred. Indeed, since late antiquity, the ritual of consecration for virgins had many conscious parallels to contemporary marriage liturgies.[20] Moreover, in the twelfth century, there was little linguistic precision in the distinction between betrothal and marriage ceremonies, or between betrothed couples and spouses.[21]

Through consecration Christina's status as a bride of Christ was assured. None the less she herself had postponed this ritual confirmation, perhaps for reasons beyond the banal expressions of humility which her hagiographer offered. This woman, who had won her independence of action by defying and successfully thwarting the wishes of her parents, may well have resisted abandoning that hard-won independence at the behest of male clerics. Whatever the truth of this hypothesis, Christina had to secure both a formal renunciation of Burthred's betrothal and an episcopal annulment of that vow before she emerged from hiding to gain full and public acceptance of her status as a bride of Christ. No less than five bishops, including the two metropolitans of the kingdom, had become involved in her case: Ranulf Flambard had suggested her betrothal to Burthred; Robert Bloet had first found her vow to Christ to be valid, only later to enforce the betrothal to Burthred; Ralph d'Escures had declared her vow of virginity valid; Thurstan of York went so far as to annul the betrothal to Burthred; Alexander of Lincoln had consecrated her.

From virtually the earliest Christian communities a vow of virginity such as that made by Christina after her visit to St Albans had been considered an impediment to marriage.[22] At several early Frankish councils, for example, the bishops had required that a marriage be annulled if it were determined that the woman had once made such a vow.[23] Moreover, the claim that one had been forced into a marriage against one's will by parents or other authorities, as in the coercion which Autti had freely admitted, had also traditionally been accepted as an impediment to a valid marriage contract.[24] Indeed, as René Metz has remarked: 'The same laws which governed the union of man and wife were themselves applied, *mutatis mutandis*, to the union of the virgin and of Christ.'[25]

Why, then, was Christina's struggle so difficult? I do not think that it is sufficient to suggest simply, as have Robert Hanning and Christopher Brooke, that ecclesiastical courts were reluctant to support a young girl against the authority of her parents.[26] It was after all possible for Fredebertus, after dismissing Autti's appeal to parental authority, to enforce Christina's betrothal to Burthred on the basis of the indissolubility of the sacrament of marriage. Indeed, over the course of the twelfth century, ecclesiastical authorities worked to lessen the familial pressures exerted over prospective couples in marital matters.

The crux of the matter was not Autti and Beatrix's wishes for Christina, but the question of whether the young woman was legally the *sponsa* of Christ or of Burthred. The debate comes into clearer focus when we consider Aelred of Rievaulx's view of a recluse's marriage to Christ.[27] He composed a *Rule for a Recluse* at almost the very time that Christina was involved in her court battle. This English abbot of a Cistercian community described the relationship between a hermitess and Christ in biblical language largely drawn from the Song of Songs, rather than the legal language used by the monk of St Albans. Aelred emphasized the completion rather than the inception of the relationship. He wrote: 'He himself has already chosen you as his bride, but he will not crown you unless you are proven.'[28] According to Aelred, a female virgin must avoid any contact with men for a lengthy period of time in order to prove her virginity. Only then, after she has been tested through the active practice of the religious life and has been 'crowned', that is, consecrated, was she a true recluse and worthy to be called a *sponsa Christi*. Thus in Aelred's view of this relationship it is arguable that Christina's betrothal to Burthred would have taken priority, for she had failed the test by accepting such a betrothal. While the marriage to Burthred had yet to be consummated, Christina's mere association with him prevented the consummation of her marriage to Christ.

Aelred's text betrays a very particular understanding of marriage, one in which actions, be they the 'proving' of a virgin or the sexual union of a married couple, rather than simple consent played a constitutive role. Over the course of the very period during which Christina lived and the monk of St Albans composed his *Life*, the definition of what constituted a valid Christian marriage underwent significant change. Marriage was a matter of deep concern to the bishops who served as judges in ecclesiastical courts. It also interested the scholarly masters who taught in the schools sponsored by those bishops, both those who were concerned with legal matters – who would later come to be known as canonists – and those concerned with the 'sacred page' of scripture – who would later come to be known as theologians. Scholars generally regard the developments between Bishop Ivo of Chartres (1090–1116) and Pope Alexander III (1159–81) as forming a decisive chapter in the evolution of the ideal of marriage in canon law. This period corresponded almost exactly to Christina's lifetime and the composition of her *Life* by the monk of St Albans. During this period there was no single understanding of marriage that was held to be normative. Bishops and masters were collectively groping towards an understanding of this sacrament and its constitutive elements as they collected together relevant scraps of authoritative texts from the works of the Christian fathers and of the Roman jurists. In order to understand Christina's legal problems, then, it is necessary to survey various strands of thought on this topic.

A valid marriage was considered by all Christian authorities to be indissoluble. According to Roman law, the consent of the partners was all that was necessary to constitute a valid marriage. A frequently used adage went: 'Consent makes a marriage (*Consensus facit nuptias*).' Most church fathers, in particular Ambrose and Augustine, were in accord and held marriages to be virtually indissoluble from the time of the *desponsatio*. Pope Leo I, however, interpreted Ephesians 5:22–32 to imply that a couple did not have the same marriage as that which existed between Christ and the church if copulation had not occurred.[29] One of the most prominent Carolingian reformers, Hincmar of Reims, used this text to argue that copulation, as well as consent, was necessary to a valid marriage. Thus marriages which had not been consummated could be dissolved.[30] There were two poles to the debate: a 'consensual' and a 'copulative' theory of marriage.[31]

When Ivo of Chartres assembled his *Panormia* in the 1090s he brought together a number of citations from both Roman law and the fathers which supported the consensual theory.[32] His rubrics are revealing. Before a text of Isidore of Seville, he noted: 'From the first making of the betrothal, they are truly called wedded.' Other rubrics, however, suggest a process which was only begun at the *desponsatio*. To this long series he starkly juxtaposed the text of Leo I stressing the importance of sexual union.[33] As a bishop, Ivo had to adjudicate marriage cases and his letters provide a picture of the theory of marriage which he developed from these authorities. In general, he dated the indissolubility of a marriage from the moment of the *desponsatio*. In a famous formula which he repeated in several guises, he said that a marriage existed 'for the most part' (*ex maiori parte*) from the consent of the two parties.[34] He held *desponsationes* to be indissoluble, even in those cases where they had been neither blessed nor consummated. Ivo did, however, allow the dissolution of betrothals which had been extracted by force and fear or in which a free man had unknowingly promised himself in marriage to a serf. In some of these cases carnal knowledge had occurred, but true consent had been lacking.[35] In practice, Ivo considered any consensual betrothal to be an impediment to a second marriage. For him *consensus* formed a valid *pactum coniugale*.

Anselm of Laon and the masters associated with him added an important refinement to this theory. During the first third of the twelfth century they produced a number of *florilegia* which included sections concerning marriage. These discussed many of the authorities collected by Ivo and agreed that marriage was a matter of consent. They distinguished, however, two types of betrothal, a *fides pactionis* and a *fides consensus*. The first was simply an agreement between two parties to be married at some unspecified point. It could be broken and the parties would merely commit the sin of giving false witness. The second involved full consent of the will and could not be broken.[36]

The Parisian master Hugh of St-Victor adopted and broadened this distinction. For him, the word *desponsatio* referred merely to the promise to become married and was to be differentiated from consent itself.[37] Hugh formulated a second distinction between two levels in the sacrament of marriage.[38] There was the 'great sacrament' (*magnum sacramentum*), similar to the relationship between Christ and the church discussed in Ephesians, which involved both consent and carnal knowledge. There was also, however, a 'greater sacrament' (*maius sacramentum*) which involved consent alone. This was the essence of marriage and was similar to the love of God for the human soul. While Hugh had in mind the marriage of the Virgin Mary and Joseph, this description could equally have applied to the relationship of Christina and Christ. Hugh was also sensitive to the problems posed by clandestine marriages, that is, marriages contracted informally and in private, away from the supervising eye of clerics. While any consensual agreement would form an indissoluble marriage, the existence of consent was almost impossible to prove in those cases which had not been witnessed. Ecclesiastical authorities could not know what was hidden and they must exercise great care in determining the truth concerning such prior betrothals before dissolving a later match.

It was Gratian who revived the copulative theory of marriage in his *Concordance of Discordant Canons*, better known as the *Decretum*, compiled around 1140. He marshalled many of the same authorities as had Ivo into a single *quaestio* devoted to the dissolution of betrothals.[39] In the first section, he gathered those authorities which indicated that 'consent makes a marriage', but he pointed out that the definition of consent required refinement: 'But it is asked what consent makes a marriage, is it consent to cohabit, or consent to have sexual relations, or both?' If it were merely the first, then brothers and sisters could be said to be married. If the second were necessary, then the Virgin Mary and Joseph could not be said to have been married.[40] In the second part of the *quaestio*, Gratian placed texts which stressed the importance of sexual union as a criterion for marriage. To the evidence of Pope Leo's letter, he added a text of Augustine, unknown to Ivo, which is now known to be pseudonymous: 'There is no doubt that a woman is not involved in a marriage when it is known that there is no sexual union.'[41] For Gratian, this text was crucial. While he accepted consent as a necessary criterion for a marriage, it was not sufficient. Consent merely initiated a process which was consummated in sexual union. Where Hugh had earlier made a distinction between the engagement itself and the betrothal or promise to become engaged, Gratian more simply distinguished any form of engagement or betrothal from the consummation of a marriage. Only such a *matrimonium perfectum* was a sacrament, and thus betrothed women (*sponsae*) were not properly called wives (*coniuges*). Hence betrothals were able to be dissolved in a number of situations.[42] These circumstances specifically included betrothed women who, prior to the consummation of their marriage, decided to enter a convent.[43]

A little over a decade later, Peter Lombard provided a creative synthesis of the views of Hugh of St-Victor and Gratian. He refined Hugh's clumsy distinction between engagements and betrothals into one between those promises to wed made for some indeterminate time in the future (*verba de futuro*) and those made with the intent of more immediately taking up the married state (*verba de presenti*).[44] The former were able to be dissolved, with suitable penance, while the latter constituted an indissoluble marriage. The Lombard also responded to the problem posed by Gratian concerning the meaning of the term 'consent'. It was not consent made specifically either for cohabitation or for sexual union, but consent to taking up a 'conjugal society' (*coniugale societas*), which could, but need not, include both those characteristics.[45]

The work of Peter Lombard provides a significant conclusion to our survey, not simply because he provided a compelling synthesis of earlier writers, but because his view was adopted by Pope Alexander III (who was not, as was once thought, a pupil of Gratian). Alexander's adjudication of marriage cases marked the victory of the consensual theory.[46] He issued approximately eighty decretals for England which dealt with matters of matrimony.[47] These helped to define the practice of English ecclesiastical courts during the time when the monk of St Albans composed his narrative.[48] Most of Alexander's decretals concerned issues such as consanguinity and concubinage, rather than those found in Christina's case. In cases involving a conflict of vows, however, Alexander regularly upheld the validity of prior betrothals made *de presenti*, including those made in secret and not blessed by clergy, over later vows.

Alexander seems to have followed a path pioneered by Innocent II, as can be seen in the celebrated case of Richard of Anstey.[49] The case originated in the promise of William de Sackville to marry Aubrey de Tresgoz. After reaching an agreement with Aubrey's father, however, William broke off their engagement and married a woman named Alice in a church ceremony, despite Aubrey's presence and her protests that she was William's lawful wife. Some years later, after he had fathered several children by Alice, William had yet another change of heart and successfully sought an annulment of his marriage to Alice in an episcopal court. Innocent II upheld the annulment, basing his decision on a distinction between the non-binding character of a promise made for the future and the binding character of one made, like that between William and Aubrey, for the present.[50] That decretal, contemporary with the work of Peter Lombard, marked the earliest explicit use of that master's language in adjudicating a marriage case. Its significance was weighty. A bishop and a pope were willing to dissolve a marriage celebrated *in facie ecclesiae* on the basis of an earlier consensual contract. The marriage of William and Aubrey was apparently childless and, on William's death, his inheritance went to Alice and his daughter Mabel. William's nephew, Richard of Anstey, eventually challenged the inheritance, claiming that Mabel was the child of an adulterous union and hence had no legal claim. Mabel's defence rested on the argument that William's first contract with Aubrey had neither been blessed in church nor consummated, whereas his contract with Alice had. The summary of the pleading includes the maxim that 'a marriage which carnal knowledge has not confirmed and perfected is not complete, although it is begun from the first pledge of betrothal'. This is a virtual quotation from Gratian.[51] Richard, for his part, based his claim on the previously unchallenged actions of the ecclesiastical courts. Alexander agreed and so, early in his pontificate in a case involving English plaintiffs, cast his lot with the advocates of the consensual theory of marriage.

The net result of this and other cases was to enforce, in England and elsewhere, the consensual theory of marriage as the basis for judgement in ecclesiastical courts. One of the most striking aspects of this academic and juridical definition of marriage was the minor role played by ecclesiastical blessings. In the twelfth century church authorities – differing from Hincmar of Reims and his Carolingian contemporaries – thought that, however desirable, such blessings were not absolutely necessary. Bishops attempted to require ecclesiastical rituals as a matter of church discipline, in France going so far as to threaten those who did not obtain them with excommunication, but in the light of this understanding of canon law they could not make marriage dependent on such blessings, as Lanfranc of Canterbury had earlier attempted. If consent made a marriage, and marriage was a sacrament, laypeople could enter into a sacramental bond without the benefit of clergy. Charles Donahue has described Alexander's policy as a new set of legal rules which continued to have force in coming centuries, allowing (if not promoting) the relative frequency of clandestine marriages. Even if such language attributes more coherence and novelty to Alexander's decisions than they in fact had, the effect of his decretals was important and wide-ranging.[52] The power of individuals to choose their own marriage partner thus received important validation from the Church.[53]

By the end of the twelfth century the court of the archbishop of Canterbury regularly endorsed the validity of betrothals made de presenti before lay witnesses, as well as those made de futuro which were later confirmed by clerical blessing.[54] Throughout the later Middle Ages, English ecclesiastical courts considered those promises of marriage which had been made with the consent of both parties to form an impediment to any later marriage, even when the first union had been neither sexually consummated nor ecclesiastically blessed.[55] The evidence suggests that a significant percentage of all marriage cases heard before those courts involved the enforcement of clandestine marriage agreements. Betrothals were also upheld as impediments to later marriages in the minority of marriage cases which were brought before the King's Bench, although civil courts were more likely to protect the rights of women while the cases were still being tried.[56] In a neat reversal of Christina's story, one such court forced a professed Cistercian monk to return to secular life when it was shown that he had promised to marry before entering the monastery.[57] Over the course of the later Middle Ages, those English clerics who served as spiritual advisors to women continued to see the celebration of their consecration in the religious life as a form of marriage. Several decades after the death of Christina, Stephen

Langton – then a university master, but later archbishop of Canterbury – addressed a community of nuns on a feast of the Virgin Mary. He described each of the various spiritual attainments of these religious women in terms of the vestments and ornaments worn by a bride at her wedding. Thus chastity metaphorically became a golden belt, while charity was the bride's gloves. Not only was each virgin a *sponsa Christi*, but Christ himself was her *contractus*.[58]

Viewing the *Life of Christina of Markyate* in the mirror of contemporary academic thought and legal practice concerning marriage indicates that the account provided by the monk of St Albans has verisimillitude. The variety of stances which he described towards Christina's two betrothals can all be found in contemporary writings. While high ecclesiastical courts would eventually have enforced Christina's prior vow to Christ over her betrothal to Burthred, it remains quite possible that certain lesser ecclesiastical authorities, more sensitive to local social standing, would originally have favoured the claims of parents and secular spouse. There is no reason to doubt the accuracy of the hagiographer's account.

In the eyes of high ecclesiastical authorities, however, the power of lords and heads of households over the marriage choices of their dependents diminished over the course of the twelfth century. This was a direct, if unintended, result of the victory of the consensual theory in academic and episcopal circles. As Duby has phrased it:

> Hence, the Church emphasized the union of two hearts in marriage and postulated that its validity rested more on the betrothal (*desponsatio*) than on the wedding, and especially on the consent (*consensus*) of the two individuals concerned. The Church thus unintentionally tended to take a stand against the power of the heads of households in matters of marriage, against the lay conception of misalliance, and, indeed, against male supremacy, for it asserted the equality of the sexes in concluding the marriage pact and in the accomplishment of the duties thereby implied.[59]

The story of Christina's insistence on a marriage partner other than the man approved by her family – an insistence which was eventually validated by the ecclesiastical courts, if only after a protracted struggle – thus becomes virtually emblematic of the almost seismic shifts which were occuring in the contemporary understanding of marriage.

A young woman originally named Theodora married Christ, and so transformed not only her name, but her entire life. It was in all ways a true marriage, but a marriage which made the holy startlingly present in human society on human terms. Christ not only chose a woman such as Theodora to become a virginal bride, she chose him to be her husband as well. Through her choice of partner, Christina endorsed a vision of society as a set of personal relationships which included the divine. God was willing to enter contractual relationships with human beings. But the human Jesus had become her spouse only through her own consent. The bond which Christina and her saviour crafted and which the monk of St Albans described was far different than that envisioned by their contemporary Aelred of Rievaulx, in which Christ had almost the sole authoritative voice. Theirs was a union 'of two hearts' rendered possible by contemporary appreciation both of Christ's humanity and of the power of wilful consent in establishing the marital bond. In a gesture redolent with the affective concerns of twelfth-century humanism, a young woman became a primary actor in the drama of her own salvation.

Afterword

The version of this article presented here is an abridgement of an article originally published in 1989.[60] I would like to thank Samuel Fanous and Henrietta Leyser, as well as the editors of *Viator*, for the chance to publish it again. I particularly would like to thank Robert Benson, since deceased, who as an editor of *Viator* and as a friend provided excellent guidance in developing this article from a paper originally delivered at the Twenty-Second International Congress of Medieval Studies at Kalamazoo, Michigan, in May 1987. Ruth Mazo Karras, Virginia Reinburg, Elizabeth Robertson and John Van Engen were all also of great help in composing the original article. In abridging the article, I have removed several whole sections, but have otherwise retained the original text without addition. I have shortened the notes much more radically than the text itself, most notably excising almost all of the Latin originals of quoted texts. The format of this volume has necessitated a number of stylistic changes from the original notes. As in the text, however, I have not made any additions. The argument therefore remains one that is some fifteen years old, based on scholarship available at that time. In the process of abridging the article, I was very pleased to find that I thought it none the less still quite sound. (I have removed one claim about the timing of Christina's change of name, the error of which is pointed out by R. I. Moore's article, Chapter 8 in this volume.[61])

I would like to add, however, in this afterword a few words on where scholarship has gone in the intervening time since the original publication of this article and which I might have very usefully added to its footnotes. In the same year as the publication of my article, Paulette L'Hermite-Leclercq began presenting her research on the *Life of Christina of Markyate*, work which was not fully published until 1992 and which came independently to many of the same conclusions as I had drawn.[62] My research was similarly done well in advance of the publication of my article, and as I was conducting the research I regretted the lack of a good synthesis on the canon law of marriage. James Brundage produced exactly that in his magisterial *Law, Sex, and Christian Society in Medieval Europe*, which appeared too late to be of use to me, but which could have been usefully cited in addition to the articles which I used in almost every footnote dealing with canon law.[63] Since that time, Dyan Elliott has intelligently explored the relationship of the marriage vow to the vow of chastity in a wider context than I have undertaken here.[64] The largest regret that I have in republishing my study is that I did not pay more attention to hagiography, in addition to canon law, in presenting the context for Christina's successful avoidance of marriage to a man in favour of marriage to Christ. The two hagiographic traditions which are most relevant, as I discuss briefly, are those of Cecilia and Alexis. Dyan Elliott has presented a convincing analysis of the Cecilia legend and its relationship to the ideal of chaste marriage in the Middle Ages.[65] Neil Cartlidge has thoroughly investigated the relationships between the *Chanson de St Alexis* and the *Life of Christina of Markyate*.[66] He has correctly chastised me for presenting too strict a division between Anglo-Saxon and Anglo-Norman cultures in twelfth-century England (although he does not take up the evidence of liturgical calendars which I have presented).[67] The place of women within the trilingual religious culture found in high medieval England has since been superbly analysed by Jocelyn Wogan-Browne.[68]

Notes

1 Ruth Mazo Karras, 'Friendship and Love in the Lives of Two Twelfth-Century English Saints', *The Journal of Medieval History* 14 (1988), 305–20 (p. 313).

2 See particularly the discussion of the evidence by Talbot in *Life*, pp. 6–8.

3 John Bugge, *Virginitas. An Essay in the History of a Medieval Ideal*, International Archives of the History of Ideas, series minor 17 (The Hague, 1975) p. 94.

4 Barbara Newman, *Sister of Wisdom: Saint Hildegard's Theology of the Feminine* (Berkeley, 1987), pp. 221–2.

5 Jean-Baptiste Molin and Protais Mutembe, *Le Rituel du mariage en France du XIIe au XVIe siècle*, Théologie historique 26 (Paris, 1974), p. 277.

6 Thomas Renna, 'Virginity in the *Life* of Christina of Markyate and Aelred of Rievaulx's *Rule*', *American Benedictine Review* 36 (1985), 79–92 (p. 91).

7 While Christina's words have the ring of a liturgical formula, no version of this particular vow is to be found among the standard liturgies for the consecration of virgins discussed by René Metz, *La Consécration des vierges dans l'Église romaine. Étude d'histoire de la liturgie* (Paris, 1954).

8 On those relationships, see Thomas Head, *Hagiography and the Cult of the Saints. The Diocese of Orléans, 800–1200*, Cambridge Studies in Medieval Life and Thought, fourth series 14 (Cambridge, 1990), ch. 4 and the bibliography discussed there.

9 On the flexibility of the term *desponsatio*, see Jean Gaudemet, *Le Mariage en Occident. Les Moeurs et le droit* (Paris, 1987), pp. 60–1.

10 Molin and Mutembe, *Le Rituel du mariage*, provides the fullest discussion of marriage rituals after the year 1000. Their treatment, while focused on French sources, includes many Anglo-Saxon and Anglo-Norman liturgical texts and can be considered accurate for twelfth-century England. During that period betrothals were not usually distinguished in a formal manner from wedding ceremonies. On the location of such ceremonies *ad ianuas ecclesiae* in twelfth-century Anglo-Norman rituals, see p. 35. On the donation of the symbolic *denarius*, see pp. 179–86. On the verification of consent, see pp. 63–9. The background to these ceremonies can be found in Korbinien Ritzer, *Formen, Riten und religiöses Brauchtum der Eheschliessung in den christlichen Kirchen des ersten Jahrtausends*, 2nd edn, Liturgiewissenschaftliche Quellen und Forschungen 38 (Münster, 1981).

11 On this process, see Gérard Fransen, 'La Formation du lien matrimonial au Moyen Âge', in *Le Lien Matrimonial*, ed. René Metz and Jean Schlick, Université de Strasbourg II, Annuaire du CERDIC, Hommes et église 1 (Strasbourg, 1970), pp. 106–26 and, in less detail, Gaudemet, *Le Mariage en Occident*, pp. 171–88.

12 *Be Wifmannes Beweddunge*, ch. 8 in *Councils and Synods With Other Documents Relating to the English Church. Part I, 871–1204*, ed. Dorothy Whitelock, Martin Brett and Christopher Brooke, 2 vols. (Oxford 1980–81), 1. 431.

13 *Canons of the Council of Winchester*, ch. 6 in *Councils and Synods*, 2: 620.

14 For a catalogue, which goes well beyond the twelfth century, see Baudouin de Gaiffier, 'Intactam sponsam relinquens. À propos de la Vie de s. Alexis', *Analecta Bollandiana* 65 (1947), 157–95.

15 Pächt, pp. 126–46. See chapter 13 in this volume.

16 See, for example, Holdsworth, 'Christina of Markyate', p. 191.

17 For editions of English calendars of saints' feasts, see *English Kalendars Before A.D. 1100*, ed. Francis Wormald, Henry Bradshaw Society 72 (London, 1934) and *English Kalendars After A.D. 1100. Volume I, A–D*, Henry Bradshaw Society 77 (London, 1939). Virtually all the published calendars include the feast of St Cecilia (November 22). None include that of Alexis (July 17). All those which date from before 1100 list November 6 as the feast of Winnocus. Of those which date from after 1100, all but two list that date as the feast of Leonard of Noblat, while none retain the mention of Winnocus.

18 On this phrase, see Giles Constable, '*Nudus nudum Christum sequi* and Parallel Formulas in the Twelfth Century. A Supplementary Dossier', in *Continuity and Discontinuity in Church History: Essays Presented to George Huntston Williams on the Occasion of His Sixty-Fifth Birthday*, ed. F. Forrester Church and Timothy George, Studies in the History of Christian Thought 19 (Leiden, 1979), pp. 83–91 and the bibliography cited there.

19 Their fears become even more comprehensible in light of an incident, recorded by William of Malmesbury in a passage excised from the final version of the *De gestis pontificum Anglorum*, in which Robert Bloet attacked Roger for harbouring, in the person of Christina, a woman whom he had ordered to be turned back over to her parents and husband. On this passage, see Elkins, *Holy Woman*, pp. 31–2.

20 On the evolution of the ritual of the consecration of virgins, see Metz, *La Consécration des vierges*, particularly pp. 118–24 on similarities to marriage ceremonies in late antiquity and pp. 386–409 on such similarities in the twelfth century. As a formal consecration (*sacracio*) this ritual had to be performed by a bishop using blessed oil. It thus belonged to the highest rank of blessing within the Christian Church, although it was not regarded as a sacrament. The marriage ceremony, on the other hand, required only a simple blessing which could be performed by any priest. Nevertheless, by the twelfth century it was generally considered to be a sacrament. The status of these two blessings was reflected in the choice of language made by the monk of St Albans: here *sacratum signum*, while earlier *sacramentum* in reference to both the betrothal and to the wedding service which was never performed. For a review of the development of the sacramental doctrine of marriage, see Gaudemet, *Le Mariage en Occident*, pp. 188–91. On its relationship to canon law, see Nicholas Haring, 'The Interaction Between Canon Law and Sacramental Theology in the Twelfth Century', in *Proceedings of the Fourth International Congress of Medieval Canon Law*, ed. Stephan Kuttner, Monumenta iuris canonici C.5 (Vatican City, 1976), pp. 484 and 490.

21 The monk of St Albans, for example, at one point seemed to make a distinction between the *desponsatio* or betrothal ceremony between Christina and Burthred which had occurred (*Life*, p. 46), and the *nupciarum celebracio* or wedding ceremony which had not (*Life*, p. 54). Later, however, he used the terms *nupciae*, *sponsalia* and *coniugium* to refer to the betrothal (*Life*, pp. 54, 108 and 112 respectively). On the relationship of these terms, see Gaudemet, *Le Mariage en Occident*, p. 61.

22 Ibid., pp. 52–4 and 199–200.

23 Gérard Fransen, 'La rupture du mariage', in *Il matrimonio nella società altomedievale*, 2 vols., Settimane di studio del Centro italiano di studi sull'alto medioevo 24 (Spoleto, 1977), 2:614–16.

24 Joseph Sangmeister, *Force and Fear as Precluding Matrimonial Consent. An Historical Synopsis and Commentary*, Catholic University of America, Canon Law Studies 20 (Washington, DC, 1932), pp. 23–71.

25 Metz, *La Consécration des vierges*, p. 121.

26 Robert Hanning, *The Individual in Twelfth-Century Romance* (New Haven, 1977), pp. 40–1; Christopher Brooke, 'Aspects of Marriage Law in the Eleventh and Twelfth Centuries', in *Proceedings of the Fifth International Congress of Medieval Canon Law*, ed. Stephan Kuttner and Kenneth Pennington, Monumenta Iuris Canonici C.6 (Vatican City, 1980), pp. 337–8.

27 Aelred of Rievaulx, *De institutione inclusarum*, chs 14–18 in *Opera Omnia*, ed. C. H. Talbot, CCCM 1 (Turnhout, 1971), pp. 649–54.

28 Ibid., ch. 14, p. 650.

29 Leo I, *Epistolae*, no. 167, part 4 in *PL* 54, cols. 1204–5.

30 The key text is Hincmar of Reims, *Epistola*, no. 136 in *MGH, Epistolae*, 8. 87–107.

31 On these developments in the early Middle Ages, see Jean Gaudemet, 'Le Lien matrimonial. Les Incertitudes du haut Moyen-Âge', in Metz and Schlick, *Le Lien matrimonial*, pp. 81–105, and 'Recherche sur les origines historiques de la faculté de rompre le mariage non consommé', in Kuttner and Pennington, *Proceedings of the Fifth International Congress*, pp. 309–31.

32 On Ivo, see particularly Rolf Sprandel, *Ivo von Chartres und seine Stellung in der Kirchengeschichte* (Stuttgart, 1962), pp. 64–77, and Yves Labonté, *Le mariage selon Ives de Chartres* (Montreal, 1965), pp. 1–56.

33 Ivo of Chartres, *Panormia*, 6.11–23 in *PL* 161, cols. 1216–18. The quoted rubric is at 6.15.

34 The formula occurs in Ivo of Chartres, *Epistolae*, nos. 99, 148, 161 and 246 in *PL* 161, 119, 153, 165 and 253.

35 Ivo of Chartres, *Epistolae*, nos. 166 and 243 (force and fear) and 213 and 242 (serfs). Unfree people could not legally give their consent.

36 On these writers and their ideas of consent, see Heinrich Reinhardt, *Die Ehelehre der Schule des Anselm von Laon. Eine theologie- und kirchenrechtsgeschichtliche Untersuchung zu den Ehetexten der frühen pariser Schule des 12. Jahrhunderts*, Beiträge zur Geschichte der Philosophie und Theologie des Mittelalters, Neue Folge 14 (Münster, 1974), particularly pp. 86–98.

37 Hugh of St Victor, *De sacramentis*, 2.11.5 in *PL* 176, cols. 176–487.

38 Ibid., 2.11.3 in *PL* 176, cols. 481–3.

39 Gratian, *Decretum*, C. 27, q. 2 in *Corpus Iuris Canonici*, ed. Emil Friedburg (Leipzig, 1881; reprint, 1959), 1: 1062–78.

40 Gratian, *Decretum*, C. 27, q. 2, post can. 2 in Friedburg, *Corpus Iuris Canonici*, col. 1063.

41 Gratian, *Decretum*, C.27, q.2, can. 16 in Friedburg, *Corpus Iuris Canonici*, col. 1066.

42 Gratian, *Decretum*, C. 27, q. 2, post can. 39 in Friedburg, *Corpus Iuris Canonici*, col. 1074. One problem with this stress on the *conmixtio sexuum* was that it excluded, as Gratian admitted, the union of Mary and Joseph from being a fully sacramental marriage.

43 Gratian, *Decretum*, C. 27, q. 2, post can. 26 in Friedburg, *Corpus Iuris Canonici*, col. 1070.

44 Peter Lombard, *Sententiae in IV libris distinctae* (Grottaferrata and Rome, 1981), 4.27.3, pp. 422–3.

45 Peter Lombard, *Sententiae*, 4.28.4, p. 435.

46 Charles Donahue, 'The Policy of Alexander the Third's Consent Theory of Marriage', in Kuttner, *Proceedings of the Fourth International Congress*, pp. 251–81; *idem*, 'The Dating of Alexander the Third's Marriage Decretals', *Zeitschrift der Savigny-Stiftung für Rechtsgeschichte, Kanonistische Abteilung* 99 (1982), pp. 69–124; Charles Duggan, 'Equity and Compassion in Papal Marriage Decretals to England', in *Love and Marriage in the Twelfth Century*, ed. Willy van Hoecke and Andries Welkenhuysen, Mediaevalia Lovaniensia 1.8 (Leuven, 1981), pp. 59–87.

47 Duggan, 'Equity and Compassion', p. 62.

48 Adrian Morey, *Bartholomew of Exeter, Bishop and Canonist. A Study in the Twelfth Century* (Cambridge, 1937), pp. 66–72; Jane Sayers, *Papal Judges Delegate in the Province of Canterbury, 1198–1254. A Study in Ecclesiastical Jurisdiction and Administration* (Oxford, 1971), pp. 204–9; Donahue, 'Policy of Alexander', particularly pp. 256–60; Brooke, 'Aspects of Marriage Law', particularly pp. 335–40; Duggan, 'Equity and Compassion', *passim*.

49 There are several extant documents relevant to the case: a decretal of Innocent II adjudicating the first appeal of the case, see *Quinque compilationes antiquae*, ed. Emil Friedberg (Leipzig, 1882; rpt., 1956), Comp. I, 4.1.10, pp. 44–5 (not included in the *Liber Extra*); a letter by John of Salisbury, on behalf of Archbishop Theobald, to Alexander III which summarizes the original pleading, see *The Letters of John of Salisbury*, ed. W. J. Millor and H. E. Butler, rev. Christopher Brooke, Nelson's Medieval Texts (Edinburgh and London, 1955), pp. 227–37; the diary of Richard of Anstey, see P. M. Barnes, 'The Anstey Case', in *Medieval Miscellany for Doris Mary Stenton*, ed. Patricia Barnes and C. F. Slade (London, 1962), pp. 17–23; and the decretal of Alexander III adjudicating the second appeal, see Barnes, 'The Anstey Case', p. 24. For commentary, see *The Letters of John of Salisbury*, pp. 267–71; Barnes, 'The Anstey Case', pp. 1–16; Brooke, 'Aspects of Marriage Law', pp. 335–6.

50 *Quinque compilationes antiquae*, p. 44 and *The Letters of John of Salisbury*, p. 229. On the text of Innocent's decretal, see *The Letters of John of Salisbury*, p. 268, n. 2.

51 'Praeterea coniugium non esse perfectum quod non confirmat et perficit commixtio corporalis, licet a prima desponsationis fide initium sortiatur', *The Letters of John of Salisbury*, p. 231. Cf. 'Ecce, quod in desponsatione coniugium initiatur, non perficitur', Gratian, *Decretum*, C. 27, q. 2, post can. 35 in Friedburg, *Corpus Iuris Canonici*, col. 1073. 'Coniunctorum permixtio matrimonium perfecit', Gratian, *Decretum*, C. 27, q. 2, can. 36, col. 1073.

52 Donahue, 'Policy of Alexander', particularly pp. 151–3 and 270–9, and 'The Canon Law on the Formation of Marriage and Social Practice in the Later Middle Ages', *Journal of Family History* 8 (1983), 144–5. In an appendix to the former article (pp. 280–1), Donahue considers the question of the cohesiveness of Alexander's policy in the light of the work of other scholars.

53 On this matter generally, see John Noonan, 'Power to Choose', *Viator* 4 (1973), 419–34, and Georges Duby, *Medieval Marriage: Two Models from Medieval France*, trans. Elborg Forster (Baltimore, 1978).

54 See, for example, 'Alice *contra* John the Blacksmith', in *Select Cases from the Ecclesiastical Courts of the Province of Canterbury, c. 1200–1301*, ed. Norma Adams and Charles Donahue, Selden Society 95 (London, 1981), pp. 25–8.

55 Most of the extant evidence on marriage cases from England courts dates from the thirteenth century or later. See, for example, William Sheehan, 'The Formation and Stability of Marriage in Fourteenth-Century England: Evidence of an Ely Register', *Mediaeval Studies* 33 (1971) 228–63; R. H. Helmholz, *Marriage Litigation in Medieval England* (Cambridge, 1974); Donahue, 'Policy of Alexander', pp. 260–70; Robert Palmer, 'Contexts of Marriage in Medieval England: Evidence from the King's Court circa 1300', *Speculum* 59 (1984), 42–67; Elaine Clark, 'The Decision to Marry in

Thirteenth- and Early Fourteenth-Century Norfolk', *Mediaeval Studies* 49 (1987), 496–516.

56 Palmer, 'Contexts of Marriage', p. 64.

57 Ibid., p. 42, n. 1.

58 Phyllis Roberts, 'Stephen Langton's *Sermo de Virginibus*', in *Women of the Medieval World. Essays in Honor of John Hine Mundy*, ed. Julius Kirshner and Suzanne Wemple (Oxford, 1985), pp. 103–18, particularly p. 107.

59 Duby, *Medieval Marriage*, pp. 16–17.

60 Thomas Head, 'The Marriages of Christina of Markyate', *Viator* 21 (1990), 71–95.

61 R. I. Moore, pp. 141–2, n. 1 in this volume.

62 Paulette L'Hermite-Leclercq, 'Enfance et mariage d'une jeune anglaise au début du XIIe siècle: Christina de Markyate', in *Les Âges de la vie au Moyen Âge: Actes du colloque du Département d'Études Médiévales de l'Université de Paris-Sorbonne et de l'Université Friedrich-Wilhelm de Bonn, Provins, 16–17 mars 1990*, ed. Henri Dubois and Michel Zink, Cultures et civilizations médiévales 7 (Paris, 1992), pp. 151–69; 'Gestes et vocabulaires du mariage au début du XIIe siècle dans un document hagiographique: La *Vita* de Christina de Markyate', in *Maisons de Dieu et hommes d'église: Florilège en l'honneur de Pierre-Roger Gaussin*, ed. Henri Duranton, Jacqueline Giraud and Nicole Bouter (Saint-Etienne, 1992), pp. 151–63; 'De l'ermitage au monastère, genèse d'une institution. Un exemple anglais de la première moitié du XIIè siècle', in *Histoire et société: Mélanges offerts à Georges Duby*, ed. Charles de la Roncière *et al.*, 4 vols. (Aix-en-Provence, 1992), iii. 49–59.

63 James Brundage, *Law, Sex, and Christian Society in Medieval Europe* (Chicago, 1987).

64 Dyan Elliott, *Spiritual Marriage: Sexual Abstinence in Medieval Wedlock* (Princeton, 1993), particularly pp. 155–67, but also more specifically on Christina of Markyate, see pp. 143, 217, n. 73, 218, n. 77 and 220, n. 83.

65 Elliott, *Spiritual Marriage*, particularly pp. 63–73, and more specifically on the relationship of Christina and the Cecilia legend at p. 209.

66 Neil Cartlidge, *Medieval Marriage: Literary Approaches, 1100–1300* (Cambridge and Rochester, 1997), pp. 76–118.

67 Cartlidge, *Medieval Marriage*, p. 106, n. 156.

68 Wogan-Browne, *Saints' Lives*, particularly pp. 41–2, 51, 65, 87, 115, 131–3, 190 and 205 for comments on Christina.

8

RANULF FLAMBARD AND CHRISTINA OF MARKYATE[1]

R. I. Moore

He [Ranulf Flambard] had the unsuspecting girl brought into his chamber where he himself slept, which was hung with beautiful tapestries, the only others present with the innocent child being members of his retinue. Her father and mother and the others with whom she had come were in the hall apart giving themselves up to drunkenness. When it was getting dark the bishop gave a secret sign to his servants and they left the room, leaving their master and Christina, that is to say, the wolf and the lamb, together in the same room. For shame! The shameless bishop took hold of Christina by one of the sleeves of her tunic and with that mouth which he used to consecrate the sacred species, he solicited her to commit a wicked deed.

(*Life*, pp. 41–3)

The story of Ranulf Flambard's overture to the young Theodora, later to be known by her name in religion as Christina of Markyate,[2] and of how she frustrated it by persuading him to allow her to bolt the door, 'for even if we have no fear of God, at least we should take precautions that no man should catch us in the act', and doing so from the outside after making her escape, is understandably a popular one with writers and lecturers, and generally loses nothing in the telling. Ranulf was no longer, in William of Malmesbury's phrase, *totius regni procurator* (manager of the whole kingdom), as he had been under William Rufus,[3] but he was still bishop of Durham, one of the wealthiest and most independent magnates of the kingdom, long since recovered from the disgrace and humiliation which the beginning of the new reign and the distrust of the new king had almost inevitably brought for the greatest servant of the old one, and the obvious scapegoat for his unpopularity.[4] Besides the elements of comedy and titillation in the story, there could hardly be a more touching image of defiance of the brutalities of conquest than a sixteen-year-old girl successfully fending off the man whose name, more than any except that of William Rufus himself, and despite the judicious reappraisal of modern scholarship,[5] stubbornly continues to evoke them. Yet, even allowing for the selectivity of memory and the improvements which doubtless occurred to the ageing Christina as she told the story to the anonymous monk of St Albans to whom we owe her *Life*,[6] the text does not quite bear out that impression. Certainly, though Christina may have feared that 'if she openly resisted him, she would certainly be overcome by force', 'attempted rape'[7] is a stronger description than the text will support. Though its recent use obviously reflects late twentieth-century distaste for the abuse of power for sexual ends, it echoes an older stereotype of the licence and inclinations of 'feudal' magnates in relation to young women 'of the people' which this story should encourage us to question, at least occasionally. The term more commonly employed, 'seduction',[8] is nearer the mark, but it does not altogether prepare us for Ranulf's response to his somewhat ignominious rebuff:[9] he continued his journey to London, and 'on his return came to Huntingdon, bringing with him silken garments and precious ornaments of all kinds' – which Christina, of course, rejected with contumely. Nevertheless, that sounds more like courtship – even, conceivably, with a hint of apology for its over-hasty beginning. At the least it suggests that Ranulf's interest was neither impetuous nor furtive, and therefore – no small point for such a man – that he was prepared to risk whatever loss of face his failure, in the circumstances, would imply.

Perhaps, then, the risk was not so very great. The acquaintance, it will be recalled, arose from Ranulf's connection with Alveva (Ælfigfu), the sister of Christina's mother Beatrix. The text says simply that he had her (*habuerat*), but the relationship was not a transient one. The connection began when Ranulf was still 'justiciar of the whole of England, holding second place after the king', so before 1099, and probably before Christina's birth. There were children (*filios*) by the union, and it seems that Ranulf took his obligations to them seriously, if Barlow was correct in identifying one of them as the twelve-year-old boy for whom he tried to secure the bishopric of Lisieux to the indignation of Ivo of Chartres, and another as Elias, clerk in Henry I's household and prebendary of St Paul's.[10] Southern's description of Ranulf's connection with Alveva as a marriage,[11] even allowing for the uncertaties attending that state in the 1090s, is not altogether easy to reconcile with the *Life*'s statement that 'afterwards he gave her in marriage (*in uxorem*) to one of the citizens of Huntingdon and for her sake held the rest of her kin in high esteem', but it does justice to the evidently public and respectable character of the liaison. Ranulf made it his habit to stay with Alveva and her husband on his journeys between London and Northumbria, and it was on one such occasion, probably around 1114, when 'Autti, his friend [and Alveva's brother-in-law], had come as usual to see him' that 'the bishop gazed intently at his beautiful daughter' (*Life*, p. 41). It does not sound as though Autti objected very strongly to the gaze, for he and his wife would hardly have become so drunk as not to notice the prolonged absence of their daughter in their host's bedroom, and Christina's conviction at the moment of crisis that it would be useless to call her parents because 'they had already gone to bed' (*Life*, p. 43) is not entirely convincing, unless there was an unexpectedly high level of soundproofing even for a substantial town house. It can hardly have been without their knowledge that Ranulf renewed his advances with the expensive gifts from London. Nor was his friendship with Autti and Beatrix soured either by his own or by Christina's behaviour, since he responded to her second rebuff by arranging her marriage to Burthred, another of his connections among the English nobility of the vicinity. Her biographer's (and presumably therefore her own) attribution of this involvement to Ranulf's malicious determination to 'gain his revenge by depriving Christina of her virginity, either by himself or by someone else', may sound pruriently plausible to the post-Freudian mind, but a more obvious explanation is that he considered it consonant with his patronal relationship with her family to help secure an advantageous match for their eldest daughter, even though she had rejected his own offer of protection. In any case, the enthusiasm with which both parents urged the consummation of the marriage over the next couple of years provided ample opportunity for the trial – and the triumph – of Christina's resolve.

In short, there was evidently mutual and continuing advantage in the connection that had been created through Alveva. Perhaps the social eminence of her family, *ex anglis nobilibus antiquis atque potentibus* ('of ancient and powerful English nobles' (*Life*, p. 82)),[12] offered something of glamour or standing as well as a good deal in helpful contacts among the conquered to the lowborn Norman who had risen so high. The shrewd observation that 'some kind of legitimation was to be sought in the co-option of the support of native heiresses and saints'[13] has wide application, and the standing of Christina's family, as well as her own distinction, was later implicitly acknowledged in Archbishop Thurstan's suggestion that she might enter Marcigny or Fontevrault (*Life*, p. 127), two of the smartest convents in Europe. Certainly Ranulf had a great deal to offer in return to Saxons of high rank who were making their way back to the wealth and standing which they had enjoyed before the conquest.

In that light the famous bedroom scene prompts the suspicion that Autti's family would not have been averse to seeing Christina succeed to the position that had brought her aunt wealth, a good marriage in the town, and friends, perhaps even sons, in high places. Christina preferred, of course, to dedicate her life to Christ, and eventually inherited the hermitage of Roger, a monk of St Albans who had lived the solitary rule under the obedience of his abbot. She might have preferred a monastic life from the outset if it had been open to her.[14] But, as Henry Mayr-Harting showed in his classic paper on the functions of the recluse in this period,[15] her refusal to succeed to Alveva's position by no means required her to dishonour her family or turn her back on friends and community. In her chosen life Christina achieved fame and influence far wider than Alveva's, not least through her intimacy with another great Norman prelate, Abbot Geoffrey of St Albans, whom King Stephen sent to Rome to secure papal confirmation of his election to the throne, and who was repeatedly advised by Christina on his relations with the royal court through the dangerous years that followed (*Life*, pp. 161–71). It was Geoffrey who built a priory at Markyate for Christina, and most probably his successor, Abbot Robert, who commissioned for her the great Psalter whose obits commemorated her family and friends, including her parents, her brothers and her sister – and Alveva.[16]

If this reading is correct it might seem that Christina did not so much refuse to take over the duties of her aunt as insist on reinterpreting them for a new generation, in a manner better suited to the sensibilities of a reformed church, a more elevated conception of female influence and the standing of her family, and even a more dignified representation of the relationship between Norman administration and a prosperous English bourgeoisie. In that case, even if scepticism of the sensational details of her story were justified,[17] it would have remained a salutary and instructive example of the qualities which enabled the hermits and recluses who were, as Mayr-Harting insisted, to be found in or near so many communities in early twelfth-century England, to provide the indispensable bridge between conquered and conquerors. As he showed, the acquisition and deployment of spiritual power might, in these circumstances, require not only pre-eminent virtue, but a measure of toughness, even bloody-mindedness, in the most unexpected ways. Christina, still in her teens, kept the keys to her father's strong-box (*Life*, p. 73). She was fitted and destined, by family, talent and upbringing, to assume a place among the leadership of the English community in Huntingdon, to whom their relations with the Normans were obviously of crucial importance, and was no doubt expected to accept the responsibilities that went with it. Her mother's fury at her obdurate determination to resist the marriage which Ranulf arranged perhaps reflected not only the chagrin of disappointed social ambition, but a sense of betrayal that her child should reject such a role. But Christina did not reject it. She was more fortunate than Alveva had been in the space for negotiation that was open to her as to the form her mediation should take, as well as skilful and determined in the use to which she put it over a long and distinguished life. Her rejection of Ranulf Flambard's bed may remind us how another young woman from Hertfordshire, Elizabeth Bennet, declined Lydia's offer to get husbands for all her sisters before the end of the winter: 'I thank you for my share of the favour, but I do not particularly like your way of getting husbands.'[18] Elizabeth, as it turned out, had a better way of her own.

Notes

This chapter was previously published as R. I. Moore, 'Ranulf Flambard and Christina of Markyate', in *Belief and Culture*.

1 I am grateful to my colleague A. E. Redgate, a friend and pupil of Henry Mayr-Harting, for comments on a draft of this paper.

2 For Christina's family and the chronology of her life I follow Talbot's 'Introduction' at pp. 10–15. The *Life* does not make it clear when she adopted the name Christina. *Pace* Thomas Head's valuable 'The Marriages of Christina of Markyate', Viator 21 (1990), 71–95 at p. 85, that she 'deserved (meruerit) to be known by the name of her creator' for her steadfastness in resisting the consummation of her marriage though apparently deserted even by her spiritual adviser Sueno (*Life*, p. 57) does not necessarily mean that

she was known by it from that time: she was addressed as Theodora in a vision and by her sister some time later, just before she ran away from home (*Life*, p. 91). At this point she took refuge with the anchoress Alfwen at Flamstead, abandoning the silk dress and luxurious furs which she had worn in her father's house for a religious habit, and living in concealment for two years (*Life*, pp. 93–5). This would have provided both a religious and a practical occasion for changing her name, the latter perhaps accounting for the rather puzzling 'nomen sibi Christinam accepit ex necessitate' of the opening paragraph (*Life*, pp. 33–5).

3 William of Malmesbury, *De Gestis Pontificum Anglorum*, ed. N. E. S. A. Hamilton, RS 52 (London, 1870), p. 274; quoted by Frank Barlow, *William Rufus* (London, 1983), p. 201, n. 173; similar characterizations from all the leading Anglo-Norman chroniclers are collected and discussed, ibid., pp. 200–1, and by R. W. Southern, 'Ranulf Flambard' in *Medieval Humanism and Other Studies* (Oxford, 1970), pp. 183–205, at pp. 184–5.

4 Southern, 'Ranulf Flambard', pp. 196–9.

5 In addition to Southern's classic paper cited above see especially Barlow, *William Rufus*, pp. 193–210 and passim, and H. S. Offler, 'Rannulph Flambard as Bishop of Durham', *Durham University Journal* 64 (1971).

6 cf. Christopher Brooke, *The Medieval Idea of Marriage* (Oxford, 1989), pp. 144–8, who suspects 'an element of fantasy' in the Flambard story.

7 Holdsworth, 'Christina of Markyate', p. 198; Elkins, *Holy Women*, pp. 28–9.

8 Southern, 'Ranulf Flambard', pp. 183–205, at 203; Brooke, *Medieval Idea of Marriage*, pp. 144–5; Head, 'Marriages', p. 120 in this volume; Barlow, *William Rufus*, p. 197, in a characteristically invigorating account of Flambard's personality and exploits.

9 The epithet is borrowed from Southern, 'Ranulf Flambard', p. 186.

10 Barlow, *William Rufus*, p. 202

11 Southern, 'Ranulf Flambard', pp. 186, 191.

12 For the likely *milieu* of Christina's pre-conquest forebears see Robin Fleming, 'Rural Elites and Urban Communities in Late Saxon England', *Past & Present* 141 (1993), 3–37.

13 Henrietta Leyser, *Medieval Women* (London, 1995), p. 200.

14 Holdsworth, 'Christina of Markyate', p. 187; but her parents, once reconciled to her refusal to marry, could certainly have afforded the necessary dowry – if they had been willing, or anxious, for her to leave the neighbourhood.

15 Henry Mayr-Harting, 'Functions of a Twelfth-Century Recluse', *History* 60 (1975), 337–52.

16 *Life*, p. 25; Pächt, pp. 27–8.

17 Brooke, *Medieval Idea of Marriage*, see n. 6 above. H. S. Offler, *Durham Episcopal Charters, 1071–1152*, Surtees Society 179 (1968), p. 105, declared himself sceptical of the whole story, but gave no reason, and saw none to doubt Ranulf's Huntingdon connection. In general the *Life*, the object of so much enthusiastic interest in recent years, has stood the scrutiny very well: see, for example, the confirmation of some of its most original elements offered coincidentally and quite independently by William of Malmesbury's account of a confrontation between Bishop Robert Bloet of Lincoln and the hermit Roger because the latter was giving shelter to a virgin who had escaped from her husband: *De Gestis Pontificum*, p. 314, noticed by Elkins, *Holy Women*, pp. 31–2.

18 Jane Austen, *Pride and Prejudice*, ch. 51, World's Classics (Oxford, 1929), p. 305.

9

DINING AT MARKYATE
WITH LADY CHRISTINA

Rachel Koopmans

Like many twelfth-century hagiographers, the writer of Christina of Markyate's *vita* knew his subject personally. Christina's establishment at Markyate was less than ten miles away from the writer's home community of St Albans, the large, powerful and ancient Benedictine abbey that dominated the surrounding region. The writer must have made the short trip from St Albans to Markyate often. From the *vita* it is clear that he dined with Christina at Markyate, questioned her at length, knew many of her quirks, spoke with her mother and siblings, and did not wait for her death to begin writing his tale of her life. This writer knew Christina well, and how we envision his relationship with and perception of the living Christina is essential to how we read and understand his text.[1] The first part of this essay is dedicated to thinking through this relationship more carefully. When did the writer come to know Christina? What was it like for him to be in her presence? What did he admire and respect in her? To what extent did Christina dictate the tone and contents of the *vita*, and to what extent the author?

The last question is central to any interpretation of the *vita*. Many scholars read in a large role for Christina: C. H. Talbot set this direction when he declared that 'the whole tone of the text is autobiographical rather than historical' (*Life*, p. 6). I would argue, though, that the *vita* needs to be read as the writer's creation, not as Christina's. When one compares the *vita* to the few other surviving documentary sources concerning Christina, it is possible to note with some precision, on one point at least, the extent to which this text is a construction of the author and not a channeling of Christina's experiences. This one point, as I will explore in the middle section of this essay, is the question of Christina's connections to religious communities besides that of St Albans. The writer presents to us a Christina who focuses all her affections on St Albans, excluding even Christina's own establishment at Markyate. The other sources strongly suggest that this picture reflects the author's desires much more than the reality of Christina's past or present connections.

Rather than thinking of the writer as acting as an amanuensis, a transparent transmitter of Christina's thoughts and actions, it is better to think of him as acting like a portrait painter, sketching out an image of Christina to his liking.

Reading the *vita* as an individualistic portrait of Christina can also help us to imagine how others might have envisioned her differently. In the concluding part of this essay, I will consider how other people acquainted with Christina could have reacted to the *vita*. While an assessment of these reactions must remain speculative, thinking about Christina from other possible perspectives can help us construct a clearer picture of her than the single viewpoint provided for us in the writer's *vita*. We can even begin to wonder how the Lady of Markyate might have responded to the *vita*'s image of herself.

It is not hidden from me

The last third of Christina's *vita*, the section in which the author details Christina's relationship with Abbot Geoffrey as she lived at Markyate, is the best place to look for clues to the writer's perception of and personal experience with Christina. It is in this section of the *vita* that the author's comments and observations take on a distinctly participatory tone. He describes, for instance, how up to the present (*usque presens*) he could not get Christina to tell him how she saw a vision concerning Abbot Geoffrey; how he heard of the punishments meted out to Christina's detractors; and how he had seen others repent of their false gossip (*Life*, pp. 150; 172–4). Earlier in the text, the author's observations tend to be cast in terms of the writer's later experience: he notes, for example, that 'we saw her cured many years later' when he discusses Christina's ailments during the time she lived with Roger (*Life*, p. 104).[2] Considering that Christina did not grow up in the region of St Albans and was in hiding for much of her young adulthood, it seems highly likely that the writer first became acquainted with Christina when she was the leader of Markyate, some time after Roger's death.

Particularly revealing is a passage found on the next-to-last page of the *vita*, a chapter devoted to the story of a meal at Markyate at which the author himself was present. Nowhere else in the *vita* does the author present himself as a direct participant in Christina's story, and the passage, though short, provides us with our best route into the writer's sense of Christina's personality and presence. In the chapter before this passage, the writer describes how Christina knew that one of her maidens was secretly thinking about doing something shameful. He then writes:

> At another time, when we were sitting down at the table with the hand-maid of Christ, the aforesaid maiden set down food for us to eat. And so we began to eat, but Christina would not touch it. Asked whether she would eat something of it with us, she firmly refused. Godit was called, for this was the girl's name [... textual damage ...].[3] For Christina had sworn up to that time that she would not eat of the neighbouring garden, whose owner, possessed by greed, had refused her chervil when she once asked for some. Christina kept silence, by and by accepting some of the salad, but she would not taste the food. Shortly after the meal she proved

144

the girl wrong by the testimony of those seeing her, and she admitted that she had gathered what was eaten in the prohibited garden.

(Life, p. 190)

For the writer from St Albans, to be in Christina's presence meant, first of all, to be with someone in charge of those around her. At the time of this meal, Markyate is clearly being run wholly by Christina's dictates. She can host guests at her table as she pleases, eat and speak as she will, and impose her will on her followers. The period in Christina's life when she was in fierce dispute with her family and hiding out with hermits is long past. Christina is now an independent and mature adult, living openly as Roger's successor at Markyate, with her female followers and even much of her family now reliant on her for leadership and support.[4] It is as 'lady' (domina) that Godit addresses Christina in the anecdote immediately preceding the story of the meal. In nearly every document concerning Christina that has come down to us, Christina appears as Domina Christina,[5] and in the vita Abbot Geoffrey too speaks of Christina as 'my lady' (dominam meam Christinam) (Life, p. 142).

Undoubtedly it was as 'lady' that the author himself addressed Christina. What pulled the author to her presence, though, was something more than her status as a community leader. The thrust of the anecdote is that the Lady of Markyate possesses a special power, the power to see into secrets, to know things, like Godit's herb gathering, that she had no means to know. The writer dedicates much of the last third of the vita to the same theme. In the writer's presentation, Abbot Geoffrey and Christina are introduced in just such an incident. Christina, although she does not know Geoffrey personally, nevertheless sends word to him about a secret design of his, warning him not to carry it out. Although Geoffrey dismisses Christina's warning as nonsense, 'nevertheless he was amazed that what he had conceived alone in his heart had been revealed to the virgin' (Life, p. 136). Later on in their relationship, as the writer reports in awestruck detail, Christina knows what Geoffrey dreams, knows when Geoffrey decides to visit her, when he will recover from illnesses and when he will and will not take a journey. She even knows what colour of clothes he is wearing. No matter what happened, Christina always seemed to be able to say, as she does at one point in the vita, 'it is not hidden from me' (nec me latet) (Life, p. 150).

Dining at Markyate, the writer had the chance to see the handmaiden of Christ in action for himself. Perhaps he had long been hoping for such a sight. The source of these marvellous powers, the author believed, was Christina's special love for God, as he tries to explain for his readers:

> ... as much as she came close to you in true love, so much she merited, with a clean heart, to penetrate more clearly the hidden things of your wisdom. Thus you gave to her to see the secret thoughts of people, and to know from far off those deliberately hidden things as if she were present.

(Life, pp. 188–90)

The writer seems unsure here exactly how God transmitted this knowledge to Christina. In two other chapters the writer states that Christina heard a voice from above, and in another he seems to think that Christina's consciousness could float around outside of Markyate while she was in prayer in her chapel (*Life*, pp. 153, 159 and 141). Abbot Geoffrey was flummoxed: the author reports how he spent many sleepless nights trying to figure it all out (*Life*, p. 151). However she did it, the writer was convinced that Christina could speak with and see God here on earth, that she could engage in secret, sweet and indescribable conversation with God (*sed secretis. sed dulcibus. sed indicibilibus cum Domino colloquiis*) far beyond that vouchsafed to most religious (*Life*, p. 180).

These conversations meant not only that Christina knew other people's secrets but also, and just as wonderful to the author, that she could affect the future in a positive way for her friends. By speaking with God, Christina had already kept Abbot Geoffrey from harm more than once. The author informs his readers, in effusive detail, how Geoffrey begged for Christina's prayers when he was assigned to go on dangerous journeys, and how Christina's intervention kept Geoffrey safely at home (see *Life*, pp. 161–71). Once, the author reports, when Geoffrey wanted to go on a certain trip on the king's business, Christina aired the matter with God nevertheless and managed to keep him at home (*Life*, p. 164). Although the author of the *vita* never reports an instance in which he himself benefited from Christina's prayers, he was clearly fascinated by this aspect of her powers, urging her, it appears, to be specific about how they actually worked, and reporting with precision in his text about the kinds of physical and visual signs that Christina received when God decided to answer her prayers (see *Life*, p. 171).

The writer's understanding of Christina's special and superior relationship with God was not, it appears, undermined by Christina's behaviour at this meal. The writer's report of the proceedings shows clearly that, however sweet Christina's spiritual conversation could be, dealing with the living Christina could be very difficult. Christina apparently sat like a stone at the beginning of this meal, eventually forcing the author and the others at the table, who must have been wondering what was the matter, to beg her to eat a bit with them. Christina refuses to explain or comply and instead causes some sort of scene with Godit there and then (unfortunately the text is damaged at this point). Afterwards, she still keeps silent, only picking a bit at the salad, holding her guests in suspense and agitation until finally at the end of the meal she formally humiliates Godit, calling in witnesses and forcing her to confess her peccadillo as if it were a great crime. And of course, all of this began with Christina taking offence at a neighbour's minor slight.

The author was quite familiar with this side of Christina's behaviour. At various points in the last third of the *vita* he comments on how Christina would not accept help from anyone unless she felt the person's motives were pure; how she only loved her family members if she approved their holiness; and how she would not curb her tongue even if it prompted jealousy in others (see

Life, pp. 133, 157–9, 149). Godit was not the only one Christina admonished for what she thought were serious failings. Abbot Geoffrey and others also clearly felt the sharp side of her tongue (see *Life*, 141, 191). In fact, the last line of the *vita* we now have speaks of Christina's reproofs. The stiffly silent and unresponsive Christina was also far from unknown to the author. He tells the reader how Christina would often go silent right in the middle of a conversation, suddenly knowing nothing of who was about her, what they were doing or what they were saying (*Life*, p. 171). Those who made the journey to Markyate, it appears, could not count on finishing a conversation with Christina, something that Geoffrey, at least, initially found quite disconcerting (see *Life*, p. 155).

Instead of deterring him, Christina's abrupt and abrasive manner seems to have enhanced her spiritual standing with the writer. He speaks of her sudden silences as something remarkable and admirable, evidence of rapt ecstasy with God (*Life*, p. 171). There is only one place in the *vita* where the author displays some irritation at Christina's manner. He describes how Christina, in a conversation with the sub-prior of St Albans, informed the sub-prior that although he had said that Abbot Geoffrey was wearing a white cope on a certain occasion, he was wrong: Geoffrey had actually been wearing a red one. The sub-prior, amazed, realized that she was right. But Christina refused to explain how she knew this: 'How she saw this vision, although she well knows, we have not been able in any way to elicit from her up to the present' (*Life*, p. 150). It appears that Christina was not only good at knowing the secrets of others: she also enjoyed keeping at least some of her own secrets to herself.

While the contents of the *vita* demonstrate that the author did, in the end, manage to elicit a great deal of personal information about Christina, it seems unlikely to have been a smooth or simple process for him. The author remarks on how Christina was always slow to respond when questioned, and how they had often found that to get what they wanted from Christina it was important to approach her carefully and gently (*Life*, pp. 165, 153). Christina seems to have liked expressing herself in pithy proverbs, such as 'Tomorrow white stones will be thrown into the pot' (*Life*, p. 147),[6] rather than in straightforward explanations, a habit of speaking that may well have impressed Christina's listeners but would not have been helpful when it came to gathering material for a *vita*. In two anecdotes in the last third of the *vita* Christina refuses to speak for herself at all, instead calling in her sister Margaret to relate to the company what Christina had told her earlier (*Life*, pp. 145, 155). If Christina did this kind of thing frequently, the author may have found himself speaking as much to Margaret as to Christina. Indeed, we need to consider that the writer may have heard many of the *vita*'s stories, even the stories of Christina's visions, second-hand, from people like Margaret or Abbot Geoffrey. Christina had a reputation to uphold that these two, intimate with Christina's concerns, did not, and it may be that the author resorted to them as more responsive and productive sources than Christina herself.

She chose our monastery above all

Writing a *vita* for Christina, a *domina* whom the author saw graced by such impressive spiritual abilities and condescension, may or may not have been the author's own idea. Christina herself may have first suggested it, in what looks to be a typically oblique manner: the writer reports how Christina, after a display of her clairvoyant powers, remarked to Margaret that 'if something like this had happened in the time of blessed Gregory he would have committed it to memory' (*Life*, p. 154). Perhaps Abbot Geoffrey picked up on such hints, or perhaps the *vita* was initially his idea. At the least, it seems that the *vita*, written by a monk who was clearly a close associate of Geoffrey's, would not have been started without the abbot's knowledge and approval. Perhaps the *vita* was someone else's idea entirely. But whoever initiated the *vita* project, the author made it his own, painting an image of Christina that would help others, especially his primary audience – the community of St Albans – to see her as he did, as a holy woman who had in the past and could in the future do great things for St Albans.

When one reads through the last third of the *vita*, it is extraordinary how often the author makes St Albans come up. At a conservative estimate, this section of the text concerns a good decade of Christina's life at Markyate. The overriding theme in this section of the *vita*, however, is Christina's concern for a single person: Abbot Geoffrey of St Albans. Once Geoffrey is introduced into Christina's story, his relationship with her, and particularly the spiritual, political and physical benefits she showers upon him, is the author's subject to the exclusion of almost everything else. He portrays for his readers a Christina who loves Geoffrey dearly, calling him her most intimate friend (*familiarissimus*), her beloved (*dilectus*), and herself his girl (*sua puella*) (*Life*, pp. 145, 149, 155). Christina puts out her very best intercessory efforts on Geoffrey's behalf, being almost always in tearful prayer for him (*Life*, p. 145). In fact, the author claims on no less than three different occasions that Christina puts more effort into praying for Geoffrey than she does for herself (*Life*, pp. 141, 145, 149). Her beneficial powers are reserved for him even when the story starts out being about something else, as in the case of the headless body found at Markyate that frightened Christina's female followers (*Life*, p. 181).

Reading through the last portion of the *vita*, one would be excused in thinking that, in the time that the author knew her, Christina cared for nothing and no-one unconnected with St Albans. Even the few 'Geoffrey-free' chapters are still always tied back to St Albans somehow, as in the story of Christina's beloved pilgrim, a pilgrim whom she sees, in a vision, standing among the choir of monks at St Albans (*Life*, p. 187). Sources besides the *vita*, however, present to us a rather different Christina, one who was not exclusively the friend of Geoffrey or of St Albans monks. The first clues to this wider range of acquaintances are in the *vita* itself. Eager to show Christina's affection for Geoffrey, the author describes how Christina confessed that 'there was no-one among the many intimates (*familiares*) she had in Christ for whom she was able to pray to God with such devotion and perseverance in prayer' (*Life*, p. 144). Eager to show Geoffrey's influence on Christina, the author describes how many of Christina's intimates and friends urged her to make her profession (*monebatur autem a multis magna sapientibus et religiosis ipsisque familiaribus et amicis suis*), but how it was Geoffrey's pleading that did the trick (*Life*, pp. 144–6). A couple of these non-St Albans *familiares* make brief appearances in the *vita* in the context of Geoffrey's relationship with Christina. In one anecdote, Geoffrey has a travelling companion on the road to Markyate, a certain Evisandus, a man whom the author refers to simply as a 'religious'. This Evisandus discusses Christina's characteristics with Geoffrey and appears to be quite well acquainted with her (*Life*, p. 153). In another anecdote, Abbot Geoffrey receives a message about a vision proving Christina's virginity from a certain Simon of Bermondsey, who, the author says, loved Christina and often felt the Holy Spirit when in her presence (*Life*, pp. 175–7).

In the author's presentation, St Albans monks are solidly and constantly in the foreground of Christina's attention, while Evisandus and Simon and the other unnamed *familiares* are consigned to a blurry existence in the background. The obits in the St Albans Psalter present a different picture. These obits include Geoffrey and the other St Albans members one would expect from the *vita*'s presentation.[7] But there is also a large number of names and figures who do not appear in the *vita*. There are two more monks, a Robert and a Richard; two hermits, Ailward and Azo; a canon, Ailward; and a man labelled simply as Godwin. There are also three new female names: *Adelaisa monialis*; *Avicia priorissa de Sopewell*; and *Matildis monialis de Marzellis*.[8] While Christina could not have been the guiding force behind these obits (hers is there too), given their reference to her (the obit for Gregory, for instance, reads *Gregorius monachus frater domine Cristine*), it seems highly likely that Christina knew these men and women well. Maybe Robert and Richard were not St Albans monks: the hermits Ailward and Azo, the canon Ailward and Godwin almost certainly were not. As the *vita* writer refused to say anything about them, we will never know just what role these men had in Christina's life or she in theirs. However, they may well have been as important to her, or more, than the abbot or monks from St Albans.

The women's names in the obits are particularly telling. The *vita* writer mentions the names of only eight women, and not once does he present Christina as having affection for any of them, not even for her sister and companion Margaret. Godit is the only woman at Markyate besides Margaret who gets named in the *vita*, and then only to be reproved. The Adelaisa and Matilda of the obits may have been, as Francis Wormald surmised for Matilda, some of Christina's first followers at Markyate, and probably, given their appearance in the obits, especially beloved.[9] Just as interesting is the appearance of the prioress of Sopwell. Sally Thompson has uncovered charter evidence which suggests that Roger of Markyate had close ties with the nuns of Sopwell; that he founded that community, in fact.[10] The writer of the chronicle of St Albans, the *Gesta Abbatum*, describes Abbot Geoffrey's involvement with the community at

Sopwell at considerable length. With these two men active in the community at Sopwell it would seem odd indeed if Christina never had any interaction with the women there. Yet the *vita* writer never whispers a word about Sopwell in his presentation of Christina's life-story.

Some of these silences may be attributed to abridgement to the text of the *vita* in the Tiberius manuscript, the basis for Talbot's edition. It is clear that the text we now have cuts out anecdotes having to do with Abbot Geoffrey and another St Albans monk, Thomas; perhaps the full text mentioned Robert, Richard, Ailward and the rest.[11] But the whole current of the story we now have would argue against a text that in its unabridged state gave serious attention to Christina's relationships with non-St Albans monks, especially serious attention to the women at Markyate. The extent of the author's disregard of Christina's networks outside of St Albans becomes even more evident when one looks at the witness lists of the two charters relating to the foundation of the nunnery of Markyate in 1145. Geoffrey and St Albans monks appear as prominent witnesses to both of these charters. But there are also many other names of men on the witness lists from a wide range of other religious communities.[12] Another monk from Bermondsey appears as a witness to the first charter; not Simon this time, but Gervase. Might Simon and Gervase have made the trip to Markyate from Bermondsey together? How many other monks in that community were acquainted with Christina? On each witness list one finds a man from Christina's home town of Huntingdon: the first, 'Simon of Huntingdon', might have been Christina's brother; the second, 'Henry archdeacon of Huntingdon', is unidentified, but these entries suggest that Christina may have retained close ties with her birthplace, something the author never mentions.

Also interesting is the appearance of Robert, the prior of Merton, whose name is present on the witness lists of both the original agreement with the canons of St Paul's and the confirmation charter by Alexander, bishop of Lincoln. On each charter Roger is accompanied by another member of his house as well. Might this Robert have been grateful for some favour Christina had obtained for him? Could Christina have had a special relationship with the canons at Merton as well as the monks of St Albans? Still another man who witnessed both charters was Ilbertus, the master of the infirmary of St Julian's. It would not be surprising if Christina had close ties with this community. As with Sopwell, the *Gesta Abbatum* chronicler states that the community of St Julian's was founded and constructed by Abbot Geoffrey.[13] Once again, though, the *vita* gives no hint of any association of Christina with this community. Also striking is the fact that the *vita* writer never relates a word about Christina's possible relationship with the canons of St Paul's in London, the community that owned the land Christina lived on and, by these charters of 1145, came to hold formal religious jurisdiction over Markyate. It is possible that Christina had no contact with these canons before 1145, but harder to believe that at the time the author knew her Christina also had no contact with St Julian's, St Mary's at Huntingdon, Merton, or Bermondsey, or the female communities in her region, such as Sopwell and Flamstead.

In the final third of the *vita*, the author paints a portrait of the Christina he knew as a woman focusing every fibre of her loving attention on his abbot and community of St Albans. He must have known of Abbot Geoffrey's dealings with Sopwell and the hospital at St Julian's, and the extent of Christina's involvement. He must have been acquainted with at least some of the women at Markyate besides Margaret and Godit. He also clearly knew that Christina hosted more than just St Albans monks at Markyate, but he did not allow any of these men or women a solid presence within his portrait of Christina's life, most probably because a clear picture of Christina as a leader of another community and the friend of many would undermine his attempts to show her special value and affection for his own.

The author also strives to show Christina's particular regard for St Albans in the period before he knew her, in her childhood and early adulthood. At the very beginning of the *vita*, just a few paragraphs in, there is the young Christina already visiting 'our monastery', brought there 'through divine providence' by her parents. The author does his best to lend great significance to this childhood visit, saying that Christina liked what she saw of the monks there, that 'she proclaimed them happy and she wished to become one of their associates'. He goes on to tell of the departing Christina scratching a cross on a door with her fingernail to show 'that she had specially hidden her affection in that monastery' (*quod in illo specialiter monasterio suum recondidisset affectum*). To add a final weighty note to this incident, the author informs his readers that this cross-scratching took place on Christina's birthday (*Life*, p. 38).

Perhaps this is precisely how the mature Christina remembered her long-ago visit to St Albans, and perhaps it is a strictly accurate reflection of her thoughts and attitudes as a girl. It seems more likely, though, that either the author or Christina or both read back considerably more significance into this visit than was present at the time. In addition to inflating the importance of St Albans here, the author also minimizes the importance of other religious communities to the youthful Christina. The Augustinian community of St Mary's in Huntingdon was founded around the time Christina was born, between 1086 and 1092. The author mentions this community numerous times in the early portion of Christina's *vita*: St Mary's is where Christina's friend Sueno lives; where Christina finds the strength to resist her marriage; where Christina's parents bring her to be questioned and look for her when they cannot find her at home (see *Life*, pp. 47–9, 59, 87–9, 95). But the author never allows Christina to express any admiration of the canons at St Mary's as she does for the monks of St Albans. She scratches no cross on its door and never desires to become associated with its inhabitants. St Mary's is introduced into Christina's story simply as the monastery in her town (*quod in civitate situm est*) (*Life*, p. 34).

Another religious locale that receives short shrift in the author's presentation is the church of Shillington. This church appears briefly in the *vita* in the context of Christina's family's visit to St Albans. Shillington is where the family stops for the evening on its way home and where, in the morning, Christina makes a secret vow of virginity before the priest. The author provides so little transition between St Albans and Shillington that it reads as though Christina was inspired to this vow by her visit to St Albans: indeed, there is so little transition here that Talbot, misreading, stated that the vow took place at St Albans itself.[14] The author then whisks the reader back to Huntingdon, never mentioning Shillington again. Christina appears to have chosen the locale of her vow carefully, however. A charter in a cartulary from Ramsey indicates that Christina's father, Autti, received the revenues of the church of Shillington at the time Christina made her vow there. As the charter speaks of Autti's unjust slanders against the church, it may even be that one of the ways Autti attempted to dissuade Christina from keeping her vow was to castigate and finally divest himself of the Shillington church.[15] Without the chance survival of this charter we would never have known that Christina made her secret vow at a place that probably meant more to her and to her immediate family at the time than St Albans.

After Christina fled from her family and before her first meeting with Geoffrey of St Albans, she was closely involved with two religious communities: Flamstead, where she first hid, and then Markyate itself, where she took refuge under the protection of Roger, the head of the community at that point. As with St Mary's and Shillington, the *vita* writer does his best to deflect attention from these other communities to Christina's (future) relationship with St Albans. Markyate itself was particularly problematic, considering that Christina stayed there the rest of her life. The author responds by portraying her pre-Geoffrey residence there as, in essence, time spent under the spiritual mentorship of a St Albans monk. In the chapter in which the author introduces Roger into Christina's story, he stresses over and over that Roger was 'ours': he was 'our monk' (*noster quidem monachus*); 'our old man' (*nostro sene*); 'our Roger' (*noster Rogerus*) living near 'our monastery' (*nostro monasterio*) (*Life*, pp. 80–2).

At the time the author was writing Roger was buried at St Albans, and probably by this time too the obit for Roger, which also declares him to be both a hermit and a monk of St Albans (*heremite monachi sancti Albani*), was written into the St Albans Psalter.[16] But Roger's actual connection with St Albans during his lifetime is questionable, as Sally Thompson has pointed out.[17] The only non-St Albans source to mention Roger, a passage erased from William of Malmesbury's *De Gestis Pontificum Anglorum*, refers to Roger simply as a holy anchorite living near St Albans, with none of the 'hermit and monk' dualism one finds in the *vita* and the Psalter obit.[18] It is also clear that Roger died at Markyate, not at St Albans, and in no source do we see Roger at St Albans as a living man. It would be marvellous to know more about when, how and why the transfer of Roger's body to St Albans took place. Roger appears to have died between 1121 and 1123, at the very beginning of Geoffrey's tenure as abbot at St Albans. Was Roger's body then immediately moved to St Albans? Was this Roger's wish? How involved were Geoffrey or Christina in this transfer?

Claiming Roger as 'ours', in any case, enabled the author to link all of Christina's time with Roger to St Albans, foreshadowing the much more intensive links the author desired in his own present. The author's treatment of Flamstead is particularly interesting in this context. Flamstead, a community very close to Markyate, was Christina's first hiding place. The writer tells us almost nothing about her time there. He never gives us a picture of Christina sharing any affection with Alfwen, nor of being guided by her. In fact, the author even declares that the reason Christina chose to go to Flamstead was because it was near Roger, eliminating, in effect, any place for Alfwen or Flamstead in Christina's personal religious landscape (*Life*, p. 87). The author hints at some friction between Alfwen and Christina, stating bluntly that after two years with Alfwen 'it was necessary for her to leave' and commenting on Roger's care not to speak directly to Christina when she arrives at Markyate to avoid giving Alfwen any justification to complain to the bishop (*Life*, 99–101). Perhaps, looking back on her life, Christina herself saw her escape to Flamstead as a mere stepping stone to Markyate, but whether the *vita* accurately reflects her thinking at the time she arrived at Flamstead is another question.

The period in Christina's life after Roger died and before she met Abbot Geoffrey was particularly tricky for the writer. It is not clear how much time elapsed here, but these months or years were obviously crucial ones: after Roger's death she seems to have left Markyate for a time, hiding in various places, finally staying with a cleric (both name and place untold) who was greatly attracted to Christina and she to him. At some point Christina left this cleric, made her way back to Markyate, and established herself as its *domina*. The author tells us nothing about how Christina accomplished all this, leaving open many tantalizing questions: how did Christina come to be accepted as the leader of a community she had, apparently, abandoned? What happened to the men living with Roger? When and why did the women begin arriving? Instead of telling us about this process, the author instead focuses on Christina's healing of a woman who came from the region of Canterbury, Christina's own recovery from various illnesses, and her triumphs over her detractors, subjects that did not threaten Christina's attachment to St Albans.

In fact, it is in this section of the *vita*, the point in her life when Christina established herself at Markyate, that the author makes his most impassioned argument for Christina's attachment to his own community. In the midst of describing how Christina was suffering greatly from illness and feared that she would die, the author states how Christina wanted to make a religious profession before she died, and how she was being asked by Archbishop Thurstan and others to leave Markyate to join a different religious community. He then writes:

> But she chose our monastery above all [*preelegit nostrum monasterium*] because the eminent athlete of Christ, Alban, bodily rested in it, whom she specially loved above the other martyrs beloved by her, because Roger the hermit was a monk and was buried in it, because she most

strongly loved you above all other pastors on earth under Christ, just as
you proved by experience, and because there were not a few in our
congregation whose souls she held more dear than in all other locations,
some of whom she had made monks. And let it be known that the most
salutary Alban, our patron, received her from God that he might have a
fellow labourer on earth in improving and providing for his community
and afterwards a partner of felicity in heaven eternally. For these
reasons she resolved to make her profession in this monastery and to
receive sacred benediction from the bishop.

(*Life*, p. 126)

It is hard to miss the author's anxiety to stress Christina's superior attachment
to St Albans in every way possible – her attachment to Alban himself, to her
former St Albans mentor, Roger, to her present living St Albans mentee,
Geoffrey, the 'pastor' addressed in this passage, and to many other St Albans
monks. What is easier to miss is how misplaced this passage is in terms of the
vita's own chronology. The author addresses Geoffrey here even though Geoffrey
has not yet been introduced in Christina's story. The author triumphantly brings
up Christina's profession at St Albans at this point even though he states that it
was many years later, after she knew Geoffrey well, that it actually occurred (*Life*,
pp. 145–7). Christina is portrayed here as choosing to stick with St Albans even
before she has any close connection with the community. Christina's feelings for
her position and followers at Markyate, surely essential to any decision she made
about whether or not to leave the area, are not even hinted at. Indeed, for
Christina to 'choose' St Albans in any meaningful sense, as in living there or
becoming a member of the community, was, of course, never an option.

Spare your monks

Whether Christina herself later viewed her decision to live her life at Markyate
as a choice to stay near St Albans is difficult to say, but what is clear is that the
vita writer chose to portray Christina's past and present life as revolving around
his community of St Albans. Our monastery, our saint, our monks, our Roger,
and you, Geoffrey, as you know from experience: these are the focal points of
Christina's affections. No other community is allowed a place in Christina's
heart. In the passage cited above, the author even envisions Christina's posthumous future for his readers, a future not within the ranks of other virgins, but
side by side with the great saint of his community, the martyr Alban, the two of
them enjoying each other's company eternally. Like other authors of hagiography before and after him, the writer from St Albans was attempting to claim
Christina's future benefits for his own community.[19]

Others at St Albans shared the writer's vision. Abbot Geoffrey, for one, must
have seen her in a similar, if not identical, light. Geoffrey's relationship with
Christina appears to have been considerably more intimate than that between

154

the writer and Christina. The *vita* writer mentions by name three other St Albans monks who treat Christina like a holy woman: the Subprior Alexander (of the cope colour business); Alvered, who knew and respected Christina even before she met Geoffrey; and a venerable Thomas, who, the *vita* writer reports, knew Christina's secrets (*Life*, pp. 151, 135–7 and 163). These monks may or may not have shared all of the *vita* writer's views, but whoever thought up the addition of a new initial for Psalm 105 in the St Albans Psalter was just as enthusiastic about Christina as the *vita* writer. This initial presents a picture of a woman interceding for monks with Christ, with the caption reading 'O Jesus, in your mercy, spare your monks, I pray' (*Parce tuis queso monachis clementia Iesu*) (Plate 1). Given the unusual circumstances of this initial's appearance within the Psalter, there seems little doubt that it was meant to be a portrait of Christina, a woman who, in the artist's presentation, can stretch her hand and break the boundary between the fields of heaven and earth, a woman whose prayers can gain favours for the monks urging her forward.[20]

For the monks enthusiastic for Christina at St Albans, she was someone through whom to experience the divine, someone who could obtain grants from heaven for the monks of St Albans. A *vita* for Christina written by Simon of Bermondsey, Avicia of Sopwell or Ilbertus of St Julian's no doubt would have portrayed her affections and told her story differently, maybe quite differently. Or might they have found the very idea of a *vita* for Christina to be excessive? And how did the Markyate women view the *vita*-writing project – as a well-deserved recognition of their mistress's powers, or as an attempt to pull her away from them?

Whatever the women of Markyate thought, the project was clearly not endorsed by everyone at St Albans. Rumours about Christina's love for her male friends being as much physical as spiritual were so widespread that the *vita* writer had to address them again and again in the course of his text. The thought of this woman – no *virgo* or *ancilla Christi* in the minds of many – being specially connected to St Albans monks appears to have horrified some of its members. Christina's mysteriously abrupt manner impressed the *vita* writer, but it is not hard to imagine others reacting quite differently, particularly with the financial and jurisdictional implications of a permanent link with Markyate. This *domina* put off her formal religious profession and the foundation of her house for many years: even if she was a virgin, such delay did not reflect well on her commitment to the religious life. As for Christina's spiritual prowess, the *vita* writer reports how some saw her visions as mere dreams, her gift from God as just worldly cleverness (*Life*, p. 173). Moreover, even if one takes the Godit story exactly as the *vita* writer tells it, spotting a servant's forbidden vegetable gathering could be seen as rather small potatoes, spiritually speaking, in the twelfth-century climate. It is not hard to imagine prior Alchinus, the reform-minded man who found many followers at St Albans after Geoffrey's death, rolling his eyes at the writer's enthusiasm for this incident.[21]

The same living woman whom the *vita* writer, Geoffrey and others painted as holy, and desired to link to their monastery, could be, and was, viewed quite differently by their contemporaries. If Abbot Geoffrey had outlived Christina by a few years, perhaps the *vita*-writing project could have been brought to completion. A dead Christina would have been easier to shape to a certain image than a living one, particularly a Christina extracted from Markyate and buried in the abbey as was Roger, a Christina who could not offend or be offended ever again, a Christina whose image was softened with time and who perhaps could have started to rain down favours on St Albans from her place in heaven. But with Geoffrey suddenly dead, Christina living, and a faction opposed to Geoffrey's policies taking charge at the abbey, the project had little chance at completion.[22]

Even as it is clear that the *vita*'s vision of Christina was not accepted by a faction of St Albans monks, and was probably also found objectionable by people outside St Albans for other reasons, it is also important to note that Christina may not have endorsed it all herself. Christina had created a religious career for herself out of remarkably inauspicious beginnings. From sheer force of will she had put aside her marriage and forged a place for herself among the religious, over the years becoming the head of her own community and earning the respect of important religious personages such as the archbishop of York. Now she had attracted an even more flattering kind of attention. Men from St Albans thought she was a saint. The abbot was visiting constantly and providing her growing community with what it badly needed: buildings, books and other forms of financial support. Then he went even further, giving one of his monks the go-ahead to start composing a *vita*. Was this Christina's hope all along: when she heard stories of saints as a girl, was she thinking she was one of them? To what extent was she consciously manipulating Geoffrey, treating him as her *familiarissimus* whenever he was around in the interests of her house and her future reputation? Or was no calculation involved at all? In any case, it would take a rare personality to reject the honour of a *vita* written about oneself, and as unusual as Christina was, she does not appear to have been unusual in that way.

Wanting a *vita* written and approving what was actually in it, though, are two different things. The text produced by the author was no disinterested gift to Christina or her house, no vanity press biography for Christina to smile over in her declining years: this was a text for 'our monastery', not for her, and certainly not for Markyate. How much of her life was spun into a web of significance that she found objectionable? It seems, at the least, that Christina would have objected to how the author portrays her feelings for the women at Markyate. In addition to the obit evidence cited above, a remarkable passage in Markyate's foundation charter signals the intensity of her concern for them. The charter explicitly states that no cleric or monk was allowed to change the Markyate women's way of life without their consent.[23] This looks like a Christina making sure, as best she could, that Geoffrey and the many other religious men who signed their names to this charter could not interfere with her followers after her death.

While Christina's *vita* is a rich text, it is no self-portrait, and no more than a shadow of the richness of Christina's lived experience. It is not just the descriptions of Christina's actions that are the author's, but her actions themselves, actions which he reports selectively and uses to shape a particular image of Christina. In fact, one wonders whether the very similar visual portrait of Christina, the initial in the St Albans Psalter, might have been posted there to shape Christina's own image of herself. This image (perhaps put on a Psalm with special meaning to Christina?) could serve as a constant reminder, even when no St Albans monk was at Markyate, that Christina was to see herself first and foremost as an intercessor for St Albans. The caption to the image even helpfully scripts her prayers for her: 'O Jesus, spare your monks' is the prayer the men want her to make. Here was how Christina could repay the gift of the marvellous Psalter, of the very buildings in which she was sitting, all paid for by St Albans. The key question is whether the Christina who saw this image was pleased, complaisant or perhaps stubbornly reluctant to see herself pictured in this single-minded way. It is just possible that the desires of the *vita* writer were rejected, or at least not embraced wholeheartedly, not just by other monks at St Albans but by the subject of the *vita* herself.

Notes

1   On these kinds of relationships between hagiographer and subject, the best introduction and analysis is by Aviad Kleinberg, *Prophets in Their Own Country: Living Saints and the Making of Sainthood in the Later Middle Ages* (Chicago, 1992). I would like to express my gratitude to Daniel Hobbins, Catherine Kaplan, David Mengel and John Van Engen for their help with this essay.

2   Unless otherwise noted, all translations of the *Life* in this essay are my own. References to translations are therefore to the Latin text.

3   Too much of the text has been lost to be confident about the wording of this passage. Talbot reconstructs and translates the mid-portion of this chapter as 'vocata est godit hoc enim erat nom[en eius. Requirit] ab ea tacite Christina [an de vetitis] olus. Composuit illa timore v[isitan]cium': 'for that was her name. Christina asked her, but quietly, out of respect for the guests, if she had made the salad from ingredients which had been forbidden.' The one who is doing things silently (*tacite*) and with fear (*timore*) in this passage could be Godit, not Christina (Talbot often softens Christina's image in his translation), and many other verbs could be supplied here besides *requirit*. Unless more of this text can be recovered from the Tiberius manuscript, it is best not to make a guess at it.

4   Christina's sister Margaret was living at Markyate at the time of the *vita*-writing project, another brother had recently died as a monk at St Albans, and yet another sibling, Matilda, would visit Christina at Markyate. Some time after Christina left home, her parents suffered a major change of fortune (*Life*, p. 97), and had to come to Christina for help (*Life*, p. 69). The author refers to himself as speaking to Christina's mother personally (*Life*, p. 35), indicating that she was alive and nearby, if not at Markyate itself, when the author was composing the *vita*.

5   Christina is termed *Domina* in the confirmation charter of the foundation of Markyate (*English Episcopal Acta, I: Lincoln 1067–1185*, ed. David M. Smith (London, 1980), no. 49, pp. 30–1); a Pipe Roll entry (see *The Pipe Rolls of 2–3–4 Henry II*

(London, 1844), p. 22); the chronicle of St Albans (see *Gesta Abbatum*, i. 127), and the St Albans Psalter obits. For other references to Christina as *domina* in the text of the *vita*, see *Life*, pp. 124, 142–4, 152, 178 and 190.

6 Talbot's translation. For another of these proverbial statements, see *Life*, p. 141.

7 For the St Albans obits, see Pächt, pp. 27–30, and the reproduction of the calendar pages, Pächt, Plates 2–13. Three and possibly four St Albans monks known from the *vita* appear in these obits. Geoffrey is found on 25 February, Alvered on 4 June, and Gregory on 12 February. The 'Thomas monachus' on 2 October is probably to be connected to the 'venerable Thomas' under the orders of Abbot Geoffrey of the *vita* (see *Life*, p. 162).

8 Adelasia's obit is found on 11 February, Avicia's on 20 March and Matilda's on 12 July.

9 See Pächt, p. 29. Talbot identified Adelisia as one of the founding members of Sopwell, which is also possible (*Life*, p. 24, n. 1).

10 Thompson, *Women Religious*, p. 23.

11 On the abridgement of the *vita* in the Tiberius manuscript, see *Life*, p. 5, and Koopmans, 'The Conclusion', p. 671.

12 For the texts and witness lists of the charters, see *Early Charters of the Cathedral of St Paul, London*, ed. Marion Gibbs, Camden 3rd series, 58 (London, 1939), nos. 154 and 159, pp. 119–20 and 121–2; the second charter is edited by Smith, *English Episcopal Acta*, p. 31.

13 *Gesta Abbatum*, i. 77–8.

14 See *Life*, p. 28.

15 *Cartularium monasterii de Rameseia*, ed. William Henry Hart, RS 79 (London,1884–93), i, no. 59, p. 138. The charter, dated between 1114 and 1123, concerns the transfer of the church of Shillington from Autinus of Huntingdon and his son Baldwin to the abbot of Ramsey. In the Ramsey cartulary, another notice about Shillington follows on this charter describing how Baldwin attempted to regain the church of Shillington after the death of his father.

16 On Roger's burial at St Albans, see *Life*, p. 127, and *Gesta Abbatum*, i. 101. For Roger's obit in the St Albans Psalter, see Pächt, pp. 29–30 and Plate 10.

17 Thompson, *Women Religious*, p. 19.

18 *De Gestis Pontificum Anglorum*, ed. N. E. S. A. Hamilton, RS 52 (London, 1870), p. 314 n. 1: 'Predixerat ei, sed ancipiti oraculo, genus mortis anachorita quidam sanctus, Rogerius nomine, qui in silva quae juxta Sanctum Albanum est, rigidam vitam, et nostro tempore parum auditam, duxit.'

19 The monks of Durham, to take one contemporary example, also cast their net around a neighbouring hermit: see Susan J. Ridyard, 'Functions of a Twelfth-Century Recluse Revisited: The Case of Godric of Finchale,' in *Belief and Culture*, pp. 236–50, and Victoria Tudor, 'Durham Priory and its Hermits in the Twelfth Century,' in *Anglo-Norman Durham, 1093–1193*, ed. David Rollason, Margaret Harvey and Michael Prestwich (Woodbridge, 1994), pp. 67–78.

20 The initial was a later addition to the Psalter (actually pasted into the book), and of a later style than the other initials. The caption to this initial, unlike the others, has no echo in the Psalm itself. See Pächt, pp. 163, 244–5; Geddes, Ch. 12, p. 198.

21 For the best recent overview of the twelfth-century religious climate, see Giles Constable, *The Reformation of the Twelfth Century*, (Cambridge, 1996). It is particularly interesting in this context to compare Christina to a contemporary like Hildegard of Bingen: see John Van Engen, 'Letters and the Public *Persona* of Hildegard', in *Hildegard Von Bingen in Ihrem Historischen Umfeld*, ed. Alfred Haverkamp (Mainz, 2000), pp. 375–420.

22 For more detail on St Albans monks' negative reactions to Christina, the campaign against Geoffrey's abbatial policies and the fate of Christina's *vita* after Geoffrey's death, see Koopmans, 'The Conclusion,' pp. 663–98.

23 Gibbs, *Early Charters*, p. 120: 'Nulli autem ibi liceat mutare ordinem sanctimonialium quia super hac tenura nec clericis nec monachis aliquam facimus concessionem nisi sanctimonialibus tantum ibi commorantibus.'

10

ALTERNATIVE INTIMACIES

Men, women and spiritual direction in the twelfth century

Dyan Elliott

> And so they saw each other, not by design and yet not by chance, but, as afterwards became clear, by divine will ... The fire, namely, which had been kindled by the spirit of God and burned in each one of them cast its sparks into their hearts by the grace of that mutual glance; and so made one in heart and soul in chastity and charity in Christ, they were not afraid to dwell together under the same roof.
>
> (*Life*, pp. 101–3)

> And loosing his fiery darts, he [the devil] pressed his attacks so vigorously that he completely overcame the man's resistance ... Sometimes the wretched man, out of his senses with passion, came before her without any clothes on and behaved in so scandalous a manner that I cannot make it known, lest I pollute the wax by writing it, or the air by saying it.
>
> (*Life*, p. 115)

These are some key moments from pivotal relationships in Christina of Markyate's life. The first concerns her initial glimpse of the man who was to become her spiritual advisor for a number of years, the hermit Roger. It is an instant blistering with the heat of their shared spiritual vocation. The second describes the behaviour of the nameless cleric to whom Christina was entrusted after Roger's death, afflicted by a different kind of heat – a demonic fire which caused his feelings for his spiritual confidante to burst their restraints and overturn his reason. Christina's life was, in fact, a veritable roller coaster of volatile emotions. Her relationships with the various clerics who offered her spiritual direction and support contributed to this tumultuous ride, and provide us with some memorable vignettes of the deeply affective turn that spiritual direction took in Christina's experience. But is the shape these relationships assume unique to her particular spiritual odyssey?

The present study examines this question by creating a loose typology for the kinds of interaction that can be assembled under the general rubric of spiritual direction, thus framing Christina's experience within the context of both past and contemporary models. For my present purposes, the term 'spiritual direction' should be understood in its widest sense, implying a situation in which one person advises another person or persons on how to live the best possible Christian life – whether by example, written or spoken word. My purview, however, will be limited to the rapport established between persons of the opposite sex who are not related by blood. In other words, Aelred of Rievaulx's manual on the anchoritic life written for his sister will only be mentioned in passing. I will also be working under the assumption that the spiritual director in this period is usually, although not invariably, a male – a patriarchal bias underwritten by the pastoral epistles' prohibition against female teaching (1 Tim. 11–12). With the notable exception of Abelard and Heloise, the people I will be considering are not united by matrimony. Finally, my focus is on the rapport established between the concerned parties rather than on the actual content of the spiritual direction imparted. Aspects of this can be glimpsed through how outsiders construe (and misconstrue) these relationships. But I am primarily concerned with the perspective of the individuals involved, particularly their initiatives to establish an alternative intimacy to marriage. I will conclude by indicating what I perceive to be the structural limitations to these efforts – the difficulty in evading a matrimonial paradigm. On the most fundamental level, Christina of Markyate was stalked by the spectre of marriage. Yet even individuals who were secure in their ascetical and, frequently, misogamic terrain could not elude parallel hauntings.

A legendary heroine of the early church

The nature of Christina's relations with her various mentors is often overshadowed by compelling literary *topoi*, a quality shared by most hagiographical works. And yet the anonymous author, probably a monk of St Albans, had to work especially hard to transform his contemporary subject – a local girl who made an early and unpropitious marriage – into a type of virgin martyr. Clearly working under the assumption that more is better, the author aimed for the maximum number of motifs in his work: the precocious vow of chastity; the evil machinations of her parents; the attempts on Christina's virtue by the 'pagan ruler', Ranulf Flambard; his delegation of Burthred as surrogate rapist; Christina's Cecilian efforts to convert Burthred to chastity; her eventual Alexian flight (not to mention her sojourn in Roger's cell and the discomfort she endured, which far outstrips Alexis' ignominious sufferings under his parents' staircase); and her spirited defence of virginity to her learned interlocuters, an incident especially evocative of Katherine of Alexandria's life.[1] But the author's success is uneven: some of Christina's early trials so doggedly track the contours of the *passio* that bathos frequently threatens to invade pathos.

Aspects of Christina's relationships with her spiritual directors likewise pay homage to earlier models. In many ways Christina is a modern Thecla with Sueno standing in for Paul as prophet of virginity.[2] Both heroines receive parallel tests: Paul keeps rejecting Thecla, dismissing her as a seductive and shallow woman. On one occasion he even abandoned Thecla to a besotted Syrian ruler, resulting in her arrest and condemnation to wild animals in the circus maximus.[3] Christina, too, is constantly tested by the disaffection of her supporters. Sueno disinvests in his holy client upon the news of her marriage – a pattern that recurs in miniature with Roger when he learns that Christina is married (*Life*, pp. 55, 83, 95).

Christina's spirituality is especially shaped by the revival of an anchoritic lifestyle in emulation of the *Vitae Patrum* – particularly the bond between the senior ascetic and the fledgling monk.[4] These relationships are depicted as rigidly hierarchical, requiring total obedience to the spiritual director. For John Cassian, even an abusive director helps to foster the quintessential monastic virtue of humility.[5]

But the relationships depicted by Cassian and his cohort were almost invariably between men. An exception occurs in the hagiographical account of Thais the Courtesan, who was rescued from the world of the flesh through the tough love of the legendary Paphnutius.[6] Gaining access to Thais through pious subterfuge, posing as a client, Paphnutius reproached Thais with her sins. The impact was instantaneous. Thais repented and submitted entirely to his direction. She was taken at her word.

> She reached the spot that he ordained for her. He led her into a little cell that is found within a monastery of virgins, and sealed the door with lead … When, moreover, he would have left with the door leaded, Thais said to him: Where do you order I should pour my urine, father. And he answered: in your cell as you deserve.[7]

Immured in the Egyptian desert, Thais remained in this penitential mode for three years until it was divinely revealed that her sins had been forgiven. She died within a fortnight.[8]

Christina also makes a voluntary move from a world of relative independence to a restricted world dominated by a patriarch. Her first experience of the religious life occurs in Flamstead where she spent two years under the protection of the anchoress, Alfwen. Then the author blandly states that 'it was necessary for her to go elsewhere' (*Life*, p. 99). No reason is provided for her removal apart from the sudden whim of Roger, her future spiritual director (*Life*, pp. 95–7, 101). When this proposition met with Alfwen's vigorous opposition, Roger, like Paphnutius, resorted to pious subterfuge for securing his hold over his future disciple. He refused to meet Christina 'in order that there might be no excuse for Alfwen to accuse him before the bishop of being a cause of dissension' (*Life*, p. 101) – presumably so he could claim no knowledge of Christina if accused.[9] It was Roger's reticence about meeting with Christina that set the stage for the climactic exchange of glances cited in the epigraph.

The conditions endured by Christina in the course of her enclosure in Roger's cell are strikingly similar to those visited upon the legendary Thais. Christina is hidden at the angle where the two walls meet in a space no bigger than a span and a half.

> In this prison, therefore, Roger placed his happy companion. In front of the door he rolled a heavy log of wood, the weight of which was actually so great that it could not be put in its place or taken away by the recluse.
>
> (*Life*, p. 103)

Thus she remained for four years in all, until Roger's death, enduring desert-like extremes of temperature.

> But what was more unbearable than all this was that she could not go out until evening to satisfy the demands of nature. Even when she was in dire need, she could not open the door for herself, and Roger usually did not come till late.
>
> (*Life*, p. 105)

Thais died as a result of her claustration; Christina was spared, but her health was permanently damaged (*Life*, pp. 103–5; 121–5). But her bizarre living arrangements – so punitive in nature and entirely of Roger's contrivance – beg the question of whether his initial disapproval of his married petitioner was ever entirely dispelled. Perhaps he believed that Christina was in some way culpable for the marriage to Burthred after all. (It is perhaps suggestive that, after Roger has refused to assist Christina and subsequently learns of her flight, he immediately assumes that a third party 'has abducted and ruined her whilst she was off her guard' (*Life*, p. 97).) Roger's solution was thus for Christina to undertake an especially rigorous penance to expiate her close brush with the world of the flesh.

The story of Thais was extremely well-known: Marbod of Rennes, a contemporary of Christina's whom we will encounter again as a critic of Robert of Arbrissel, actually wrote a metric life of the famed courtesan.[10] But even if the parallels between Christina and Thais are accidental, the depiction of Roger is rooted in the austere spirituality of the desert: he is even occasionally referred to as the 'old man' (*senex*) in the manner of the early chroniclers of those wizened desert heroes. Roger 'trained her [Christina], first by word, then by example' in the requisite spiritual exercises that were at the basis of the solitary life (*Life*, pp. 104–5). Christina's total submission to Roger is depicted as central to her spiritual growth.

The counsel of reconciliation

Early Christian *topoi* aside, one wonders why Christina, clearly embodying the most highly esteemed model of Christian womanhood, encountered so much resistance from the clergy – even those who were not corrupted by lust. Why is it that these clerics so readily fit the bill as pagan tyrants?

In fact, their behaviour conforms with the clergy's traditional role as guardians of marriage and upholders of the husband's prerogatives. Even in the time of Augustine, when the clergy tended to distance themselves from marriage owing to its unabashed ties with the world, Augustine intervened with the matron Ecdicia, who, after obtaining a vow of chastity from her husband, assumed both the clothing and independence of a widow. Augustine informed her that her marriage did not cease with sexual activity and that she must continue to submit to her husband.[11] In the ninth century, Bishop Hincmar of Reims would vigorously resist Lothair II's attempts to rid himself of his infertile wife, upholding the validity of the marriage tie even after the wife, eventually fearing for her life, begged to be released.[12] When the tenth-century St Godelive appealed to the bishop concerning the ill-treatment she received at the hands of her husband, she was sent home to where she literally became a martyr to her marriage.[13] In other words, the clerics who resisted Christina's vocation and attempted to reconcile her to her married lot in life were just doing their job. Even Roger, one of the most committed engineers of Christina's escape from marriage, had a conventional response when he learned of Christina's marital status: 'Roger, straightway turning his glaring eyes upon him [Edwin], said angrily: "Have you come here to show me how to dissolve marriages? Get out of here quickly and think yourself lucky if you get away safe and sound: you deserve a whipping"' (*Life*, p. 83). With the exception of the contemporary attack on clerical marriage, a reckless separation of couples was going against the ecclesiastical current.[14]

Even non-traditionalists understood what was owed to the institution. Thus Robert of Arbrissel, founder of the famed double monastery of Fontevrault which it seems made overtures to Christina, advised Countess Ermengard of Brittany to return to her marriage. Ermengard had been married in 1092 to Alan Fergent, count of Brittany. Around 1105, however, she fled the notorious violence of Brittany and sought refuge in Fontevrault under the pretext of a consanguinous marriage.[15] Robert's letter of 1109 was intended to ease her reluctant return to the world, instilling resignation, after her petition for an annulment was denied. His initial efforts are unorthodox, however: he begins with a warning against simulated piety and false inspiration, perhaps intending to challenge the ostensibly pious impulse which prompted Ermengard's flight. He is then at pains to justify some of the sterner mechanisms of justice such as corporal punishment, the confiscation of goods, and even the death penalty.[16] It may be that Robert was attempting to reconcile Ermengard with the implacable and often brutal ramifications of secular law, which she doubtless had witnessed at first hand. But in doing so, he simultaneously sent a warning concerning its efficacy and the gravity of transgressing against its strictures. For, as Robert reminds Ermengard, even if her husband was in his own way an infidel, she was nevertheless required to take Queen Esther as a model, who remained married to a pagan ruler. 'You are married [*coniunga*]: you cannot be unbound [*disiungi*] by law.'[17] To have the marriage dissolved, she must furnish legitimate witnesses. This insistence on marriage as a binding contract, and on legal forms generally, harkens back to his disquisition on the legality of secular punishments. Thus his defence of the marriage bond is premised upon its subtle alignment with the most punitive aspect of law. So if Ermengard's marriage is a punishment to her, this punishment is not simply licit but also just – this is in spite of the fact that Robert seems to acknowledge at the end of the letter that Ermengard's marriage (as well as that of her daughter) was truly incestuous.[18] Robert's alternative counsel of reconciliation sharply contrasts with this legalistic argument. He provides her with a set of guidelines for living a religious life in the world:[19] a revolutionary concept that anticipates the later penitential orders.

Variants on the spiritual counsel offered by the clergy as upholders of marriage are attempts to enforce the monastic vow which renders a woman bride of Christ – a much holier and hence more serious bond than its mundane counterpart. In 1093, the year of his elevation to the see of Canterbury, Anselm of Bec wrote an exceptionally stern letter to a nun of royal birth who entered her community upon the death of her betrothed with the expectation of being made abbess. When this hope was dashed, she intended to leave the community to marry. Anselm depicts her situation as a struggle between good and evil. 'Sister, you are trapped. From this snare, Christ draws your soul on the one side, and the devil pulls in the opposite direction from the other side.'[20] Marriage to Christ could be every bit as grim, and as legally binding, as Ermengard's troubled union.

Finally, Abelard's entire correspondence with Heloise could be construed as a set of strategies intended to reconcile his estranged spouse to her religious vocation. At times he theologizes. Thus he justifies placing Heloise's own name before his own by stressing the superiority of the nun's condition as bride of Christ, following the lead of his hero, Jerome.[21] A similar approach informs his letter of direction discussing the origin and efficacy of the order of nuns.[22] At other times he enlists brutally direct reproofs. In response to Heloise's 'perpetual complaint … in which you presume to blame God for the manner of our entry into religion', he cautions that 'if it persists you can neither please me nor attain bliss with me'. Yet occasionally he comforts Heloise with the voice of her beloved spouse: 'Come, too, my inseparable companion, and join me in thanksgiving, you who were made my partner in guilt and in grace … At one time I desired to keep you whom I loved beyond measure for myself alone, but he [God] was already planning to use this opportunity for our joint conversion to himself.'[23] While acknowledging to his 'inseparable companion' that the marriage bond endured beyond their conversion, it nevertheless pales in comparison with the greater marriage to Christ.

Testing the limits: from syneisaktism
to 'a fruitless martyrdom'

Christina's relationships with her different mentors were not simply intimate from the perspective of a spiritual rapport: they were physically intimate as well. She literally shared the same space with Roger and, less successfully, cohabited with the nameless smitten cleric. This is hardly in keeping with the contemporary counsel of authorities like Aelred of Rievaulx, who attempted to limit the anchoress's contact with men to a single priest:

> ... an elderly man of mature character and good reputation. To him she may speak infrequently and solely for the purposes of confession and spiritual direction, receiving advice from him when in doubt and encouragement when depressed. Never must she let him touch or stroke her hand, for the evil within our bodies is always to be feared; it can so often arouse and unman even the oldest.[24]

But this kind of rigour had not always prevailed. There are a number of precedential experiments in cohabitation that were comparable to Christina's experiences. The early church had confronted the threat of syneisaktism: a living arrangement in which male ascetics and their female companions (*syneiskatoi*, in Greek; *virgines subintroductae*, in Latin) would cohabit, providing one another with domestic and spiritual support. These unions were especially popular before female communities were widespread and ascetical options for women were still sparse.[25]

The couples in question vehemently protested that their relationships were not based on sex. Few believed them. But while the attacks on syneisaktism focused mainly on the physical threat such relations presented to the couple's chastity, certain perspicacious authors would argue that mere technical chastity was insufficient. John Chrysostom recognized that sexual gratification was not restricted to mere carnal acts, averring that the pleasure generated by female company was sexual in nature.[26] Yet behind threats to chastity stood another peril of which Chrysostom was also aware: that shared accommodation, free from the restraints of marriage and unimpeded by physical relations, was uncharted territory with the capacity to disrupt traditional gender roles. He expressed concern that clerics would become womanly, too comfortable with gossip and distaffs, while the virgins would, in turn, become lordly and domineering.[27] This erosion of rigid gender boundaries would doubtless take its toll on the normative model of spiritual direction as well: rather than a hierarchical relationship with a one-way flow of advice from male director to female disciple, syneisaktism may also have facilitated a more egalitarian two-way flow.

John was only one of a series of powerful figures in orthodoxy who vigorously denounced syneisaktism. The Council of Nicaea (325) officially forbade the presence of *virgines subintroductae* in clerical households, further stipulating those women who would be admissible.[28] And thus orthodoxy drew a line for the level of intimacy permitted between female ascetics and the clergy.

It is clear that Christina and her clerical companions failed to toe the Nicaean line – nor were they alone in their insubordination. We know of a number of heterosexual ascetical configurations in which the individuals involved actively chose the terms of their intimacy, in contrast to Christina's arrangements of expediency. Moreover, far from being censured, such relationships frequently met with sympathy and even admiration.[29] A person of no lesser consequence than Anselm in his capacity as archbishop of Canterbury writes to a certain Robert with considerable warmth, and to

> ... his sisters and daughters the most beloved Seit, Edit, Thydit, Lwerun, Dirgit, Godit.... I rejoice and give thanks to God for your holy proposition and holy way of life, which you have together in love of God and a life of sanctity ... I seek your dear love, dearest daughters, as I write some admonitions which should teach and elevate you to living well, although you have our beloved son Robert with you, whom God inspired to have care of you, and teach you daily how you ought to live by word and example, according to God.[30]

Furthermore, the spiritual direction that Anselm himself proffers in this context has nothing to do with the potential dangers of heterosexual cohabitation, as one might expect. Rather he addresses the kinds of issues that had traditionally preoccupied desert solitaries: the human will versus God's will; what to do when afflicted by a 'depraved will'; and how to address unbecoming movements of body or soul.[31] His concluding message to Robert anticipates the divine reward he will receive for undertaking the care of these women.[32]

Some time in the late eleventh or early twelfth century, Eve, originally a nun at Wilton, abandoned both her community and her country to live in Angers with the monk Hervé, a follower of Robert of Arbrissel, who was now living as an anchorite.[33] Moreover, far from being disgraced, we learn that Hervé was still relied on by his community to train new recruits after Eve's death. Around 1102, the couple was warmly commended in a letter by Geoffrey of Vendôme, abbot of La Trinité, who encouraged them to persist in their holy way of life, thereby winning salvation.[34] Eve and Hervé's relationship did not entirely escape criticism, however. In a poem commemorating Eve, Hilary of Orléans, a former student of Abelard, writes:

> Eve lived a long time with her companion Hervé./ As to you who hears these things, I feel that I disturb you with this utterance./ Brother drive off [the impulse] to suspect, nor should you be suspicious in this case,/ For this love was not of this world, but in Christ.[35]

Hilary fondly lingers over the strength of their bond: 'a wonderful love of such a man and such a woman,/which is found proven without any crime.' Furthermore, despite the apprehensions of patristic authors like Chrysostom, Hilary describes their relationship in terms of a traditional gender hierarchy, with Hervé preceding 'in words and works', and Eve following along the same path. Their attachment to each other was absolute: Hervé was left desolate by Eve's death.[36] If Hilary's representation is accurate, this relationship may have fulfilled some of the church's lofty expectations for chastity, initiating the couple into a different and more profound order of intimacy.

A controversial variant of chaste heterosexual relations was attributed to Robert of Arbrissel, who was repeatedly accused of sleeping alongside his female followers. We first catch wind of this behaviour sometime between 1098 and 1100 in a censorious letter from Marbod, bishop of Rennes. Like his early Christian predecessors, Marbod puzzles over why Robert would have any contact with women at all, having already spurned the opportunity for a wife.[37] Even if by some miracle Robert could maintain physical purity, indulging in the sight and speech of a woman is still a form of lust. Otherwise, Marbod reasons, why would anyone tolerate female company?[38] Marbod again follows the lead of syneisaktism's most savage critics in a devolution into misogynist polemic. Thus he compares women to hissing serpents and the like. Solicitude for clerical purity (in this instance, Robert's) typically unleashed virulent attacks on the women perceived as undermining this purity. This anxiety, first articulated in the early church, returned with a vengeance in Marbod's time with the Gregorian reformers' parallel aggressions against clerical wives.

Robert apparently failed to heed Marbod's warning, since the accusation resurfaces around 1106, this time impelled by Geoffrey of Vendôme. The tone is more respectful than was Marbod's. Yet Geoffrey shows none of the sympathy apparent in his letter to Hervé and Eve:

> It seems to you, as you asserted, that you carry the cross of our Lord Saviour worthily when you try to extinguish the evil burning ardour of the flesh. If this is the way you act, or at some time acted, you have invented a new and unheard of, but fruitless kind of martyrdom.[39]

Although Geoffrey recognizes that the initiative is Robert's, women again bear the brunt of his displeasure. A biblical miscellany on the evils of woman is thus offered up.[40]

Aspects of Christina's relations with her clerical advisors resonate with some current efforts at heterosexual cohabitation and even refract the near-contemporary experiment of Robert of Arbrissel. Certainly it would be impossible to live in closer quarters with one's partner in the religious life than was the case with Christina and Roger. And yet Roger sometimes represents the anchoritic life as a singular one, conducted in isolation from the opposite sex. He even plays on this perception when the bewildered Burthred shows up, looking for his reluctant spouse: 'Who do you think you are, expecting to find a woman here at this hour? It is with the greatest difficulty that a woman is allowed here even in broad daylight and accompanied' (*Life*, p. 95).

This is not to say that Roger himself was known for his strict avoidance of women, as were so many of the desert fathers. In fact, we later learn that he was extremely close to a couple 'who lived a happy married life under Roger's direction' (*Life*, p. 111). Moreover, Christina would eventually become co-participant in Roger's profound spirituality. On one occasion when Roger's inner spiritual heat made him oblivious to the fact that the devil had set his cowl on fire, the anonymous author adds: 'It should therefore be believed that Christina also was no less on fire when she stood by the side of the man in prayer' (*Life*, pp. 105–7). Moreover, Roger ordains his beloved 'Sunday daughter' as successor to his hermitage, and hence his spiritual heir (*Life*, pp. 107–9). Even so, there are aspects of the hierarchical desert model that linger: the old man and his disciple ultimately prevail over the more egalitarian household of the *virgines subintroductae* and their descendants.

Roger's seniority was doubtless an assistance in maintaining this hierarchical distinction which, in turn, helped to ensure that spiritual fire never metamorphosed into carnal flames. Of course, as Aelred cautions above, age is no barrier to lust. This uncomfortable truth was brought home to Christina early on in her relationship with her aged mentor Sueno. He was expounding on the struggles and glory inherent in virginity when 'someone said to her that he [Sueno] was still so stimulated by lust that unless he were prevented by the greater power of God he would without any shame lie with any ugly and mis-shapen leper' (*Life*, pp. 37–9). Disgusted, Christina reproached the man for this unedifying comment, although she did not see fit to challenge it.

But it is in the course of her cohabitation with Archbishop Thurstan's friend, the anonymous cleric, that the situation spun out of control, fulfilling the worst fears of critics of syneisaktism. He was 'a religious and a man of position in the world' (*Life*, p. 115) – attributes which secured Christina's trust. Yet, while designated her patron, he seems to have been possessed of no particular spiritual ascendancy. In fact, unlike her earlier experiences with Sueno and later Roger, this relationship was premised upon a spiritual egalitarianism that proved to be extremely volatile, with the unhappy results alluded to above.

It was also under these circumstances that the unhappy couple achieved the dubious dissolution of gender roles that Chrysostom had anticipated and feared. The cleric did everything he could to win Christina's love: he begged; he pleaded; he appeared before her naked; he even turned into a bear! 'And though she herself was struggling with this wretched passion, she wisely pretended that she was untouched by it. Whence he sometimes said that she was more like a man than a woman, though she, with her more masculine qualities, might more justifiably have called him a woman' (*Life*, p. 115).

Even after her patron had triumphed over his passion, Christina continued to be assailed by hers. And so, by virtue of daily contact with the object of her desire, she was involuntarily subjected to the kind of martyrdom that Robert of Arbrissel had so confidently solicited for himself. But fortunately she would eventually attain the triumph over the flesh that Robert sought. When the Virgin Mary appeared and handed Christina the Christ-child to hold, the fire of lust departed from her forever (*Life*, pp. 117–19).

Just friends

Even when spiritual direction entirely skirted the quagmire of cohabitation, and gender roles remained more or less intact, these relations never ceased to be a source of contention. This point is epitomized by the response to Jerome's intense rapport with his spiritual disciple and close confidante, the patrician widow Paula.

> Of all the ladies in Rome but one had the power to subdue me, and that one was Paula. She mourned and fasted, she was squalid with dirt, her eyes dim from weeping ... The only woman who took my fancy was one whom I had not so much as seen at table. But when I began to revere, respect, and venerate her as her conspicuous chastity deserved, all my former virtues forsook me on the spot [i.e., in the eyes of Rome].[41]

Jerome is in full command of his considerable rhetorical resources in this letter. For, while serving as a sharp riposte to those suspecting him of illicit sexual activity, the letter also contains a provocative acknowledgement that such suspicions of intimacy were not entirely gratuitous. Jerome did not approve of the domestic familiarity implicit in syneisaktism, however, and had added his voice to the many orthodox critics of such relations;[42] hence his care to stipulate that he had never even dined with Paula. Elsewhere in a letter to Paula's daughter, Eustochium, he pens a scathing satire of the rich widow who dines with the clerics in her entourage.[43] Since Jerome was not given to self-parody, we can only assume that he reckoned himself to be in an entirely different category than such clerical hangers-on.

After the patristic period, equivalent expressions of intensity to those which Jerome had once used to characterize his spiritual bond with Paula seem to disappear. Perhaps the very emotional ties that had prompted these expressions of commitment were likewise in abeyance. It is impossible to know. But a parallel fervent tenor once again begins to appear in the later eleventh century. The timing is no surprise. Both John Boswell and Brian McGuire have drawn attention to the deep bonds of love and friendship which appear and flourish in monastic milieux at the time.[44] The rise of vernacular love lyric adds additional testimony. And other, less comfortable, sentiments are also brought to the fore. The emergent penitential movement suggests that contrition and remorse also begin to be felt in a new way.[45] In short, this was the beginning of a period that might well be labelled 'the Age of Affect'.

Peter Damian – the radical reforming monk who was later made cardinal – is on the cusp of these changes. On a devotional level, Peter was an early promoter of the cults of the Eucharist and the Virgin Mary, key zones for the rising religious feeling of the age, while, from the perspective of introspection and the personal burden of guilt, he was fully the equal of Augustine.[46] Peter's correspondence with religiously inclined women, particularly the Empress Agnes, reflect this interstitial position.[47]

Peter's relationship with Agnes is also a harbinger of a dogmatic shift that provides a new zone of intimacy between a clerical spiritual director and his female charge: the rise of auricular confession. In a letter to Agnes, written some time between 1063 and 1065, Peter evokes the confession she made to him in front of the altar of St Peter's in Rome. This was no ordinary confession, moreover, but a life confession. The empress's narrative of self-accusation begins at five years of age – two years before she would be held culpable by canon and civil law.

> And there, just as if the blessed apostle corporeally presided, whatever subtle or smallest thing was able to titillate the inner parts of your nature, whatever vain thing in thoughts, whatever superfluous thing stole into speech, was rolled out in faithful recountings.[48]

Any evidence for lay confession is unusual prior to Lateran IV (1215) when annual confession was mandated. Agnes's level of scrupulosity seems especially precocious.[49]

The role of confessor will eventually come to dominate the spiritual director's persona. And this change would, in turn, reinforce the association of spiritual direction with masculine prerogative – a tendency that will increase as the theological understanding of absolution progressively assimilates the confessor with God.[50] But the gender hierarchy has clearly never been a barrier to certain kinds of intimacy. And there is every reason to believe that Peter's epistolary salutation to Agnes is not simply formulaic, but bespoke a sincere feeling of loss.

> Dejected, I mourn daily while you are absent; indeed I sigh with a singular grief that my heart is far away from me. It is certain that where my heart is, there lies my treasure (Matt. 6:21). For my treasure is beyond doubt Christ. Because I am not unaware that he is hidden in the treasury of your breast, I appoint you as the parlour of the celestial treasure and on that account, though I may turn from you to whatever place, I do not in fact go away.[51]

After Agnes left Rome, Peter was in constant anxiety that she would be drawn back into the worldly ambit of the court.[52] He also wrote to his brother, Damianus, praising the empress's piety and her recent conversion. Clearly relishing his time with Agnes, Peter relates an anecdote which she shared with him just the night before concerning two captive princesses and their ingenious strategies for preserving their virginity.[53]

But Peter's expressions of sorrow pale in comparison with his slightly later contemporary, Goscelin of St Bertin, and the grief sustained at the absence of his spiritual daughter Eve, the former nun of Wilton who had gone to live as a recluse in Northern France with the monk Hervé. While still in England she had been befriended and undoubtedly dominated by the older monk, Goscelin, who was probably about twenty years her senior.[54] We do not know the reasons behind Eve's departure. The poet Hilary suggests that the community at Wilton was lax.[55] In any event, Eve left England without a word to Goscelin, a show of independence which occasioned a long treatise entitled *Liber confortatorius*. It is a book laced with bitter reproaches, rendering the title something of an enigma as to who was in need of comfort. In the opening, painful reminiscences flow thick and fast: he first beheld Eve when she received the veil and somehow arranged a second meeting at the dedication of a church.[56] He sent her a present of fish. Eve, in her turn, had once told him a dream of how he gave her the whitest bread which turned into gold in her mouth.[57] Yet Goscelin characterizes her departure as an act against love, a serious crime indeed since God himself is love. Goscelin is unrestrained in his expression of indignation. 'I praise the strength of your profession, but mourn the cruelty of your silence.' And later, 'You performed parricide against him who regarded you as a daughter.'[58] From his perspective, not one of the saints, let alone Christ himself, would have transgressed in this way against those who loved them. Goscelin further cites with approval the holy Paula's reflection that love has no measure, a statement which she puts to good use in her salutation to absent friends.[59]

Eventually, however, Goscelin seems to resign himself to the inevitable, seeking comfort in the thought that he now has an effective intercessor working on his behalf: 'So be it that now I have a daughter as a patron.'[60] Yet this statement of Eve's alleged spiritual ascendancy signals a turn to instruction, suggesting his reluctance to let go of the reins. He thus presents a series of edifying instances of saints doing battle with the devil and admonishes Eve to do likewise; he discusses the significance of the anchoress's cell; he advises her on readings, urging her to emulate the female friends of Jerome whom the latter referred to as 'Christ's library'; he instructs her on how to meditate on Christ's suffering during the recital of the hours; and he upholds monastic virtues like humility and patience.[61] Goscelin also uses every opportunity to remind her of his role as spiritual advisor: 'Remember what I used to bawl [*personare*] in your ear ... that all things are possible with God'?[62] Even when this familiar territory is regained, however, the role of spiritual director only vies with – it cannot subdue – the slighted friend. His work concludes much as it started. He asks that Eve, 'the sweet part of my soul',[63] show compassion and 'have mercy on the bereavement of Goscelin, whom you loved as the domicile of your soul in Christ, but you shook completely to the foundations with your departure'.[64]

For sheer emotionality, Christina of Markyate's relationship with Abbot Geoffrey was a match for the one Goscelin had sought to establish with Eve. In this case it was Christina who was spiritual director and Geoffrey the disciple, however. Like Goscelin, her feelings for her spiritual subordinate were expressed in quasi-romantic endearments: Christina referred to Geoffrey as 'her beloved' (*dilectum suum*), or her 'most familiar one' (*sibi familiarissimum*) (*Life*, pp. 145, 149). But fortunately for Christina, her feelings were a requited version of the unfortunate Goscelin's passionate devotion to Eve.

> Their affection was mutual, but different according to their standards of holiness. He supported her in worldly matters: she commended him to God more earnestly in her prayers. If anything, she was more zealous for him than for herself and watched over his salvation with such care that, surprising to say, the abbot, whether near or far, could not offend God, either in word or deed, without her knowing it instantly in spirit.
>
> (*Life*, p. 145)

Although this intimacy generated gossip, Christ had a way of visiting afflictions on her detractors (*Life*, p. 173). It is in this context that we encounter everyone's favourite late-antique couple, Jerome and Paula, though a different set of associations seems to be evoked than in Goscelin's work: 'Some of them gossiped about things neither true nor having the appearance of truth, so that listening to them you might think one was Jerome, the other Paula, had one not been a virgin and the other the mother of a virgin.'[65] The tone is wry, but so is the meaning. One assumes that the author is alluding to the gossip that Paula and Jerome excited in Rome. Yet the phrasing is murky: scandal, not sanctity, seems to be the basis of comparison. Buried in the remark may be a tacit acknowledgement that this was a dangerous model to emulate.

From carnal to spiritual love: the limits of sublimation

When a carnal love is sublimated and transformed into its spiritual counterpart, an erstwhile lover could emerge as spiritual director. There were some famous contemporary instances of this model. Gilbert of Sempringham struggled with his sexual desire for the beautiful daughter of his landlord. One night he had a dream of placing his hand on her breasts. Interpreting this dream as a warning against future fornication, the distraught Gilbert promptly fled his hostel.

> But what he saw in his dream heralded not future sin but glorious merit, for this girl was later one of the seven original persons with whom the father founded the communities of his order. Her bosom into which your pastor and assiduous friend put his hand was like the mysterious peace of the church, of which he was the foundation.[66]

The kind of love was changed, but the sexual imagery remained.

This highly esteemed transition from carnal to spiritual love was at the very centre of the Church's teaching on marriage since, from the time of Augustine, the unconsummated marriage of Mary and Joseph was upheld as the ideal.[67] The lives of saints were teeming with instances of individuals who successfully diverted their partner's desire into a spiritual marriage. Generally, these couples separated to enter religious institutions, but some persisted in living in the world. We have seen that Christina of Markyate was mindful of such exemplars and was clearly prepared to assume the dominant role generally ordained for the one who does the converting. Thus she temporarily convinced her husband, Burthred, to forego consummating the marriage, explicitly evoking the model of Cecilia and Valerian.[68] But her efforts at spiritual direction came to naught when her carnal family intervened and hectored the already harried husband into attempting a forced consummation.[69]

The correspondence of Abelard and Heloise painfully chronicles the difficulties of transforming a carnal relationship into a spiritual one. But, as we have seen in the case of Christina and the unknown cleric, the process could happen in reverse.

> At the beginning they had no feelings about each other, except chaste and spiritual affection. But the devil, the enemy of chastity, not brooking this for long, took advantage of their close companionship and feeling of security to insinuate himself first stealthily and with guile, then later on, alas, to assault them more openly.
>
> (*Life*, p. 115)

In other words, it happened just like the ancient critics of syneisaktism said it would: the devil fosters an 'unfriendly friendship', removing all feelings of lust, 'and so for a long time the sleeping fire hides without any flame, until joining the two torches together he lights them both'.[70]

By the same token, Goscelin's *Liber confortatorius* could subtly mark a parallel devolution. This is a difficult point to sustain because the expressions of carnal and spiritual love are basically interchangeable. We have seen that Goscelin described his former condition of intimacy with Eve in similar terms to those employed by Peter Damian to describe his feelings for Agnes: love created a domicile for the soul – a shared domicile erected in Christ. But Goscelin also comforts himself by the constant expectation of reunion in the afterlife.[71] Abelard had held out this hope to the desolate Heloise in the prayer: 'Now, Lord, what thou hast mercifully begun, most mercifully end, and those whom thou hast parted for a time on earth, unite forever to thyself in heaven.'[72] Peter the Venerable's anticipation of unity is even more complete when he reassures Heloise: '... him [Abelard], I say, in your place, or as another you, God cherishes in his bosom and keeps him there to be restored to you through his grace at the coming of the Lord.'[73]

Is there something inherently conjugal in this expectation? There may well be, in spite of the fact that Christ intoned that the marriage bond would not endure in heaven (Matt. 22:30).[74] But even if the hope itself is matrimonially neutral, there is no mistaking Goscelin's efforts to paint his desire for a heavenly reunion with Eve in terms of marriage: 'in that homeland [*patria*] we will pant and hasten to be united, where for eternity we can never be parted.'[75] The verb Goscelin uses to describe their union is *coniungere* – a word with unmistakably matrimonial overtones. Still, there is nothing shocking in this portrayal – especially considering the proliferation of nuptial metaphor in monastic letters. Moreover, even if Goscelin regarded Eve as a spouse of sorts, his perspective on marriage might be sufficiently spiritualized as to render this an appropriate way of understanding relations between a spiritual director and his female disciple. Goscelin's much earlier life of Edward the Confessor, completed by 1067, describes the spiritual marriage of the king and his wife, Edith, who would sit in filial piety at the feet of her older and wiser husband.[76] Perhaps Goscelin had come to regard his relationship with Eve in a similar light.

And yet, the frantic tenor of the *Liber confortatorius* is unsettling, while one tale in particular, mixed in with various spiritual directives to Eve, is particularly alarming. The story, ostensibly demonstrating the devil's relentless attacks on the holy and God's mercy on the truly penitent, concerns a certain Alexander, an anchorite in the forest who was 'already great, able to touch the heavens with his virtues'.[77] The infant daughter of a neighbouring king was stolen and entrusted to the hermit by a demonic monk. Alexander raised her, seduced her, and ultimately impregnated her. Fearing exposure, the panic-stricken hermit confessed his sin to his demonic friend who, in turn, convinced him to murder the hapless girl, arguing that a single murder was far preferable to the scandal ensuing from the fall of someone reputedly so holy. Then Alexander's friend, 'the good master of perdition', helped to bury the girl.

Eventually this pastiche of lust, sin and crime is put to rights: Alexander's hand is miraculously stuck in a tree for some fifteen years to facilitate his penance; the girl (who has managed to survive in her grave all this time) is exhumed, pardons her abusive guardian, and is joyfully reunited with her father.[78] And yet the errant hermit continues to hover in this reader's mind as an ominous instance of projection. Moreover, any exculpatory vision of marriage that might have been inspired by Edward the Confessor's union with Edith is undermined by the fact that the poor murdered girl is referred to as the hermit's 'dead wife' (*extinctamque coniugem*). The presence of this tale is hardly nugatory: it is undoubtedly one of the longest exempla in the entire work. Soon after, when Goscelin admonishes Eve that 'by loving that lovable one [Christ] completely you conceive, give birth, bring forth, and nourish', the wall between metaphorical and physical birth has been rendered uncomfortably thin.[79]

A woman's orientation: he for God and she for God in him

Goscelin's relentless focus on Eve is something of an anomaly among the men discussed. Even Jerome's affection for Paula, the orthodox prototype for a type of spiritualized heterosexual intimacy, observed certain bounds that seem constantly in danger of being breeched by Goscelin. But in general, men were not nearly so emotionally or spiritually preoccupied with their female charges. In this context, it is significant that a number of the celebrated founders of various female communities often stumbled upon their destinies by accident, without any apparent desire to benefit women. The foundation of Fontevrault resulted from expediency: the women of Robert's following needed somewhere to go. As Jacques Dalarun has argued, moreover, women seemed to have been purely instrumental in Robert's unusual sexual discipline.[80] Gilbert of Sempringham initially looked for a community of men to patronize without success. He soon discovered that the women of the area were both more pious and in greater need. Abelard's role as founder was accidental. Heloise and her nuns had been expelled from Argenteuil and needed somewhere to go; Abelard himself was anxious that someone attend to his oratory. The letters of direction and the rule were all written at Heloise's specific behest.

This rather cavalier attitude contrasts sharply with the level of female dependence among the individuals discussed – one which was clearly over-determined by patriarchal structures, particularly the institution of marriage. Although the women in question may have set aside carnal marriage, their spiritual commitments nevertheless often retain or assume a marital aspect. The consecration of a nun is the most obvious example. But there is sometimes a covert impulse for female disciples to regard their spiritual directors as marriage brokers or even surrogates for the celestial bridegroom, Christ. The emotional and spiritual profundity of the ensuing dependency is often surprising. Ermengard of Brittany is a case in point. With her husband's eventual monastic conversion, Ermengard was at last permitted to enter Fontevrault licitly. But the resulting vocation was every bit as troubled as her marriage probably was. The source of this vocational unease may have been the virolocal attitude adopted by Ermengard with regard to her spiritual directors, in keeping with the usual expectations of an aristocratic marriage. For example, Ermengard never permanently settled at Fontevrault, leaving and re-entering probably three or four times.[81] On the basis of her subsequent behaviour, it seems probable that these comings and goings were prompted by Robert's movements. Fontevrault had never been his permanent residence. Robert's death in 1118, however, seems to have left Ermengard shaken, resulting in still more compelling proof of how her religious vocation was contingent upon her personal relations with masculine figures of authority. The following year marked the death of her husband, the former count of Brittany (who, somewhat ironically, had managed to remain true to his monastic vows). Ermengard then proceeded to launch a complaint against her first husband, William of Aquitaine, for having abandoned her.[82] When this pathetic attempt to regain the count failed, she left Fontevrault. Some years later, Ermengard was captivated by the preaching of that mellifluous doctor, Bernard of Clairvaux. She thereupon followed Bernard to Dijon where she took the veil as a Cistercian nun.[83] Bernard wrote letters to his avid disciple – the ardent tenor of which has troubled a number of scholars, clearly leaving Peter Damian's fervent admiration for Agnes in the dust.[84] When Bernard departed for Italy, however, Ermengard, probably close to sixty years of age, once again left the religious life in order to follow her half-brother to the holy land, where he had been made king of Jerusalem.[85]

Although an extreme case, Ermengard was not unusual in her male-centric orientation. Heloise clearly revered Abelard as the intellectual, spiritual and emotional centre of her universe – the husband who forced her into the religious life and then forgot her. Anselm's anonymous addressee took the veil when she lost one man, and attempted to re-enter the world when she found another. Even Eve, despite her spirited show of independence in unilaterally leaving England and her spiritual director, could be perceived as merely exchanging Goscelin for Hervé.

Christina provides a refreshing exception to this pattern in a number of ways. Her accession to Roger's cell seems to represent a move from discipleship to mastery, suggesting a diminished need for a specific spiritual director. This view is supported by the fact that a community of women sprang up around her hermitage. Moreover, she is further presented as a spiritual mentor to Abbot Geoffrey. And yet, if Christina's potential as a director of others seems to imply a degree of spiritual independence, this is clearly a scenario in which the whole is less than the sum of its parts. Rather than moving towards spiritual autonomy, the relationship with Geoffrey actually provides a new focus for Christina's spirituality. The text is relentless and (somewhat monotonously) laced with proof of her preoccupation. Aware of any errors he might commit in his absence, 'she was more zealous for him than for herself' (*Life*, p. 141). 'She was so zealous on his account that she prayed for him tearfully almost all the time and in God's presence considered him more than herself … There was none of those who were dear to her for whom she could plead to God with such devotion and instant prayer' (*Life*, p. 145). An inner voice asked if she would like to be able to see Geoffrey during an absence – an offer she gratefully accepted 'as she was in some ways more anxious for him than herself' (*Life*, p. 149). The *Life* itself breaks off with an account of various measures Christina took to ensure that she could intercede more effectively on Geoffrey's behalf (*Life*, p. 193). Furthermore, Christina's obsession with Geoffrey accords with some of the larger structural determinants of her life. It evokes her earlier rejection of Alfwen's community in favour of a virolocal move to Roger's cell. And it anticipates her eventual acquiescence to Geoffrey's insistence that her community be amalgamated with his.

The subordination of Christina's presumably more potent spirituality to Geoffrey's wellbeing parallels the emerging pastoral discourse which designates the husband's salvation as the wife's primary concern.[86] Geoffrey's appropriation of Christina's spiritual energy is epitomized in a dream he relates:

> One night … he saw himself holding a flowering herb in his hands, the juice of which was very efficacious for driving away maladies. If he

squeezed it strongly, little juice came out, but if gently and quietly he would get what he wanted.

(*Life*, p. 153)

A hermit friend tells him that the herb represents Christina; the flower her virginity; and that she should be approached carefully and treated gently. But whatever meaning the hagiographer may attach to this dream, the perception that Christina has been commodified to meet Geoffrey's needs is inescapable – a spiritualized herbal remedy.[87]

As Stephen Jaeger points out, the passion between Christina and Geoffrey is presented as a kind of climax to a love story.[88] (In fact, Geoffrey's possession of the Christina-flower anticipates the actions of the amorous, but predatory, dreamer in the *Romance of the Rose*.) And yet, as suggested above, the ancillary nature of Christina's spirituality is in many ways counter-intuitive, actually resisting the larger narrative momentum of the *Life*. This begs the question of whether the interdependence between Christina's spirituality and her relationship with Geoffrey may have been purposefully exaggerated or distorted in some way. Could this have been the anonymous monk's homage to his abbot? Or was the author instead conflicted about the growing visibility of contemporary holy women, despite his apparent partisanship of Christina? There are other indications of his relative indifference to depicting Christina's independent spiritual achievement. Most telling, perhaps, is the absence of any real description or discussion of the community that had sprung up around Christina. We only learn about its existence incidentally (*Life*, p. 145).

The various emphases, de-emphases and downright omissions give the impression of a text that is divided against itself: one which is bent on promoting the reputation of a particular holy woman by chronicling her progression towards spiritual mastery, while simultaneously downplaying the autonomous or independent aspects of her religious development that seem intrinsic to the achievement of this mastery. Yet it is through the fissures of this divided text that a distinct alternative to female dependency does fleetingly emerge. It assumes the form of the audible marvel that was experienced by Roger's companions:

The sound of virgins singing was heard by Roger's two companions, Leofric and Acio his friend, as they were rendering their due praises to God. They wondered what it was and, being enchanted by the melody, they did not sing alternately, as was their custom, but sang the same verse in unison. At the end of the verse they kept silent and listened to the following verse being sung to a sweet melody by the opposite choir. Quite often a whole psalm would be sung completely by the men and the maidens in this way. They spent much time trying to find out the meaning of this, and finally it was partially revealed to Roger in prayer.

(*Life*, pp. 99–101)

At the time of this occurrence, Christina was a member of Alfwen's community, dwelling in a small cell of her own (*Life*, pp. 93ff.). The marvel seems to pay tribute to the autonomy of this community. The respectful interaction of the two men with the mysterious female choir is represented as a melodious and balanced antiphon: all in all, a striking figure of gender equity.

This image of independent, but complementary, choirs is not permitted to remain, however, and is very soon subverted. From Roger's perspective, the marvel signifies that God will send a great treasure to Markyate. The treasure turns out to be Christina who, once at Markyate, will undertake a discipleship that contrasts sharply both with the spirit of Alfwen's community and with the above marvel. And so the visionary alternative almost immediately begins to disappear from view. It is finally eclipsed by the dream in which Geoffrey garners Christina's spiritual juices.

Notes

1 Cf. Jocelyn Wogan-Browne, 'Saints' Lives and the Female Reader', *Forum for Modern Language Studies* 27 (1991), 318–21.

2 *The Acts of Paul*, c. 5–6, *The Apocryphal New Testament*, trans. M. R. James (Oxford, 1924; rpt., 1966), p. 253.

3 Ibid., c. 26, p. 277. See Stevan Davies's analysis of this work in terms of proto-feminist revolt against church patriarchy in *The Revolt of the Widows* (Carbondale, Ill, 1980), pp. 58–61. In contrast, Peter Brown sees no such direct relation but perceives the male authors of the apocryphal acts as using women 'to think with'. See *The Body and Society: Men, Women, and Sexual Renunciation in Early Christianity* (New York, 1988), pp. 153–4; on Thecla, see pp. 156–9.

4 On the impact of the desert tradition, see Ann Warren, *Anchorites and Their Patrons in Medieval England* (Berkeley, 1985), pp. 7–14; Henrietta Leyser, *Hermits and the New Monasticism* (London, 1984), pp. 7–17.

5 John Cassian, *Conférences* 2.10, 2.13, ed. and trans. E. Pichery, Sources chrétiennes 42 (Paris, 1955), 1:120, 124–6. Cf. John Climacus, who places the spiritual director's will *above* God's in *Scala paradisi* Step 4, PG 88, cols. 727–8; *The Ladder of Divine Ascent*, trans. Colm Luibheid and Norman Russell (New York, 1982), p. 119.

6 See the section on Paphnutius in Rufinus of Aquileia's version of the anonymous *Historia monachorum in Aegypto*, c. 14; *The Lives of the Desert Fathers*, trans. Norman Russell (London, 1980), pp. 95–8.

7 *AA.SS*, IV October, 225. Cf. the account from Jacobus of Voragine's incredibly popular *Golden Legend*, trans. William Granger Ryan (Princeton, 1993), 2:234. See Ruth Karras, 'Holy Harlots: Prostitute Saints in Medieval Legend', *Journal of the History of Sexuality* 1 (1990), 3–32.

8 *AA.SS*, IV October, 225.

9 See Talbot's unsubstantiated speculation on a possible rupture between Alfwen and Christina (*Life*, pp. 19–20).

10 *AA.SS*, IV October, 226–8. Marbod tactfully refrains from all mention of bodily functions, although they are integral to most accounts.

11 See Dyan Elliott, *Spiritual Marriage: Sexual Abstinence in Medieval Wedlock* (Princeton, 1993), pp. 57–8.

12 See Jane Bishop, 'Bishops as Marital Advisors in the Ninth Century', in *Women of the Medieval World: Essays in Honor of John Mundy*, ed. Julius Kirshner and Suzanne Wemple (Oxford, 1985), pp. 53–84.

13 Georges Duby, *The Knight, the Lady, and the Priest: The Making of Modern Marriage in Medieval France*, trans. Barbara Bray (New York, 1983), pp. 130–5.

14 For the attack on clerical marriage, see Elliott, *Spiritual Marriage*, pp. 98–104; Dyan Elliott, *Fallen Bodies: Pollution, Sexuality, and Demonology in the Middle Ages* (Philadelphia, 1999), pp. 107–26.

15 'Une lettre inédite de Robert d'Arbrissel à la Comtesse Ermengarde', ed. J. de Petigny, *Bibliothèque de l'Ecole des Chartres* ser. 3, 5 (1854), 213–14; Therese Latzke, 'Robert von Arbrissel, Ermengard und Eva', *Mittellateinisches Jahrbuch* 19 (1984), 122–5. Bruce Venarde has recently translated writings by Robert (including the letter to Ermengard) or ones concerning him in *Robert of Arbrissel: A Medieval Religious Life* (Washington, D.C., 2003).

16 'Une lettre', ed. Petigny, p. 226.

17 *Ibid.*, p. 227. Unless otherwise indicated, all translations are mine.

18 *Ibid.*, pp. 232–4.

19 *Ibid.*, pp. 232–5.

20 'Une lettre inédite de S. Anselme à une moniale inconstante', ed. André Wilmart, *Revue Bénédictine* 41 (1928), 319–32 (p. 323).

21 'The Personal Letters Between Abelard and Heloise', ed. J. T. Muckle, *Mediaeval Studies* 15 (1953), 47–94; trans. Betty Radice, rev. M. T. Clanchy, *The Letters of Abelard and Heloise* (London, 2003), pp. 72–3; cf. 'The Letter of Heloise on Religious Life and Abelard's First Reply', ed. J. T. Muckle, *Mediaeval Studies* 17 (1955), 240–81, p. 267, where Abelard cites additional remarks of Jerome on this subject.

22 'The Letter of Heloise', ed. Muckle, pp. 253ff. See Mary McLaughlin, 'Peter Abelard and the Dignity of Women: Twelfth Century "Feminism" in Theory and Practice', in *Pierre Abélard/ Pierre le Vénérable: les courants philosophiques, littéraires et artistiques en occident au milieu du XIIe siècle*, Colloques internationaux du centre national de la recherche scientifique 546 (Paris, 1975), pp. 287–333.

23 'The Personal Letters', ed. Muckle, pp. 87, 90; trans. Radice rev. Clanchy, pp. 79, 83.

24 Aelred of Rievaulx, *De institutione inclusarum* c. 6, in *Opera omnia*, ed. A. Hoste and C. H. Talbot, CCCM 1 (Turnhout, 1971), 1.642; *A Rule of Life of a Recluse*, trans. Mary Paul Macpherson, in *Treatises and the Pastoral Prayer*, Cistercian Fathers series 2 (Kalamazoo, Mich., 1972), 1.51–2.

25 The classic work on this practice is Hans Achelis, *Virgines subintroductae: ein Beitrag zum VII. Kapitel des I. Korinthebriefs* (Leipzig, 1902).

26 John Chrysostom, *Instruction and Refutation Directed against Those Men Cohabiting with Virgins*, ch. 1, in *Jerome, Chrysostom, and Friends: Essays and Translations*, trans. Elizabeth Clark (New York, 1979), p. 165. See also Elizabeth Clark, 'John Chrysostom and the Subintroductae', *Church History* 46 (1977), 171–85.

27 Chrysostom, *Against Those Men Cohabiting with Virgins*, ch. 10, p. 195. See also Clark, 'John Chrysostom and the *Subintroductae*', pp. 181–2.

28 Nicaea, ch. 3, in *Conciliorum oecumenicorum decreta*, ed. G. Alberigo *et al.* (Freiburg, 1962), p. 6.

29 Elkins, *Holy Women*, pp. 38–46.

30 Anselm of Bec, Ep. 414, *S. Anselmi Cantuariensis archiepiscopi opera omnia*, ed. F. S. Schmitt, 6 vols. (Edinburgh, 1946–61), 5.359–60; cf. an earlier letter in which only Seit and Edit are mentioned (Ep. 230, *Opera*, 4.134–5). See Elkins, *Holy Women*, p. 40; Warren, *Anchorites and their Patrons*, p. 105.

31 Anselm, Ep. 414, *Opera*, 5.360–1. Anselm basically says that an individual should not struggle with such thoughts but rout them with useful ones. Cf. Cassian's discussion on concupiscence of the flesh and spirit (no. 4) and on chastity (no. 12) in *Conférences*, Sources chrétiennes 42, 1.166–87; Sources chrétiennes 54, 2.120–46.

32 Anselm, Ep. 414, *Opera*, 5.361–2.

33 Elkins, *Holy Women*, pp. 24–7; see André Wilmart, 'Eve et Goscelin', *Revue Bénédictine* pt. 1, 46 (1934), 414–38; pt. 2, 50 (1938), 42–83. On Hervé's association with Robert, see Latzke, 'Robert von Arbrissel', p. 141.

34 Geoffrey of Vendôme, Ep. 27, *Oeuvres*, ed. and trans. Geneviève Giordanengo (Brussels, 1996), p. 47; see Wilmart, 'Eve et Goscelin', pt. 1, pp. 417–19; Latzke, 'Robert von Arbrissel', pp. 143ff.

35 Hilarius, *Versus et Ludi, Epistolae, Ludus Danielis Belouacensis*, ed. Walther Bulst and M. L. Bulst-Thiele (Leiden, 1989), p. 23. Hervé was also criticised on an unrelated matter after Eve's death. See Geoffrey of Vendôme, Ep. 45, *Oeuvres*, p. 80.

36 Hilarius, *Versus*, p. 24.

37 Marbod of Rennes, Ep. 6, *PL* 171, col. 1482. For the early church, see the anonymous *De singularitate clericorum*, in *S. Thasci Caecili Cypriani opera omnia*, ed. W. Hartel, CSEL 3,3 (Vienna, 1871), pp. 173–220.

38 Marbod of Rennes, Ep. 6, *PL* 171, cols. 1482–3.

39 Geoffrey of Vendôme, Ep. 79, *Oeuvres*, p. 148. In fact, Geoffrey is wrong in his assumption that this practice was unprecedented. See Roger Reynolds, '*Virgines subintroductae* in Celtic Christianity', *Harvard Theological Review* 61 (1968), 559–60. Note hagiographer Baldric of Dol's discussion of Robert's constant testing of canonized boundaries, such as gender and class (*Vita B. Roberti de Arbrissello, PL* 162, cols. 1054–5). Cf. Jo Ann McNamara's theory of a crisis in masculinity in 'The *Herrenfrage*: The Restructuring of the Gender System, 1050–1150', in *Medieval Masculinities: Regarding Men in the Middle Ages*, ed. Clare Lees (Minneapolis, 1994), pp. 3–29.

40 Geoffrey of Vendôme, Ep. 79, *Oeuvres*, p. 150.

41 Jerome, Ep. 45, *Epistulae*, expanded edition, ed. I. Hilberg, CSEL 54 (Vienna, 1996), 1.325; trans. W. H. Fremantle, *St. Jerome: Letters and Select Works*, Library of Nicene and Post-Nicene Fathers of the Church, 2nd ser., vi (Oxford and New York, 1893), p. 59. On Jerome's circle of female friends, see Clark, 'Friendship between the Sexes: Classical Theory and Christian Practice', in *Jerome, Chrysostom, and Friends*, pp. 35–106. Also see Jo Ann McNamara, *Sisters in Arms: Catholic Nuns through Two Millennia* (Cambridge, Mass., 1996), pp. 61–8. For parallels between these early ascetical circles and those appearing in the late eleventh century, see ibid., pp. 236–9. For a later period, see Ann Bartlett, '"A Reasonable Affection": Gender and Spiritual Friendship in Middle English Devotional Literature' in *Vox Mystica: Essays for Valerie M. Lagorio*, ed. Ann Bartlett *et al.* (Woodbridge, Suffolk, 1995) pp. 131–46.

42 See Jerome's letter to a nameless mother and daughter cohabiting with clerics in Gaul, Ep. 117, *Epistulae*, CSEL 55, 2.422–34; trans. Fremantle, pp. 215–20.

43 Jerome, Ep. 22, c. 16, *Epistulae*, CSEL 54, 1. 164; trans. Fremantle, p. 28.

44 John Boswell, *Christianity, Social Tolerance, and Homosexuality: Gay People in Western Europe from the Beginning of the Christian Era to the Fourteenth Century* (Chicago and London, 1980), pp. 207ff.; Brian Patrick McGuire, *Friendship and Community: The Monastic Experience 350–1250*, Cistercian Studies Series 95 (Kalamazoo, Mich., 1988), pp. 194ff.

45 See G. Meersseman and E. Adda, 'Pénitents ruraux communautaires en Italie au XIIe siècle', *Revue d'histoire ecclésiastique* 40 (1954), 343–90.

46 Elliott, *Fallen Bodies*, pp. 104, 110, 115, 119. Rachel Fulton, *From Judgment to Passion: Devotion to Christ and the Virgin Mary, 800–1200* (New York, 2002), pp. 89–118; Lester Little, 'The Personal Development of Peter Damian', in *Order and Innovation in the Middle Ages: Essays in Honor of Joseph R. Strayer*, ed. William C. Jordan *et al.* (Princeton, 1976), pp. 330–2.

47 On Peter and his friendship with men, see McGuire, *Friendship and Community*, pp. 205–10. McGuire sees Damian as a transitional figure with respect to monastic friendship.

48 Damian, Ep. 104, *Die Briefe des Petrus Damiani*, ed. Kurt Reindel, *MGH, Die Briefe der Deutschen Kaiserzeit* (Munich, 1989), 3.151.

49 On the relationship between women and confessional scrupulosity, see Elliott, 'Women and Confession: From Empowerment to Pathology', in *Gendering the Master Narrative: Women and Power in the Middle Ages*, ed. Mary Erler and Maryanne Kowaleski (Ithaca, NY, 2003), pp. 31–51.

50 See Dyan Elliott, *Proving Woman: Female Spirituality and Inquisitional Culture in the Later Middle Ages* (Princeton, 2004), pp. 41–2.

51 Damian, Ep. 149, *Die Briefe*, 3.547. For similar laments to Agnes, see Ep. 130, 3.435; Ep. 144, 3.526. For the chronology of Agnes's comings and goings, see Little, 'Personal Development', p. 324.

52 Damian, Ep. 124, *Die Briefe*, 3.410. Cf. his admonishment that she would soon be exchanging her purple robes for a tomb where she would be food for worms (Ep. 130, ibid., 3.436).

53 Ep. 123, ibid., 3.400–1. Peter corresponded with other women as well. See, for example, his letter to Countess Beatrice of Tuscany commending her recent transition to a spiritual marriage with her husband, Godfrey, and urging her to greater acts of hospitality and bequests to the church (Ep. 51, ibid., 2.132–7; *Letters*, trans. Blum, 2.335–40). Cf. the correspondence of Pope Gregory VII, who was especially close to Beatrice and her daughter Mathilda (McNamara, *Herrenfrage*, p. 11).

54 Thus Goscelin recounts an incident from his novitiate: 'I was an adolescent, you an infant', *Liber confortatorius* bk. 4, ed. C. H. Talbot, *Studia Anselmiana* 37, *Analecta Monastica*, ser. 3 (Rome, 1955), p. 102. On his age, see Wilmart, 'Eve et Goscelin', pt. 2, p. 51.

55 Hilarius, *Versus*, p. 23.

56 Goscelin, *Liber confortatorius*, bk. 1, p. 28.

57 Ibid., p. 29.

58 Ibid., pp. 30–1.

59 Ibid., p. 31; see Jerome, Ep. 46, ch. 1, *Epistulae*, CSEL, 54, 1.329; trans. Fremantle, p. 60. Cf. Goscelin, *Liber confortatorius*, bk. 1, pp. 34–5, where he again refers to this passage. Goscelin seems to have a deep sympathy with Jerome, perhaps because of his friendship with Paula, and cites him at every opportunity. See, for example, ibid., bk. 1, p. 43; bk. 2, pp. 61, 74, 81. He also misattributes Rufinus's work to Jerome: see bk. 2, p. 56 (bis), bk. 2, pp. 59–61, and *passim*.

60 Ibid., bk. 1, p. 34.

61 Ibid., bk. 2, pp. 49ff.; bk. 3, pp. 79, 81, 83; bk. 4, 91ff.

62 Ibid., bk. 4, p. 107. Likewise, he still sees it as his job to arm her with 'the munition of total virtue' (p. 103).

63 Ibid., bk. 4, p. 116; cf. the opening where he calls her 'beloved light of my soul' and 'my sweetest soul' (bk. 1, p. 27).

64 Ibid., bk. 4, p. 117.

65 *Life*, pp. 174–5; cf. 144–5; 172–3. Cf. Abelard who, when slandered for his efforts to help Heloise and her nuns, sought comfort in the parallel trials of Jerome, *Historia calamitatum*, ed. J. Monfrin (Paris, 1959), p. 101; *The Letters*, trans. Radice rev. Clanchy, p. 42.

66 *Life*, ch. 4, in *The Book of St. Gilbert*, ed. Raymonde Foreville and Gillian Keir (Oxford, 1987), pp. 18–19.

67 See Penny Gold, 'The Marriage of Mary and Joseph in the Twelfth-Century Ideology of Marriage', in *Sexual Practices and the Medieval Church*, ed. Vern Bullough and James Brundage (New York, 1982), pp. 102–17, 249–51.

68 *Life*, pp. 50–1. For the influence of Cecilia, see Elliott, *Spiritual Marriage*, pp. 64–7.

69 *Life*, pp. 72–3; Elliott, *Spiritual Marriage*, pp. 104–6; 208–9.

70 *De singularitate clericorum*, pp. 194, 195. Cf. Bartlett's "A Reasonable Affection", p. 135.

71 Goscelin, *Liber confortatorius*, bk. 1, p. 33; bk. 4, p. 117.

72 'The Personal Letters', ed. Muckle, p. 94; *The Letters*, trans. Radice, p. 89. See M. T. Clanchy, *Abelard: A Medieval Life* (Oxford, 1997), p. 153.

73 Peter the Venerable, Ep. 116, *The Letters of Peter the Venerable*, ed. Giles Constable (Cambridge, Mass., 1967), 1.308; *The Letters*, trans. Radice rev. Clanchy, p. 223. See Clanchy's discussion of Peter the Venerable's vision of love (*Abelard*, pp. 158–61).

74 On the popular projection of the marriage bond beyond the grave, see Elliott, *Spiritual Marriage*, pp. 69–73.

75 Goscelin, *Liber confortatorius*, ed. Talbot, bk. 1, p. 27.
76 Goscelin of St Bertin, *The Life of King Edward who Rests at Westminster*, ed. and trans. Frank Barlow (London, 1962), p. 60; cf. pp. 42, 76. See Elliott, *Spiritual Marriage*, pp. 120–3.
77 Goscelin, *Liber confortatorius*, ed. Talbot, bk. 4, p. 104.
78 Ibid., pp. 104–5.
79 Ibid., p. 107.
80 See Jacques Dalarun, *Robert d'Arbrissel: fondateur de Fontevraud* (Paris, 1986), pp. 67–71; idem, 'Robert d'Arbrissel et les femmes', *Annales ESC* 39 (1984), 1146–51; see also idem, *L'Impossible sainteté: La vie retrouvée de Robert d'Arbrissel* (Paris, 1985), pp. 183ff.
81 Petigny, 'Une lettre', pp. 220–1; Regine Pernoud, *Women in the Days of the Cathedrals*, trans. Anne Côté-Harriss (San Francisco, 1989), p. 126.
82 Pernoud, *Women*, p. 125. Petigny says that the marriage was dissolved as consanguinous and probably never consummated ('Une lettre', p. 214).
83 Petigny, 'Une lettre', p. 222; Pernoud, *Women*, pp. 124–6.
84 On this exchange see Jean Leclercq, *Women and Saint Bernard of Clairvaux*, Cistercian Studies 144 (Kalamazoo, Mich., 1989), pp. 45–52. Leclercq mentions modern scholars' discomfort with Bernard's exuberance (p. 45). One wonders how contemporaries regarded this relationship – especially since Ermengard was once a famed beauty whose graces were celebrated poetically by none other than Marbod of Rennes (but then again, so was Thais). Petigny cites Marbod's poem in full ('Une lettre', p. 216). It is translated by Pernoud in *Women*, pp. 124–5.
85 Petigny, 'Une lettre', p. 223; Latzke, 'Robert von Arbrissel', pp. 135–6.
86 See Sharon Farmer, 'Persuasive Voices: Clerical Images of Medieval Wives', *Speculum* 61 (1986), 517–43. For the clergy's subordination of the wife's physical and spiritual health to that of the husband, see Elliott, *Spiritual Marriage*, pp. 146ff.
87 *Life*, pp. 126–7. This absorption of female into male communities is a common pattern in this period. See Elkins, *Holy Women*, pp. 46–50.
88 See chapter 6 in this volume.

11

CHRISTINA'S TEMPTING

Sexual desire and women's sanctity

Kathryn Kelsey Staples and Ruth Mazo Karras

Around the age of twenty, Christina of Markyate faced the scorching fires of lust in an ultimate challenge from the devil. Her triumph, with God's help, proved to be the turning point in her sanctity. Christina's *vita* provides the modern audience with a window onto a time of shifting ideas and standards about sexual temptation, highlighting important issues about women's roles and their sexuality in monastic life.

According to her *vita* Christina felt the call to chastity at an early age. Before her birth, a dove appeared to her mother as an omen of her holy birth (*Life*, p. 35). When Christina had decided to adhere to the directives of a chaste life, she secretly vowed virginity in Shillington, near St Albans. Yet her parents had other plans for her. After evading the sexual advances of the bishop of Durham, Christina was betrothed and married to Burthred, the son of a local noble family. She persisted in her virginal vow and refused to consummate the marriage. Christina finally escaped and took refuge in Flamstead with Alfwen the anchoress, and two years later with the hermit Roger. Here, she lived in a very small cell adjacent to Roger's and endured numerous physical trials. After Roger's death, Christina, through a petition to the archbishop of York, lived secretly with an unnamed cleric to continue to avoid Robert, the bishop of Lincoln, who had tried to enforce her marriage to Burthred and from whose ruling she escaped. Later, the archbishop secured the annulment of her marriage and she made her formal vows around 1131. After this date, Christina led an independent and public life and became the prioress of Markyate and the spiritual advisor to, and good friend of, Geoffrey, the abbot of St Albans.

Before her formal vows and her subsequent duties as a prioress, Christina's life was filled with physical and spiritual tests. Yet one trial rose above the rest. After she overcame the gruelling trials that she faced as a hermit – the extreme cold and heat, the close quarters, the constant fasting, and the subsequent illnesses (*Life*, pp. 103–5) – the devil forced upon Christina perhaps her greatest battle, endured while she lived with the unnamed cleric: sexual temptation. According to her hagiographer, seeing Christina and the cleric grow close in spiritual friendship enraged the devil, the 'enemy of chastity', who then attacked them both and 'assailed her flesh with incitements to pleasure and her mind with impure thoughts' (*Life*, p. 115).

Although the cleric succumbed to these ideas of pleasure, Christina withheld her consent and resisted the temptations, the form of which was so impure her hagiographer deemed them too dangerous to record in writing: 'Sometimes the wretched man, out of his senses with passion, came before her without any clothes on and behaved in so scandalous a manner that I cannot make it known' (*Life*, p. 115). Christina fasted and scourged herself, and prayed for help. She felt the temptation, however, only when the cleric was not present: 'for in his absence she used to be so inwardly inflamed that she thought the clothes which clung to her body might be set on fire. Had this occurred whilst she was in his presence, the maiden might well have been unable to control herself' (*Life*, p. 117). God sent a vision to the cleric warning him to stop troubling Christina, but her own lust still persisted. Eventually Jesus appeared to Christina in a vision as a small child, comforted her, and stifled the temptation of lust in her forever afterwards (*Life*, p. 119). This chapter will focus on the inclusion of this crucial trial of sexual temptation in Christina's *vita* and its role in the presentation of Christina's sanctity.

The physical and spiritual test of desire, which she fought off with prayer and harsh self-punishment and deprivation, is significant in two aspects. First, Christina's temptation reflects a development in Christian thought in the twelfth century and, second, the trial of her sexual temptation serves a vital narrative function in the portrayal of Christina herself. The inclusion of the trial of sexual temptation in her *vita* coincided with a shift in attitudes within the medieval church towards sexual temptation for women. While commentators discussed the topic of sexual temptation throughout the Middle Ages, until the twelfth century they primarily emphasized the threat of it for men. In this century and beyond, many priests, monks and scholars became preoccupied with issues of chastity for both men and women and became increasingly alarmed by the growing proximity between male and female religious. The theme of sexual temptation began to apply as much to women as to men. Many of these concerns appear in Christina's *vita* in general and in her triumph over sexual temptation in particular.

Christina's sexual temptation becomes a key issue in her *vita* and serves to enhance her sanctity. After she triumphs over the ordeals of hunger, physical discomfort and sickness, Roger considers her worthy to inherit his hermitage (*Life*, p. 109). Yet she needs to face and conquer lustful bodily temptation for good in order to become a spiritual guide, prophetess and 'faithful protectress' (*Life*, p. 147) to Abbot Geoffrey later in the *vita*. Christina's *vita* is distinctive because it deals concretely with the issue of sexual temptation for the saint herself and the inclusion of this issue is necessary for the portrayal of Christina's sanctity to her twelfth-century audience.

Treatments of sexual temptation in the late antique period and the early Middle Ages can help us understand how and to what end Christina's hagiographer uses it in her *vita*. In the late antique period the topic of sexual temptation captured the attention of many authors. The particular dangers of lust are elucidated in the *Vitae*

Patrum tradition, a group of sayings, biographies and anecdotes of the first desert hermits often cited by later medieval authors.[1] The desert fathers became holy through struggling against a variety of temptations, including the sexual. Pelagius' sixth century translation of the *Sayings of the Fathers*, part of the *Vitae Patrum*, includes a number of anecdotes in which sexual temptation is an issue for hermits and monks.[2] Many late antique authors discussed the need for controlling sexual temptation. This was an important topic for Augustine (*c.* 353–430) in his writings on the human will and what constituted sin. In his view, which helped shape Western Christian beliefs, sexual temptation was a spiritual danger, particularly because sexual organs could not be controlled by human will ever since Adam's original disobedience to God.[3]

The control of sexual desire also featured in views on sainthood and in the composition of saints' lives. John Climacus (*c.* 525–*c.* 606) believed that one must vanquish sexual desire in order to achieve sanctity, stating: 'I do not think anyone should be classed as a saint until he has made holy his body, if indeed that is possible ... To have mastered one's body is to have taken command of nature, which is surely to have risen above it. And the man who has done this is not much lower than the angels, if even that.'[4] As the genre of saints' lives developed, authors frequently demonstrated the great holiness of their subjects by emphasizing their triumphs over sexual temptation. In the *Life* of the first desert father, Antony, written by Athanasius in 356, the saint resisted 'seductive dreams', the suggestion of impure thoughts and an apparition of a beautiful woman.[5] The late sixth- to early seventh-century Celtic saint, Columbanus, was tempted by the devil to desire 'lascivious maidens' and, upon the advice of a holy woman, overcame this lust by running away.[6] In the early tenth century *Life* of Gerald of Aurillac, God enabled Gerald to overcome his desire for a woman by making her seem deformed and perhaps also by rendering him impotent.[7]

In these *vitae*, and many more besides,[8] the saints' struggle against sexual temptation is emphasized and their sanctity is strengthened by their ability to overcome and control their lust. This control is sometimes achieved by force of will, sometimes, as with Gerald of Aurillac (and eventually Christina), as a gift of God through prayer. Sexual temptation appears often either as the only temptation the saint suffers or as outranking the lure of other temptations, such as money or secular power. The trial of sexual temptation also frequently serves as the gateway trial to a saintly life. For example, St Columbanus faces the trial of sexual temptation early in his life and his defeat of this trial sets him onto his pious life marked by his miracle-working powers and apostolic enthusiasm.

Despite its centrality in many *vitae*, for the most part only male saints wrestle with sexual temptation. While the issue may appear in female saints' lives, or in other writings about virtuous women, the women are usually temptations to men but are not subject to temptation themselves. Traditional Christian thought held virginity as an important virtue for women, but women needed to be protected from threats to their virginity by men rather than protected from their own thoughts which might lead them astray. In the *Sayings of the Fathers*, a nun lying ill prevents her brother from visiting her at her convent lest the sight of her or her sisters bring him into temptation.[9] In his letter to Eustochium on virginity, Jerome stresses her importance as the bride of Christ and advises her to remain hidden from view so as not to incite the lust of men and subsequently lose her virginity.[10] Later, in Hrotsvitha's tenth-century play, *Calimachus*, Drusiana is the subject of Calimachus' desire and she dies in order to end Calimachus' lust for her, saying, 'Permit me to die so that I won't become the ruin of that charming young man!'[11] Jane Tibbetts Schulenburg argues convincingly that hagiographers before the twelfth century attempted to portray their female subjects as 'dead to earthly desires', in order to emphasize their virginal perfection and spiritual purity. Only by protecting their virginity could women 'transcend their unfortunate sexuality and free themselves from their corporeal shackles'.[12] While churchmen of the early Middle Ages emphasized virginity for women as a way to rise above their carnal nature and as an avenue for sainthood, the emphasis was on defending their virginity from male pursuers rather than on an internal struggle against sexual temptation. In the *vitae* before Christina's, female saints are either the objects of desire or never face situations in which sexual temptation figures. It appears that sexual temptation was not a very important issue in female sanctity before the twelfth century.[13] This makes it all the more noteworthy that, when the cleric is inflamed with lust for Christina, her biographer expresses no concern about her having incited it. Christina is concerned to protect her own virginity, but does not feel responsible for the chastity of another.

In the central Middle Ages the topic of sexual temptation and the threat women posed to holiness among monks and clerics intensified and continued to expand beyond hagiography. In the tenth century, monks tried to distance themselves from female monastics who would join Cluny's ranks, claiming the Benedictine rule to be too challenging for women to follow because of their lack of self-control and declaring their female charm dangerous to the order's monks.[14] In the eleventh century, the concern over the lust of monks and clerics for women remained ever-present.[15] Finally, the twelfth century witnessed a return to the monastic debate over nocturnal emission, a specific manifestation of lust not discussed on such a scale since the seventh century.[16] This was due to the ecclesiastical reform movement, which emphasized the importance of the Eucharist and of a 'ritually pure clergy' to celebrate the Eucharist, as part of an effort to formalize the sacraments.[17]

Although sexual temptation remained a focus of concern in male saints' lives, in the twelfth century scholars and clerics began to place more emphasis on women as subject to the dangers of desire. During this century, there was an increase in writings emphasizing that women, too, were susceptible to perilous feelings of lust. The second redactor of Gratian's *Concordance of Discordant Canons*, writing between 1140 and 1158, viewed sexual temptation as a weakness of the human body and claimed that women were especially vulnerable to sexual suggestions.[18] The importance of Gratian's view lies in the fact that he made a relatively obscure earlier opinion (of Cyprian of Carthage) more prominent.

Although earlier authors had occasionally seen women as susceptible to sexual temptation, the emphasis shifted distinctly in the twelfth century because of a combination of factors: an increase in women religious, the movement for monastic reform, and the movement for the strict claustration of nuns. This context is essential to understanding the presence and role of sexual temptation in Christina's *vita*.

The eleventh century witnessed a growth of female monasticism.[19] The increase in women joining religious houses was initially met with lay and ecclesiastic approval. However, by the twelfth century the number of women religious augmented the pressure placed on monasteries to provide spiritual direction and sacramental support to these women, and monks became less enthusiastic in their acceptance of female counterparts. The visits that many monks were required to make to women's houses took away from their contemplative and prayerful lives of solitude and brought them into contact with the world from which they had sought to distance themselves.[20] The church reform movement of the eleventh and twelfth centuries centred on the interpretation and importance of the sacraments and had attendant concerns of ritual purity – the monks' 'levitical ritual purity from the pollution of the world'[21] – which materialized in invectives against simony and clerical marriage. In particular, the emphasis on clerical celibacy and the denunciation of clerical wives led to a negative view of women, because it emphasized the danger that contact with women held for the spiritual well-being of clerics. Jo Ann McNamara explains the cause and effect in this manner: 'In the eleventh century, zealots transformed the respectable relationships of the married clergy into a swamp of corruption and led at last to a revolution in the structure of the church itself, forever separating the male clergy, monks and seculars, from the imperfect laity, stigmatized by its association with women.'[22] By the twelfth century, the movement for clerical celibacy worked to hinder female monasticism and prompted concern over women's sexuality.

The expression of female religiosity through acceptable avenues was also curbed by the trend towards standardization of religious orders, which in turn led to a discussion of sexual temptation for women. Women of the eleventh and twelfth centuries who inclined to the spiritual way of life had the choice of entering a double monastery or joining an independent female community, often working to gain entrance into an established order. Entry into orders such as the Cistercians gave female institutions clout, recognition and official endorsement in a religious world that often refused to recognize independent houses. It also gave them certain exemptions and a level of freedom that the mainstream orders enjoyed. As a response to this religious zeal, the newly strengthened church sought standardization among these new orders in an effort to suppress heresy and encourage orthodox belief. Concerned in particular with women's orthodoxy, popes applied pressure on monks to provide for female religious communities to prevent heresy.[23] The 'provision for' and standardization of women's communities led to their control.

During the twelfth century, a sense of distrust grew of spiritual friendships between men and women in double monasteries, and in female religious communities between nuns and their provisioning priests.[24] Sally Thompson uses St Albans and its connections with surrounding female communities as an example of the suspicion of these spiritual friendships. She claims that Christina's *vita* evidences friendly connections between male and female communities and mutual visits between male and female religious. However, by the end of the twelfth century, as seen in the lack of involvement of St Albans monks with the priory at St Mary de Pré at this time, there was less contact between monks and nuns.[25]

In the thirteenth century, individual orders began to shut their doors to female religious communities seeking affiliation. Orders offered a variety of reasons for this, including financial strains, the weak and heterodox nature of women religious,[26] and the issues of sexual temptation and female sexuality. While the risk of sexual temptation was ever-present to men, as it had been since the desert fathers, increased contact between male and female religious led to a new emphasis on *women's* sexual temptation. This concern is illustrated well in Aelred of Rievaulx's twelfth-century account of the nun of Watton who, as a nun of a Gilbertine double monastery in Yorkshire, became pregnant and who, as a punishment for her surrender to sexual temptation, was forced to castrate her lover, and was beaten and imprisoned.[27]

During the following century, this concern about the sexual temptation of women led to increased calls for claustration. Already in the mid-twelfth century, the Cistercian Idung of Prüfenung argued against female religious houses enjoying the same exemptions as male houses because of their natural vulnerability to lust:

> ... in the first place it must be said that, because the feminine sex is fragile, it requires greater protection and tighter enclosure ... the protection presented by tighter enclosure is more necessary for consecrated virgins than for monks ... Indeed, it is not expedient for that sex to make use of the freedom of its own governance because of both its natural changeableness as well as because of nearby outside temptations which womanly weakness is not sufficient enough to resist.[28]

Idung argues that virgins needed to be enclosed for protection from the four enemies that plague the feminine sex: their own lust, the lust of men, their curiosity and the devil.[29] Peter Abelard also suggested isolation for religious women because of their greater susceptibility to desire. In a letter to Heloise, in which he promotes the virtues of monastic life, he instructs her: 'Solitude is indeed all the more necessary for your [woman's] frailty, in as much as for our part we are less attacked by the conflicts of carnal temptations and less likely to stray towards bodily things through the senses.'[30] The case for strict surveillance, 'protection' and 'solitude' because of the inherent powerlessness of women monastics in the face of sexual temptation was a new point of contention.

Monks and secular clerics pursued similar lines of thought and discovered that claustration was the answer to these burdensome, numerous and potentially polluting and polluted religious women. These concerns culminated in 1298, when Pope Boniface VIII (c. 1235–1303) finally ordered in his bull, *Periculoso*, the strict claustration of religious women in every order, specifying that nuns could neither leave their houses nor ask unofficial visitors to their houses.[31] Among other concerns, this thirteenth-century tract reflects the transformation of twelfth-century individuals' anxieties about female temptation into far-reaching church policy. Boniface argued for claustration in order that 'the nuns be able to serve God more freely, wholly separated from the public and worldly gaze and, occasions for lasciviousness having been removed, may most diligently safeguard their hearts and bodies in complete chastity'.[32] In Boniface's mind, then, claustration would prevent women from being tempted by men and other enticements. In Elizabeth Makowski's words, Boniface had a care to 'safeguard nuns from themselves; to diminish, if not completely remove, worldly temptations'.[33]

The shift between the eleventh and the thirteenth centuries in the attitude towards women and sexual temptation, from women as temptresses to women as tempted, is also visible in saints' lives. Before the twelfth century, some hagiographers depict female saints as seeking to embody virginal perfection by protecting their own bodies, by keeping out of the sight of men, or by disfiguring themselves to ward off would-be rapists.[34] Other hagiographers emphasize the role of God in protecting their bodies for them, as in the case of St Agnes.[35] According to Schulenburg, by attaining this virginal perfection these saints, through either their own actions or divine intercession, became more man-like, and they transcended their gender.[36] In Christina's *Life* and in female saints' lives after hers, women are portrayed as still seeking to attain virginal perfection, but they do so often by overcoming sexual temptation. This triumph over sexual temptation is a new element in female *vitae* beginning with Christina's *vita*, and it continues to be prominent in hagiographic compilations produced in the thirteenth century.

This shift in the depiction of saintly women can be elucidated by considering two female saints whose *vitae* were popular both before and after the twelfth century, Justina and Agatha. In a fifth-century work, the 'Martyrdom of St. Cyprian', written by Eudokia, a Byzantine empress, Justina faced temptations sent by the magician Cyprian at the behest of a man named Aglaides who was smitten with Justina. In this early version, Justina triumphed over every demon sent by Cyprian to trick her. Each time demons approached her, she recognized their tricks, which included one demon 'fanning a flame in her heart to divide her against herself', one who was to give her a magic drink, and one who disguised himself as another holy virgin and tried to talk her out of virginity. Justina recognized the demons and turned them away with lengthy prayers to God. The author focuses on Justina's prayerful response and very little on the temptations. Indeed, there is no mention of Justina struggling with lustful feelings. Instead, she recognized the demons and prayed for protection, for her body to remain unharmed.[37] However, in *The Golden Legend*, completed in 1266, Jacobus de Voragine focuses on the attempts by the devil and various demons to incite 'raging heats of passion'[38] in St Justina for Cyprian, who aimed to take her saintly virginity. He also emphasizes the struggle Justina faced when she felt 'the flames of fleshly desire burn so strongly within her',[39] and how she freed herself from all temptation. Likewise, in *The South English Legendary*, contemporaneous with *The Golden Legend*, St Justina is beset with wanton thoughts.[40]

St Agatha likewise appears in *The South English Legendary*, and she too is introduced as a saint who rejected 'sin and fornication',[41] through facing the temptations of foul thoughts presented by Aphrodosia and her nine prostitute daughters.[42] Whereas the thirteenth-century narrator of *The South English Legendary* emphasizes Agatha's resistance to sexual temptations, Ælfric, the late tenth-century author of a compilation of saints' lives, portrayed Agatha's sanctity through her resistance to promises of riches and honours. Ælfric explains that Aphrodosia is to take Agatha and teach her 'the enticements of harlots', but in Ælfric's account these enticements are defined as material objects rather than foul thoughts. When Aphrodosia admits her defeat to Quintianus, she claims: 'I promised her gems and golden apparel, and other honours and a great house, estates and servants.'[43] The aspirations of sanctity for women may have remained constant, but the new conduit was the trial of sexual temptation.

The dangers of sexual temptation for women were not limited to hagiography. The author of the thirteenth-century advisory guide, *Ancrene Wisse*, cautions anchoresses that the more spiritual the female religious, the more she should expect to feel the fiery blasts of temptation. Furthermore, the author comforts and encourages the anchoresses in their trials by claiming that all the holy saints, their role models, were fiercely tempted.[44] The author of the *vita* of Christina of Markyate, writing in the twelfth century, anticipates these concerns in his discussion of Christina's sexual temptation. Furthermore, the way in which the author uses this trial in Christina's *vita* is quite original. Since sexual temptation does not appear as a crucial trial (if it appears at all) in female saints' lives before the twelfth century or in saints' lives contemporaneous to Christina's, it is not likely that Christina's hagiographer followed a specifically female model. This leaves two possibilities.

First, Christina's *vita* can be viewed as the genuine chronicle of a life, and her trial of desire sent by the devil as an exceptional event. Judging by the many other biographical aspects of her *vita*, for example, the details of her childhood, family and marriage problems, which seemingly divorce the text from hagiographical *topoi*, the author may have recorded the actual experience of a pious individual to whom he had a close proximity. Unusually, the author probably recorded his subject's life as he heard it from her own mouth, instead of rewriting a pre-existing *vita* or writing a *vita* in the interests of canonization.[45] It is very possible that Christina's desire for the unnamed cleric is an authentic experience which this author chose to detail for his audience. Yet this is only half the story. Even if the monk faithfully recorded Christina's experiences as she told them to him, why did she have *these* experiences and why did she shape them in the manner she did? Furthermore, why did she not face other temptations, perhaps more similar to those of her earlier counterparts? To answer these questions, one must look at the historical context.

The second and perhaps more convincing possibility is to consider Christina's *vita* as a product of her time, one which reflects both the concerns among the St Albans community directly and the anxieties among wider twelfth-century religious circles. First, Christina's hagiographer may have been using his work, and the inclusion of her struggle against sexual temptation, to argue against the cynical rumours that surrounded Christina and Geoffrey's friendship and to dispute popular views which denounced relationships between male and female religious in general. The concern over the friendship between Christina and Geoffrey is highlighted in the hagiographer's mention of the rumours spread about them. He writes: '[Other people] who could think of nothing better to say spread the rumour that she was attracted to the abbot by earthly love ... the abbot was slandered as a seducer and the maiden as a loose woman' (*Life*, pp. 173–5). In addition, other evidence suggests that the St Albans community frowned upon their relationship and especially on Abbot Geoffrey's financial endowments to Christina and her community at Markyate.[46] Although the author of the *vita* places the blame for these slanderous rumours at the door of the devil, who planted them in people's minds, their inclusion in the *vita* reflects contemporary concerns about companionship between male and female religious. Furthermore, by first detailing Christina's struggle against, and victory over, the lust-inciting devil, the author strengthens the validity of their friendship. After overcoming her desire for the unnamed cleric, Christina's lust dissipated forever (*Life*, p. 119) and she was subsequently able have a pure and chaste spiritual friendship with Geoffrey. With the inclusion of, and her triumph over, the trial of sexual temptation, and with the positive portrayal of Christina and Geoffrey's relationship afterwards, the *Life* as a whole speaks very favourably to spiritual friendships and works to alleviate the condemnation of Christina and Geoffrey's particular relationship by the St Albans community.

In writing about the sexual temptation that Christina faced, it is conceivable that her hagiographer also wished to communicate a larger message of clerical celibacy to his audience. Christina's and the unknown cleric's triumph over temptation, and her success later as a visionary and spiritual guide to an abbot, is a testimony to the value and viability of cross-gendered monastic friendship. Finally, and most compellingly, the author possibly used the popular anxieties over sexual temptation among the members of his religious audience to underscore his subject's sanctity. In triumphing over the foul thoughts and feelings the devil sent her, Christina's trial echoes those of the desert fathers and other earlier male saints. She resists through denial (scolding the cleric, even though she has the same desires as he), physical punishment and prayer. In doing so, she presents an example not of a woman who is so virtuous that she need only fear physical violation (or the harm she might cause by tempting others), but of one who deals with the feelings of lust that later writers especially would attribute to women, and overcomes them. Like the stories of these earlier male saints, Christina's *vita* does not present the overcoming of temptation as her triumph alone. It is God who makes her desire the cleric only in his absence. The author here adopts the Pauline notion that God 'will not let you be tested beyond your strength, but with the testing he will also provide the way out so that you may be able to endure it' (1 Cor. 10:13), and it is God himself who, at her prayer, removes the temptation.[47]

With regard to male clergy, John Arnold has recently drawn a useful distinction between lust controlled by bodily chastisement or an effort of will on the one hand, and by external intervention on the other. The first, which he calls 'chastity', is a continual struggle; the second, 'virginity', is the result of God's grace, 'the state for only a blessed few, those who have lost all desire and have transcended human pleasure.'[48] If these categories are applicable to women as well – and there seems no reason why they should not be – one might say that the earlier female saints, whose chastity was threatened by external forces but not by their own desires, fell into the second category.

Christina represents both. Her struggle led her to the higher state through God's grace, and her story thus becomes more compelling. It also becomes more exemplary: not everyone can confidently expect the gift of sexual anaesthesia through God's grace, but everyone can participate in the very human struggle against temptation. Henrietta Leyser comments that the twelfth century sees a shift from the tradition of resisting temptation to internalizing it and developing spiritually from the struggle.[49] Christina, withstanding both the advances of the cleric and the passions inflamed within her own heart, experiences with God's help both the internal struggle and the external resistance. With the inclusion of her struggle to overcome sexual temptation, Christina appears as a woman of her time while her hagiographer emerges as an author conscious of current issues and capable of adapting his subject's experiences to the anxieties prevalent among male and female religious.

Notes

The authors wish to thank the Graduate Research Partnership Program, College of Liberal Arts, University of Minnesota, for funding the research for this article.

1   Constance Rosenthal, *The Vitae Patrum in Old and Middle English Literature* (Philadelphia, 1936).

2   See, for example, Pelagius, *Verba Seniorum*, 'Liber Quartus: De Continentia', 68, *PL* 73, col. 873B. Also see 4:61 and all of Book Five, 'De fornicatione'. For a translation, see *The Desert Fathers*, ed. and trans. Helen Waddell (New York, 1998).

3   Augustine, *Civitate Dei*, 14.24, *PL* 41, cols. 432–3. For a translation, see *Augustine: The City of God Against the Pagans*, ed. and trans. R. W. Dyson (Cambridge, 1998), pp. 625–7.

4 John Climacus, *Scala Paradisi*, *PG* 88, cols. 631–1164, translated in *The Ladder of Divine Ascent*, trans. Colm Luibheid and Norman Russell (London, 1982), pp. 178, 181.

5 *Early Christian Lives*, trans. Carolinne White (London, 1998), pp. 11–12; the version known in the West in the Middle Ages was the Latin translation by Evagrius, *PL* 73, cols. 125–68 (129). Cf. *Das altenglische Martyrologium*, ed. Günter Kotzor, 2 vols. (Munich, 1981), 17 January, ii. 17–19, in which 'devils tempted him there beyond measure with impure desires, even so that at night they came to him in the form of adorned women'.

6 Jonas Bobiensis, *Vita Columbani*, *PL* 87, cols. 1015B-1016C. For a translation, see *Life of St. Columban by the Monk Jonas*, ed. Dana Carleton Munro (Felinfach, 1993), pp. 12–15.

7 Odo of Cluny, *Vita S. Geraldi Comitis Aurillac*, 1.9, *PL* 133, cols. 648–9. For a translation, see *St. Odo of Cluny*, ed. and trans. Gerard Sitwell (New York, 1958), pp. 101–3. For the suggestion of impotency, see Jacqueline Murray, ' "The law of sin that is in my members": The problem of male embodiment', in *Gender and Holiness: Men, Women and Saints in Late Medieval Europe*, ed. Samantha J. E. Riches and Sarah Salih (New York, 2002), p. 14.

8 For more examples of sexual temptation in male saints' lives, see Jane Tibbetts Schulenburg, *Forgetful of Their Sex: Female Sanctity and Society ca. 500–1100* (Chicago, 1998), pp. 311–14.

9 Pelagius, *Verba Seniorum*, 4:61, *PL* 73, col. 872B.

10 Jerome, *Epistola XXII*, 'De custodia virginitatis' *PL* 22.5, cols. 411–12. Although Jerome warns Eustochium elsewhere in the letter against her own lust and explains the ways in which she can avoid inciting lust in herself, women's lustfulness was not a prominent theme in the *vitae* of women. For a translation, see Charles Christopher Mierow, ed. and trans., *The Letters of St. Jerome* (London, 1963), pp. 134–79.

11 *The Dramas of Hrotsvit of Gandersheim*, trans. Katharina M. Wilson (Saskatoon, 1985); *Hrotsvithae Opera*, ed. Helena Homeyer (Munich, 1970), p. 286.

12 Schulenburg, *Forgetful of their Sex*, p. 127.

13 St Radegund (*c.* 522–87) is an example where sexual temptation is not an integral part of sanctity. See Venantius Fortunatus, *De Vita Sanctae Radegundis*, ed. Bruno Krusch, *MGH SRM* (Hanover, 1984), ii. 358–95. For a translation, see *Sainted Women of the Dark Ages*, ed. Jo Ann McNamara, John E. Halborg and E. Gordon Whately (Durham, 1992), pp. 70–105.

14 Jo Ann Kay McNamara, *Sisters in Arms: Catholic Nuns through Two Millennia* (Cambridge, Mass., 1996), p. 210.

15 For example, Burchard of Worms, *Decretum*, *PL* 140, col. 977B–C.

16 For a full discussion of the concerns of emissions and pollution among writers in the Middle Ages, see Dyan Elliott, *Fallen Bodies: Pollution, Sexuality, and Demonology in the Middle Ages* (Philadelphia, 1999), pp. 14–34. See also James A. Brundage, 'Obscene and Lascivious: Behavioral Obscenity in Canon Law', in *Obscenity: Social Control and Artistic Creation in the European Middle Ages*, ed. Jan M. Ziolkowski (Leiden, 1998), pp. 246–59; and Marie Theres Fögen, 'Unto the Pure All Things Are Pure: The Byzantine Canonist Zonaras on Nocturnal Pollution' in Ziolkowski, *Obscenity*, pp. 260–78.

17 Elliott, *Fallen Bodies*, pp. 15, 21–2 (quotation at p. 21). The intention and consent of the person, in this case of the sleeping offender, played a large role in the discussions of this time. See Peter Abelard, *Peter Abelard's Ethics*, ed. and trans. D. E. Luscombe (Oxford, 1971), pp. 32–7; Brundage, 'Obscene and Lascivious', p. 256; Hildegard of Bingen, *Hildegardis Causae et curae*, ed. Paul Kaiser (Leipzig, 1903), p. 83.

18 *Decretum Magistri Gratiani*, ed. Emil Friedberg, C. 27, q. 1, c. 4, vol. 1 of *Corpus Iuris Canonici* (Leipzig, 1874; rpt 1959), cols. 1047–8. See Anders Winroth, *The Making of Gratian's Decretum* (Cambridge, 2000), Appendix, p. 221, for absence of this section in the first redaction.

19 Many scholars have speculated on the reason for this increase. See Jo Ann McNamara, 'The Herrenfrage: The Restructuring of the Gender System, 1050–1150' in *Medieval Masculinities: Regarding Men in the Middle Ages*, ed. Clare A. Lees (Minneapolis, 1994), pp. 3–29. See also McNamara, *Sisters in Arms*, pp. 233–4, 260–1; Brenda Bolton, 'Mulieres Sanctae', in *Women in Medieval Society*, ed. Susan Mosher Stuard (Philadelphia, 1976), pp. 147–8; Elkins, *Holy Women*, p. xx; Bruce L. Venarde, *Women's Monasticism and Medieval Society: Nunneries in France and England, 890–1215* (Ithaca, 1997), p. 57. In England in 1130 there were 20 female religious communities, but by 1165 there were over 100. In France and England together in 1070 there were about 100 female religious communities, and in 1170 there were four times that number. See Elkins, *Holy Women*, p. xiii, and Venarde, *Women's Monasticism*, p. 54.

20 However, Constance Berman suggests that 'it was sometimes the nuns themselves who actively opposed being incorporated into the Order' (*The Cistercian Evolution: The Invention of a Religious Order in Twelfth-Century Europe* (Philadelphia, 2000), p. 43).

21 Phyllis G. Jestice, *Wayward Monks and the Religious Revolution of the Eleventh Century* (New York, 1997), p. 18.

22 McNamara, *Sisters in Arms*, p. 246, quotation at p. 220.

23 McNamara, *Sisters in Arms*, p. 304; Venarde, *Women's Monasticism*, pp. 161–2.

24 Elkins, *Holy Women*, p. 156.

25 Thompson, *Women Religious*, pp. 60–1.

26 See McNamara, *Sisters in Arms*, pp. 299, 304, 310, 315; Elizabeth Makowski, *Canon Law and Cloistered Women: Periculoso and Its Commentators 1298–1545* (Washington, 1997), p. 12.

27 Aelred of Rievaulx, 'De Sanctimoniali de Wattun', *PL* 195, cols. 789–96. For a translation, see John Boswell, *The Kindness of Strangers: The Abandonment of Children in Western Europe from Late Antiquity to the Renaissance* (London, 1989), pp. 452–8.

28 *Le Moine Idung et Ses Deux Ouvrages: 'Argumentum Super Quatuor Questionibus' et 'Dialogus Duorum Monachorum'*, ed. R. B. C. Huygens (Spoleto, 1980), pp. 70, 74, 75. For a translation see *Cistercians and Cluniacs, The Case for Cîteaux: A Dialogue between Two Monks, An Argument on Four Questions*, ed. and trans. Joseph Leahey (Kalamazoo, 1977), pp. 168, 174, 176.

29 Huygens, *Le Moine Idung*, p. 70.

30 *The Letters of Abelard and Heloise*, trans. Betty Radice, rev. M. T. Clanchy (London, 2003), p. 142; 'Abelard's Rule for Religious Women', ed. T. P. McLaughlin, *Mediaeval Studies* 18 (1956), 241–92, quotation at 250. Radice translates 'vestrae infirmitati' as 'your woman's frailty'. While 'vestrae' does indicate that he is talking about the frailty of a group of women, he does not necessarily mean it to apply to women in general.

31 Makowski, *Canon Law and Cloistered Women*, pp. 1, 2.

32 Boniface VIII, *Periculoso*, MS. Vat. Borghese 7, Liber Sextus fol. 56v-57v, cited in Makowski, *Canon Law and Cloistered Women*, p. 30.

33 Makowski, *Canon Law and Cloistered Women*, p. 30.

34 For example, the nuns of Coldingham (*c.* 870) cut off their noses to discourage the Danish attackers from raping them. See Roger of Wendover, *Flores Historiarum*, ed. Henry O. Coxe (London, 1841) i. 301–2. For a translation see Roger of Wendover, *Flowers of History: Comprising the History of England from the Descent of the Saxons to A.D. 1235*, trans. J. A. Giles (New York, 1968) i. 191–2. See also Schulenburg, *Forgetful of their Sex*, pp. 145–55.

35 See *Ælfric's Lives*, i. 170.

36 Schulenburg, *Forgetful of their Sex*, p. 128.

37 Eudokia Aelia, *De Martyrio S. Cypriani*, in *Eudociae Augustae, Procli Lycii, Claudiani: Carminum Graecorum Reliquiae*, ed. A. Ludwich (Leipzig, 1897). For a translation, see Eudokia, 'The Martyrdom of St. Cyprian', trans. G. Ronald Kastner, in *A Lost*

Tradition: Women Writers of the Early Church, ed. Patricia Wilson-Kastner *et al.* (New York, 1981), pp. 149–69.

38 Jacobus de Voragine, *The Golden Legend*, trans. William Granger Ryan, 2 vols. (Princeton, 1993), ii. 193–4; *Legenda Aurea*, ed. Giovanni Paolo Maggioni (Sismel, 1998), ii. 973.

39 Ibid.

40 Although Justina is absent from the earliest manuscripts of *The South English Legendary*, this representation of her sanctity is significant none the less. Karen Winstead, *Chaste Passions: Medieval English Virgin Martyr Legends* (London, 2000), p. 28, and appendix A, pp. 173–8. For her translation see pp. 35–9.

41 *The South English Legendary*, ed. Charlotte D'Evelyn and Anna J. Mill, 2 vols., EETS OS 235, 236 (1956–59), ii, p. 54, ll. 1–2, trans. Winstead, *Chaste Passions*, p. 28.

42 Although Aphrodisia and her daughters promise her fancy things and flatter her, the emphasis is on Agatha's rejection of the temptations of foul and evil thoughts. *The South English Legendary*, i. 54–5, ll. 9–10, 26.

43 Ibid., 196–9, ll. 13, 35–7.

44 *Ancrene Wisse: Guide for Anchoresses*, trans. Hugh White (London, 1993), pp. 86, 110, using the example of St Sarah.

45 See Rachel M. Koopmans, 'The Conclusion'.

46 See the *Gesta Abbatum* i. 95, 103; Koopmans, p. 695. Thompson, *Women Religious*, pp. 57–9, points out additional indications of disapproval by the St Albans monks (or by the later St Albans historians) towards connections between the monastery and nearby nunneries.

47 For the erotic nature of the vision with which he does so, see Ruth Mazo Karras, 'Friendship and Love in the Lives of Two Twelfth-Century English Saints', *Journal of Medieval History* 14 (1988), 305–20.

48 John Arnold, 'The Labour of Continence: Masculinity and Clerical Virginity', in *Medieval Virginities*, ed. Anke Bernau, Ruth Evans and Sarah Salih (Aberystwyth, 2003).

49 Henrietta Leyser, 'Two concepts of Temptation', in *Belief and Culture*, pp. 318–26.

12

THE ST ALBANS PSALTER

The abbot and the anchoress

Jane Geddes

The St Albans Psalter is one of the most spectacular illuminated manuscripts of twelfth-century England. It consists of five separate sections involving several scribes and artists: the calendar; the miniatures of the Life of Christ; the Alexis Quire; the Psalms; and finally a diptych of St Alban and David. Because her name appears in the calendar, the book has been, to varying degrees, associated with Christina of Markyate. Research stretching back over many decades has suggested numerous links and scholars are able now to piece together an increasingly rich context for the production of the book.[1] The theme to have emerged most prominently from current investigations is this: in almost all aspects, the Psalter is a book created for Christina, but its contents are strongly controlled by her mentor and patron, Abbot Geoffrey de Gorran.[2] Once a worldly French schoolmaster, now an ambitious but troubled administrator,[3] Geoffrey was creating not exactly the book Christina wanted, but the book he thought she should have. In some instances the images seem even to contradict her own stated preferences. Using the wealth of personal information which is available about the abbot and the anchoress,[4] I will be looking at each section of the Psalter to explore motives for its creation, and its reception.

Christina in the calendar

The objective evidence for Christina's connection with the book is to be found in the calendar section. Here the deaths of Christina and her family, the death of Christina's mentor Roger the Hermit, and the foundation of Markyate Priory, are all added at later dates. At the very least, these entries show that the calendar was important in the context of Christina and of Markyate, after her death.[5] However, it is also possible to show that the calendar was based on a model from the Fenland Abbey of Ramsey, which was near Christina's home in Huntingdon, and had strong connections with Christina's family.[6] A monk from St Albans copied out this calendar, and added a few saints' names from his own abbey, including that of St Alban (though he managed to misspell it). Since we know that Christina brought with her a psalter from Huntingdon, it is likely that this calendar was copied from her original model (*Life*, p. 99).

197

The image of Christina in the Psalter

Identifying references to Christina in the Psalm section is a more complicated process because, basically, the 211 initials were intended to illustrate the words of the Psalms. Here it is necessary to bring in evidence from events which are described in Christina's *Life* in order to identify personal details. The basic design of the Psalms consists of an initial with figures which illustrate the words absolutely literally. Adjacent is a short rubric taken from the Psalm, which explains the picture. So, for example, in Psalm 2, the rubric is 'Why have the nations raged?', and the initial shows a group of armed warriors. Facing the warriors is Christ brandishing a rod, illustrating the words which follow later in the Psalm: 'Thou shalt rule them as an iron rod'. Clearly, if the artist followed this literal rule all the way through, the reader would only learn how to study the Psalms, but that was not the case. It is through the few initials which break the rule that one can detect an element of choice on the part of the patron.

The Psalms have several oddities, of which two are important here. Stitched into the back of the book are two leaves showing St Alban and David, the musician (Plate 6).[7] Normally David is placed at the beginning of the Psalms, and a patron saint should also normally come at the start. These pages look like the beginning of a book of Psalms prepared for use at St Albans, which for some reason were relegated to the back. Second, out of a rigorously planned sequence of 211 initials, just one was left out. It is not at the beginning or the end, but at an arbitrary point in the middle, Psalm 105, and it happens to be the letter C (Plate 1). The space is covered by a glued-in patch, with nothing visible underneath. This initial shows a woman, presumably Christina, leading some monks to Christ. It is by a sophisticated artist who made no other illuminations in the book. Why was the gap left? Why was this patch made by a special artist? And why is the rubric different from all the other initials? The text does not come from the Psalm but says in a hexameter, 'Spare your monks I beseech you, merciful kindness of Jesus'.

There are three possibilities. The first, proposed by Peter Kidd,[8] is that the patch was a trial piece commissioned from this special artist, before the book format was decided. He did not get the job but his sample was used because the book was being prepared for Christina from the start. But if the book was intended for Christina, why stick her picture obscurely in the middle of the book? It is not even the first initial C.

The second possibility, which has a great deal of support for stylistic reasons, is that this patch was added several years later, in a style which is perceived as 'more advanced' than the strident designs of the other initials.[9] This theory assumes that the Psalms were only given to Christina long after they were made, and for some obscure reason just one initial, which happened to be the letter C, was left blank when all the others were complete. If the space was not left blank, then the original initial was totally scraped off and the damaged parchment covered by the patch. Even C. R. Dodwell who supported this theory wrote that this late insertion was 'difficult to understand'.[10]

The third possibility is that the patch was commissioned while the book was in progress, to mark a new destination. It began as a book of Psalms for St Albans, with the Martyrdom and David the Musician at the front, and then something happened which diverted the book to Christina, and, I shall argue, fundamentally changed the remainder of its contents. The patch was made by a special artist working outside St Albans, who never saw the rest of the book and did not know how the letter C was normally written.[11] The letter C was specially chosen for Christina, and the elegant style was preferred, to complement her elegant and spiritual nature.

There is a further clue to support this theory. The steady neat writing of the tag, in red and green, is by the same scribe who produced the calendar.[12] It was noted above that the calendar was specially made for Christina, with her local saints from the Fens. The parchment behind the patch, on p. 286, shows that when the patch was stuck in, its paint was already dry, but the scribe wrote his inscription with wet ink after the patch was applied. The green ink of the writing has seeped intensely through two layers of parchment whereas the imprint of the initial is much fainter. In other words, the addition of the C initial happened at the same time as Christina's calendar was being penned.

Christina as intercessor

The next question is why did Geoffrey decide to present this costly book to Christina, and the answer seems to lie in the initial's rubric which uniquely diverges from the words of the Psalms: 'Spare your monks I beseech you'. Christina is meant to utter these words aloud as she looks at the picture. Her main spiritual function is to act as intercessor for Geoffrey and his monks (*Life*, pp. 127, 139–41); in this picture she is thus shown crossing over the boundary between heaven and earth, in order to bring the monks to Christ.[13] Christina has the power to act as a conduit, crossing into the sacred space, but tenderly linked by touch to Geoffrey and his monks.

Christina's function as intercessor is shown again in the Litany (p. 403) (Figure 2). The importance of this initial is emphasized by its extraordinary size. The words of the Litany itself pray for intercession, invoking a notable number of virgin and female saints.[14] Christina is still reaching through to heaven, but this time in the company of her nuns at Markyate and, without doubt on this occasion, Geoffrey is the most important person present. This scene must be understood as a depiction of the powerful vision which Christina and Geoffrey had shared,[15] as described in the *Life*:

> [She] saw herself in a kind of chamber ... with two venerable and very handsome personages clothed in white garments. Standing side by side, they differed neither in stature nor beauty. On their shoulders a dove far more beautiful than other doves seemed to rest. Outside she saw the abbot trying without success to gain entrance to her.
>
> (*Life*, p. 157)

Note the insistence on this particular moment: it is clear from close examination of the manuscript that the artist had originally drawn the dove with spread wings, about to fly; evidently he was corrected, and told to make the bird rest. Geoffrey, flapping his arms, is failing to attract Christina's attention. The *Life* continues, describing this situation: 'Giving her a sign with his eyes and head, he[Geoffrey] humbly begged her to introduce him to the persons standing by her side in the divine presence' (*Life*, p. 157). After this the dove descends and Geoffrey is filled with the Holy Spirit. The experience is deeply moving for both of them.

> Filled with joy at this, she cherished him and venerated a fellow and companion of heavenly, not earthly glory and took him to her bosom in a close bond of holy affection. Who shall describe the longings, sighs, the tears as they sat and discussed heavenly matters? Who shall put into words how they despised the transitory, how they yearned for the everlasting?'
>
> (*Life*, p. 157)

For Geoffrey, this introduction to the divine was clearly a climactic moment in his life. Later on, in 1145, when the priory was formally established, it was quite naturally dedicated to the Holy Trinity, the focus of this vision.[16]

It is argued here that this episode prompted Geoffrey to divert his psalter from the library at St Albans to Christina. Psalm 105 thus represents its turning point, but the impact of the experience reverberates through many further sections of the book, as will be discussed below. But it is first necessary to consider whether the Psalms, after Psalm 105, reflect this change of destination, whether they become more specifically tailored for Christina's needs, and whether Geoffrey started to incorporate any special messages for her.[17] There are a few clues about this: I shall examine first the attitude to women, and then the layout of the initials together with the issue of literacy.

Women and the Psalter

Twenty initials in the Psalter depict women. In some cases they are a necessary part of the Psalm content and cannot be avoided. However, where female figures are deliberately chosen when none is mentioned in the text then clearly an intellectual and artistic decision has been made. In Psalms 8, 50, 122, 148, the Canticle of Anna, the Magnificat and the Apostles Creed, for example, women are an essential part of the text and are therefore illustrated. In Psalm 71, the Kings of Tharsis bringing gifts are simply translated into a New Testament context, illustrated by the adoration of the Magi before Mary and Christ. This reflects the Psalm's recitation at the mass of the Epiphany. Sometimes women are merely included as part of 'the World' or the 'Children of Israel', as in Psalms 92, 109 and 136. But in the Canticle of Symeon (p. 395), on the other hand, Joseph is omitted from the Presentation at the Temple, being replaced by a woman. (The same scene in the full-page miniatures, p. 28, also replaces Joseph with female dove bearers.) In the

Canticle of Moses (p. 377) and Psalm 149 a clear choice is being made to include women. In the canticle there is no mention of men and women praising God with timbrels as shown in the picture. Moses with his rod and a female leader direct segregated groups of men and women in their praise. In Psalm 149, the penultimate song of praise, the words are gender-neutral: 'Let his praise be in the church of the holy ones ... The holy ones shall rejoice in glory', but a group of women is shown within a church. The text implies that the holy ones are the same people as the soldiers with swords, but the illustration makes a pointed distinction to depict women as the holy ones. Other contrary examples show that in this location, Psalm 149, the choice of women as 'the holy ones' is deliberate, providing a female coda to the Psalms. A similar text, in Psalm 133, shows only men: ' ... all servants of the lord. Who stand in the house of the lord.'

A sense of gender inclusion is reflected also in the prayers. C. H. Talbot misleadingly stated: 'It is true that all the prayers in the psalter were written in the masculine as if the text was meant to be read by a man' (*Life*, p. 22). In fact, where a suppliant is suggested, it is plural (usually *famuli*/servants, as in collects 1, 2, 3, 10 and 11, or *servi* as in collect 4). This, coupled with the specific references to *domo tua* (collect 7) and *ecclesiae tuae* (collect 8), indicates that the prayers would be appropriate for those living within a community. Specific reference to *famulae* (handmaidens) in collects 3 and 10 suggests that these prayers are appropriate to both male and female communities.[18]

In a number of cases, however, women are used to personify sins, even when they are not in the text. Psalm 36 refers to 'delight in the Lord'. A woman, excluded from intimacy with the Psalmist and God, holds the word 'delight' as a reminder of the sins of the flesh. Psalm 51 discusses malice, personified as a woman ensnared between greed and lust. Psalm 67 refers to God breaking the heads of his enemies: they are represented by embracing couples. The massive design for Psalm 118 (p. 315), clearly intended to arrest the reader (Figure 3), has a text which warns in general terms 'Avert your eyes from vanity', but the figures chosen to represent 'vanity' are a carefully thought-out selection. One man flaunts fine garments (pomp) and the falcon of aristocratic leisure pursuits.[19] The attributes of the second man signify avarice and lust. The particular sins selected are not dependent on the Psalm but are based on the commentaries of Ambrose and Augustine, and are given a female twist.[20] They can be applied to Christina. She dressed well before running away from home and the many details recorded about her clothing suggest she found them important enough to remember. At the feast of the Gild Merchant she took off her mantle 'so that, with her garments fastened to her sides with bands and her sleeves rolled up to her arms, she should courteously offer drinks to the nobility'. Eventually she replaced her 'silk dresses and luxurious furs' with a rough habit (*Life*, pp. 49, 93). Bishop Ranulf Flambard, 'a slave to lust' himself, perhaps knew her predilections when he attempted to buy her favours with rich gifts. From London he brought her 'silken garments and rich ornaments ... but she looked on them as dirt and despised them' (*Life*, p. 45). Finally, lust affected even the pious Christina, who was sorely tempted by a

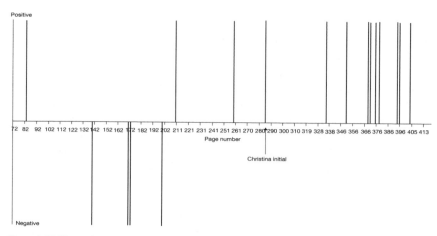

Figure 1 Table to show position of good and bad women in the Psalm initials

'certain cleric', but throughout she 'violently resisted the desires of her flesh' (*Life*, pp. 115–17). Yet, whereas Psalms earlier in the book show women ensnared by vice (Psalms 51 and 67), a close look at this initial shows that the women are tempted but resisting. The first woman holds a flowering branch, like the one given to Christina in a vision by the Virgin. This enabled her to repel her husband's grasping hands and demands (*Life*, p. 77). The second holds up her hand to bless and quell the lustful man. A table (Figure 1) underscores this change of direction, showing that although relatively few women are depicted in the initials they are much more frequent after p. 285.[21] More significantly, before p. 285, women, as demonstrated above, are shown in a bad light, personifying sin, but after p. 285 they are always good, resisting evil and praising God.[22]

Layout and literacy

The next issue is a subtle change in the layout of the initials which becomes apparent after the pasted Christina initial. Many scholars have observed that the initials include a lot of pointing.[23] These excitable fingers direct the reader's eye to the key words. They do so in three ways: some point to the black Psalm text; some point to the red rubric; and some point to the red writing in the little books within the initial (for example, pp. 133, 319 and 373). It should be noticed that the Psalms were written by Scribe 2, while the rubrics and little books are written by Scribe 3 (based on Rodney Thomson's analysis of the scribes).[24] Scribe 3 set to work after the Psalms and initials were complete. In the early Psalms, characters mainly point to the black Psalm text adjacent to the picture. After p. 285, the pointing is much more insistent, and the fingers virtually ignore the black text, instead indicating the jolly red captions. The short catch-phrases have suddenly become more important for the reader. Spotting them becomes almost an entertaining game of 'look and say'. They are certainly a dynamic way of holding the reader's attention. A table (Figure 2)

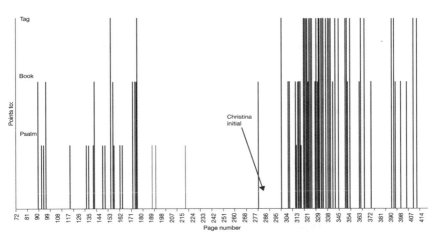

Figure 2 Table to show fingers pointing in the initials: to the black text, to the rubric, to the little books

shows that, in the latter part of the book, the artist has clearly been instructed to emphasize the contribution of the rubricator. In turn, the rubricator encourages the reader to understand his short phrases by looking at the picture. These observations about the pointing have two implications: one about the physical tasks of reading, remembering and meditating on the image; and the other about the identity of the rubricator who is so clearly drawing attention to himself. The significance of the change needs to be understood in the context of literacy and of how the book may have been 'read'.

Could this be a book designed by one-time schoolmaster Geoffrey to improve Christina's reading of both Latin and French? We have no way of gauging the extent of Christina's literacy. She is likely to have known the Psalms by heart, but that does not indicate how well she could read, write or understand Latin. If – as will be suggested later – the quire containing the Alexis *Chanson* was specially made as a gift to Christina, how much of its French or Latin could she understand? If she could not read the words, perhaps she was already familiar with the story.[25] Great efforts are expended to make the French words arresting by using coloured inks,[26] but the captions explaining the picture of the grieving bride are in Latin. The letter by Pope Gregory (p. 68), on the importance of pictures to aid the illiterate, is written twice, in both Latin and French, to make sure it is fully understood, perhaps as a teaching exercise. The letter provides three points for the reader's guidance: through a picture, one may learn what is to be worshipped; pictures help the illiterate to understand; and pictures are not idolatrous nor should they be destroyed, because their use has been sanctioned by antiquity. This suggests Geoffrey and Christina may have had some discussion about the extravagance of the initials and particularly the miniature section in the book. She, out of modesty, perhaps felt they were too lavish, but he felt they were a suitable offering to the woman who was both his language pupil and his spiritual mentor.[27]

A tiny detail may indicate that for Christina, the recipient, these illustrations were indeed more important than carefully reading the black text. Several of the notable paintings were once protected by little silk curtains which were stitched on to the parchment. The needle holes are frequently visible and sometimes even the crimson thread remains. Usually the stitching is kept neatly in the margin, but on at least six occasions the curtain was stitched directly onto the text itself.[28] This indicates that the user did not mind if the text was obscured, so long as the pictures were safe. Of course, these curtains could have been added at any time, but it is likely they were applied as soon as the psalter, calendar and miniatures were ready. The Alexis quire, which seems to be a later addition to the book, does not have any curtains. That suggests Christina herself may have stitched them in before she received the Alexis quire.

Miniatures of the life of Christ

The miniature section, forty full-page paintings showing the Fall and the Life of Christ, is the artistic glory of the book. The sequence of images is very carefully selected to provoke meditation on the Bible, but there are no accompanying words for guidance. The scenes show a great deal of interest in women. Many are particularly suitable as a meditation for a female recluse. Within the context of Christ's life, women play a relatively small though significant role. During the eleventh and twelfth centuries the cult of the Virgin gathered momentum, generally increasing awareness of both the Virgin Mary and Mary Magdalen.[29] It is thus notable that women feature in eighteen out of these thirty-nine narrative miniatures (David, p. 56, excluded). In almost every case the women are active participants, if not star performers.

The following selection emphasizes the active female role. At the Fall, Eve both receives and gives the apple; at the Annunciation, the reading Virgin is both intellectually and emotionally alert; the Visitation is enhanced by two female attendants; Mary's finger is raised in speech at the Nativity while Joseph sits dumbstruck; Joseph is absent from the Presentation, replaced by women; the mothers of Bethlehem unusually fight back at the Massacre of the Innocents;[30] Mary Magdalen introduces and completes the Passion with her foot-washing and her exceptional annunciation of the Resurrection to the Apostles; the two Marys assist at the Descent from the Cross; the composition of the Entombment is based upon the swooping curve of Mary's back. The patron made a deliberate choice to include the Virgin at the Ascension as well as at Pentecost, although there is no explicit mention in the Bible of Mary's presence at either occasion.

In terms of her own experiences, Christina often acted as witness to Christ, following the model of Mary Magdalen. She too held Christ as a baby, saw him with the Trinity, and served him as a pilgrim (*Life*, pp. 119, 157 and 183–9). Like the Virgin at Pentecost, she experienced the descent of the dove of the Holy Spirit (*Life*, p. 157), and like the disciples at Emmaus, she experienced the mysterious disappearance of Christ (*Life*, p. 189). She also suffered humiliation and slander, being called a 'loose woman' (*Life*, pp. 173–5), accused like Mary Magdalen at the house of Simon the Pharisee.

Some scenes occur out of sequence, jolting the viewer to reassess their significance. For instance, The Agony in the Garden (pp. 39–40) is placed before the Last Supper (p. 41), to give extra impact. Moreover, the episode is divided into two scenes, Christ praying alone, facing a chalice and an angel on the hilltop; and Christ awakening the disciples. The unusual doubling of these Gethsemane scenes allows a solitary reflection on the chalice of the Eucharist. Appropriately for an anchoress, Christ's blood sacrifice is pictured alone rather than at a communal male feast. It allows a private female communion, uninterrupted by the presence of the disciples or an officiating priest. By contrast, the Last Supper is depicted not as the Eucharist, but as the betrayal by Judas and denial by Peter.

The female reader was intended to meditate on these images, and to participate on a strong emotional and spiritual level in Christ's experiences.[31] It was clearly easier if scenes were chosen where women were involved. This cycle shows a distinctly feminine bias. As such, it provides an instructive contrast to the cycles from the Eadwine Psalter which George Henderson considers is strictly textual and chronological; and the Bury cycle, part of which is 'overtly that of Church versus Synagogue'.[32]

Abbot Geoffrey and the Psalter

C. R. Dodwell has shown that many of the initials have a priestly and often Benedictine slant which would have suited the world of Abbot Geoffrey. Be that as it may, the illustration to Psalm 132 gives the reader as much of a shock as Psalm 105 where Christina leads the monks to Christ, because in this case the illustration shows the exact opposite to the text (Plate 4). The words describe how 'pleasant it is for brothers to dwell in unity'. The tag refers to the unction of blessing being poured on the head of Aaron the priest, a reward for his priestly leadership. This Psalm was interpreted by SS Augustine and Jerome as a eulogy for corporate life in the monastery.[33] The picture does indeed shows some happy brothers, but one is clearly excluded and resentful. Aaron is *not* receiving any unction but is being instructed to look at the factions above him. In comparative Psalm cycles with a similar scene, Aaron *is* anointed.[34]

Under Abbot Geoffrey there can be no doubt that St Albans suffered factional strife, both because of his high-handed behaviour and because of the money he spent, and not least the money he spent on Markyate. His leadership was criticised, particularly by his own monks. 'He began to grow more haughty than was right and relied more on his own judgement than on that of his monks. He decided to carry out a project which he knew could not be accomplished without the annoyance of his chapter' (*Life*, p. 35). The *Gesta Abbatum* records that 'he impetuously conceded [to Markyate] without the convent's consent the whole of our toll'.[35] After Geoffrey's death, the *Epistola* mentions 'how that contrary part of his congregation suddenly and furiously laboured to undo those exterior things [which he had done]'.[36] The initial to Psalm 132 is therefore a vivid allegory of strife within the monastery, and the withholding of divine approval from the abbot. Choosing this interpretation for the initial reflects those moments of administrative despair when Geoffrey rode down to Markyate for solace. 'Feeling disgusted [by his worldly affairs] he went to the handmaid of Christ as to a place of refuge and received her answer as if it were a divine oracle' (*Life*, p. 138).[37]

The interpolation of the St Martin page (p. 53) within the Christ cycle, left even Pächt baffled, but it may also be connected to Geoffrey.[38] Sandwiched betwwen Doubting Thomas and the Ascension, it jolts the reader to ask why it is there and to ponder its connection with the rest of the sequence. It is clearly inserted at the patron's request, to impart a particular message to the reader. Perhaps in some way it is standing as a substitute for the Emmaus scenes which are dislocated from this part of the sequence, being depicted on pp. 69–71, in the Alexis quire. St Martin gives his cloak to the unknown beggar; at Emmaus the disciples give supper to a stranger. Underlying both these deeds of charity to a stranger are Christ's words in Matthew 25: 35: 'For I was an hungred and ye gave me meat; I was thirsty and ye gave me drink; I was a stranger and ye took me in, naked and ye clothed me ... Inasmuch as ye have done it unto one of the least of these my brethren, ye have done it unto me.' To relieve the poor and clothe the naked are among the Good Works prescribed for monks in the Rule.[39]

St Martin performing his act of charity thus creates an implied reference *back* to Matthew 25 at this point. This serves to wrap up and close all the terrestrial scenes of Christ's passion on the preceding pages. Matthew 26 continues immediately with the anointing at Simon's house, and on to the Last Supper, creating a continuous circle of meditation on the Passion as told by the Evangelists. However, in Matthew, Christ's words about charity are uttered in the context of explaining the Last Judgement. They therefore point *forward* to the subsequent celestial scenes which are described in Acts.[40]

St Martin, a soldier who became a monk and later a bishop, has ostensibly little connection with Christina, but his life provided more of a model for Geoffrey. Geoffrey also entered the church after an earlier career, as a teacher, and rose to become an abbot, a great administrator. St Anselm, archbishop of Canterbury (1093–1109) compared himself to St Martin, saying that they both had been taken from their monks and put over clerics, monks, laymen and women.[41] Geoffrey also became a leader of men and women. Before Christina met Geoffrey she was 'tried in the crucible of poverty', but through his generous intervention she and her little community were succoured. 'One consolation gladdened him that, unknown to the world, he could bestow his earthly riches on the poor of Christ' (*Life*, pp. 133, 139, 151).

Cloaks and clothing played an important part in Geoffrey's life. He borrowed some copes from St Albans in order to put on a play about St Katherine. When these were burnt in an accident he offered himself in recompense, literally as a burnt offering, to St Albans Abbey. Ordained on St Katherine's day, he subsequently arranged for a magnificent conventual feast to be held on that day.[42] As abbot, Geoffrey 'diligently' provided costly vestments, including seven copes covered in gold and gems, and five gold chasubles.[43] Like St Martin, he therefore gave copes to Christ. His own clothes were also given to the poor, through the intervention of Christ: Christina made him special undergarments to comfort him on an arduous mission, but when his journey was cancelled she was advised in a vision to give them to the poor, 'because Christ will obtain for him more gracious comfort on his journey' (*Life*, pp. 161–3). St Martin's appearance at this point in the cycle is unprecedented but, displaying virtues which Geoffrey sought to emulate, he is elevated among the apostles and Christ himself.

The Alexis quire

It is in the Alexis quire that Geoffrey has space to contribute his most personal messages, free from the constraints of the otherwise standard liturgical material. The quire consists of the *Chanson of St Alexis*, with a prologue, written in French (Plate 5); the letter of Pope Gregory to the hermit Secundinus recommending the use of pictures in worship, written in both Latin and French; three full-page illustrations from the Emmaus story; and an extraordinarily convoluted prologue, a Discourse on Good and Evil, leading up the 'Beatus Vir', the start of Psalm 1.[44]

Before analysing the contents, we need to examine the activities of its scribe, objectively known as Scribe 3.[45] This is the same scribe who added the rubrics to the psalter, increasingly drawing attention to his words by the pointing fingers. He also added the obit of Roger the Hermit to the calendar, and he penned the entire Alexis quire. He could write a sedate book hand, which he produces for the *Chanson of St Alexis* text. However, he seems to have the authority frankly to mess up several pages produced by other scribes and even by the Alexis Master himself. His handling of space becomes passionate and intense, with the impact of his words taking precedence over their orderly delivery. Roger's obit (p. 11) sprawls across the page and has a spelling mistake; Pope Gregory's letters (p. 68) ignore the ruling of the page and are unnecessarily cramped. The text on the Emmaus scene and Psalm 1 (pp. 69, 72) creeps around and bumps into the Alexis Master's illustration (Plate 8). He plays visual games with the almost lurid alternation of inks (green, blue, red) in the Alexis quire, and there is certainly a playful element in the use of tags in the Psalms. In the Discourse on Good and Evil which serves as a preliminary to the Psalms, he muses in the first person: 'it seems to me ... '. Otto Pächt thought this was the holograph of the Alexis Master.[46] Rodney Thomson, Malcolm Parkes and the present author prefer a tentative identification with Abbot Geoffrey himself.[47] All the things this scribe writes are of special interest to Christina or himself; the lively presentation and helpful translations are the sign of an encouraging schoolmaster; his words are both copied and composed in Latin and French.[48] His hand has also been identified in another St Albans manuscript. The closest comparison is with a St Albans calendar, London, BL Egerton, MS. 3721, ff. 1v-7v, notably written to include the feasts upgraded by Geoffrey.[49]

The cult of St Alexis at St Albans seems to have been relatively short-lived; his feast only appears in the Egerton calendar (penned by Scribe 3 of the St Albans Psalter), the St Albans Psalter litany and in St Petersburg, Public Library MS. Q.v.I, 62.[50] However, his story, about a holy man who on his wedding night renounced his marriage to become a hermit, must have been frequently discussed in Christina and Geoffrey's day. His cult was introduced by Abbot Richard (1097–1119) and his chapel in the abbey had recently been dedicated by Bishop Ranulf Flambard of Durham. The dedication took place between 1115 and 1119.[51] It is quite possible that Christina was introduced to the story of Alexis by Bishop Flambard himself, on one of his conjugal visits to Christina's aunt's household.[52] From Christina's account, one may perhaps picture Flambard, feasting with a few flagons of ale in the home of his mistress, flanked by his illegitimate children, entertaining Autti and Beatrix (Christina's parents) and the delectable Christina, even recounting his recent task of dedicating the Alexis chapel at St Albans.

Most illustrations of the life of Alexis concentrate on the later part of his story, the years when he returned home as a beggar to live unrecognized by his family in seclusion under the stairs.[53] But in the St Albans Psalter, the choice was made to place the grieving, bereft bride at centre stage, flanked by tender scenes of her departing love (Plate 5). Captions are necessary to explain the bride's importance in these scenes, because she remains mute at this point in the *Chanson* (ll. 61–75). Scribe 3 has no choice about the rather harsh words with which Alexis addresses his stunned bride in the poem: 'Hearken to me, maiden' (ll. 66), but in the caption he is free to make a more personal and sympathetic address. Whereas the other captions employ the third person, the direct vocative address is used for 'O blessed bride, forever bound to grief'. The bride, pivotal in the picture, plays a smaller part in the poem, always following her husband's parents. She does not even have a name; although she laments poignantly (l. 468–95), her eternal grief is nothing compared to that of his mother.[54]

Superficially the illustration and *Chanson*, with the chaste wedding night and departure for an ascetic life far from home, fit Christina's circumstances, and indeed the theme of the life of St Alexis was suggested by C. H. Talbot and Otto Pächt as a parallel for Christina's own. However, evidence on every level suggests that the entire insertion of the Alexis quire was Abbot Geoffrey's idea, and reflects *his* relationship with Christina rather than her own preferences. He, too, left his home, in Northern France, and found a new life serving God in a foreign land. He sustained a lifelong, pure and spiritually enlightened relationship with Christina, where many previous men in her life had been overcome by her physical attractions. Both Geoffrey and Alexis gave away their riches to the poor.[55] The poem certainly does not fit Christina's life in detail. Alexis was, after all, a continental male cult figure recently adopted by the Abbey of St Albans whereas St Cecilia was the female equivalent, familiar to Anglo-Saxons and indeed invoked by Christina. Alexis complied with his father's wish for the marriage and enjoyed a splendid wedding; Christina fought all the way. Alexis, over the untouched wedding bed, tenderly hands his wife gifts symbolizing fidelity, and she pines for ever like a turtle dove after he departs; Christina sat her husband firmly down on the bed and lectured him about the virtuous marriage not of Alexis but (more naturally) of St Cecilia. She made desperate attempts to escape, even jumping over a fence. She certainly did not weep for her spouse. The prologue mentions those 'who take delight in virginal marriage'; her unconsummated marriage to Burthred was far from delightful (*Life*, pp. 45–55). All these features suggest that the choice of illustration may have a different meaning. Historical events may explain the unusual iconography of the illustration and explain why the distraught, grieving woman is the centre of the composition.

In 1136 Geoffrey was summoned to Rome, and he went to consult Christina about the journey. 'He admitted his sadness and shed tears as proof of his grief.' Christina's 'countenance was bathed with tears, her heart torn with sighs', and she prepared gifts for his departure (the cosy, personally-stitched undergarments) (*Life*, p. 161). This was indeed a chaste and sorrowful parting, with gifts. A second visit to Rome, proposed in 1139, met with equal resistance from Christina, who once more summoned up the powers of divine visions to underline her anxiety. Her prayers to prevent the journeys succeeded because 'she knew how to love to supreme advantage', a phrase which even suggests emotional blackmail (*Life*, p. 165). As it turned out, Christina's divine prescience and a change of events prevented Geoffrey's journeys altogether (*Life*, pp. 161–3).

The bride of the Alexis poem experiences her noblest moment when, after years of grieving for her absent love, she realizes that true fulfilment is found in loving God: as a reward she is united with Alexis in heaven.[56] The poem thus offers consolation for the abandoned bride and perhaps a gentle reminder for Christina to release Geoffrey to perform his duties with less emotional pressure. The titles *beatus/beata* in the captions indicate that the couple achieve beatitude in the afterlife. Christina's *Life* asks of Geoffrey and Christina: 'Who shall put into words how they despised the transitory, how they yearned for the ever-lasting?' (*Life*, p. 157). They too could be united in heaven.

The three Emmaus scenes (*Life*, pp. 69–71) are, like the Alexis *Chanson*, a male gloss on Christina's experience. According to the *Life* (pp. 183–9), an unknown pilgrim once came to her cell and Christina entertained him. On a second visit, she and her sister Margaret rushed around to give him a meal, an event which Christina likened to Mary and Martha (Luke 10:39–40). They provided him with bread and fish (as shown in the illustration, p. 70), not the meat which Christ was offered at Emmaus (Luke 24:30). On his third visit he vanished mysteriously through the locked doors of her chapel, as Christ vanished from the Emmaus supper. The strongly feminine scene of Christ with Mary and Martha, obviously cherished by Christina, is notable by its absence from the Psalter.

The final Discourse in the Alexis quire (pp. 71–2) provides an intense and passionate justification for both the appearance of the Psalter and Geoffrey's some-what scandalous relationship with Christina.[57] It begins describing the war against evil fought by monastics in their cloister. Then comes the pregnant sentence:

You [singular] recently heard our word and that verse which shall be written [future tense] in the name of heavenly love, and honour of the spiritual war, lest any one of those talkers, who investigate, should rebuke us.[58]

The 'verse which shall be written' presumably refers to the title which was about to be penned at the conclusion of the page, and was then repeated as a caption in David's book. The words of the caption are 'The blessed Psalmist David, whom God has chosen, has gushed forth the annunciation of the Holy Spirit'. The sentence is couched in very defensive terms. This discussion was seemingly to rebut criticism from gossip-mongers. Knowing the connection which this book has with Christina and Geoffrey, this rather tortuous passage seems to reflect the scandalized murmurings which their companionship provoked. Christina's *Life* refers to the jealous rumours with similar words, borrowed from Horace: her intimacy with Geoffrey did not happen 'without the wagging of spiteful tongues' (*Life*, p. 149).[59] Gossips called her a dreamer, a seducer of souls, a worldly-wise business woman, a loose woman attracted to the abbot by earthly love, while Geoffrey was also a seducer (*Life*, pp. 173–5).[60] The *Gesta Abbatum* provides a view from the abbey: 'so great was the affection of mutual charity between them that, unless the whole multitude had known how holy both were, it may be that evil suspicion would have arisen from so great love'.[61]

If malicious people should enquire what was going on between the abbot and the anchoress, then these pages would provide justification, perhaps even an alibi. Although their minds were no doubt focused on spiritual issues, Christina's *Life* (p. 157) recalls their shared moments at a high emotional key. 'Who shall describe the longings, the sighs, the tears they shed as they sat and discussed heavenly matters?' Those outside Christina's cell, perhaps hearing the tears and sighs, might well jump to salacious conclusions, but the Psalter survives as evidence of the spiritual sincerity expressed by this introductory passage.

This passage culminates in a portrait of David holding his harp and displaying the Psalter inscribed with the prophecy of Christ's Annunciation by the Holy Spirit (Plate 8). The writer comments that David's book, 'which he held in great affection, signifies the wisdom of prophecy, and that divine prediction, and for that reason spiritual people love the psalter and desire its own divine teaching, because it sows sweetness in their hearts'.[62] These are Geoffrey's last words before the Psalms begin. Christina also revered the Psalter (*Life*, pp. 98–9),[63] and after all these coded messages, Geoffrey at last declares the sweetness of her heart.

The David portraits

There are three portraits of David. They can be called three false starts, because each one fails to make the impact of a correct frontispiece to the Psalms.[64] However, each in their own way reflects Geoffrey's developing commitment to the book and to Christina. The first version forms the last bifolio of the book (pp. 416–17). It is simply stitched onto the end of the Psalms and prayers as a separate sheet and looks out of place. However, it is clearly painted by the same artists who worked on the Psalm initials. The diptych shows first the martyrdom of St Alban and then a rather cheery David with his musicians (Plate 6). This would be a very suitable preliminary to a book destined for the Abbey of St Albans. Geoffrey was an ardent promoter of St Alban's cult. These scenes might have been designed at the start of the project and would seem to support the theory proposed here that the book began as a book for the abbey, rather than as one for Christina, and only later changed its destination.

The second David is painted as the last leaf of the Life of Christ cycle (p. 56), a completely separate group of gatherings from the Psalms. It follows the Ascension, and is placed on a verso, anticipating Psalm 1 to begin on the facing recto. In fact it faces the Alexis *Chanson* (p. 57). But here David has sobered up (Plate 7). He is still primarily a musician but is now flanked by the sheep and goat, anticipating the Judgement which follows the Ascension on the previous page. But more significantly he is being inspired by the dove of the Holy Spirit. This dove has played a vital role. In Christina's momentous vision where she beheld the Trinity, she first saw the dove at rest above the two figures, and Geoffrey gestured frantically to join her. 'Outside she saw the Abbot trying without success to gain entrance to her.' She was then able to summon the Holy Spirit by the power of her prayer to flap around Geoffrey's head and fill him with divine inspiration:

> She saw the dove glide through the chamber with a fluttering of its wings … she would not stop pleading until she saw [Geoffrey] either possessing the dove or being possessed by it. And then she realised that the dove meant the holy spirit, and the abbot, once filled with it, was able to aspire only to things above.
>
> (*Life*, p. 157)

It was this moment of spiritual inclusion which inspired Geoffrey to dedicate the book to Christina and change its subsequent appearance. The new, spiritually charged David is a testimony to this. This third David (p. 72) is the most personal of all, uniting the composer of the Psalms with the writer/scribe of this book (Plate 8). It shows David holding the book of Psalms with Scribe 3's (Geoffrey's) own writing in them. The passive dove has changed into something as powerful as a goose, reflecting what happened in the vision. The bird almost besieges his head. Once again, as with the Litany picture, one detects the patron reminding the artist that this was no ordinary bird. Geoffrey and David have become united in their inspiration to create the book of Psalms.[65]

A comparison between the first and last Davids reflects the spiritual journey which Geoffrey had undertaken with Christina's help, between starting and finishing the Psalter. The wording of Roger's obit (p. 11), added by Scribe 3

(Geoffrey) to the calendar probably at the same time as he added the rubric to the Psalms, may reflect many of the problems which Geoffrey had to overcome on the way. Roger, the original occupant of the cell at Markyate, befriended Christina and acted as her loving mentor until he died *c.* 1121–2. Previously he had served as a monk at St Albans and was highly venerated by the brethren. His exceptionally long obit, misspelt and poorly spaced, reads: 'The death of Roger the Hermit, monk of St Albans; whoever has this psalter should hold his memory in honour on this day'.[66] Perhaps the monks of St Albans felt resentful about the extravagant waste of resources and their abbot's infatuation with the 'loose woman'; perhaps Christina felt embarrassed by the honour, guilty about the luxury. This obit wording allowed the monks, who venerated Roger sufficiently to bury him in the abbey,[67] to accept the project as a mark of respect for him while Christina could own the book humbly in Roger's honour. Christina's ambivalent relationship to the book is hinted at by the words of Pope Gregory's letter, encouraging her to accept the images; by this dedication to Roger; by the curtains stitched over the text; by no mention of her name in the book until after her death; and finally by its pristine condition. The book shows only very light signs of use, even after 900 years.[68]

Dating the Psalter

If the visions were so important, they should help to date the production of the Psalter. Whereas the historical events in Christina's *Life* unfold in a reasonable chronological order, the visions belong to another realm, and their temporal occurrence cannot be pinned down easily. Many suggestions about the Psalter's date have been made, ranging from 1115 to 1145/6.[69] A suitable occasion might have been when Christina made her profession as a nun, an episode which required 'frequent pleadings and humble sweetness' from Geoffrey. The douceur of a psalter would have been appropriate but the timing seems to be wrong. This ceremony took place around 1131. However, the vision of the Trinity, with Geoffrey and the Dove, is recorded some time 'after the fourth year of her profession', i.e. *c.* 1135. This date allows the sophisticated style of the pasted initial to coexist with the rest of the work. It also ties in with episodes which I believe may have prompted the Alexis quire made shortly after the rest of the book, namely Geoffrey's proposed journeys to Rome in 1136 or 1139.

This book has previously been called the Albani Psalter; more recently, in a feminist climate, the Psalter of Christina of Markyate. However it is clearly infused with Geoffrey's passionate commitment to participate in Christina's spiritual and mental welfare, with his priorities often overruling her own. He seems to have diverted a book intended for the Abbey of St Albans, and instead completed it as a token of love and respect for his 'Beata Christina … suae dilectricis',[70] in order to stimulate her essential prayers of intercession. It was not necessarily the book she needed to receive, but it was undoubtedly the book Abbot Geoffrey needed to create, for the salvation of his soul and his abbey.

Notes

1 Adolf Goldschmidt, *Der Albani-Psalter in Hildesheim und seine Beziehung zur symbolischen Kirchensculptur des XII.*Jahrhunderts (Berlin, 1895); Pächt; Holdsworth; T. A. Heslop, 'The Visual Arts and Crafts' in *The Cambridge Guide to Arts in Britain*, II, ed. Boris Ford *The Middle Ages* (Cambridge, 1988) pp. 164–70; Ursula Nilgen, 'Psalter der Christina von Markyate (sogenannter Albani-Psalter) in Diözesan-Museum Hildesheim, *Der Schatz von St Godehard*, [exhibition catalogue Hildesheim Diözesan-Museum], no. 69, (Hildesheim, 1988), pp. 160–3; M. H. Caviness, 'Anchoress, Abbess, Queen: Donors and Patrons or Intercessors and Matrons?', in *The Cultural Patronage of Medieval Women*, ed. J. H. McCash (Athens, Georgia, 1996) pp. 105–53. Kristine Haney, *The St. Albans Psalter, an Anglo-Norman Song of Faith* (New York, 2002), pp. 334–9.

2 Essays by Jane Geddes, on the St Albans Psalter web site: <http://www.abdn.ac.uk/stalbanspsalter>

3 The troubled administrator, see Koopmans, 'The Conclusion'.

4 In addition to the *Life, Gesta Abbatum*, i. 72–105; 'Epistola ad amicum', in *Analecta Dublinensia: three medieval Latin texts in the library of Trinity College, Dublin*, ed. Marvin L. Colker (Cambridge, Mass., 1975) pp. 91–160.

5 Francis Wormald in Pächt, pp. 27–30.

6 Geddes at <http://www.abdn.ac.uk/stalbanspsalter/english/essays/calendar.shtml#calendar>.

7 See pp. 416–17. All page references to the Psalter are cited in the text.

8 Pers. comm.

9 Dodwell in Pächt, p. 200; Pächt in ibid., p. 163; C. R. Dodwell, *The Pictorial Arts of the West, 800–1200* (New Haven and London, 1993), pp. 328–9; *Life*, p. 25; Larry M. Ayres, 'The Role of an Angevin Style in English Romanesque Painting', *Zeitschrift für Kunstwissenschaft* 37 (1974), 216–17; Caviness, 'Anchoress, Abbess, Queen', p. 112; Haney, *The St Albans Psalter*, p. 4.

10 Dodwell, in Pächt, p. 244.

11 The letter is formed from a single gold band. Other Cs have foliage in their swollen bows.

12 Thomson's Scribe 4. Rodney M. Thomson, *Manuscripts from St Albans Abbey, 1066–1235* (Woodbridge, 1982) i. 119.

13 Psalm 105:23 refers to Moses in this position, acting as a bulwark between the Israelites and the wrath of God.

14 Wormald in Pächt, pp. 30–2.

15 Nilgen, 'Psalter der Christina von Markyate', pp. 160–3.

16 Pächt, Plate 169. The foundation charter, London, BL, MS Cotton Ch. xi. 8.

17 Caviness, 'Anchoress, Abbess, Queen', p. 108. 'Only the internal evidence of the pictures can help us decide whether their messages were encoded for, and perhaps by or 'against', a female virgin.'

18 Sue Niebrzydowski at <http://www.abdn.ac.uk/stalbanspsalter/english/essays/calendar.shtml#collects>.

19 A stole of this type is used to depict Pomp in an Anglo-Saxon *Psychomachia*, London, BL Add. MS 24199, f. 21v; Dodwell in Pächt, p. 251.

20 St Augustine, *Enarrationes in Psalmos*, CCSL, 10 (3) (Turnholt, 1956) pp. 1698–9, 1700, 1703 (avarice, worldly desire); St Ambrose, *Expositio Psalmi* 118, ed. M. Petschenig, CSEL, 62, section V, 1–47 (Vienna, 1999) V, 97, para. 28, 29; 98, para 30 (secular pomp, looking at a woman to desire her). This source is confirmed by the trees and water at the end of the initial. Ambrose advises the reader to look instead at God's earth and sea. I would like to thank Barbara Raw for these references.

21 If these extra women were 'normal' in other literally illustrated Psalters, then the element of choice by the patron diminishes. Haney provides a close comparative

study of the following: Utrecht Psalter (Utrecht, University Library, MS 32), Stuttgart Psalter (Württembergische Landesbibliothek, MS Biblia folia 23), the Byzantine Chuldov Psalter (Moscow, State Historical Museum, MS 129) and Hamilton Psalter (Berlin, Kupferstichkabinett, MS 78.A.9). From these it is clear that the St Albans women of 'the World' (Psalms 92, 109, 136) and those writ large in Psalm 118:33 are originals, while the canticles of Symeon and Moses are unusual. (Haney, *St. Albans Psalter*, pp. 439–654).

22 Caviness, 'Anchoress, Abbess, Queen', p. 108. Caviness was struck by the misogynist nature of some of the initials, made 'against' Christina. The current explanation shows that these negative images are only in the first part of the book, created when it was initially destined for the monks at St Albans.

23 Heslop, 'The Visual Arts and Crafts', p. 169; Haney, *St Albans Psalter*, pp. 60–2.

24 Thomson's analysis: *Manuscripts from St Albans Abbey*, i. 119.

25 <www.abdn.ac.uk/stalbanspsalter/english/translation/trans057.shtml> 'del quel nus avum oit lire e canter'.

26 These coloured inks carry the story from p. 57 to p. 59, precisely the section which was relevant to Christina and Geoffrey. The remainder of the *Chanson* is in black ink.

27 It is notable that no silk curtain was sewn over Christina's 'own' picture on p. 285, perhaps as a sign of humility, whereas Geoffrey's significant moment in the Litany (p. 403) was protected.

28 St Albans Psalter, pp. 101, 115, 123, 129, 133, 135.

29 M. E. Carrasco, 'The Imagery of the Magdalen in Christina of Markyate's Psalter (The St Albans Psalter)', *Gesta* 37 (1999), 67–80.

30 Sophie Oosterwijk, '"*Long lullynge haue I lorn!*" The Massacre of the Innocents in Word and Image', in *Reading Images and Texts: Medieval Texts and Images as Forms of Communication*, ed. Marco Mostert and Mariëlle Hageman (forthcoming).

31 The significance of the miniature cycle as a means of meditation is discussed in greater detail by Geddes at
<http://www.abdn.ac.uk/stalbanspsalter/english/essays/miniatures.shtml>.

32 George Henderson, 'The Textual Basis of the Picture Leaves' in *The Eadwine Psalter*, ed. M. Gibson, T. A. Heslop, R. W. Pfaff (London and University Park, PA), pp. 41–2.

33 Jerome, *PL* 26, col. 1217; Augustine, *PL* 37, col. 1730; Dodwell in Pächt, p. 260.

34 Utrecht, University Library, MS 32, f. 75v; Stuttgart Psalter, Württembergische Landesbibliothek, MS Biblia folia 23, f. 149v; London, British Library, MS Harley 603, f. 68v. Haney, *St Albans Psalter*, p. 617.

35 *Gesta Abbatum*, i. 95: 'absque consensu Conventus, violenter concessit'.

36 'Epistola ad amicum', in *Analecta Dublinensia*, ed. Colker, p. 108: 'maliciose partis subiectorum conspirauit inuidia, quamque repentino furore exteriora quae pro cari-tate et dignitatis honore absque detrimento substantie fecerat pars congregationis contraria cassare nitebatur'.

37 'Que fastidiens, et ancillam Christi ac si asilum suum adeundo consulens.responsum illius pro divino suscipiebat oraculo.' (Talbot translates 'Que fastidiens' rather meekly as 'growing weary'.)

38 Pächt in Pächt, p. 50.

39 <http://www.ccel.org/b/benedict/rule2/rule.html> *The Holy Rule of St. Benedict*, trans. Rev. Boniface Verheyen, OSB, 1949, St. Benedict's Abbey, Atchison, Kansas. Electronic text (with added scripture references) prepared by Br Boniface Butterworth, OSB, ch. 4.

40 K. E. Haney, 'The St Albans Psalter and the new spiritual ideals of the twelfth century', *Viator* 28 (1997), 152–63. Haney points out that the Martin scenes face Doubting Thomas, and she links the two in terms of colour, composition and theology: Martin represents Charity, and Thomas, Faith. He is also sandwiched

between the few scenes of the book which depict the assembled apostles. In this way Martin, a pre-eminent monk, visually joins the ranks of the apostles. Exhortations for monks to become like the apostles were part of the monastic reforms of the eleventh and twelfth centuries.

41 Ibid., p. 155.

42 *Gesta Abbatum*, i. 73, 75.

43 Ibid., p. 93.

44 For full text: Pächt, pp. 163–4. Translation at <http://www.abdn.ac.uk/stalbanspsalter/english/translation/trans057.shtml>.

45 Thomson, *Manuscripts from St Albans*, i.119; Wormald in Pächt, pp. 276–7. <http://www.abdn.ac.uk/stalbanspsalter/english/essays/scribes.shtml#scribe3>. The hand is small and neat but somewhat nervous and intense. The 'g' is not usually closed, so it looks rather like an 's'. The ampersand has its downward diagonal stroke pulled smartly to the left at the bottom; the upper diagonal may or may not touch the upper bowl. The 'ct' ligature surmounts the letters with a circumflex stroke which can be pointed and angular. The 'e' and 'r' often have a hairline ending. The 'a' is usually headless. The words themselves seem more important than their sedate arrangement. Thus the metrical poem of St Alexis is written as continuous lines of prose instead of stanzas; its first three pages (pp. 57–9) are a riot of alternating blue and red lines with green initials, but the remainder sobers up with black ink.

46 Pächt, p. 161, and as scribe-author in the Alexis quire, p. 137.

47 Thomson, *Manuscripts from St Albans*, i. p. 42; Malcolm Parkes in Nilgen, 'Psalter der Christina von Markyate', p. 162.

48 The holograph Latin is the Discourse on Good and Evil (pp. 71–2), and the labels to the Alexis illustration; Jubb considers that, although Geoffrey 'may well have commissioned both the translation of the letter and the prologue to the poem for this manuscript, the linguistic evidence suggests that he is unlikely to have composed either himself' (Jubb,
<http://www.abdn.ac.uk/stalbanspsalter/english/essays/frenchgreg.shtml> and <http://www.abdn.ac.uk/stalbanspsalter/english/essays/oldfrenchlife.shtml>.

49 Thomson, *Manuscripts from St Albans*, ii. pl. 139. Wormald in Pächt, p. 24.

50 However, St Alexis is not in the St Albans Psalter calendar which, as noticed above, was based on Ramsey rather than on St Albans. The St Petersburg calendar, made at St Albans in the mid-twelfth century, also included St Christina. By the end of the century it was at Wherwell Nunnery (Thomson, *Manuscripts from St Albans*, i. 37, 123).

51 *Gesta Abbatum*, i. 148.

52 Talbot, in *Life*, pp. 41–2.

53 Pächt, pp. 135–40.

54 All quotations of the *Alexis Chanson* are from <http://www.abdn.ac.uk/stalbanspsalter/english/translation/trans057.shtml>, by Margaret Jubb. 'Oz mei pulcele'; 'O Sponsa beata se[m]p[er] gemebunda'.

55 ll. 91–7; *Life*, p. 151.

56 ll. 493–5, 606–10.

57 Pächt, pp. 163–4;
<http://www.abdn.ac.uk/stalbanspsalter/english/translation/trans072.shtml> and <http://www.abdn.ac.uk/stalbanspsalter/english/translation/trans071.shtml>. For a fuller discussion of this passage: Geddes at <http://www.abdn.ac.uk/stalbanspsalter/english/essays/alexisquire.shtml>.

58 <http://www.abdn.ac.uk/stalbanspsalter/english/translation/trans072.shtml> 'Modo audisti n[ost]r[u]m dictu[m] & illu[m] v[e]rsu[m] / q[ui] erit sc[ri]pt[u]s in no[m]i[n]e celestis amoris & in honore sp[irit]ualis belli ne aliq[u]is illo[rum] locuto[rum] q[ue] scrutant[ur] nos rep[re]hendant'.

59 'Nec sine multorum livido dente', a phrase taken from Horace, *Epodes*, 5.47.

60 Koopmans, 'The Conclusion', pp. 681–5.

61 *Gesta Abbatum*, i.105. 'tantaque fuit inter eos mutuae caritatis affectio, ut nisi notissima fuisset toti vulgo sanctitas utriusque, fortassis orta fuisset de tanta dilectione mala suscipio'.

62 'suus lib[er] / que[m] habuit in magna dilectione significat sapienta[m] p[ro]phetie & illa[m] divina[m] p[re]dictione[m]. & id[e]o spirituales amant / Psalteriu[m] & cupiunt sua[m] divina[m] doctrina[m]. id[e]o q[ui]a dulcedine[m] inserit cordib[us] eo[rum]'.
<http://www.abdn.ac.uk/stalbanspsalter/english/translation/trans072.shtml>.

63 'spalterio vendicantes medium locum in gremio virgi(nis) quor propemodum omnibus horis iacebat expansum in usum sponse Christi', ' ... the Psalter which lay open on her lap at all hours of the day for her use'.

64 For a detailed discussion of how each section of the St Albans Psalter was put together, see Geddes at
<http://www.abdn.ac.uk/stalbanspsalter/english/essays/conclusion.shtml>.

65 Pächt compares this extraordinary dove to earlier examples, Pächt, p. 148, n. 3.

66 'Obiit] Rogeri heremite monac/hi s[an]c[t]i albani· ap[ud] que[m]c[um]q[ue] fuerit h[oc] psalt[er]iu[m]· fiat ei[us] memoria maxime / hac die.'
<http://www.abdn.ac.uk/stalbanspsalter/english/translation/trans011.shtml>.

67 *Gesta Abbatum*, i. 105.

68 The pages are very clean except the start of the Alexis *Chanson*, p. 57, where one suspects additional wear from more recent French scholars.

69 Goldschmidt, *Der Albani-Psalter in Hildesheim*, pp. 29–33, connected with the dedication of the chapel to St Alexis at St Albans Abbey 1115–19; *Life*, p. 26, 'somewhat later than the consecration of Holy Trinity, Markyate' in 1145; Holdsworth, 'Christina of Markyate' pp. 193–5, 'after 1140–1 and before the death of Abbot Geoffrey in 1146'.

70 *Gesta Abbatum*, i. 98, 103.

13

THE *LIFE* OF ST ALEXIS,
475–1125[1]

Tony Hunt

The St Albans Psalter contains the first known version in Old French of the story of St Alexis. How and why this story of an Eastern holy man spread to the West to become particularly popular in the eleventh and twelfth centuries, and what connections the story might have with Christina, are highly complex questions.

The evolution of the story of the anonymous 'man of God' before it first finds literary expression in a European vernacular encompasses a number of stages which are reflected quite clearly in the emergent Old French redactions of the legend six centuries after it is first recorded. The legend seems to originate with a fifth-century Syriac text of what is a largely historical account of the 'man of God', an ascetic known in this version as Mar Riscia ('[my lord] Prince'),[2] who, anonymous, poor and devout, lives in Edessa in Mesopotamia and collects the alms of the faithful at the church door, further distributing to the needy all that exceeds the strict necessities for his own survival. Nothing is generally known about him save by the sacristan of the church to whom, shortly before his death, the solitary beggar confides the story of his life. Born in Constantinople (the 'new Rome'), the child of wealthy parents, he is destined to be married, but when the day comes he flees his home, without even seeing the intended bride, and lives incognito in Edessa where he is dependent on begging for his living. On his death his corpse is buried in the communal grave, but the sacristan intercedes with Rabbula (bishop of Edessa 412–35) to have his remains transferred. When the grave is duly visited by the bishop it is found to be open and vacant, the body of the 'man of God' having miraculously disappeared, leaving only his rags behind. Soon after the events thus described this austere and pious tale began to circulate and was committed to writing in Syriac *c.* 450–75. The three surviving manuscripts, strikingly, date from no more than fifty years later. A Greek version of substantially the same tale survives in a twelfth-century manuscript in Venice, Marcianus VII 33 (ff.177r–179r), discovered and printed by Margarete Rösler,[3] who took the view that this was the original version of the legend, preceding Amiaud's Syriac version, a contention which, in the nature of things, is difficult to prove.

Meanwhile, a comparable story was evolving in Constantinople concerning John the Calybite (i.e. John the Hut-Dweller), born in Rome, who was inspired by a monk whom his family knew to enter a Bithynian monastery. Eventually a heavenly voice summons him to return to his parents in Rome, which he does incognito, living in a little outhouse ('hut') near the main residence of his parents with whom he is openly reunited shortly before his death. In 868 Anastasius Bibiothecarius translated the story as *Vita Johannis Calybitae* (BHL 4358)[4] at the instigation of Bishop Formosus of Porto (d. 896).[5]

The next stage in the story's evolution is marked by the emergence of a somewhat embellished, composite Greek version, which amalgamates the main lines of the Syriac account with the story of John the Calybite and in which the 'man of God' returns home to his parents in Constantinople and lives with them incognito, so that only after his death does a miracle reveal to them his identity.[6] This version gives greater prominence to the theme of the marriage, but the protagonist, now called Alexis, still abandons his bride and departs for Edessa. After seventeen years a statue of the Virgin issues the command 'seek the man of God', which precipitates Alexis' flight and his sojourn incognito with his parents, with whom he stays for seventeen years. The Emperors and the Pope seek him and find him dead, clasping a roll relating his experiences. His funeral takes place in St Peter's. This amplified version of the legend is found in Syriac versions of not earlier than the ninth century which deserve more detailed scrutiny than has so far been accorded to them. It was then combined with the earlier Syriac version, in which the 'man of God' died in Edessa, so that a way had to be found for him to be revived and continue his wanderings. Further investigation is needed of the manuscripts which transmit this Graeco–Syrian composite. A number of odes singing the praises of Alexis are also found in the ninth century in Joseph the Hymnographer's 'canon'.

Since Duchesne[7] it has been thought that the cult of Alexis was not introduced to the West until late in the tenth century, when Sergios, archbishop of Damascus, taking refuge in Rome (977), established it in the church of St Boniface where he had created a Graeco–Roman community, and popularized the story in its Graeco–Syriac form, though the exact details of it are almost impossible to fix.[8] Alexius became the second patron of this Benedictine abbey in 986[9] (his relics were transferred to Montecassino in 1023). As a result his story was translated into Latin, substituting Rome for Constantinople. Of the various texts of this *Vita* one of the most important was published by the Bollandists.[10] Nevertheless, Ulrich Mölk pointed out that, before the cult of Alexis is attested in Rome, he is already (as simply 'famulus Dei', the servant of God) the subject of a Latin prose life surviving in four manuscripts, most significantly in a Passionary of the Abbey of San Pedro de Cardeña (Burgos), written as early as the second quarter of the tenth century (now London, BL MS Add. 25600 ff.253va-258va),[11] and in a version in Madrid, Academia de la Historia, MS Aemilianensis 13, from San Millán de la Cogolla, which seems to be the most faithful witness to the original. This Life seems to have reached Spain without any Italian intermediary and before Alexis was associated with Boniface on the Aventine. The widely known Latin *Vita* on which the Old French Lives are based, published by the Bollandists, was composed probably at the beginning of the eleventh century, and no fewer than nineteen manuscripts date from that century.[12] In the evolution of the Alexis tradition, however, a complication was introduced by the existence of a Latin rhythmic poem *Pater Deus ingenite*, consisting of 348 octosyllables arranged in stanzas of six lines, rhyming *aabbcc*, which was copied in the last quarter of the eleventh century, in MS 644 of the Stiftsbibliothek at Admont (Steiermark) and at the beginning of the next century in Vatican Library, MS palat. lat. 828. For a long time the predominant view was that the poem preceded, and even influenced, the earliest Old French *Vie*, but Jean Rychner's conclusion that the Latin poem is an abridged adaptation of the French and that the Latin prose *Vita* in Rome, Bibl. Casanatense, MS 719 (BHL 290) was the intermediary between the *Vita* and the *Pater Deus*[13] is now widely preferred. Perugi (*La Vie de saint Alexis*, p.70) observes that this intermediary is 'nécessaire mais non suffisante pour expliquer *St Al*' and that the Latin manuscript (Stiftsbibliothek, Admont MS 664) reflects a transitional stage in the *Vita* tradition between the type represented by the Madrid manuscript and that of the Casanatense (p. 93).

The eleventh century is thus a key period in the genesis of the Old French poem, but one for which further research is needed regarding the circulation of texts, notably the *Vita* and the *Deus Pater ingenite*. At the same time considerable importance attaches to the surviving evidence for the cult of Saint Alexis in France, and this has been gathered by Mölk.[14] The three twelfth-century MSS of the Old French *Vie* all give textual indications (ed. Perugi , l.542) of a connection with the day of the saint's festival (17 July). Mölk has shown that no clearly defined pattern of diffusion of the cult of Alexis can be discerned in France. A breviary from the Abbey of Saint-Loup at Troyes (Troyes Bibl. mun. MS 571, *c.* 1100) mentions the office of Saint Alexis and offers some parallels to the ordinary of Rheinau, the oldest liturgical book north of the Alps to provide information on that cult. Mölk also lists thirty manuscripts of two versions of the *Vita* of known French provenance dating from the eleventh and twelfth centuries, the evidence being particularly common in passionaries from the Walloon region, and shows how the original name form 'Alexius' was frequently replaced by 'Alexis', as in the Old French *Vie* and in the *Deus Pater ingenite*. Mölk also notes that a Norman document records the death of an 'Alexis monachus' around the year 1113 (with another document reporting the death of an 'Alexis canonicus' of Soissons in the same period). So there is evidence from the Ile-de-France, N-E France (specially important), the Champagne (particularly striking) and the S-E. The Old French *Vie* could in principle have been written in any of these areas where there is evidence that Alexis was venerated.[15] Nevertheless Mölk sticks with Gaston Paris's preference for a Norman origin of the *Vie* and here we naturally look to the Abbey of Bec.[16] One of its English foundations, the priory of Saint-Neots, contains the saint's festival in its calendar, but Bec itself, although making the feast a solemn one (with twelve lessons), does not record such an observance before the thirteenth century. An attractive conjecture would be that the cult of the saint had been introduced by Lanfranc (born in Pavia) who was in close contact with Italy, spent some time in Rome in 1050, and is known to have introduced certain liturgical practices from Montecassino, where the cult of Saint Alexis existed in the eleventh century. But evidence for Bec is unfortunately lacking until the thirteenth century. Mölk's useful survey of the diffusion of the *Vita* is the essential preliminary to the next step, a consideration of the Old French *Vie de saint Alexis* itself.

Like 'La Chanson de Roland', the title 'La Vie de Saint Alexis' is conferred par excellence on a single-manuscript version, respectively, Oxford, Bodleian Library, MS Digby 23 and the St Albans Psalter (St Godehard, Hildesheim), of which the fifth quire, containing the Alexis material, is accorded the siglum L.[17] In both cases their 'precellence', to use the term applied to the Oxford manuscript of the *Roland*, rests on aesthetic qualities rather than any criterion of authenticity, and the editors' titles are also applied more generally to a constellation of closely related texts which may be said to constitute the 'tradition'.[18] In the case of the *Alexis* in stanzas of decasyllabes there are seven manuscripts representing six distinct versions. Despite some chronological uncertainties, the view is gaining ground that the *Vie de Saint Alexis* as presented in L was influenced by the *Roland*[19] and was in turn adapted in the abbreviated *Pater Deus ingenite*,[20] and later had a clear influence on the *Vie de sainte Euphrosine*.[21] The Hildesheim text has certainly been the subject of a great deal of attention, and editions based on this text alone number over twenty and involve some of the most celebrated editors of Old French texts. Nevertheless, attempts to consider the text *in situ* have been rare. Though it is unlikely that the Hildesheim text was copied, as is sometimes maintained, in the period 1115–19, it is certainly the oldest copy to survive. It cannot for that reason, however, be equated with the 'original'. The whole genesis of the Old French *Vie* is extremely complicated and defies the straightforward composition of a *stemma codicum*. The art of textual genetics was until recently still somewhat in its infancy, so far as the *Alexis* is concerned, though tribute should be paid to the insights of Wendelin Foerster,[22] however unacceptable some of his conclusions may have become. Great progress in this domain has now been made by Gianfranco Contini,[23] and by Maurizio Perugi in his new edition of the *Alexis*, which offers a 'stratified' text. Perugi recognizes in L 'le résultat d'un accroissement progressif' (p. 96), which 'par un souci de complétude' and in the manner of a 'véritable manuscrit-réceptacle', seeks to preserve as much as possible in a *version intégrante* which has no special authenticity but a distinctively inclusive character. For Perugi, L is the end-product of a three-stage development which can be discerned in a trio of surviving witnesses, APL. First there was a 'short' original, consisting solely of the life, now approximately represented by A (concluding at st.110),[24] Paris, BNF nouv. acq. MS 4503 which also includes the *Voyage de saint Brendan* by Benedeit and the *Vie de sainte Catherine* by Clemence of Barking, two texts the transmission of which has been associated with the Abbey of Bec. This early version may well have been produced in the 1090s.[25] Next came a continuation which incorporated the translation of the saint's relics to the church of

St Boniface: this is now reflected in P (Paris, BNF MS fr.19525). Then came a text augmented by miracles (L st.111–13) found in four manuscripts (VLMS). This procession of *vita, translatio* and *miracula* follows well attested processes of accretion in hagiography. Finally, the text now represented by L was subject to a number of revisions and assembled, probably in Lower Normandy, where the earliest Old French *Vie* was most likely composed, though Burger (see n. 15 below) has suggested the Franco–Provençal area of SE France.

The inescapable and intriguing problem remains that of the status of L, accepting the fact that it is the oldest surviving copy of the Old French *Vie*. Pächt believed that it was based directly on the original, which was itself, he supposed, composed at St Albans during the period 1115–19 when a chapel or altar was dedicated to St Alexis. But this idea inadmissibly truncates the textual history of the Old French *Vie*, not least by excluding the evidence that L's model is the result of the conflation of the first-stage or shorter version (like A) with a second version which included the Bonifatian material. Certainly the association of L's model with St Albans is logical: not only was a chapel or altar in the abbey church dedicated to St Alexis, but the abbey owned copies of the Roman and Montecassino versions of the Latin *Vita* (BHL 286 and 287), and July 17 was the saint's festival (though its observance seems not to have lasted very long, his feast appears once in two St Albans calendars, and in the litany of the St Albans Psalter). A French *Vie* was most likely imported from Normandy by Geoffrey of Gorham (Gorran) who came from Maine, was Abbot of St Albans from 1119 to 1146, and had himself composed for the school at Dunstable a play, the *Ludus de sancta Catherina*, which perhaps resembled the fragment of a dramatic narrative which survives in Manchester, John Rylands University Library, MS French 6.[26]

Once a text of the French *Vie* was to hand, how was it incorporated in the Psalter? Legge felt that it was written *c.* 1115 and sung at the dedication – by the bishop of Durham, Ranulf Flambard – of the chapel of St Alexis constructed by Richard de Albini, who introduced the cult of St Alexis at St Albans. Dodwell pointed out that the Psalter must have been written some time before 1123, as the *obit* of Christina of Markyate's protector, Roger the Hermit, is written on the manuscript in a hand different from the main hand and dated 12 September 1123. But this all seems rather early. We cannot know exactly what adjustments were needed to adapt the *Vie* to its new context. The Psalter proper seems to have been the first stage of the St Albans project, written in the hand of scribe 2 for use at the Abbey.[27] When the quite radical decision was taken, probably by Abbot Geoffrey, to make the book into a presentation volume for Christina – and we do not know when that was – a new initial for Psalm 105, depicting Christina, was inserted and the plan of the book changed to incorporate her calendar followed by pictures for her contemplation. Some time later quire 5, including the Alexis material, suggesting a significant extension of the project, was added, again probably under the direction of Abbot Geoffrey. This could have happened during the 1130s when, against Christina's wishes, Geoffrey was asked to travel to Rome in 1136 and 1139 (invitations

symbolized, perhaps, by the illustration on p. 57 of Alexis entering the ship).[28]
The scribe here employed (scribe 3) intervened in two other places in the book
and worked on other manuscripts at St Albans (e.g. the calendar in London, BL,
MS Egerton 3721 ff.1v-7v) and could possibly be Abbot Geoffrey himself. The
Vie is sandwiched between a prose prologue and a translation of a defence of
the pictorialization of narrative as expressed in a letter of Gregory the Great to
the recluse 'Secundinus'.[29] This letter, first given in Latin and then in French
translation, seems to be a defence of the forty textless full-page miniatures in an
earlier section which are by another hand from that responsible for the *Vie*, and
is not necessarily related specifically to the Alexis illustration, which has, of
course, its own text. The prologue is in prose, but the question of whether it is
written in 'Reimprosa' or 'de-rhymed prose' remains open.[30] The introductory
phrase *Ici cumencet* is not necessarily to be understood as the rubric for a written
copy of the prologue, nor simply as 'Boniment de présentateur avec résumé
rapide des événements du récit et éloge du poème qui va être exécuté'.[31] A
possibility is that it is 'de-rhymed' prose, because a contributor to the Psalter, as
we have suggested probably Abbot Geoffrey himself, was working from memory
and could not accurately recall the verse prologue of which he was mindful. He
therefore wrote as much as he could (the language is thought by Tyssens and
Mölk to be slightly younger and more insular than that of the *Vie*, with its continental origins), with the assonances acting as an *aide-mémoire*, but apparently
insufficient to enable him to recall the full text. At any rate neither this prologue
nor the text of the *Vie* is to be regarded as originating with the Psalter, but
rather as already existing before its compilation.

The presence of French, commonly used in the convents and monasteries of
Britain, should not be taken as necessarily connected with Christina. Certainly
some adjustments to the *Vie* must have been introduced at St Albans, but there
is little justification for pursuing imagined parallels with Christina's predicament
too far, as if L were essentially created to meet her case. It is the additions,
notably the prose prologue and the illustrations on p. 57 of the Psalter, which
weigh more heavily in departing from normal hagiographical conventions
(including the iconographical tradition of the 'beggar under the stairs', representing the *conclusion* of the hagiographical narrative).[32] There is undeniably
something appropriate about the illustration on p. 57 in the context of 'le grand
tournant dans le passé personnel de Christina', as Maddox puts it, 'le moment
de la renonciation au mariage et le début d'une vie spirituelle'. Maddox justifiably concludes: 'Au lieu donc de souligner le rôle d'Alexis en tant que pèlerin,
comme le fait le manuscrit A, ou en tant qu'intercesseur, comme c'est le cas
surtout à la fin du ms. L, est ici thématisé le refus du mariage – dans un
contexte mondain, charnel, du moins – au profit d'une ascèse rigoureuse, sans
que soit pour autant négligée la consolidation du rapport spirituel chez le
couple', and, one might add, their final reunion in heaven (L ll.608–9). It is easy
to sympathize with Peter Damian's observation on 'new martyrdom', in his *De
sancto Alexio confessore* in which the 'new martyr' is presented not as the victim of

physical torment inflicted by an executioner or judge, but by the beauty of his wife![33] The prose prologue reinforces the idea of a commemorative use of the *Vie*, 'del quel nus avum oït lire e canter' ('[extracts of which] we have heard spoken and sung'), a phrase which in itself suggests little more than the reading in church of the *Vie* on the saint's feast-day, a feature which marks the genesis of many Old French saints' lives. As it stands in the manuscript, the prose prologue does not support Maddox's interpretation (based on the reconstituted version by Williman) of a direct injunction by Alexis to his bride, but, rather, makes it clear that Alexis' action eases the way for her to be united with the 'spus vif de veritét, ki est un sul faitur e regnet an trinitiet' ('the living Bridegroom of Truth who is sole Creator and who reigns in the Trinity) and evokes those who 'digne-ment sei delitent es goies del ciel ed es noces virginels' ('worthily delight in Heavenly joys and virgin marriages') as well as providing a parallel to lines 66–7 of the *Vie*: 'Oz mei, pulcele! Celui tien ad espus / Ki nus raenst de sun sanc precius' ('Hear me, maiden! Take as your spouse Him who redeemed us with His precious blood'). It should be noted that to the version represented by A the text of L adds 15 stanzas, but these are also present in some form in the other five manuscripts (LVPMS) even though the two 'endings' are scarcely compat-ible. L was not a version specifically created for the Psalter, but the embellishments, particularly the pictures, are a sign of adaptation to new circumstances, and are hence defended by the letter, in Latin and in French, of Gregory to 'Secundinus'. But even this is of broader relevance (e.g. to the forty-page, pictorial, Christological cycle, which is textless, and the three miniatures of the Supper at Emmaus) than a straight reference to the individual case of Christina.[34] The Latin letter seems to have been written by a different scribe from that of the prose prologue,[35] but small differences between the prose prologue, the Latin letter and its French translation may simply be the result of the small periods of time separating the copies.[36]

We are gradually led to the view that, in the St Albans Psalter, the *Vie de saint Alexis* is revived, along with a prologue here rendered in prose, through the patronage of Abbot Geoffrey some time after 1124 and equipped with two supple-mentary pieces on the value of pictures. C. H. Talbot saw the *Vie* as primarily a 'pièce justificative' for Christina's abandonment of her husband (*Life*, p. 26), although for Legge there was no essential connection with Christina at all.[37] However, once we adopt the perspective of a parallel between Alexis and Geoffrey it is easy to see that the nuptial theme is foregrounded by the artist on p. 57 and is also present in the prose prologue. In this perspective the bride has a pivotal role, as if to mark up the parallel with Abbot Geoffrey's own relationship to Christina. In manuscripts LAPV marriage is associated with attachment to the world and is thus renounced, whereas this opposition is greatly reduced in later versions where there are some signs of alarm at Alexis' treatment of his bride.[38] This is all under-standable in the context of the complex relationship of Geoffrey and Christina. The role of a saint's Life in the celebration of the Saint's feast, after the office, is entirely conventional, often attracting the phrase 'paraliturgical' and undergoing a gradual process of emancipation as interference with the *chansons de geste* takes place.[39] Attempts to make the *Vie de saint Alexis* part of a more strictly liturgical ceremony are unconvincing.[40] If the prose prologue refers to the life of Eufemien's son 'del quel nus avum oït lire e canter', ('[extracts of which] we have heard spoken and sung') and line 542 (LA) declares 'pur oec en est oi cest jurn oneurét' ('for that reason he is honoured on this day') (altered in P to 'Por ceo est ore el ciel coroné'), this simply suggests a commemorative reading which need not imply a precise liturgical context. Indeed, the well-known tale of the conversion of a wealthy citizen of Lyon, Peter Valdès in 1173, on hearing the story recited by a jongleur[41] offers clear evidence of the story's emancipation from such a context.

In short, the relationship of Christina of Markyate and Abbot Geoffrey led to the preservation in a prestigious codex of a mature version of the *Vie de saint Alexis*, which remains the only complete witness before 1200, but is certainly not the *Urtext*.

Notes

1   Essential bibliography in L. J. Engels, 'The West European Alexius Legend: With an Appendix presenting the Medieval Latin Text Corpus in its Context (Alexiana Latina Medii Aevi, I)' in *The Invention of Saintliness*, ed. A. B. Mulder-Bakker (London and New York, 2002), pp. 93–144; C. Storey, *An Annotated Bibliography and Guide to Alexis Studies (La Vie de Saint Alexis)*, Histoire des idées et critique littéraire 251 (Geneva, 1987) and *La Vie de Saint Alexis*, ed. M. Perugi, Textes Littéraires Français 529 (Geneva, 2000).

2   See the study of Arthur Amiaud, *La Légende syriaque de saint Alexis, l'homme de Dieu*, Bibliothèque de l'Ecole des Hautes Etudes 79 (Paris, 1889) who prints in an appendix the Syriac text and his own translation of it, which is in turn put into English in C. J. Odenkirchen, *The Life of Saint Alexius in the Old French Version of the Hildesheim Manuscript: the original text reviewed, with comparative Greek and Latin versions, all accompanied by English translations; and an introductory study, and bibliography and appendices*, Medieval Classics: Texts and Studies 9 (Brookline, Mass. and Leyden, 1978), pp. 13–20. Amiaud's account is essentially summarized by C. E. Stebbins, 'Les Origines de la légende de saint Alexis', *Revue Belge de Philologie et d'Histoire* 51 (1973), 497–507 and the early Syriac text is summarized and commented upon in Karl D. Uitti, *Story, Myth and Celebration in Old French Narrative Poetry 1050–1200* (Princeton, 1973), pp. 28–31.

3   M. Rösler, 'Alexiusprobleme', *Zeitschrift für romanische Philologie* 53 (1933), 508–28, repr. with English translation in Odenkirchen, *The Life of Saint Alexius*, pp. 21–9.

4   Texts are identified according to their appearance in BHL (*Bibliotheca Hagiographica Latina antiquae et mediae aetatis*) t.1 (Brussels, 1898–99, repr. 1992) and 2 (*Novum Supplementum* ed. H. Fros, 1986).

5   *Analecta Bollandiana* 15 (1896), 257–67.

6   See M. Rösler, *Die Fassungen der Alexiuslegende mit besonderer Berücksichtigung der mittelenglischen Versionen* (Vienna and Leipzig, 1905). The composite Byzantine life is summarized and commented upon in Uitti, *Story, Myth and Celebration*, pp. 31–4.

7   L. Duchesne, 'Notes sur la topographie de Rome au Moyen Age, VII (1): Les légendes chrétiennes de l'Aventin', *Mélanges d'Archéologie et d'Histoire de l'Ecole Française de Rome* 10 (1890), 225–50.

8   Max Friedrich Blau, *Zur Alexiuslegende* (Vienna, 1888) confirmed Duchesne's view that Sergius introduced the cult of Alexis in Rome. From a document of 987 relating to

the church it is clear that an association with St Alexis had been established and the church on the Aventine Hill became that of San Bonifazio e Alessio.

9 See K. F. Werner, 'La légende de saint Alexis: un document sur la religion de la haute noblesse vers l'an mil?' in *Haut Moyen-Age, Culture, Education et Société, Etudes offertes à Pierre Riché*, ed. Cl. Lepelley *et al.* (Paris, 1990), pp. 531–46.

10 Most easily accessible in J.-M. Meunier, *La Vie de saint Alexis, poème français du XIe siècle* (Paris, 1933), pp. 11–17. The text printed in W. Foerster and E. Koschwitz, *Altfranzösisches Übungsbuch*, 6th edn. (Leipzig, 1921), cols. 299–308 is reprinted in G. Rohlfs, *Sankt Alexius. Altfranzösische Legendendichtung des 11. Jahrhunderts*, 4th edn. (1963), pp. 14–23 and Odenkirchen, *The Life of Saint Alexius*, pp. 34–51. C. E. Stebbins, *A Critical Edition of the 13th and 14th Centuries Old French Poem Versions of the 'Vie de Saint Alexis'*, Beihefte zur *Zeitschrift für romanische Philologie* 145 (Tübingen, 1974), pp. 149–53 prints, like Meunier, the text of the Bollandists, *AA.SS* t.31, Iul IV (t.4 of July), pp. 251–3. The Bollandists listed nine different versions of the *Vita* in BHL i. no. 286–91, ii. no.291a–c. See also the summary and commentary by Uitti, *Story, Myth and Celebration*, pp. 35–42. Léon Hermann was persuaded that a Latin verse version (Brussels Bibl. Roy. 8883–8894, 12th C.) was closer to the Hildesheim text, but this view has not found favour.

11 See U. Mölk, 'Die älteste lateinische Alexiusvita (9/10 Jahrhundert), Kritischer Text und Kommentar', *Romanistisches Jahrbuch* 27 (1976), 293–315.

12 M. Sprissler, *Das rhythmische Gedicht 'Pater Deus Ingenite' (11 Jh.) und das altfranzösische Alexiuslied*, Forschungen zur romanischen Philologie 18 (Münster, Westf., 1966), pp. 28–9 lists them and on pp. 106–53 prints and analyses the text synoptically according to his division of the MSS into four groups. The first group, closest to the version published by the Bollandists, is not sufficient to account for all the features of the Old French poem. Here there is further work to be done.

13 'La *Vie de saint Alexis* et le poème latin *Pater Deus ingenite*' in J. Rychner, *Du Saint-Alexis à François Villon: études de littérature médiévale*, Publications romanes et françaises 169 (Geneva, 1985), pp. 21–37.

14 U. Mölk, 'La *Chanson de saint Alexis* et le culte du saint en France aux XIe et XIIe siècles', *Cahiers de civilisation médiévale* 21 (1978), 339–55 and 'Das Offizium des heiligen Alexius nach französischen Brevierhandschriften des XI–XIII Jahrhunderts' in *Lebendige Romania. Festschrift für Hans-Wilhelm Klein* (Göppingen, 1976), pp. 231–44.

15 The twelfth-century (*c.* 1140?) fragment of the *Alexis* in Rome, Vatican, Cod. Lat. 5334 is the work of a Walloon scribe copying a Franco–Provençal model, see M. Burger, 'La langue et les graphies du manuscrit V de la *Vie de saint Alexis*' in *Et multum et multa. Festschrift für Peter Wunderli zum 60. Geburtstag*, ed. E. Werner *et al.* (Tübingen, 1998), pp. 373–86. Burger considers that the home of French versions of the *Alexis* is the Franco–Provençal South-East. MS V is of some importance in attesting to the 'continuation' of the *Vie* through the inclusion of the miracles.

16 See S. M. Cingolani, 'Normandia, Le Bec e gli esordi della letteratura francese' in *Lanfranco di Pavia e l'Europa del secolo XI*, ed. G. D'Onofrio (Rome, 1993), pp. 281–93.

17 There is an excellent colour facsimile of the *Alexis* text in U. Mölk, *La Chanson de saint Alexis: facsimilé en couleurs du ms. de Hildesheim publié avec introduction et bibliographie*, Nachr. d. Akad. d. Wiss. in Göttingen 1. Phil.-Hist. Kl. 1997 nr.2 (Göttingen, 1997). The whole manuscript can be inspected on the University of Aberdeen's website *www.abdn.ac.uk/stalbanspsalter* and Margaret Jubb's presentation of the *Chanson* at www.abdn.ac.uk/stalbanspsalter/english/essays/oldfrenchlife.shtml. Individual illustrations are also contained in M. Camille, 'Philological Iconoclasm: Edition and Image in the *Vie de saint Alexis*' in *Medievalism and the Modernist Temper*, ed. R. Howard Bloch and S. G. Nichols (Baltimore, 1996), pp. 371–401. The manuscript was in England during the Reformation, but the flyleaf records that in 1657 it belonged to the Anglican Benedictine congregation of Lamspringe not far from Hanover and

Hildesheim in Lower Saxony. When the monastery was secularized in 1803, it was acquired by the parish church of St Godehard, Hildesheim.

18 Seven versions of the *Roland* (and three fragments) and six versions of the decasyllabic *Alexis*. For a general study of the latter see the introduction to A. G. Elliott, *The Vie de Saint Alexis in the Twelfth and Thirteenth Centuries: an edition and commentary*, North Carolina Studies in the Romance Languages and Literatures 221 (Chapel Hill, NC, 1983).

19 See J. Rychner, 'La *Vie de saint Alexis* et les origines de l'art épique' in Rychner, *Du saint Alexis à François Villon*, pp. 47–63. M. Burger, 'Les traits formels communs de l'*Alexis* et du *Roland*: témoins d'emprunts intentionnels ou témoins d'une langue poétique en formation?', *Ensi firent li ancessor. Mélanges de philologie médiévale offerts à Marc-René Jung* 1 (Alessandria, 1996), pp. 199–225 argues for the second alternative of his title.

20 See n. 13 above.

21 See C. Storey, '*La Vie de Sainte Euphrosine* – a reminder of a neglected thirteenth-century poem', *French Studies* 31 (1977), 385–93.

22 W. Foerster, *Sankt Alexius. Beiträge zur Textkritik des ältesten französischen Gedichts (Der Aufbau, Nachweis von Lücken und Einschiebseln* (Halle, 1915).

23 G. Contini, *Breviario di ecdotica* (Milan and Naples, 1986). Contini produces a tripartite stemma L-AV-PSM.

LAPV = The 'eleventh century' *Chanson de Saint Alexis*
L   St Albans Psalter, Hildesheim (mid-C.12)
A   Paris, BN, MS nouv acq. fr. 4503 (C.12)
P1   Paris, BN, MS fr. 19525 (C.13)
P2   Manchester, John Rylands Library, MS fr. 6 (mid-C.13)
V   Vatican, Cod. Lat. 5334 (mid-C.12)

Related Thirteenth-Century Versions
S   Paris, BN fr. 12471
M   (a) Paris, BN MS fr. 1553
       (b) Carlisle Chapter Library

24 See the edition by T. D. Hemming, *La Vie de Saint Alexis: Texte du manuscrit A (B.N. nouv.acq.fr.4503)*, Textes Littéraires 90 (Exeter, 1994). The merits of A are proclaimed in H. Sckommodau, 'Zum altfranzösischen "Alexiuslied"', *Zeitschrift für romanische Philologie* 70 (1954), 161–203, D. L. Maddox, 'Pilgrimage Narrative and Meaning in Manuscripts L and A of the *Vie de saint Alexis*', *Romance Philology* 27 (1973), 143–57 and H. S. Robertson, '*La Vie de Saint Alexis*: Meaning and Manuscript A', *Studies in Philology* 67 (1970), 419–38. For further discussion and bibliography see M. Burger, 'Existait-il au XIe siècle deux versions de la *Vie de saint Alexis*, une longue et une courte?', in *Le Moyen Age dans la Modernité: Mélanges offerts à Roger Dragonetti*, ed. J. R. Scheidegger (Paris, 1996), pp. 173–81. Burger believes the original, like L, was composed of 125 stanzas. A. G. Elliott, 'The Ashburnham Alexis again', *Romance Notes* 21 (1980), 254–8 argues that L is the recasting of an earlier poem close to A and that the final 15 stanzas were composed at St Albans on the occasion of the dedication of the Alexis chapel.

25 Gaston Paris's view, based on a reconstruction of the language of the poem, was that the earliest version of the *Vie de saint Alexis* was probably produced in Normandy *c.* 1050 and that the Hildesheim text was copied some hundred years later, but these views have never been verified. See G. Paris and L. Pannier, *La Vie de saint Alexis, poème du XIe siècle et renouvellements des XIIe, XIIIe et XIVe siècles* (Paris, 1872, repr. 1887), p. 45 (hypothetical intermediaries between the original and L are indicated in the stemma given on p. 45). Paris's dating has been supported by M. Burger, 'Le Mariage de saint

Alexis' in '*Ce est li fruis selonc la letre*'. *Mélanges offerts à Charles Méla*, ed. O. Collet, Y. Foehr-Janssens and S. Messerli (Paris, 2002), pp. 227–34, who argues that the omission in the *Vie* of the *Vita*'s reference to the wedding taking place in church with officiating priests, and the emphasis on the couples' fathers instigating the marriage in a lay, public ceremony suggest a mid-eleventh-century context.

26 See E. C. Fawtier-Jones, in *Romania* 56 (1930), esp. 86–7. For the possibility that this portion of the manuscript was once part of London, BL MS Egerton 2710 see D. W. Russell, 'The Manuscript Source of the Fragment Rylands French MS 6', *Bulletin of the John Rylands University Library* 71 (1989), 41–7. On the *Alexis* fragment in this manuscript see now M. Burger, 'Le manuscrit P2 et sa position dans la tradition manuscrite de la *Vie de saint Alexis*' *ITALICA – RAETICA – GALLICA: studia linguarum litterarum artiumque in honorem Ricarda Liver*, ed. F. Wunderli *et al.* (Tübingen and Basel, 2001), pp. 489–501.

27 For Legge (*Anglo-Norman in the Cloisters: The Influence of the Orders Upon Anglo-Norman Literature* (Edinburgh, 1950)) the Psalter may have been begun at St Albans for the cell of Wymondham, founded by Abbot Richard's kinsman, William de Albini pincerna. The second prior of Wymondham, Alexius, is recorded as being in office in 1139.

28 See L. Kendrick, '1123? A Richly Illustrated Latin Psalter Prefaced by a Vernacular *Chanson de saint Alexis* is produced at the English Monastery of St Albans for Christina of Markyate', in *A New History of French Literature* (Cambridge, Mass. and London, 1989), ed. D. Hollier, pp. 23–30, who states, 'Composed earlier, probably for the dedication of a chapel to St Alexis, the St Albans *Alexis* is made, through the pointing of (these) visual and verbal glosses, to apply more clearly to the life of Christina of Markyate' (p. 29).

29 In reality to Serenus, bishop of Marseille, the error emanating from Burchard of Worms's collection of canons (Lib.III, c.36). See the assessment of U. Mölk, 'Bemerkungen zu den französischen Prosatexten im Albanipsalter', *Zeitschrift für französische Sprache und Literatur* 87 (1977), 289–303. Irritatingly, his significant contribution is omitted from Storey, *Annotated Bibliography* and situated in the wrong journal by Perugi, *La Vie de Saint Alexis*.

30 See M. Tyssens, 'Le Prologue de la Vie de Saint Alexis dans le manuscrit de Hildesheim', in *Studi in onore di Italo Siciliano* (Florence, 1966), pp. 1165–77. Quite unacceptable is the attempt of J. P. Williman, 'The Hidden Proeme in Verse of the *Vie de saint Alexis*', *Romance Notes* 14 (1972/73), 606–12, to argue the Picard character of the prologue.

31 Tyssens, 'Le Prologue', p. 1175.

32 See D. Maddox, 'Exordes, épilogues, et réécriture hagiographique: *La Vie de Saint Alexis* (XIe s.–XIVe s.)' in *Seuils de l'oeuvre dans le texte médiéval*, ed. E. Baumgartner and L. Harf-Lancner (Paris, 2002), pp. 129–57. Maddox comments 'En outre, la mise en manuscrit de la *Vie de Saint Alexis* suggère un effort pour mettre en relief dans la vie d'Alexis la crise analogue à celle vécue par Christina. Il s'agissait en premier lieu de pallier l'insuffisance thématique du prologue interne qui … met l'accent sur l'*imitatio Christi* du saint dans le contexte de l'*historia*. L'intégration de cette *materia remota* hagiographique posait non seulement le problème de le situer, et même de la mettre en relief, dans le contexte d'un psautier, pour lequel elle était peu convenable du point de vue générique, mais aussi la nécessité d'en faire un *corpus non alienum*, parfaitement adapté aux convictions du destinataire'.

33 *PL* 144, col. 658.

34 Maddox, 'Exordes, épilogues,' pp. 141–2 concludes: 'la réorchestration que subit la *Vie de saint Alexis* dans le *Psautier de Saint Albans* accomplit deux objectifs: établir une analogie thématique entre Alexis et Christina en ce qui concerne le mariage spirituel, et replacer ces deux figures exemplaires, ainsi "spécularisées", dans le contexte maximal de la textualité eschatologique. Ainsi l'insertion systématique de la *Vie de saint*

Alexis au sein du *Psautier* rejoint-elle la visée de l'*historia* déjà établie par le prologue interne du poème. Dans le contexte signifiant du *Psautier*, c'est le seul début du poème qui est mis en relief, c'est-à-dire la crise de conscience qui oppose diamétralement deux voies, la temporelle et la spirituelle, mais non sans ouvrir celle-ci à l'accommodation de l'"autre" conjugal, afin d'initier la montée réciproque du couple vers le Tiers médiateur'.

35 See K. E. Haney, 'The St Albans Psalter: A Reconsideration', *Journal of the Warburg and Courtauld Institutes* 58 (1995), 1–28 (2).

36 See Mölk, *Bemerkungen*, p. 302.

37 See the discussion in L. Gnädinger, *Eremitica: Studien zur altfranzösischen Heiligenvita des 12. und 13. Jahrhunderts*, Beihefte zur *Zeitschrift* 130 (Tübingen, 1972), pp. 44–53. The marriage motif was borrowed into the Alexis story from the *Passio SS. Iuliani et Basilissae*, see B. de Gaiffier, 'Source d'un texte relatif au mariage dans la *Vie de saint Alexis*, BHL 289', *Analecta Bollandiana* 63 (1945), 48–55 and '*Intactam sponsam relinquens*. A propos de la *Vie de saint Alexis*', *Analecta Bollandiana* 65 (1947), 157–95. On the marriage theme see D. Robertson, *The Medieval Saints' Lives: Spiritual Renewal and Old French Literature* (Lexington, 1995), pp. 216ff. and J. Pinder, 'Transformations of a Theme: Marriage and Sanctity in the Old French St Alexis Poems', in *Shifts and Transpositions in Medieval Narrative: A Festschrift for Dr Elspeth Kennedy*, ed. K. Pratt (Cambridge, 1994), pp. 71–88. M. Glasser, 'Marriage in Medieval Hagiography', *Studies in Medieval and Renaissance History* n.s. 4 (1981), 3–34 refers to four saints who flee from their wives on their wedding nights: Macarius the Roman (23 October), Abraham of Kidunja (16 March), Alexis (17 July) and Simon of Crépy (30 September; d.c.1080) and draws attention to the parallel between the sorrow of Alexis' rejected spouse and family and the *Passio SS. Perpetuae et Felicitatis*. On the parallel with Simon of Crépy see E. Walberg, *Deux anciens poèmes inédits sur saint Simon de Crépy* (Lund, 1909), pp. 14–15. The stories of Alexis and Simon of Crépy are both found in the fourteenth-century Carthusian compilation *Le Tombel de Chartrose*, see Ch. Kriele, *Untersuchungen zur Alexiuslegende des 'Tombel de Chartrose' (14. Jhd.)* diss. Münster, Westf., 1967. The Latin *Vita* of Simon contains a remark by the author 'Cui melius similem quam sancto Alexio dixerim?'. Delphina of Sabran (1284–1360) cited the legend of Saint Alexis as a plea for a chaste marriage (*Vies occitanes de Saint Auzias et de Sainte Dauphine*, ed. J. Cambell, (Rome, 1963)).

38 See J. Pindar, 'The Intertextuality of Old French Saints' Lives: St Giles, St Evroul and the Marriage of St Alexis', *Parergon* n.s. 6a (1988), 11–21.

39 See J. W. B. Zaal, '*A lei francesca*' (Sainte Foy, v.20): étude sur les chansons de saints gallo-romanes du XIe siècle* (Leiden, 1962).

40 See the amateurish study of R. Bullington, *The 'Alexis' in the Saint Albans Psalter: A Look into the Heart of the Matter*, Garland Studies in Medieval Literature 4 (New York and London, 1991). Her thesis is further vitiated by her view that Alexis is to be seen as a leper (*mezre* l.441) and a Lazarus figure.

41 See *Chronicon universale anonymi Laudunensis, von 1154 bis zum Schluss 1219*, ed. A. Cartellieri and rev. W. Stechele (Leipzig, 1909), pp. 20–2: 'Currente adhuc anno eodem Incarnationis MCLXXIII, fuit apud Lugdunum Galliae civis quidam Valdesius nomine, qui per iniquitatem faenoris multas sibi pecunias coacervaverat. Is quadam die dominica cum declinasset ad turbam quam ante joculatorem viderat congregatam, ex verbis ipsius compunctus fuit, et eum ad domum suam deducens intense eum audire curavit. Fuit enim locus narrationis eius qualiter beatus *Alexius* in domo patris sui beato fine quievit'.

14

CHRISTINA OF MARKYATE AND *THE HERMITS AND ANCHORITES OF ENGLAND*

E. A. Jones

When Rotha Mary Clay wrote her ground-breaking, and still unsuperseded, *Hermits and Anchorites of England*,[1] C. H. Talbot had not yet performed the feat of textual recovery without which this volume would probably not have come into existence. Her knowledge of Christina's life was based on Nicholas Roscarrock's plot summary of *c.* 1600, as printed by Hortsman, and the St Albans-centred highlights included (by a later hand) in the *Gesta Abbatum Monasterii Sancti Albani*, printed in the Rolls Series sequence of chronicles of the Abbey.[2] Had she had access to the far more richly detailed text of the *Life* which, thanks to Talbot, we are now able to read, Christina would undoubtedly have featured more prominently in Clay's book than she did.[3]

As it is, Clay's fullest discussion of Christina amounts to no more than a few pages in her chapter on 'Forest and Hillside Hermits', where she notes that, in the twelfth century, 'a group of fen and forest recluses were dwelling miles apart in the counties of Huntingdon, Bedford, and Hertford, whose lives were interwoven in a singular manner'.[4] The agent of their interweaving is, of course, Christina, whose story is briefly recounted, together with mentions of the hermit Edwin and the recluse Alfwen, and rather more on Christina's protector, mentor and predecessor at Markyate, Roger. Other than this, Christina appears only in passing in the rest of the book. Her austerities during her time of concealment in Roger's cell (*Life*, pp. 103–5) are noticed in the chapter on 'Trial and Temptation'; Godit, her maid (*Life*, p. 191),[5] is one of Clay's examples showing that it 'was customary for the enclosed person to have servants', and both Christina and Roger feature in the chapter on 'Prophets and Counsellors', though here Clay (following the emphasis of the *Gesta Abbatum*) gives the lion's share of the two paragraphs to Roger.[6]

The aims of this essay are threefold. At its heart, as part of my ongoing project to complete the revision of *Hermits and Anchorites* begun by Clay herself, and continued after her death by Basil Cottle, I present updated county lists of hermits and anchorites in what the local tourist boards are not yet calling 'Christina country'. Closer examination of the earlier entries on the lists will provide the opportunity to place Christina's experiences as a solitary in the context of other men and women close to her in time, place and vocation. More critically, several aspects of Christina's life, as it is now more fully known to us, may be seen to challenge a number of the assumptions and methodologies which lay behind Clay's original work, and need to be taken into account in its revision.

Clay's approach throughout *Hermits and Anchorites* is taxonomical. That the model is derived ultimately from the biological sciences may be seen most clearly in the first part of the book, which offers a kind of natural history of solitaries, in which Clay classifies her specimens according to habitat into chapters on 'Island and Fen Recluses', 'Forest and Hillside Hermits', 'Cave Dwellers', 'Light-Keepers on the Sea Coast', 'Highway and Bridge Hermits', 'Town Hermits' and 'Anchorites in Church and Cloister'. As we have already seen, Christina finds herself among the 'Forest and Hillside Hermits' (on the strength, perhaps, of *Christina de bosco*, as she is called in Henry II's grant to Markyate). *Hermits and Anchorites* is, however, less whimsical than I am making it sound. The book's real substance is found in the gazetteer or repertory of solitaries which forms a lengthy and scholarly appendix to the text, and lists references to the more than 750 hermits and anchorites that Clay's researches had discovered, tabulating them by county.[7]

In general, this system of classification is a convenient and unobtrusive way of organizing a potentially bewildering mass of material. But Christina presents a problem: where to place the Huntingdon girl whose spiritual journey saw her work her way up Watling Street from St Albans (Herts.) to Markyate, which until 1897 was in the parish of Caddington (over the border in Bedfordshire), but is now reckoned in Hertfordshire? (Clay puts her at 'Markyate (in Caddington)', in her list of Bedfordshire sites.) Her case highlights two shortcomings of classification by county. First, as will be apparent from the List of Sites and Hermits (see below), a number of solitaries dwelt quite precisely on the boundary between two counties. Indeed, the first element in the name Markyate is the Old English word for boundary or margin ('march').[8] In addition to Christina, examples include Great Staughton (Hunts.), Sudbury (Beds.) and Royston (Herts.); if the hermit at Royston occupied Royston Cave, then he would have been situated 'exactly across the line which … separated the parish of Barkway [in Herts.] from the parish of Bassingbourne [Cambs.]'.[9] This is probably not a coincidence. Roberta Gilchrist has drawn parallels between solitaries' liminal status, 'placed between the living and the dead, this life and the next', and their frequent siting at physical boundaries – between the church and the graveyard, between land and sea or river, or (as here) between administrative units.[10] (Is it merely coincidence that Christina makes her youthful vow of virginity at Shillington, 'a village on the Bedfordshire/Hertfordshire border'? (*Life*, p. 38 n. 1.)) If the county line seems rather less tangible or impressive a *limen* than the others, we should remember that such boundaries very often coincided with more obviously real and symbolic frontiers, including roads (at Royston, the

Icknield Way) and rivers. Bridge- or causeway-keeping hermits, in particular, by straddling an administrative division, pose an especial problem for the hermit-classifier. Examples from the region studied here are Turvey, where in the early fifteenth century the hermit John Combes was responsible for the upkeep of the bridge over the Ouse at the point where it forms the boundary between Bedfordshire and Buckinghamshire, and Earith, on the causeway over Ouse Fen which linked Huntingdonshire to Cambridgeshire.

But such problems also offer the opportunity to consider alternative configurations of our data on medieval solitaries. Ten miles or so below Earith, the Ouse is joined by the Cam. If we trace the latter from its source near Widdington in Essex to the point where it flows into the Ouse, we encounter late-medieval hermits maintaining bridges at the majority of crossings: Whytford Bridge at Hinxton, Whittlesford Bridge (in Duxford), Shelford Bridge and Smallbridges in Cambridge.[11] The region studied here is, however, notable less for its rivers than for its dense concentration of Roman and later roads leading out of London.[12] We have already noted that the sites associated with Christina – Markyate, Flamstead and St Albans – extend along Watling Street, and we might continue this line up to Dunstable, where a thirteenth-century anchorite and fifteenth-century hermit are recorded. Further east, sites on Ermine Street include Salbourne, Braughing, Royston, the hermit 'between Arrington and Royston', Huntingdon and Alconbury. The hermit 'between Barkway and Ware', if he was on the southern half of that route, would also have been on Ermine Street, and Coppingford (Hunts.) was on the Great North Road at a point where it had temporarily left the old line of Ermine Street.[13] Configuring the data in this way does not, perhaps, have the neatness of following the course of a river. The hermits engaged on bridge-work along the Cam are more obviously and causally tied to the river than the solitaries strung out along a medieval thoroughfare, who might include road-mending hermits (like the hermit 'between Arrington and Royston'), but also anchorites, some of whom might be closely linked to the route itself (for example those living in cells at town and city gates), but who, in perhaps the majority of cases, will have been at best only indirectly connected with the road, the primary consideration in the choice and approval of their sites being the presence of a conducive urban environment. This type of configuration does, however, have the advantage of reflecting an important way in which medieval people encountered solitaries. We remember that the hermit Edwin, returning from Canterbury to Huntingdon (presumably by Watling Street to London and thence via Ermine Street), stops at various places en route to speak with anchorites (*Life*, pp. 85–7). Sir Henry Willoughby of Wollaton (Notts.) travelled down to London in the summer of 1523. On 13 June he made an offering of 4d. at Our Lady of Brickhill, on the Buckinghamshire stretch of Watling Street. The next evening he arrived in London, but not before he had broken his journey at St Albans, where his servant John Levissey disbursed another 4d. 'in rayward to the ancres of Sent Talbonse'.[14] Three years earlier, Sir Thomas Lestrange of Hunstanton (Norf.) had given a penny to a hermit he encountered between Barkway and Ware (Herts.). The hermit may have been waiting in his roadside hermitage to importune the passer-by for alms. (If so, a plausible candidate for his cell might be the chapel of All Saints, Puckeridge.) But it is as likely that the hermit, as well as the nobleman, was on the move.

This is the second problem which the case of Christina throws up for Clay's decision to classify her solitaries by county. To resume the biological imagery, Clay's county lists are rather like the display-case of a Victorian butterfly-collector, with the specimens transfixed in orderly rows. There is, perhaps, a distinction to be made between solitaries like Christina, who occupied a number of sites in a series of locations (Richard Rolle is another celebrated example who comes to mind), and those like the hermit 'between Barkway and Ware', or the hermit of Earith causeway, whose particular calling seems to have been to an errant eremitism. It is not clear, however, into which category we should place Thomas Jolye, hermit, who died in London in 1487, but who, in his extant will, requested burial in the church of SS Peter and Paul, Dunstable (Beds.), along with bequests to that church and a number of others in (what we may assume to have been) his home town.[15]

The peregrinations of the would-be nun-on-the-run Christina should not, perhaps, be likened lightly to the gyrovagations of Rolle. But if a sensitivity to the charges (whether real or imagined) that Rolle perennially worried about – that is, of a scandalous instability of life – lay behind Clay's preference (however subconscious) for recording her solitaries under a single site, I should not be surprised. Tellingly, Clay decides to list Rolle under Hampole (Yorks.), though there is no evidence that, at least in life, he was ever more than loosely associated with the Cistercian nunnery, or that he ever resided there.[16] A different way of accounting for Christina and Rolle, and perhaps the only satisfactory way of incorporating the hermit Thomas Jolye, is to abandon altogether the topograph-ical configuration of the data for a listing by individual solitary. A history based on data thus classified would perhaps emphasize, rather than their quasi-institu-tionality, the *ad hoc*, impermanent nature of the vocations. The sites themselves are, after all, characterized by impermanence. The endowed hermitage or reclu-sorium was exceptional;[17] it was more usually the individual than the site which attracted funding. Solitaries' dwellings must often have been as rudimentary as the hut made 'of the branches of trees, and of bark-covered stakes, wattled with twigs' built by two twelfth-century women at Eywood (near St Albans).[18] The surviving remains of an anchorite's cell at St Leonard's, Bengeo (Herts.), suggest a small, lean-to affair made of wood; the structure has disappeared, leaving only the opening into the chancel, a recess in the exterior chancel wall, and holes for two roof timbers. But these are more substantial traces than any other anchorite in the region has left to posterity, or even perhaps to his successors. There is no evidence that Thomas Fishbourne felt himself to be in any way the heir of Ulf and Eadfrith, who had occupied the chapel of St German, St Albans, some six centuries earlier, nor that there is any continuity between the thirteenth-century anchorites attached to the churches of St Michael and St Peter, in the same town, and the anchorites who start to appear there again from the first part of the fifteenth century. On the other hand, at St Michael's there is clear evidence of continuity from one fifteenth-century anchoress to the next: Katherine Ditton, who was anchorite in 1421, died in 1437 and was succeeded (perhaps after an intervening incumbent) by one of her servants, Agnes Vertesans (or Vertesawce), who was still living in 1472. Such relationships *between* individuals – to which, of course, we should add that between Christina and Roger – would very quickly get lost in such an arrangement.

If Clay may be guilty of the wishful stabilization of Christina's life, as of Rolle's, she is, however, not alone. The same tendency is undoubtedly there in the medieval sources for Christina's life. Although its atelous state makes it difficult to offer critical comment with absolute confidence, the *Life* seems to be moving inevitably towards the (monastically-speaking) happy ending of her adoption of regular Benedictinism. In the version of her biography in which the shaping hand of St Albans can be seen even more certainly – that is, the account in the *Gesta Abbatum* – the stability which characterizes the end of the story also infiltrates earlier episodes. The first parts of Christina's story are told in sections headed *De Sanctitate et Actibus Rogeri Heremitae* and *Miraculum factum per Rogerum Heremitam*.[19] In fact (as the titles suggest) Christina's trials with her family and Burthred, and the abortive residence with Alfwen, are not recorded; we meet her first as Roger's disciple, being placed by him in the cell adjoining his hermitage. When she finally assumes centre-stage, it is under the heading *De virtutibus Christianae, Priorissae de Markʒate*, even though none of the events recounted there belong to this phase of Christina's life, and the priory itself does not come into being until the next section of the narrative, *De causis et fundatione Domus de Markʒate*. There is, tellingly, no section headed *De Sanctitate et Actibus* Christianae *Heremitae*. The story of Christina's regularization may be paralleled in another of Abbot Geoffrey's foundations. A few years earlier, he had learnt of the two 'holy women' (*mulieres sanctae*) living a life of piety, chastity and abstinence in their hut in Eywood. When the abbot learns of 'their novel religious life' (*novellam religionem suam*), he assumes responsibility for them and encloses them under lock and key and the abbot's seal, turning the *mulieres sanctae* into *sanctimoniales*, and thereby founding the priory of Sopwell.[20] Once again, however, there is some evidence that the *Gesta Abbatum* may have imposed a teleological neatness on a foundation narrative of rather greater complexity and institutional untidiness, and that the (to Benedictine eyes) shapeless eremitical phase of the priory's history may have been more substantial than the author allows.[21]

The same kind of regularization can also be seen in modern accounts of Christina. In the marginal commentary to his edition of the *Gesta Abbatum*, beside Christina's first appearance at Roger's hermitage, Riley sets 'St. Christina, a recluse, joins him'. The text here describes her less specifically as 'the blessed Christina, a virgin from Huntingdon' (*Beata Christina, virgo de Hontyngdona oriunda*).[22] In fact, both the *Life*, and the account in the *Gesta* which is based on it, although they show themselves to be aware of the technical vocabulary of religious solitude, seem to be taking pains to avoid applying it to Christina's case.[23]

Clay's account of Christina follows the pattern we have been observing. She, of course, did not have the advantage that the *Gesta*-author had, of access to the full text of the *Life*, and is relying on Roscarrock, whom she goes on to quote:

> Christina was destined to become the devoted disciple of Roger, but family claims and church order had first to be satisfied:
>
>> But before she came thither, Edwine, by Roger's means, whoe refused to admitt her, imparted her case to Radulfe, Archb. of Canterburie … After this Burfred her husband together with the Preist whoe had maried them, came with others to the Ermitage of the foreneamed Roger, and there in the presence of five Ermittes gave her leave, notwithstanding that which had passed, to dispose of her self as she pleased; and Thurstane Archb. of Yorke disolving the Match with their consent, permitted him to Marrie, and shee to enter into Religion.[24]

It is only after this, in Clay's version of events, that Christina begins her period of painful concealment in the house adjoining Roger's cell, though this confusion of the chronology may have arisen from an ambiguity in Roscarrock.[25] As a result, a number of separate events have been collapsed together to form a credible prelude to Christina's enclosure, with the emphasis on 'church order'. The passage is indeed remarkable for the procedurality with which it invests one of the most arduous and anfractuous routes to the religious life that we have on record.[26] In fact, Clay manages to make the sequence of events leading up to Christina's enclosure sound remarkably like the procedures of episcopal inquisition and approval of postulants to the anchoritic life which were developed during the thirteenth century and remained in force through the rest of the Middle Ages.[27]

As a consequence, the celebrated description of the hardships which Christina endures in her early years with Roger becomes, in Clay's account, part of her experience as an anchoress.[28] But the identification is far from clear. As we have already seen, the sources themselves avoid describing Christina in these terms. Indeed, while her strict bodily enclosure may be hagiographically apposite (one thinks of the harlot Thais, for example, as an antecedent),[29] the emphasis of the text is on enclosure not as ascetic desideratum but as fearful necessity. The language of enclosure (*clausula*) and imprisonment (*carcer*), familiar from later anchoritic texts, does occur a few times in this passage; but it is outweighed by references to concealment (*celari, latens, abscondita, latebras*): 'she would rather die in the cell than make her presence known to anyone at that time' (*Life*, pp. 103–5).[30] Significantly, once Burthred has renounced his claim on her (*Life*, p. 109), and the danger is past, the language of fear and concealment disappears, and Christina is recognized openly as Roger's successor in the hermitage.

Here is a challenge to the most fundamental of Clay's taxonomies. The epigraph to *Hermits and Anchorites* is a couple of stanzas from *Friar Daw's Reply*:

For sum fleen from the world and closen hemsilf in wallis,
And steken hem in stones, and litil wole thei speken,
To fleen sich occasiouns as foly wole fynden;
And thees we clepen ancres in the comoun speche.

Also in contemplacion there ben many other,
That drawen hem to disert and drye … muche peyne,
By eerbis, rootes, and fruyte lyven for her goddis love,
And this maner of folk men callen hermytes.[31]

Clay's first act, on identifying a site connected with a solitary, is to classify it as either a hermitage or an anchor-hold. Making the description a property of the site rather than of its occupant is not always straightforward: here, the chapel of St Mary Magdalene in St Albans was occupied by an anchorite in 1484 but by a hermit in 1530. In the *List of Sites* at the end of this chapter, I label the solitary, not the site. But individuals can be as difficult to classify. The author of *Friar Daw*, writing in the fifteenth century, was confident of being able to distinguish between the two vocations, and two hundred years earlier Gerald of Wales makes the same distinction: hermits wander about alone, while anchorites are strictly enclosed.[32] If we believe that Christina lived with Roger as an anchorite, then her succession to his hermitage (as a transition to a less strict form of religious life) may seem quite irregular. Even if we do not accept her enclosure as formally anchoritic, we may be unprepared to countenance a female hermit (Clay lists none in her book).[33] Such anxiety may explain why the account in the *Gesta Abbatum* is so vague about where and how Christina lives between Roger's death and the foundation of Markyate, supplying the *De virtutibus Christianae, Priorissae de Markʒate* rubric already discussed to fill the lacuna.[34] But Roger himself, designated a hermit in both the *Life* and the *Gesta*, is called an anchorite by William of Malmesbury.[35] In the *List of Sites* there is a twelfth-century grant of the hermitage (*eremitagium*) of Salbourne (Herts.) which was built by William the anchorite (*inclusus*).

The confusion here is partly terminological and partly taxonomical (though the two are, of course, necessarily related). The terms 'hermit' and 'anchorite' are not historically fixed: they are used synonymously by early authors (perhaps most influentially in the *Rule of St Benedict*), but gradually undergo a process of disambiguation during the medieval period.[36] It therefore makes little sense to try to differentiate early solitaries like St Arnulf (of Eynesbury (Hunts.)) or the first occupants of the chapel of St German in St Albans as either hermits or anchorites, when that distinction had no meaning for them or their contemporaries. The uncertainty in the designation of later figures like Roger and the founder of Salbourne may, however, testify to a terminology in flux. That the process of semantic separation seems to have been complete by Gerald of

Wales's time is probably no coincidence. He was writing in 1215, the year of the Fourth Lateran Council, which (among other things) was concerned to stabilize and rationalize the many new forms of more or less regular religious life which had sprung up in the preceding two centuries. Before this date, there is evidence of a greater fluidity and flexibility, not only in the terminology but in the practice of the solitary vocations, than would be permissible thereafter. A good example from outside the region is the 'very pious virgin' (*uirgo … religiosa ualde*) who, at the end of the twelfth century, gives counsel to Edmund, monk of Eynsham. While praying in a church in Oxford, he has just heard a divine voice:

> At the door of the church I met a certain pious virgin, who served God day and night by prayer and fasting, and in cold and nakedness, and rarely [*rarissime*] left the church, being almost always in its precincts [*atriis*]. When I heard the voice she had been praying as was her custom in a remote corner [*in remoto… angulo*] of the church.[37]

Similarly vague is the precise vocation of the Guido whom Christina's parents are visiting when she makes her escape: he lived 'in a secluded spot' (*locum … solitudinis*) about six miles from Huntingdon (*Life*, p. 89). Talbot subsequently translates his *solitud[o]* as 'the hermitage' (*Life*, pp. 93–5), and he is indexed as 'Guido, hermit' (*Life*, p. 203), which is to be more definite than the author of the *Life* chooses to be.

If Christina is to be classified, perhaps she belongs with solitaries like these. But this would be to de-emphasize her role as monastic founder.[38] As the central figure and inspiration behind an eremitic community, who also guided her followers through the transition to cenobitism, Christina perhaps needs to be considered also alongside the eleventh- and twelfth-century hermit-founders who have been studied by Henrietta Leyser.[39] At any rate, she has much in common with the women at Eywood, later Sopwell, or Ralph, the hermit of Moddry (Beds.) – probably like Christina a visionary – whose hermitage also came into the possession of St Albans in the time of Abbot Geoffrey, when it became the cell of Beadlow. The hermit who, according to Leland, was venerated by the monks of Bushmead (Beds.) as their founder, seems likely to have been Joseph the chaplain, whose hermitage at Coppingford (Hunts.) was granted to the priory in the first half of the thirteenth century. Other hermitages passed into the ownership of monastic houses, perhaps on the death of their occupants – Bodsey (Hunts.) to Ramsey Abbey, Salbourne (Herts.) to distant Stoke by Clare – while others were transferred as going concerns into the control of regular cenobites (Bletsoe Wood, Beds.). Perhaps closest to the degree of leadership that must have been shown by Christina is the example of Simon the hermit of Wellbury (Beds.) who, around the time of Lateran IV (and perhaps as a consequence of its reforms), arranged that, after his death, his hermitage, its endowments and the community of brethren which had gathered about him would be conveyed to the Augustinian priory of Newnham (Beds.). Although the usage is without medieval authority, it would seem to make most sense to designate Christina as a hermit, and this is the description adopted for the *List of Sites*.

In her lifetime, Christina seems to have been difficult to classify. Prelates, fellow-hermits and members of her own family all approached her with a particular set of preconceptions, but came away from the encounter having had those assumptions challenged and in many cases confounded. It is perhaps little wonder that later commentators have struggled to fit her into their conception of the solitary life. While Christina was undoubtedly an extraordinary woman, however, as solitary, visionary and monastic founder she was not unique. What sets her apart from her contemporaries above all is her *Life*, in its richness and often surprising frankness. The challenge she poses for a comprehensive account of hermits and anchorites in England is twofold: first, that the methods of analysis employed by such an account should be sufficiently flexible to incorporate her, in both her extraordinariness and her representativeness; and second, that we do not forget that, behind the names, dates and place-names of the *List of Sites* appended to this essay, there lie another fifty lives of possibly equal richness and complexity that even ultra-violet light will not bring back.

Notes

Research for this essay was begun during my tenure of a Post-Doctoral Fellowship from the British Academy held at St Anne's College, Oxford: my deep gratitude to both. For access to the papers of Miss Clay I am indebted to Bristol University Library. I am also grateful for particular assistance from the staff of the Bedfordshire and Luton Archives and Records Service and Hertfordshire Archives and Local Studies.

1 (London, 1914).
2 *Nova Legenda Anglie*, ed. C. Horstman, 2 vols. (Oxford, 1901), ii. 532–7. For details of the *Gesta*'s complex textual history, see Koopmans, 'The Conclusion', at pp. 668–9; Michelle Still, *The Abbot and the Rule: Religious Life at St Albans, 1290–1349* (Aldershot, 2002), pp. 4–5.
3 Her 'Further Studies on Medieval Recluses', *Journal of the British Archaeological Association*, 3rd ser. 16 (1953), 74–86, which opens with a brief mention of Christina's circle (p. 74), also predates Talbot.
4 Clay, *Hermits and Anchorites*, pp. 20–1. The discussion extends to p. 23.
5 Clay follows Roscarrock, who gives her name as Doet: cf. *Nova Legenda*, ii. 536.
6 *Hermits and Anchorites*, pp. 119–20, 131, 150.
7 Appendix C, on pp. 203–63.
8 J. E. B. Gover, Allen Mawer and F. M. Stenton, *The Place-Names of Hertfordshire*, English Place-Name Society 15 (Cambridge, 1938) (hereafter *PN Herts.*), p. 47.
9 J. Beldam, *The Origin and Use of the Royston Cave* (Royston, 1904), p. 46. Clay assigns the hermit to Cambridgeshire. For further details of the solitaries mentioned in this essay, and bibliographical references for them, see the *List of Sites*.
10 *Contemplation and Action: The Other Monasticism*, The Archaeology of Medieval Britain (Leicester, 1995), pp. 6–7. See also pp. 162, 190. See also Holdsworth, 'Christina of Markyate', pp. 203–4. Holdsworth develops his discussion of liminality in 'Hermits and the Power of the Frontier', *Reading Medieval Studies* 16 (1990), 55–76.

11 These are nos 14, 24, 18 and 6 in Clay's list of Cambridgeshire sites: *Hermits and Anchorites*, pp. 206–7. There was also a hermit at the chapel of St Mary, Duxford, though he is not identified as a bridge-hermit.

12 This may be seen very clearly from the map of Roman roads in Britain given by Christopher Taylor, *Roads and Tracks of Britain* (London, 1979), p. 40. It should also be noted, however, that this is the region which has been most extensively investigated (Taylor, *Roads and Tracks*, p. 50).

13 Taylor, *Roads and Tracks*, pp. 120–1. The site in Cheshunt known only as 'Wogoboliche' could also have lain on or near Ermine Street.

14 *Report on the Manuscripts of Lord Middleton, preserved at Wollaton Hall, Nottinghamshire*, ed. W. H. Stevenson, Historical Manuscripts Commission (Hereford, 1911), p. 357.

15 Guildhall Library, London, Ms 9171/7, ff. 125v–126r. Listed in *Testamentary Records in the Commissory Court of London ... vol. I 1374–1488*, ed. M. Fitch, Index Library 82 (London, 1969), p. 105.

16 *Hermits and Anchorites*, pp. 256–7.

17 For a few examples of endowed reclusoria, see Ann K. Warren, *Anchorites and their Patrons* (Berkeley, 1985), pp. 46–50.

18 *Gesta Abbatum*, i. 80.

19 The headings occur in the body of the text, in red ink, in the hand of the main scribe. See the facsimile inserted as the frontispiece of the first volume of Riley's edition.

20 *Gesta Abbatum*, i. 80–1. See also Elkins, *Holy Women*, p. 47. Something similar happened (this time to a male hermit) under Geoffrey's direction at Moddry (Beds.), as noted by Talbot in the *Life*, p. 29; see further below.

21 See the *List of Sites*, s. v. Sopwell, and Thompson, *Women Religious*, pp. 23–4.

22 See *Gesta Abbatum*, i. 98.

23 Elkins, *Holy Women*, p. 28. There is one possible exception: the use of *inclusa* at *Life*, p. 102 (and *Gesta Abbatum*, i. 98). It would be possible to argue, however, that in context the translation is (*pace* Talbot) most appropriately not 'recluse' but 'enclosed' or even 'locked-up woman'. See further the discussion below of Christina's 'enclosure'.

24 *Hermits and Anchorites*, p. 21.

25 'She lived in great Austeritie with fasting and prayer, sitting 4or yeres vppon a bare stone. But before she came thither ... ' etc. See *Nova Legenda*, ed. Horstman, ii. 535.

26 The ellipsis in Clay's quotation from Roscarrock, tellingly, is its most disorderly element: Edwin 'imparted her case to Radulphe [sic] Archb. of Canterburie, and howe her parentes indeavoured to inforce her: whoe answered, he Could not iudge that Act less then murder.' Clay has, however, briefly told of Christina's difficulties in having her vocation accepted a little earlier in her account.

27 The process is described by Warren, *Anchorites and their Patrons*, pp. 61–76. See also F. D. S. Darwin, *The English Mediaeval Recluse* (London, n. d.), pp. 42–52. For an authoritative fifteenth-century statement of procedure, see William Lyndwood, *Provinciale (seu Constitutiones Angliae)* (Oxford, 1679), III.20.2 at pp. 214–15.

28 *Hermits and Anchorites*, p. 22 and cf. p. 119.

29 See also Wogan-Browne, *Saints' Lives*, pp. 132–3.

30 Similar language is used in the description of Christina's time with Alfwen at Flamstead: e.g. *Necnon in secretissimam amarissimamque cameram ... multo tempore diligenter occultata delituit* (p. 92).

31 P. xiv.

32 *Heremitae solivagi aut Anachoritae conclusi*. Cited by Darwin, *English Mediaeval Recluse*, p. 4.

33 A late-fourteenth–early fifteenth-century example has since come to light. See N. P. Tanner, *The Church in Late Medieval Norwich*, Pontifical Institute of Mediaeval Studies, Studies and Texts 66 (Toronto, 1984), pp. 60 and 202.

34 See *Gesta Abbatum*, i. 101. Christina lives with Roger *in heremo usque ad ejus obitum*, but thereafter the account focuses on her supernatural life of visions and prophecy rather than her material circumstances, until she is safely installed in her priory.

35 As noted by Thompson, *Women Religious*, p. 23, n. 49.

36 See Warren, *Anchorites and their Patrons*, p. 8; Darwin, *English Mediaeval Recluse*, pp. 1–4 (still one of the best discussions), and my 'Langland and Hermits', *Yearbook of Langland Studies* 11 (1997), 67–86 at pp. 71–2.

37 *Magna Vita Sancti Hugonis*, ed. D. L. Douie and D. H. Farmer, Oxford Medieval Texts (Oxford, 1985), ii. 89. I would not now be as quick to reject this woman for inclusion in a list of sites as I was in 'The Hermits and Anchorites of Oxfordshire', *Oxoniensia* 63 (1998), 51–77 at p. 77.

38 That this is commonly done is pointed out by Wogan-Browne, *Saints' Lives*, p. 30 n. 42 (with a slip making Christina foundress of Sopwell rather than Markyate).

39 *Hermits and the New Monasticism* (London, 1984). The *Life*, so far as it goes, is, however, silent on any reforming ambitions Christina may have had; she was, after all, fleeing *to* rather than *from* established Benedictinism.

LIST OF SITES AND HERMITS

On the day of Christina's disappearance, her parents' first instinct is to look for her 'among the recluses of Huntingdon' (*anchoretas Huntendonie*) (*Life*, pp. 94–5). After the death of Christina's beloved Abbot Geoffrey, as Rachel Koopmans notes in 'The Conclusion' (p. 689), he is remembered amongst other things for his supervision of no fewer than twenty-four anchorites. I have not found twenty-four twelfth-century anchorites, nor have I managed to identify a single recluse in the town – or indeed the county – of Huntingdon before the fourteenth century. There is no doubt that this list of sites in Bedfordshire, Hertfordshire and Huntingdonshire is not complete. The traces left by medieval solitaries are as slight archivally as they are architecturally. Sites as extensively recorded as the reclusories at the St Albans churches of St Michael and St Peter are quite exceptional. It is a sobering exercise to run through this List of Sites, noting how many entries rely on the witness of a single source.

Nevertheless, the fifty sites (and four unlocated solitaries in St Albans) listed here represent a considerable advance in our knowledge of the hermits and anchorites of the region since the first edition of Clay's book. She knew of fifteen sites in Bedfordshire, seven in Huntingdonshire and twelve in Hertfordshire: twenty-four in all. I hope that, by the time the second edition of *Hermits and Anchorites* appears, more will have been found again, and thank readers of this essay in advance for any additions and corrections that they may be able to supply.

As far as the hermits and anchorites are concerned, I have simplified Clay's tables. I have omitted columns headed 'Description' and 'Patron' – the first because the information is given just as well under the place-name or the description or both, the second because (with the exception of some anchorites) it is often not relevant or recoverable, and indeed for the majority of sites Clay was forced to leave it empty. County boundaries are those in force prior to 1974; place-names, where identified, are regularized and given in modern spelling. I have kept the classification into hermits (H) and anchorites (A), going wherever possible by the terminology of the documents: H for *heremita*, A for *anachorita, inclusus/a, reclusus/a* and (in late texts) English equivalents. Where the sources permit, I have further distinguished anchorites by gender. Unless marked H (f) – for which, see the discussion above – all hermits are male. The date given for each entry is the date of the first document referring to a solitary at a site. Further dates in this column within an entry indicate a change in occupancy. In the description I give a summary of the document(s) referring to the solitary, and any subsequent references apparently to the same individual. For exceptionally well-documented entries such as the St Albans anchorites, limited space and a reluctance to distort the tables beyond readability have not permitted the recording of every reference. (I hope to return to the St Albans anchorites in a more detailed study of Hertfordshire hermits and anchorites in the future.) For similar reasons, bibliographical references in the tables are by short-title or abbreviation only; full details will be found in the specialized 'Bibliography' at the end of this chapter.

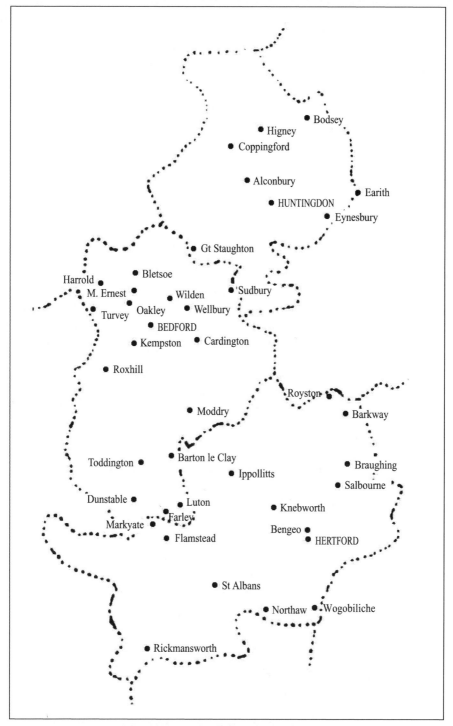

Figure 3 Map showing approximate location of sites.

Table 14.1 Bedfordshire[1]

Barton le Clay	H	1044	Ralph Gerarde held 1 croft at the H/age of Ramsey Abbey at rent of 6d. (*Ramsey Cart.* i.480; for date, see *VCH Beds.* ii.309–10).
Bedford: St Mary's	A (m)	1184–85	Royal grant to A of a penny a day for food plus 32d. for clothing (*PR 31 Hen. II*, p. 130). The next year he received 3s. 10d. before his death (*PR 32 Hen. II*, p. 20).
Bedford	H	1536–37	6d. from H of Bedford among rents of Caldwell in parish of St Peter Dunstable, Bedford (*Court of Augmentations Beds.* i.11; ii.140).
Bletsoe Wood	H	1188x 1212	Grant by Robert de Broi to Br Robert Parage of H/age in wood of Bletsoe and brothers in same of their H/age, land and pasture (*Anc. Deeds*, vi.176).
			Other grants to same, *Anc. Deeds*, i.531, i.561, ii.491, vi.272.
			1219. H/age that Robert Parage holds conveyed by Robert de Broy to Hospital of Holy Trinity outside Northampton (*Feet of Fines Beds.* pp. 55–6).
Cardington	A (f)	1199	Agreement between Wardon and Newnham includes 2 acs at the enclosure ('Ho') of A of Cardington (*Newnham Cart.* pp. 75–6). c. 1180x1206. Grant to Newnham of (*inter alia*) the *curia* which Isabella A held (ibid. pp. 17–18; cf. ibid. p. 25).[2]
Dunstable	A	1222	Simon A translated from Lichfield to Dunstable priory (*Annales Mon.* iii.77). Died 1228 (ibid. iii.109).
Dunstable	H	1442	John Smyth of Toddington bequeathes 12d. to H of Dunstable, and 2d. for making of his well (Linc. Reg. Alnwick, f. 38r; *Early Lincoln Wills*, p. 172).
Farley	H	1431	H/age robbed; relics of St Luke stolen (*Amundesham*, i.59).[3]
Harrold	H	1467–68	H/age held at rent of 4d. by prioress of Harrold (*Grey of Ruthin Valor*, p. 81).
Kempston	A	1242	Br Walter, chaplain, presented to *inclusorium* by Elstow Abbey and enclosed therein; the Abbey to find his food and clothing (*Reg. Grosseteste*, p. 320).
Luton	H	1382	Grant to John the brother H, prior of hospital of St Mary Magdalene and his brethren (Beds. Archives DW 12).
		1552	Grant of messuage called 'le armytage', or free chapel with H/age adjoining (Beds. Archives, DW 8).
Milton Earnest	H	c.1227	Land at head of 'Cestreleye' is nr H/age (*Newnham Cart.* p. 208).
			1271. H/age and grange belong to Caldwell Priory (*Beds. Coroners' Rolls*, pp. 15–6).
Moddry (in Clophill)	H	–1146	H/age and church of B.V.M. built by Ralph H granted by Robert d'Albini to St Albans, becoming site of cell of Beadlow (*VCH Beds.* i.351; Dugdale, *Monasticon*, iii.276).
			May be same as Ralph de Nuers, formerly a professed monk of Lichfield, who lived solitary life in Moddry Wood and had vision of St Cuthbert ('Cuthbertus', pp. 84–5).

242

Oakley	H	1339	Brother of John chaplain of H/age murdered (*VCH Beds*. iii.141–2).
Roxhill	H	–1205	Grant to Newnham Priory of land held by William *heremarus* (*Newnham Cart*. pp. 229–30).
Sudbury	H	1227	John son of Hermite among defendants found to have disseised plaintiffs of tenement (*Bedford Eyre*, p. 35).
		1231	Elyas de Mundavilla bequeathes 2s. 8d. to H of Sudbury ('Huntingdon Cart.' p. 265).
		1254	Raymond chaplain presented by Roger de Sudbury to H/age of Sudbury and instituted therein (*Reg Grosseteste*, p. 299).[4]
Toddington	H	1200x 1230	H/age in abuttals of grants to Dunstable Priory (*Dunstable Cart*. pp. 194; 217).[5]
Turvey	H	1405	Indulgence for repair of chapel, bridge and causeway and John Combes H, good for 1 yr (*EDR 1900*, p. 217). Similar indulgence 1408 (*EDR 1901*, p. 75).
Wellbury	H	s. xiii[6] [1]	Grant by Br Simon H of Wellbury to Newnham Priory of his H/age and its endowments and of the brethren there received by him, he to retain custody of them for life (*Newnham Cart*. p. 196). Newnham cartulary records numerous grants to H/age of B.V.M. and/or Simon H, *c*. 1197–*c*. 1227 (*Newnham Cart*. s.v. Wellbury).
Wilden	A (f)	1194	Fixed alms of 6d. from farm of Wilden which was Robert of St Remigio's (*PR 7 Ric. I*, p. 36).

Rejected: Bushmead: the H who, according to Leland, was venerated as founder was almost certainly the H of Coppingford, Hunts. See *VCH Beds*. i.385.

For Markyate see Herts.

Newnham Priory, in or near: this is Wellbury.

Notes

1 Cardington, Wilden, Welbury, Milton, Sudbury, Bletsoe, Luton, Barton, Dunstable, Moddry, and the rejected Bushmead and Markyate are noted in Godber, *Bedfordshire*, pp. 41-3. Bletsoe, Moddry, Farley, Milton Ernest, Oakley, Turvey, plus Bushmead and Markyate are noted by Owen, 'Beds Chapelries'.

2 It is not clear whether Isabella is to be identified with the A mentioned in 1199.

3 This may be the site of the hospital of the order of St William in the Desert, presumably abandoned since the suppression of the alien houses in 1414. See *VCH Beds*. i.400; Knowles and Hadcock, *Medieval Religious Houses*, p. 359.

4 The registers of the bishops of Lincoln contain numerous subsequent institutions to Sudbury, but not apparently as a H/age; none of the men presented were Hs.

5 Fowler suggests that 'it is probable, though not proved, that at an early date it was held by "Patric the priest"' (*Dunstable Cart*. p. 333), but his evidence is not compelling.

Table 14.2 Hertfordshire

Barkway	H	s. xvi	1550. Late chapel or H/age with a garden or plot of land of ½ ac. in grant of lands to Robert Chester, king's servant (*Pat. 1550–1553*, p. 29).[1]
Bengeo: St Leonard's	A	?	Traces of penthouse cell on N side of chancel: opening 120cm. x 50cm. approx., recess of similar size and two holes for roof timbers (Micklethwaite, 'Remains').
Braughing	A (f)	s. xii[ex]	A has vision of Robert, subprior of Holy Trinity Aldgate, deceased (Lambeth Palace Library MS 51, ff. 124rb–124va).
Flamstead	A (f)	s. xii[1]	Alfwen, recluse connected with Roger, with whom Christina of Markyate took refuge, *c.* 1115–18 (*Life*, p. 14 and *passim*).
		s. xii[med]	Grant by founder Roger de Tony to Flamstead Priory includes the land which belonged to the recluse of Flamstead ('Flamstead Cart.', pp. 24–5).
Hertford: hospital of H Trinity?	H	1359	H/age 'of the brother of the Trinity' visited by King John of France (currently captive at Hertford Castle) on Weds. before Easter, where he offered 5 nobles (Andrews, 'John, King of France', pp. 169–70).
[St] Ippollitts	H	s. xvi	1576. H/age and lands called 'Lampelande' in manor of Maden Crofte in hamlet of Goose More in grant of concealed lands (*Pat. 1575–1578*, p. 284).
Knebworth	H	1307	Alexander Heremita assessed at 11d. for the lay subsidy (*Hertfordshire Lay Subsidy Rolls*, p. 82).
Markyate	H	–1122	Roger, monk of St Albans, visionary and mentor of Christina (below), with up to five fellow Hs, incl. Leofric and Azo (*Life*, p. 16 and *passim*).
	H (f)	c. 1118–1555 x 66	Christina of Markyate lived with Roger until his death, viz. c. 1118–22. She returned to Markyate c. 1123, and founded the priory there 1145 (*Life*, pp. 14–15 and *passim*).
			1155. As *Christina de bosco*, granted 50s. in grain (*PR 2–4 Hen. II*, p. 22).
			She was dead by 1166.
Northaw	H	s. xii[1]	Sigar, H connected with St Albans, lived in H/age in a wood (*Gesta Abbatum*, i.105–6).

Rickmansworth	A (f)	1251	Received 13s. 4d. of Queen Eleanor's private gift (PRO E 101/349/8).
Royston[2]	H	–1250	Grant to Royston Hospital of 5s. rent as formerly received from Robert Vintner (not identified as H) for H/age (Palmer, *John Layer*, p. 45; for dating see ibid. p. 35).
		1467	Resolution of dispute between Royston Hospital and Priory over (*inter alia*) H/age (Palmer, *John Layer*, pp. 50–1).
		1506	Churchwardens of Bassingbourne (Cambs.) received 20d. of 'a Hermytt dep(ar)ting at Roiston' (Beldam, *Royston Cave*, p. 46).
St Albans: St Michael's[3]	A (f)	c. 1235	Corrody of St Albans granted to *inclusa* (*Gesta Abbatum*, i.305).
		1416	Bequest to A (Brigg, *Herts. Geneal.* i.64). Another bequest 1421 (ibid. i.67).
		1421	Katherine A received into confraternity of St Albans (*Amundesham*, i.66).
			1424–37. Many bequests to Katherine A, some also to her servants or *consodalibus*, incl. Agnes Vertesans, 1424 (Brigg, *Herts. Geneal.* i.67 and *passim*).
			1437 Will of Katherine Ditton, A of St Albans (ibid. ii.237).
		1445	1445–49. Many bequests to unnamed A (Brigg, *Herts. Geneal.* iii, *passim*), incl. to A of St Michael's and Elizabeth the poor woman there, 1449 (ibid. iii.278).
			1458 Henry VI pays visit and gives generously (BL Cotton Nero D VII, f. 73v).
			1471 Bequest to A (*St Albans Wills*, p. 1).
		1472	Bequest to Agnes Vertesawce A (PRO PROB 11/6, ff. 41r-v). Further bequest to A 1473 (*St Albans Wills*, p. 21).
		1483	Next vacancy of house of A adjoining St Michael's currently held by Dame Margaret Smythe granted to Simon Appulby (*Whethamstede*, ii.257–8).[4]
		1485– 1514	Many bequests to unnamed A (*St Albans Wills*, HALS 2AR, *passim*). 1503 Received 26s. 8d. of Queen Elizabeth's private gift (*Privy Purse Expenses*, p. 102).

	A (m)	1531	Bequest to 'the Ancur of saint Myghellis to syng a trentall for my soule & all cristen soules' (HALS 2AR, f. 215v).
St Albans: St Peter's	A (f)	1235x 1258	A has vision warning of impending famine (*Gesta Abbatum*, i.388–9).
		1412	Alice received by proxy into confraternity of St Albans Abbey (BL Cotton Nero D VII, f. 139r).
			1424–49 Many bequests (Brigg, *Herts. Geneal. passim*)
			1426 Bequest of Thomas Beaufort, Duke of Exeter (*Royal Wills*, p. 250).
			1458 Henry VI pays visit and gives generously (BL Cotton Nero D VII, f. 73v).
	A (m)	1471–76	Many bequests to 'anachorite' (sometimes opposed to 'anachorisse' of St Michael), incl. for a trental (*St Albans Wills, passim*; PRO PROB 11/6, ff. 41r–v).
	A (f)	1479	Admission by abbot of St Albans of Katherine Holsted, widow, as A, at instance of king, queen, *et al.* (*Whethamstede*, ii.202).
			1486–1528 Many bequests and gifts (*St Albans Wills, passim*; Dugdale, *Monasticon*, iii.360; *Privy Purse Expenses*, p. 1; HALS 2AR, *passim*; *Beds Wills 1383–1548*, p. 111.
St Albans: St German's chapel	H	s. ix	Ulf (Wulfa), prior of St Albans, built chapel on supposed site of St German's dwelling, and of discovery of St Alban's body (*VCH Herts.* iv.369).
		s. ix	Succeeded by Eadfrith, who resigned his office of abbot to retire here (ibid.).
	A (m)	–1428	Thomas Fishbourne lived as A before his election as Confessor General of Syon Abbey (*Amundesham*, i.27–8).[5]
St Albans: St Mary Magdalene's chapel[6]	A	1484	A of 'Mawdelens' left 12d. by Agnes Mayr (*St Albans Wills*, p. 70).
	H	1530	Bequest to Sir Nicholas Insley H for a trental (*VCH Herts.* ii.401).
St Albans: Eywood (Sopwell)	H (f)	–1140	Grant by Henry de Albini to handmaidens (*ancillis*) and servants (*servis*) of God at the cell which Br Roger the solitary rebuilt (Dugdale, *Monasticon*, iii.365).

		−1140	Abbot Geoffrey regularized the life of two *sanctae mulieres* living the ascetic life in a hut in Eywood, thereby founding Sopwell O.S.B. (*Gesta Abbatum*, i.80–1).[7]
St Albans: beyond Sopwell mill	H	1489	John Ferrers bequeathes 12d. to the H who lives beyond Sopwelmyll (*St Albans Wills*, pp. 94–5).
St Albans: unlocated	A (f)	?s. xii	Obit of Matilda anachorita in St Albans Book of Benefactors (BL Cotton Nero D VII, f. 123r).
St Albans: unlocated	H	?s. xii	Obit of Ailwardus H in St Albans Psalter and Book of Benefactors (BL Cotton Nero D VII, f. 72v; *Life*, p. 24 n. 1).
St Albans: unlocated	H	1499	Thomas Ale H died intestate (*St Albans Wills*, p. 163).
St Albans: unlocated	A	1509	Bequest of Lady Margaret Beaufort to A of St Albans (*Collegium, Divi Johannis Evangelistae*, p. 121).
St Albans: unlocated[8]	A (f)	1523	4d. paid by John Levissey, servant to Sir Henry Willughby, kt, 'in rayward to the ancres of Sent Talbonse' (Stevenson, *Manuscripts of Lord Middleton*, p. 357).
Salbourne (in Standon)[9]	H	−1178	Grant by Richard de Clare Earl of Hertford to H and brothers of Salbourne (BL MS Add. 6041, f. 73r).
		1173x 1178	Grant by Richard Earl of Clare to Priory of Stoke by Clare (Suffolk) of H/age built by William *inclusus*. Abandoned by Stoke by s. xivl (*VCH Herts*. iv.421–2).
		1185x 1264	Papal confirmation of grants to Richard le H (BL MS Add. 6041, f. 73r, noted *VCH Herts*. iv.422).[10]
		1357	Br John H in manor court for debt (PRO SC 2/178/44, m. 7r; noted *VCH Herts*. iv.422).
		1398	Grant of H/age (now a royal free chapel) to John Benewell H (*Pat. 1396–1399*, p. 416).
'Wogoboliche' (in Cheshunt)	H	1156x 1158	Grant by Conan earl of Richmond to the church and brethren of St John Baptist (unidentified) of the H/age of Wogobiliche in wood of Cheshunt (*Early Yorkshire Charters IV*, pp. 40–1).
'between Arrington & Royston'[11]	H	1401	Indulgence for repair of road and William Brown, poor H there (EDR 1900, p. 160).

'between Barkway & Ware'[12]	H	1520	Sir Thomas Lestrange en route to London gave 1d. to a H 'betwyx Barkwaye and Ware' (Gurney, 'Household and Privy Purse Accounts', p. 432).

Rejected:

Watford: Katherine Talemache A of s. xiv[med] (*VCH Herts*. ii.466) is Watford (Northants.).

Hitchin: 'The Hermitage' in Bancroft is a much -altered 'building of irregular plan which incorporates a large barn, probably of the 16th century' (*RCHME Herts*. p. 123). I have found nothing to place a medieval hermit here.

Radwell: alms to recluse of Radeswella (1st edn. no. 5). This is Ridgewell (Essex). See *PN Essex*, p. 453, and cf. *PN Herts*. p. 160.

Rowney: Thompson speculates on possible eremitic origins and links to 'Wogobiliche' (*Women Religious*, pp. 27–8), but the evidence is slight.

Notes

1 This could be the same as Royston, below, but is perhaps a site at Newsells, par. Barkway; see Beamon, *Royston Cave*, pp. 68–70.

2 This site may, but need not, be *Royston Cave*, a man-made subterranean structure whose origins and later use have been controversial since its rediscovery in 1742. See most recently Beamon, Royston Cave, who notes these references but disputes Palmer's identification of the H/age with the Cave (p. 63). It is also not certain that the three references are to the same site (cf. Barkway, above).

3 There are a number of unusual features in the exterior of the S wall of the chancel (low side window, tomb recess, coffin lid and small, locker-like recess), some or all of which may be connected with the A (*VCH Herts*. ii. 403).

4 Appulby in fact went to Allhallows in London Wall. See Clay, 'Further Studies', pp. 82–4.

5 The same account also states that, temp. Abbot William [Heyworth] (1401–20), *Hic ... domum reclusae fieri ordinavit* (ibid.), but the reference of hic is vague. There is no record of another reclusory in St Albans; it is possible that Fishbourne was the (re)founder of either St Michael's or St Peter's.

6 Susan Flood identifies the chapel of St Mary Magdalene as the home of the A of St Michael's (*St Albans Wills*, p. 14 n. and p. 73 n.). But the description of her house given in 1483 (*aedificatam et annexam Ecclesiae Sancti Michaelis – Whethamstede*, ii. 257) and the remains at St Michael's suggest otherwise; the 1531 bequest noted here is 'to the heremyte of saint Mary Magdalens & to the Ancur of saint Myghellis', which would seem to confirm that the two sites are distinct.

7 These may be the Avicia and Adelaisa whose obits are recorded in the St Albans Psalter. See, *Life*, p. 24 n. 1. These two records of the prehistory of Sopwell are not easy to reconcile with each other, and the origins of the priory remain obscure.

8 Since the anchorite at St Michael's in 1531 (and for an unknown period before) was male, the reference here to the anchoress of St Albans may perhaps be taken to indicate St Peter's. But the donor's local knowledge may have been limited, and the identification is not certain.

9 'The cottage called the Hermitage at Old Hall Green, now belonging to [St Edmund's College], may mark the site of the original hermitage, local tradition having preserved the name' (*VCH Herts*. iii.351).

10 The pope is Urban. Given the C14th date of the cartulary, this is likely to be either Urban III (1185–7) or IV (1261–4).

11 The road is Ermine Street. Arrington is in Cambs., as is almost all of this stretch of road.

12 A possible identification would be the chapel of All Saints Puckeridge, which by this date was associated with the H/age of Salbourne. Puckeridge is approximately halfway between Barkway and Ware; 'the exact site of this chapel is not known, but it was situated on the main road' (*VCH Herts*. iii.352).

Table 14.3 Huntingdonshire

Alconbury Weston	H	1325	H/age among lands of Segrave family. Location perhaps a moated site in Hermitage Wood (*Cal. Inq. VI*, p. 428; *VCH Hunts.* iii.4–5; *PN Beds. & Hunts.* p. 250).
Bodsey	H	–1231	Grants of H/age to Ramsey Abbey (*Ramsey Cart.* i.87; ii.221). Bodsey House retains some C13th. features (Haigh, *Relig. Houses Cambs.* pp. 72–3).
Coppingford	H	1225x 33	Grant to Bushmead Priory (Beds.) of H/age with chapel, buildings, etc. which Joseph the chaplain (probably first prior of Bushmead) had (*Bushmead Cart.* pp. 202–3).
Earith[1]	H	1397	Indulgence for Richard de Grymston H in repairing Earith causeway (*Ely DR 1900*, p. 117).
		1401	Indulgence for Earith causeway and Henry Bourne, H there (*Ely DR 1900*, p. 160).
		1491	Profession of John Thomson, H of Earith causeway; indulgence for same (*Ely DR 1908*, pp. 180–1).
Eynesbury	H	s. viii	St Arnulf lived and died in, and gave his name to, Eynesbury (Farmer, *Oxford Dictionary of Saints*, s.n.; Gorham, *Eynesbury*, pp. 16–19).
Higney Island	H	–1147	Grant to Edwin *domno* and Gilbert *Socius* his deputy of site of their H/age (*Ramsey Cart.* i.159). Edwin later in boundary dispute with Sawtry Abbey (*Ramsey Cart.* i.162; Ladds, 'Sawtry', pp. 356–62).[2]
Huntingdon: Holy Trinity	A (f)	1312	Indulgence for contributors to Alice, A in a place adjoining church (Linc. Reg. Dalderby, f. 258r).
		1319	Similar indulgence for Sara A (Linc. Reg. Dalderby, f. 403v).
Huntingdon: St John Baptist	A (f)	1346	Bp inquires into conduct of Maud de Algarkirk A for introduction of suspect doctrines; outcome unknown (Linc. Reg. Bek, f. 84r; *VCH Hunts.* i.361).
Huntingdon: SS Anne & Clement	H	1399	Licence to William H of Huntingdon to celebrate divine service in chapel (Linc. Reg. Beaufort, f. 23r).
Great Staughton	H	–1220	Land held by H alleged to have been seized after his death (*CRR*, ix.358). Rectory Farm was formerly known as the H/age (Watson, 'Great Staughton', p. 39).[3]

Rejected:	Godmanchester: some traditions put St Tibba here, but Ryhall (Rutland) seems the stronger candidate.

Notes

1 *VCH Hunts.* concludes from the indulgence for John Spenser given there that Earith causeway was entirely maintained by the Hs of Haddenham (ii.153 n. 9). This is not necessarily the case. It should be noted that the old river crossing in Earith is known as Armitage or Hermitage (*PN Beds* & *Hunts.* 205); see also Haigh, *Relig. Houses Cambs.*, p. 22.

2 Talbot identifies this as the hermit Edwin, the cousin of Roger, and helper of Christina of Markyate (*Life*, pp. 16, 80–1).

3 *CRR* identifies the 'Stocton' where the H held land as Little Staughton, a few miles away but in Beds. (one of the defendants was the archdeacon of Bedford). That a H based at Great Staughton would hold land in the neighbouring parish does not seem improbable. Above all, this is perhaps further evidence that Hs were no great respecters of county boundaries.

BIBLIOGRAPHY

Manuscripts

Bedfordshire Archives DW 8, 12, 14, 15
Hertfordshire Archives and Local Studies, 2AR
Linc. Reg. Dalderby; Lincolnshire Archives Office, Episcopal Register II
Linc. Reg. Bek: Lincolnshire Archives Office, Episcopal Register VII
Linc. Reg. Beaufort: Lincolnshire Archives Office, Episcopal Register XIII
Linc. Reg. Alnwick: Lincolnshire Archives Office, Episcopal Register XVIII
London, Guildhall Library, MS 9171/7
London, BL, MS Cotton Nero D VII
——, MS Add. 6041
London, Lambeth Palace Library, MS 51
Public Record Office, E 101/349/8
——, PROB 11/6
——, SC 2/178/44

Primary works

Amundesham: Annales monasterii S. Albani a Johanne Amundesham, ed. H. T. Riley, Chronica Monasterii S. Albani V, RS, 2 vols. (London, 1870–71).

Anc. Deeds: A Description Catalogue of Ancient Deeds in the Public Record Office, ed. H. C. Maxwell-Lyte, 6 vols. (London, 1890–1915).

Annales Mon Dunstable: Annales Prioratus de Dunstaplia, Annales Monasteri de Bermundeseia, ed. H. R. Luard, Annales Monastici, iii, RS (London, 1866).

Bedford Eyre: Roll of the Justices in Eyre at Bedford, 1277, ed. G.H. Fowler, Bedfordshire Historical Record Society 3 (1916).

Bedfordshire Coroners' Rolls, ed. R. F. Hunnisett, Bedfordshire Historical Record Society 41 (1961).

Bedfordshire Wills Proved in the Prerogative Court of Canterbury 1383–1548, ed. M. McGregor, Bedfordshire Historical Record Society 58 (1979).

Bushmead Cartulary, ed. G. H. Fowler and J. Godber, Bedfordshire Historical Record Society 22 (1945).

Cal. Inq. VI: Calendar of Inquisitions Post Mortem ... vol. VI. Edward II (Hereford, 1910).

Court of Augmentations Accounts for Bedfordshire, ed. Y. Nicholls, 2 vols., Bedfordshire Historical Record Society 63–4 (1984–85).

Curia Regis Rolls Richard I to Henry III, 19 vols. (London, 1923–2002).

'Cuthbertus, Episcopus Lindisfarnensis' in *Miscellanea Biographica*, ed. J. Raine, Surtees Society 8 (1838).

Dunstable Cart: A Digest of the Charters Preserved in the Cartulary of the Priory of Dunstable, ed. G. H. Fowler, 2 vols., Bedfordshire Historical Record Society 10 (1926).

Early Lincoln Wills, ed. A. W. Gibbons (Lincoln, 1888).

Early Yorkshire Charters, vol. IV, ed. C. T. Clay, Yorkshire Archaeological Society Record Series, Extra Series 1 (Wakefield, 1935).

Ely DR: The Ely Diocesan Remembrancer (Cambridge, 1885–1915).

Feet of Fines Beds: Calendar of the Feet of Fines for Bedfordshire ... of the Reigns of Richard I, John, and Henry III, ed. G. H. Fowler, 2 vols., Bedfordshire Historical Record Society 6, 12 (1919–28).

'Flamstead Cart': 'The Cartulary of Flamstead Priory', ed. C. Butterill, unpublished MA thesis, University of Manitoba (1988).

Gesta Abbatum Monasterii S. Albani, a Thoma Walsingham, ed. H. T. Riley, Chronica Monasterii S. Albani IV, RS, 3 vols. (London,1867–69).

Grey of Ruthin Valor, ed. R. I. Jack, Bedfordshire Historical Record Society 46 (1965).

Hertfordshire Lay Subsidy Rolls 1307 and 1334, ed. J. Brooker and S. Flood, Hertfordshire Record Publications 14 (1998).

'Huntingdon Cart': 'The Cartulary of the Priory of St. Mary, Huntingdon', ed. W. M. Noble, *Transactions of the Cambridgeshire and Huntingdonshire Archaeological Society* 4 (1930), 89–280.

Newnham Cart: The Cartulary of Newnham Priory, ed. J. Godber, 2 vols., Bedfordshire Historical Record Society 43 (1963).

Pat. 1327–1330: Calendar of the Patent Rolls ... A.D. 1327–1330 (London, 1893).

Pat. 1388–1392: Calendar of the Patent Rolls ... A.D. 1388–1392 (London, 1902).

Pat. 1391–1396: Calendar of the Patent Rolls ... A.D. 1391–1396 (London, 1905).

Pat. 1396–1399: Calendar of the Patent Rolls ... A.D. 1396–1399 (London, 1909).

Pat. 1550–1553: Calendar of the Patent Rolls ... A.D. 1550–1553 (London, 1926).

Pat. 1575–1578: Calendar of the Patent Rolls ... 1575–1578 (London, 1982).

PR 2–4 Hen. II: The Great Roll of the Pipe for the second, third and fourth years of the reign of King Henry the Second, A.D. 1155, 1156, 1157, 1158, Record Commission (London, 1844).

PR 31 Hen. II: The Great Roll of the Pipe ... A.D. 1184–1185, Pipe Roll Society 34 (London, 1913).

PR 32 Hen. II: The Great Roll of the Pipe ... A.D. 1185–1186, Pipe Roll Society 36 (London, 1914).

PR 7 Ric. I: The Great Roll of the Pipe ... Michaelmas 1195, Pipe Roll Society n.s. 6 (London, 1929).

Privy Purse Expenses of Elizabeth of York, ed. N. H. Nicolas (London, 1830).

Ramsey Cart: Cartularium Monasterii de Rameseia, ed. W. H. Hart and P. A. Lyons, 3 vols., RS (London, 1884–93).

Reg Grosseteste: Rotuli Roberti Grosseteste, episcopi Lincolniensis, 1235–1253 necnon rotulus Henrici de Lexington, episcopi Lincolniensis, 1254–1259, ed. F. N. Davis, *Lincoln Record Society* 11 (1914).

Royal Wills: A collection of all the wills known to be extant of the Kings and Queens of England etc., ed. J. G. Nichols (London, 1780; repr. New York, 1969).

St Albans Wills 1471–1500, ed. Susan Flood, Hertfordshire Record Publications 9 (1993).

Magna Vita Sancti Hugonis, ed. D. L. Douie and D. H. Farmer, OMT (Oxford, 1985).

Whethamstede: Registra quorundam abbatum monasterii S. Albani, qui saeculo XV^{mo} floruere, ed. H. T. Riley, *Chronica monasterii S. Albani* VI, RS, 2 vols. (London, 1872–73).

Secondary works

Andrews, H. C., 'John, King of France: A prisoner at Hertford Castle', *Transactions of the East Hertfordshire Archaeological Society* 6 (1916–18), 160–79.

Beamon, S. P., *The Royston Cave: Used by Saints or Sinners?* (Baldock, 1992).

Beldam, J., *The Origin and Use of the Royston Cave* (Royston, 1858).

Collegium, Divi Johannis Evangelistae (Cambridge, 1911).

Dugdale, W. *et al.* (eds), *Monasticon Anglicanum*, 6 vols. in 8 (1655–1723, repr. Farnborough, 1970).

Gorham, G. C., *History and Antiquities of Eynesbury and St. Neot's*, 2 vols. (London, 1820–24).

Gurney, D., 'Extracts form the Household and Privy Purse Accounts of the Lestranges of Hunstanton, from AD 1519 to AD 1578', *Archaeologia* 25, 411–569.

Haigh, D., *The Religious Houses of Cambridgeshire* (Cambridge, 1988).

The Herts Genealogist and Antiquary, ed. W. Brigg, vols. 1–3 (all published) (Harpenden, 1895–99).

Ladds, S. Inskip, 'Sawtry Abbey, Hunts', *Transactions of the Cambridgeshire and Huntingdonshire Archaeological Society* 3 (1909–14), 295–322; 339–74.

Lyndwood, William, *Provinciale (seu Constitutiones Angliae)* (Oxford, 1679).

Micklethwaite, J. T., 'On the remains of an anker-hold at Bengeo Church, Hertford', *Archaeological Journal* 44 (1887), 26–9.

Owen, Dorothy, 'Bedfordshire Chapelries: an essay in rural settlement history' in *Worthington George Smith and Other Studies presented to Joyce Godber*, Bedfordshire Historical Record 57 (1978), 9–20.

Palmer, W. M., *John Layer (1586–1640) of Shepreth, Cambridgeshire: A Seventeenth-Century Local Historian*, Publications of the Cambridge Antiquarian Society, octavo series 53 (Cambridge, 1935).

PN Beds & Hunts: The Place-Names of Bedfordshire & Huntingdonshire, ed. A. Mawer and F.M. Stenton, English Place-Name Society 3 (Cambridge, 1926).

PN Essex: The Place-Names of Essex, ed. P. H. Reany, English Place-Name Society 12 (Cambridge, 1935).

PN Herts: The Place-Names of Hertfordshire, ed. J. E. B. Grover, Allen Mawer and F. M. Stenton, English Place-Name Society 15 (Cambridge, 1938).

Report on the Manuscripts of Lord Middleton, preserved at Wollaton Hall, Nottinghamshire, ed. W. H. Stevenson, Historical Manuscripts Commission (London, 1911).

RCHME Herts.: Hertfordshire: An Inventory of the Historical Monuments in Hertfordshire, Royal Commission on Historical Monuments England (London, 1911).

Testamentary Records in the Commissory Court of London … vol. I, 1374–1488, ed. M. Fitch, Index Library 82 (London, 1969).

VCH Beds: The Victoria History of the County of Bedford, ed. H. Arthur Doubleday and William Page, 5 vols. (London, 1904–20).

VCH Herts: The Victoria History of the County of Hertford, ed. William Page, 6 vols. (London, 1902–14).

VCH Hunts: The Victoria History of the County of Huntingdon, ed. William Page, Granville Proby and H. E. Norris, 4 vols. (London, 1926–38).

Watson, H. G., 'Great Staughton, Hunts.', *Transactions of the Cambridgeshire and Huntingdonshire Archaeological Society* 3 (1909–14), 23–42.

SELECT BIBLIOGRAPHY

Primary texts

Abelard and Heloise. 'The Personal Letters Between Abelard and Heloise', ed. J. T. Muckle *Mediaeval Studies* 15 (1953), 47–94.

——, 'The Letter of Heloise on the Religious Life and Abelard's First Reply', ed. J. T. Muckle, *Mediaeval Studies* 17 (1955), 240–81.

——, Mews, Constant J., *The Lost Love Letters of Abelard and Heloise* (New York, 1999).

——, *The Letters of Abelard and Heloise*, trans. Betty Radice, rev. M. T. Clanchy (London, 2003).

Ælfric's Lives of Saints, ed. and trans. W. W. Skeat, 4 vols. rpt. in 2, EETS OS 76, 82, 94, 114 (1881–1900; 1966).

Aelred of Rievaulx, *De institutione inclusarum*, in *Opera omnia*, ed. A. Hoste and C. H. Talbot, CCCM 1 (Turnhout, 1971).

——, *A Rule of Life of a Recluse*, trans. Mary Paul Macpherson, in *Treatises and the Pastoral Prayer*, Cistercian Fathers series 2 (Kalamazoo, Mich., 1972).

The St Albans Psalter (Albani Psalter), ed. Otto Pächt, C. R. Dodwell and Francis Wormald, Studies of the Warburg Institute (London, 1960).

——, <http://www.abdn.ac.uk/stalbanspsalter> [accessed 4 June 2004].

Aldhelm, *Aldhelmi Opera*, ed. Rudolph Ehwald, MGH AA 15 (Berlin, 1913–19).

——, *Aldhelm: The Prose Works*, trans. Michael Lapidge and Michael Herren (Cambridge, 1979).

——, *Aldhelm: The Poetic Works*, trans. Michael Lapidge and James L. Rosier (Cambridge, 1985).

Alexis, St. *La Vie de Saint Alexis*, ed. Maurizio Perugi, Textes littéraires français (Geneva, 2000).

——, for further references, see Louk J. Engels, 'The West European Alexius' in *The Invention of Saintliness*, ed. Mulder-Bakker, pp. 93–144.

Ancrene Wisse, ed. Robert Hasenfratz (Kalamazoo, Mich., 2000).

Andreas Capellanus, *On Love*, ed. and trans. P. G. Walsh (London, 1982).

'Anglo-Norman Rules for the Priories of St Mary de Pré and Sopwell', ed. Tony Hunt, in *De Mot en mot: Aspects of Medieval Linguistics. Essays in Honour of William Rothwell*, ed. Stewart Gregory and D. A. Trotter (Cardiff, 1997), pp. 93–104.

The Anglo-Saxon Chronicle, ed. and trans. M. Swanton (London, 1996).

S. Anselmi Opera omnia, ed. F. S. Schmitt, 6 vols. (Edinburgh, 1946–61).

Athanasius, St., *Life of St Antony*, trans. Evagrius, *PL* 73, cols. 125–70.

——, in *Early Christian Lives*, trans. Carolinne White (London, 1998).

Carmina Burana: Die Lieder der Benediktbeurer Handschrift: Zweisprachige Ausgabe, ed. A. Hilka, O. Schumann and B. Bischoff, trans. C. Fisher and H. Kuhn (Munich, 1979).

Cassian, John, *Conférences*, ed. and trans. E. Pichery, Sources chrétiennes 42 (Paris, 1955).

K[C]atherine of Alexandria. 'Les Vies de sainte Catherine d'Alexandrie en ancien français,' ed. E. C. Fawtier-Jones, *Romania* 56 (1930), 80–104.

The Life of Christina of Markyate: A Twelfth Century Recluse, ed. and trans. C. H. Talbot (Oxford, 1959; rpt. 1987).

Councils and Synods, with Other Documents Relating to the English Church, 871–1204: Part I, 871–1066, ed. Dorothy Whitelock, M. Brett and C. N. L. Brooke, 2 vols., 2nd edn., (Oxford, 1981).

Dugdale, W. *et al.*, *Monasticon Anglicanum*, 6 vols. in 8 (1655–1723, rpt. Farnborough, 1970).

Early Christian Lives, trans. Carolinne White (London, 1998).

English Historical Documents c. 500–1042, ed. Dorothy Whitelock, 2nd edn. (London, 1996).

Geoffrey of Burton, *Life and Miracles of St Modwenna*, ed. and trans. Robert Bartlett, OMT (Oxford, 2002).

Gesta Abbatum Monasterii S. Albani, a Thoma Walsingham, ed. H. T. Riley, 3 vols., RS 28 (London,1867–69).

Gilbert of Sempringham. *The Book of St. Gilbert*, ed. Raymonde Foreville and Gillian Keir, OMT (Oxford, 1987).

Goscelin of St Bertin, *Liber confortatorius of Goscelin of St Bertin*, ed. C. H. Talbot, Analecta monastica, ser. 3, *Studia Anselmiana* 37 (Rome, 1955), 1–117.

——, *Writing the Wilton Women: Goscelin's Legend of Edith and Liber Confortatorius*, ed. Stephanie Hollis, forthcoming.

Gui de Warewic, ed. Alfred Ewert, Classiques français du moyen âge, 2 vols. (Paris, 1932–33).

Hali Meiðhad, ed. Bella Millett, EETS OS 284 (Oxford, 1982).

Historia monachorum in Aegypto, ed. Norman Russell, Cistercian Studies 34 (London, 1981).

——, trans. Norman Russell, *The Lives of the Desert Fathers* (London, 1980).

The Romance of Horn, by Thomas, ed. Mildred K. Pope, ANTS 9–10 (Oxford, 1955), revised and completed T. B. W. Reid, ibid., 12–13 (Oxford, 1964).

Jacobus of Voragine, *Golden Legend*, trans. William Granger Ryan, 2 vols. (Princeton, 1993).

Jerome, *Epistulae*, ed. I. Hilberg, CSEL 54 (Vienna, 1996).

——, trans. W. H. Fremantle, *St. Jerome: Letters and Select Works*, Library of Nicene and Post-Nicene Fathers of the Church, 2nd ser., vi (Oxford and New York, 1893).

——, *Vita Pauli, PL* 23, cols. 17–28.

——, in *Early Christian Lives*, trans. White (London, 1998).

——, *Vita Hilarionis, PL* 23, cols. 29–54.

——, in *Early Christian Lives*, trans. White (London, 1998).

The Book of Margery Kempe, ed. S. B. Meech and H. E. Allen, EETS OS 212 (London, 1940).

Le Mystère d'Adam: (Ordo representacionis Adè), ed. Paul Aebischer, Textes littéraires français (Geneva and Paris, 1963, rpt. 1964).

Nova Legenda Anglie, ed. C. Horstman, 2 vols. (Oxford, 1901).

(*Old English Martyrology*) *Das altenglische Martyrologium*, ed. Günter Kotzor, 2 vols. (Munich. 1981).

Orderic Vitalis, *The Ecclesiastical History*, ed. and trans. Marjorie Chibnall, 6 vols., OMT (Oxford, 1968–80).

Sir Orfeo, ed. A. J. Bliss, 2nd edn. (1966; rpt. Oxford, 1971).

Palladius, *Die Lateneinische Ubersetzung der Historia Lausiaca des Palladius*, ed. Adelheid Well-hausen, Patristische Texte und Studien 51 (Berlin, 2003).

The Peterborough Chronicle 1070–1154, ed. Cecily Clark, 2nd edn. (Oxford, 1970).

Rufinus, *Historia monachorum sive de Vita Sanctorum Patrum*, ed. Eva Schuz-Flügel, Patristische Texte und Studien 34 (Berlin, 1990).

Le Folie Tristan d'Oxford, ed. E. Hoepffner (Paris, 1943).

Venantius Fortunatus, *De Vita Sanctae Radegundis*, ed. Bruno Krusch, *MGH SRM* (Hanover, 1984), ii. 358–95.

——, in *Sainted Women of the Dark Ages*, trans. Jo Ann McNamara, John E. Halborg and E. Gordon Whately (Durham, 1992), 70–105.

Verba seniorum, PL 73, cols. 855–1022.

——, *The Desert Fathers: Sayings of the Early Christian Monks*, trans. Benedicta Ward (London, 2003).

Virgin Lives and Holy Deaths: Two Exemplary Biographies for Anglo-Norman Women, ed. and trans. Jocelyn Wogan-Browne and Glyn S. Burgess (London, 1996).

William of Malmesbury, *De Gestis Pontificum Anglorum*, ed. N. E. S. A. Hamilton, RS 52 (London, 1870).

Secondary texts

Altman, Charles, 'Two Types of Opposition and the Structure of Latin Saints' Lives', *Medievalia et Humanistica* 6, ed. Paul Clogan (Cambridge, 1975), 1–11.

Auerbach, Erich, *Mimesis: The Representation of Reality in Western Literature*, trans. W. R. Trask (Princeton, 1953).

Bartlett, Robert, 'The Hagiography of Angevin England', in *Thirteenth Century England V*, ed. P. R. Coss and S. D. Lloyd (Woodbridge, 1995), 37–52.

Belief and Culture in the Middle Ages: Studies Presented to Henry Mayr-Harting, ed. Richard Gameson and Henrietta Leyser (Oxford, 2001).

Brooke, Christopher N. L., *The Medieval Idea of Marriage* (Oxford, 1989).

Brown, Peter, *The Body and Society: Men, Women, and Sexual Renunciation in Early Christianity* (New York, 1988).

Brundage, James, *Law, Sex, and Christian Society in Medieval Europe* (Chicago, 1987).

Bugge, John, *Virginitas, An Essay in the History of a Medieval Ideal*, International Archives of the History of Ideas, series minor 17 (The Hague, 1975).

Bullington, Rachel, *The Alexis in the St Albans Psalter: A Look into the Heart of the Matter* (New York, 1991).

Bynum, C. W., *Holy Feast and Holy Fast: The Religious Significance of Food to Medieval Women* (Berkeley, 1987).

Carrasco, M. E., 'The Imagery of the Magdalen in Christina of Markyate's Psalter (The St Albans Psalter)', *Gesta* 37 (1999), 67–80.

Cartlidge, Neil, *Medieval Marriage: Literary Approaches 1100–1300* (Cambridge, 1997).

Caviness, M. H., 'Anchoress, Abbess, Queen: Donors and Patrons or Intercessors and Matrons?', in *The Cultural Patronage of Medieval Women*, ed. June Hall McCash (Athens, Georgia, 1996), 105–53.

Clanchy, M. T., *Abelard: A Medieval Life* (Oxford, 1997).

Clay, R. M., *The Hermits and Anchorites of England* (London, 1914).

Clayton, Mary, 'Hermits and the Contemplative Life in Anglo-Saxon England', in *Holy Men and Holy Women: Old English Prose Saints' Lives and their Contexts*, ed. Paul Szarmach, (Albany, NY, 1996), 147–75.

Clopper, Lawrence M., *Drama, Play and Game: English Festive Culture in the Medieval and Early Modern Period* (Chicago and London, 2001).

Dalarun, Jacques, *Robert d'Arbrissel: fondateur de Fontevraud* (Paris, 1986).

Darwin, F. D. S., *The English Mediaeval Recluse* (London, n. d.).

Dean, Ruth J., with Maureen B. M. Boulton, *Anglo-Norman Literature. A guide to Texts and Manuscripts*, ANTS OPS 3 (London, 1999).

Delehaye, Hippolyte, *Les Passions des martyrs et les genres littéraires*, Subsidia hagiographica 20 (Brussels, 1921; rpt. 1996).

——, *Les Légendes Hagiographiques*, 4th edn. (Brussels, 1955).

Dickson, Morgan, 'Verbal and Visual Disguise: Society and Identity in Some Twelfth-Century Texts', in *Medieval Insular Romance*, ed. Weiss, Fellows and Dickson, 41–54.

Dodwell, C. R., *The Pictorial Arts of the West, 800–1200* (New Haven and London 1993).

Duby, Georges, *The Knight, the Lady, and the Priest: The Making of Modern Marriage in Medieval France*, trans. Barbara Bray (New York, 1983).

Elkins, Sharon K., *Holy Women of Twelfth-Century England* (Chapel Hill, N.C., 1988).

Elliott, Alison Goddard, *Roads to Paradise: Reading the Lives of the Early Saints* (Hanover, NH, 1987).

Elliott, Dyan, *Spiritual Marriage: Sexual Abstinence in Medieval Wedlock* (Princeton, 1993).

——, *Fallen Bodies: Pollution, Sexuality, and Demonology in the Middle Ages* (Philadelphia, 1999).

——, 'Women and Confession: From Empowerment to Pathology', in *Gendering the Master Narrative: Women and Power in the Middle Ages*, ed. Mary Erler and Maryanne Kowaleski (Ithaca, NY, 2003), 31–51.

——, *Proving Woman: Female Spirituality and Inquisitional Culture in the Later Middle Ages* (Princeton, 2004).

Engels, Louk J., 'The West European Alexius Legend: With an Appendix presenting the Medieval Latin Text Corpus in its Context (Alexiana Latina Medii Aevi, I)' in *The Invention of Saintliness*, ed. A. B. Mulder-Bakker (London and New York, 2002), 93–144.

Farmer, Sharon, 'Persuasive Voices: Clerical Images of Medieval Wives', *Speculum* 61 (1986), 517–43.

Field, Rosalind, 'The King Over the Water: Exile-and-Return in Insular Tradition', in *Cultural Encounters in Medieval Romance*, ed. Corinne J. Saunders (Cambridge, forthcoming).

——, '*Waldef* and the Matter of/with England,' in *Medieval Insular Romance*, ed. Weiss, Fellows and Dickson, pp. 25–39.

Foot, Sarah, *Veiled Women*, 2 vols. (Aldershot, 2000).

de Gaiffier, Baudouin, '*Intactam sponsam relinquens*. À propos de la Vie de s. Alexis', *Analecta Bollandiana* 65 (1947), 157–95.

Geddes, Jane, <http://www.abdn.ac.uk/stalbanspsalter> [accessed 4 June 2004].

Gilchrist, Roberta, *Contemplation and Action: The Other Monasticism*, The Archaeology of Medieval Britain (Leicester, 1995).

Glasser, M., 'Marriage in Medieval Hagiography', *Studies in Medieval and Renaissance History* n.s. 4 (1981), 3–34.

Goldschmidt, Adolf, *Der Albani-Psalter in Hildesheim und seine Beziehung zur symbolischen Kirchensculptur des XII. Jahrhunderts* (Berlin, 1895).

Gray, Douglas, 'Popular Religion and Late Medieval Literature' in *Religion in the Poetry and Drama of the Late Middle Ages in England*, ed. Piero Boitani and Anna Torti (Cambridge, 1990), pp. 1–28.

Halpin, Patricia, 'Women Religious in Late Anglo-Saxon England', *Haskins Society Journal* 6 (1994), 97–110.

Haney, Kristine E., 'The St Albans Psalter: a reconsideration', *Journal of the Warburg and Courtauld Institutes* 58 (1995), 1–28.

——, 'The St Albans Psalter and the new spiritual ideals of the twelfth century', *Viator* 28 (1997), 145–73.

——, *The St Albans Psalter: An Anglo-Norman Song of Faith* (New York, 2002).

Hanning, Robert, *The Individual in Twelfth-Century Romance* (New Haven, 1977).

Head, Thomas, 'The Marriages of Christina of Markyate', *Viator* 21 (1990), 75–101.

——, *Hagiography and the Cult of the Saints. The Diocese of Orléans, 800–1200*, Cambridge Studies in Medieval Life and Thought, fourth series 14 (Cambridge, 1990).

Heffernan, T. J., *Sacred Biography: Saints and Their Biographers in the Middle Ages* (Oxford, 1988).

Henderson, George, 'The Textual Basis of the Picture Leaves', in *The Eadwine Psalter*, ed. M. Gibson, T. A. Heslop and R. W. Pfaff (London, 1992), 35–42.

Heslop, T. A., 'The Visual Arts and Crafts' in *The Cambridge Guide to Arts in Britain II, The Middle Ages*, ed. Boris Ford (Cambridge, 1988), pp. 164–70.

Holdsworth, Christopher, 'Christina of Markyate' in *Medieval Women: dedicated and presented to Rosalind M. T. Hill on the occasion of her seventieth birthday*, ed. Derek T. Baker, Studies in Church History: Subsidia 1 (Oxford, 1978), pp. 185–204.

——, 'Hermits and the Power of the Frontier', *Reading Medieval Studies* 16 (1990), 55–76.

Hollis, Stephanie, *Anglo-Saxon Women and the Church: Sharing a Common Fate* (Woodbridge, 1992).

Hostetler, Margaret, 'Designing Religious Women: Privacy and Exposure in the *Life of Christina of Markyate* and *Ancrene Wisse*', *Medievalia* 22 (1999), 201–31.

Jaeger, C. Stephen, *Ennobling Love: In Search of a Lost Sensibility* (Philadelphia, 1999).

Jones, E. A., 'Langland and Hermits', *Yearbook of Langland Studies* 11 (1997), 67–86.

——, 'The Hermits and Anchorites of Oxfordshire', *Oxoniensia* 63 (1998), 51–77.

Jubb, Margaret, <http://www.abdn.ac.uk/stalbanspsalter/english/essays/oldfrenchlife.shtml> [accessed 4 June 2004].

Karras, Ruth Mazo, 'Friendship and Love in the Lives of Two Twelfth-Century English Saints', *The Journal of Medieval History* 14 (1988), 305–20.

——, 'Holy Harlots: Prostitute Saints in Medieval Legend', *Journal of the History of Sexuality* 1 (1990), 3–32.

Knowles, David, *The Monastic Order in England*, 2nd edn. (Cambridge, 1963).

Knowles, David and R. Neville Hadcock, *Medieval Religious Houses: England and Wales* (London, 1971).

Koopmans, Rachel M., 'The Conclusion of Christina of Markyate's *Vita*', *Journal of Ecclesiastical History* 51 (2000), 663–98.

Legge, Dominica, *Anglo-Norman in the Cloisters: The Influence of the Orders Upon Anglo-Norman Literature* (Edinburgh, 1950).

——, *Anglo-Norman Literature and its Background* (Oxford, 1963).

L'Hermite-Leclercq, Paulette, 'De l'ermitage au monastère, genèse d'une institution. Un exemple anglais de la première moitié du XIIè siècle', in *Histoire et société: Mélanges offerts à Georges Duby*, ed. Charles de la Roncière *et al.*, 4 vols. (Aix-en-Provence, 1992), iii. 49–59.

Leyser, Henrietta, 'Two concepts of Temptation', in *Belief and Culture*, pp. 318–26.

——, *Hermits and the New Monasticism: A Study of Religious Communities in Western Europe, 1000–1150* (London, 1984).

——, *Medieval Women: A Social History of Women in England, 450–1500* (London, 1995, rpt. 2002).

McGuire, Brian, *Friendship and Community: The Monastic Experience* (Kalamazoo, Mich., 1988).

McNamara, Jo Ann, 'The *Herrenfrage*: The Restructuring of the Gender System, 1050–1150', in *Medieval Masculinities: Regarding Men in the Middle Ages*, ed. Clare Lees (Minneapolis, 1994), pp. 3–29.

——, *Sisters in Arms: Catholic Nuns through Two Millennia* (Cambridge, Mass., 1996).

Maddox, D. L., 'Pilgrimage Narrative and Meaning in Manuscripts L and A of the *Vie de saint Alexis*', *Romance Philology* 27 (1973), 143–57.

Mayr-Harting, Henry, 'Functions of a Twelfth-Century Recluse', *History* 60 (1975), 337–52.

Medieval Insular Romance: Translation and Innovation, ed. Judith Weiss, Jennifer Fellows and Morgan Dickson, (Cambridge, 2000).

Medieval Women's Visionary Literature, ed. Elizabeth Petroff (Oxford, 1986).

Millett, Bella, 'Women in No Man's Land: English Recluses and the development of vernacular literature in the twelfth and thirteenth centuries', in *Women and Literature in Britain*, ed. C. M. Meale, pp. 86–103.

Mölk, U., 'La *Chanson de saint Alexis* et le culte du saint en France aux XIe et XIIe siècles', *Cahiers de civilisation médiévale* 21 (1978), 339–55.

Morse, Ruth, *Truth and Convention in the Middle Ages: Rhetoric, Representation and Reality* (Cambridge, 1991).

Mulder-Bakker, Anneke, *Lives of the Anchoresses* (Philadelphia, forthcoming).

Newman, Barbara, *Sister of Wisdom: Saint Hildegard's Theology of the Feminine* (Berkeley, 1987).

——, *From Virile Woman to Woman Christ: Studies in Medieval Religion and Literature* (Philadelphia, 1995).

Nicoll, Donald, *Thurstan, Archbishop of York (1114–1140)* (York, 1964).

Niebrzydowski, Sue,
<http://www.abdn.ac.uk/stalbanspsalter/english/essays/calendar.shtml#collects>
[accessed 4 June 2004].

The Oxford Dictionary of Saints, ed. D. H. Farmer, 5th edn. (Oxford, 2003).

Pächt, Otto, The *Rise of Pictorial Narrative in Twelfth-Century England* (Oxford, 1962).

Pindar, Janice M., 'The Intertextuality of Old French Saints' Lives: St Giles, St Evroul and the Marriage of St Alexis', *Parergon* 6A (1988), 11–21.

Renna, Thomas, 'Virginity in the *Life* of Christina of Markyate and Aelred of Rievaulx's *Rule*', *American Benedictine Revue* 36 (1985), 79–92.

Rigg, A. G., *A History of Anglo-Latin Literature 1066–1422* (Cambridge, 1992).

Robertson, D., *The Medieval Saints' Lives: Spiritual Renewal and Old French Literature* (Lexington, 1995).

Rosenthal, Constance, *The Vitae Patrum in Old and Middle English Literature* (Philadelphia, 1936).

Schulenburg, Jane Tibbetts, *Forgetful of Their Sex: Female Sanctity and Society ca. 500–1100* (Chicago, 1998).

Sharpe, Richard, *Handlist of the Latin Writers of Great Britain and Ireland before 1540* (Turnhout, 1997).

Short, Ian, 'Bi-lingualism in Anglo-Norman England', *Romance Philology* 33 (1980), 467–79.

Southern, R. W., *The Making of the Middle Ages* (London, 1953; rpt. 1993).

——, *Medieval Humanism and Other Studies* (Oxford, 1970).

Storey, C., *An Annotated Bibliography and Guide to Alexis Studies (La Vie de Saint Alexis)*, Histoire des idées et critique littéraire 251 (Geneva, 1987).

Thompson, S., *Women Religious: The Founding of English Nunneries after the Norman Conquest* (Oxford, 1991).

Thomson, Rodney M., *Manuscripts from St Albans Abbey, 1066–1235*, 2 vols. (Woodbridge, 1982).

Uitti, Karl D., *Story, Myth and Celebration in Old French Narrative Poetry 1050–1200* (Princeton, 1973).

Venarde, Bruce L., *Women's Monasticism and Medieval Society: Nunneries in France and England, 890–1215* (Ithaca and London, 1997).

The Victoria County History, see bibliography in chapter 14.

Warren, Ann, *Anchorites and Their Patrons in Medieval England* (Berkeley, 1985).

——, 'The Nun as Anchoress, England 1100–1500', in *Medieval Religious Women I: Distant Echoes*, ed. John A. Nicholas and Lillian Thomas Shank (Kalamazoo, 1984), 197–212.

Whatley, Gordon, 'Late Old English Hagiography, ca. 950–1150', in *Hagiographies*, ed. Guy Philippart (Turnhout, 1994 –), 429–99.

——, 'An Introduction to the Study of Old English Prose Hagiography: Sources and Resources', in *Holy Men and Holy Women: Old English Prose Saints; Lives and their Contexts*, ed. Paul E. Szarmach (Albany, NY, 1996), 3–32.

Wogan-Browne, Jocelyn, 'Saints' Lives and the Female Reader', *Forum for Modern Language Studies* 27 (1991), 318–21.

——, 'Clerc u lai, muïne u dame': women and Anglo-Norman Hagiography in the twelfth and thirteenth centuries', in Meale, *Women and Literature*, 61–85.

——, *Saints' Lives and Women's Literary Culture* (Oxford, 2001).

——, '"Reading is good prayer": Recent Research on Female Reading Communities', *New Medieval Literatures* 5 (Oxford, 2002), 229–97.

Women and Literature in Britain, 1150–1500, ed. Carol Meale (Cambridge, 1993).

Young, Karl, *The Drama of the Medieval Church*, 2 vols. (Oxford, 1933; rpt. 1962).

Zatta, Jane, 'The Vie Seinte Osith: Hagiography and Politics in Anglo-Norman England', *Studies in Philology* 96 (1999), 367–93.

INDEX OF
NAMES AND PLACES